The Colleen Bawn. ... A domestic drama, etc. (Founded on G. G.'s Irish Story, "the Collegians.")

Gerald Griffin

GUIDE TO FOLD-OUTS, MAPS and OVERSIZED IMAGES

In an online database, page images do not need to conform to the size restrictions found in a printed book. When converting these images back into a printed bound book, the page sizes are standardized in ways that maintain the detail of the original. For large images, such as fold-out maps, the original page image is split into two or more pages.

Guidelines used to determine the split of oversize pages:

• Some images are split vertically; large images require vertical and horizontal splits.
• For horizontal splits, the content is split left to right.
• For vertical splits, the content is split from top to bottom.
• For both vertical and horizontal splits, the image is processed from top left to bottom right.

SIXTEENPENCE, COMPLETE.

THE COLLEEN BAWN;

OR,

THE COLLEGIAN'S WIFE.

WITH ILLUSTRATIONS BY PHIZ.

ONLY ILLUSTRATED AND UNABRIDGED EDITION.

LONDON: GEORGE VICKERS, ANGEL COURT, STRAND.

17

THE

COLLEEN BAWN;

OR,

THE COLLEGIAN'S WIFE.

A Tale of Garryowen

ORIGINALLY ENTITLED "THE COLLEGIANS."

BY

GERALD GRIFFIN, Esq.

AUTHOR OF "TALES OF THE MUNSTER FESTIVALS;" "GISIPPUS;" "TALES OF THE JURY ROOM," ETC., ETC.

LONDON:

GEORGE VICKERS, ANGEL COURT, STRAND.

MDCCCLXI.

WINCHESTER:
PRINTED BY HUGH BARCLAY,
HIGH STREET.

CONTENTS.

———◆———

LIST OF ILLUSTRATIONS.

THE COLLEEN BAWN;
OR,
THE COLLEGIAN'S WIFE.

HARDRESS CREGAN RESCUES THE COLLEEN BAWN.

CHAPTER I.

HOW GARRYOWEN ROSE, AND HOW IT FELL.

THE little ruined outlet, which gives its name to one of the most popular national songs of Erin, is situate on the acclivity of a hill near the city of Limerick, commanding a not unpleasant view of that fine old town, with the noble stream that washes its battered towers, and a richly cultivated surrounding country. Tradition has preserved the occasion of its celebrity, and the origin of its name, which appears to be compounded of two Irish words signifying " Owen's garden." A person so called was the owner, about half a century since, of a cottage and plot of ground on this spot, which, from its contiguity to the town, became a favourite holiday resort with the young citizens of both sexes—a lounge presenting accommodations somewhat similar to those which are offered to the London mechanic by

the Battersea tea-gardens. Owen's garden was the general rendezvous for those who sought for simple amusement or for dissipation. The old people drank together under the shades of trees—the young played at ball, goal, or other athletic exercises on the green; while a few, lingering by the hedgerows with their fair acquaintances, cheated the time with sounds less boisterous, indeed, but yet possessing their fascination also.

The festivities of our fathers, however, were frequently distinguished by so fierce a character of mirth, that, for any difference in the result of their convivial meetings, they might as well have been pitched encounters. Owen's garden was soon as famous for scenes of strife, as it was for mirth and humour; and broken heads became a staple article of manufacture in the neighbourhood.

This new feature in the diversions of the place was encouraged by a number of young persons of rank somewhat superior to that of the usual frequenters of the garden. They were the sons of the more respectable citizens, the merchants and wholesale traders of the city, just turned loose from school, with a greater supply of animal spirit than they had wisdom to govern. These young gentlemen, being fond of wit, amused themselves by forming parties at night, to wring the heads off all the geese, and the knockers off all the hall-doors in the neighbourhood. They sometimes suffered their genius to soar as high as the breaking a lamp, and even the demolition of a watchman; but perhaps this species of joking was found a little too serious to be repeated over frequently, for few achievements of so daring a violence are found amongst their records. They were obliged to content themselves with the less ambitious distinction of destroying the knockers and store-locks, annoying the peaceable inmates of the neighbouring houses with long-continued assaults on the front doors, terrifying the quiet passengers with every species of insult and provocation, and indulging their fratricidal propensities against all the geese in Garryowen.

The fame of the "Garryowen boys" soon spread far and wide. Their deeds were celebrated by some inglorious minstrel of the day, in that air which has since resounded over every quarter of the world, and even disputed the palm of national popularity with "Patrick's Day." A string of jolly verses were appended to the tune, which soon enjoyed a notoriety similar to that of the famous "Lillibulero, bullum-a-la," which sung King James out of his three kingdoms. The name of Garry-owen was as well known as that of the Irish Numantium, Limerick, itself, and Owen's little garden became almost a synonyme for Ireland.

But that principle of existence which assigns to the life of man its periods of youth, maturity, and decay, has its analogy in the fate of villages, as in that of empires. Assyria fell, and so did Garryowen! Rome had its decline, and Garryowen was not immortal! Both are now an idle sound, with nothing but the recollections of old tradition to invest them with an interest. The still notorious suburb is little better than a heap of rubbish, where a number of smoked and mouldering walls, standing out from the masses of stone and mortar, indicate the position of a once populous row of dwelling-houses. A few roofs yet remain unshaken, under which some impoverished families endeavour to work out a wretched subsistence, by maintaining a species of huckster trade, by cobbling old shoes, and manufacturing ropes. A small rookery wearies the ears of the inhabitants at one end of the outlet, and a rope-walk, which extends along the adjacent slope of Gallows Green (so called for certain reasons), brings to the mind of the conscious spectator, associations that are not calculated to enliven the prospect. Neither is he thrown into a more jocular frame of mind, as he picks his steps over the insulated paving-stones that appear amid the green slough with which the street is deluged, and encounters, at the other end, an alley of coffin-makers' shops, with a fever hospital on one side, and a churchyard on the other. A person who was bent on a journey to the other world, could not desire a more expeditious outfit than Garryowen could now afford him, nor a more commodious choice of conveyances, from the machine on the slope above glanced at, to the pest-house at the farther end.

But it is ill talking lightly on a serious subject. The days of Garryowen are gone, like those of ancient Erin; and the feats of her once formidable heroes are nothing more than a winter's evening tale. Owen is in his grave, and his garden looks dreary as a ruined churchyard. The greater number of his merry customers have followed him to a narrow play-ground, which, though not less crowded, affords less room for fun, and less opportunity for contention. The worm is there the reveller—the owl whoops out his defiance without answer (save the echo's)—the best whiskey in Munster would not now "drive the cold out of their hearts"—and the withered old sexton is able to knock the bravest of them over the pate with impunity. A few, perhaps, may still remain to look back with a fond shame to the scene of their early follies, and to smile at the page in which those follies are recorded.

Still, however, there is something to keep the memory alive of those unruly days, and to preserve the name of Garryowen from utter extinction. The annual fair which is held on the spot presents a spectacle of gaiety and uproar which might rival its most boisterous days; and strangers still inquire for the place with a curiosity which its appearance seldom fails to disappoint. Our national lyrist has immortalised the air by adapting to it one of the liveliest of his melodies—the adventures of which it was once the scene constitute a fund of standing joke and anecdote, which are not neglected by the neighbouring story-tellers—and a rough voice may still occasionally be heard by the traveller who passes near its ruined dwellings at evening, to chant a stanza of the chorus which was once in the mouth of every individual in the kingdom:—

> " 'Tis there we 'll drink the nut-brown ale,
> An' pay the reck'nin' on the nail;
> No man for debt shall go to jail
> ₃From Garryowen na gloria."

CHAPTER II.

HOW EILY O'CONNOR PUZZLED ALL THE INHABITANTS OF GARRY-OWEN.

But while Owen lived, and while his garden flourished, he and his neighbours were as merry together, as if death could never reach the one, nor desolation waste the other. Among those frequenters of his little retreat, whom he distinguished with an especial favour and attention, the foremost was the handsome daughter of an old man who conducted the business of a rope-walk in his neighbourhood, and who was accustomed on a fine Saturday evening to sit under the shade of a yellow osier that stood by his door, and discourse of the politics of the day—of Lord Halifax's administration—of the promising young patriot, Mr. Henry Grattan—and of the famous Catholic concession of 1773. Owen, like all Irishmen, even of the humblest rank, was an acute critic in female proportions, and although time had blown away the thatching from his head, and by far the greater portion of blood that remained in his frame had colonised about his nose, yet the manner in which he held forth on the praises of his old friend's daughter was such as to put to shame her younger and less eloquent admirers. It is true, indeed, that the origin of the suburban beauty was one which, in a troubled country like Ireland, had little of agreeable association to recommend it; but few even of those to whom twisted hemp was an object of secret terror, could look on the exquisitely beautiful face of Eily O'Connor, and remember that she was a rope-maker's daughter; few could detect beneath the timid, hesitating, downcast gentleness of manner, which shed an interest over all her motions, the traces of a harsh and vulgar education. It was true that she sometimes purloined a final letter from the King's adjectives, and prolonged the utterance of a vowel beyond the term of prosodical orthodoxy, but the tongue that did so seemed to move on silver wires, and the lip on which the sound delayed,

> " long murmuring, loath to part,"

imparted to its own accents an association of sweetness and grace, that made the defect an additional allurement. Her education in the outskirts of a city had not impaired the natural tenderness of her character; for her father, who, all rude as he was, knew how to value his daughter's softness of mind, endeavoured to foster it by every indulgence in his power. Her uncle, too, who was now a country parish-priest, was well qualified to draw forth any natural talent with which she had been originally endowed. He had completed his theological education in the famous university of Salamanca, where he was distinguished as a youth of much quietness of temper and literary application, rather than as one of those furious gesticulators, those "figures Hibernoises," amongst whom Gil Blas, in his fit of logical lunacy, could meet his only equals. At his little lodging, while he was yet a curate at St. John's, Eily O'Connor was accustomed to spend a considerable portion of her time, and in return for her kindness in presiding at his simple tea-table, Father Edward undertook to bestow a degree of attention on her education, which rendered her in a little time as superior in knowledge as she was in beauty to her female associates. She was remarked likewise at this time as a little devotee, very regular in her attendance at chapel, constant in all the observances of her religion, and grave in her attire and discourse. On the coldest and dreariest morning in winter, she might be seen gliding along by the unopened shop windows to the nearest chapel, where she was accustomed to hear an early mass, and return in time to set everything in order for her father's breakfast. During the day, she superintended his household affairs, while he was employed upon the adjacent rope-walk; and, in the evening, she usually slipped on her bonnet, and went across the street to

Father Edward's, where she chatted away until tea was over; if he happened to be engaged in reading his daily office, she amused herself with a volume of moral entertainment, such as *Rasselas, Prince of Abyssinia,* or Mr. Addison's *Spectator,* until he was at leisure to hear her lessons. An attachment of the purest and tenderest nature was the consequence of those mutual attentions between the uncle and niece, and it might be said that if the former loved her not as well, he knew and valued her character still better than her father. Father Edward, however, was appointed to a parish, and Eily lost her instructor. It was for her a severe loss, and most severe in reality when its effects upon her own spirits began to wear away. For some months after his departure, she continued to lead the same retired and unobtrusive life, and no eye, save that of a consummate observer, could detect the slightest alteration in her sentiments, the least increase of toleration for the world and worldly amusements. That change, however, had been silently effected in her heart. She was now a woman—a lovely, intelligent, full-grown woman—and circumstances obliged her to take a part in the little social circle which moved around her. Her spirits were naturally light, and, though long repressed, became readily assimilated to the buoyant tone of the society in which she happened to be placed. Her father, who, with a father's venial vanity, was fond of showing his beautiful child among his neighbours, took her with him to Owen's garden at a time when it was unusually gay and crowded, and from that evening might be dated the commencement of a decided and visible change in the lovely Eily's character.

As gradual as the approach of a spring morning, was the change from grave to gay in the costume of this flower of the suburbs. It dawned at first in a handsome bow-knot upon her head-dress, and ended in the full noontide splendour of flowered muslins, silks, and sashes. It was like the opening of the rose-bud, which gathers around it the winged wooers of the summer meadow. "Lads, as brisk as bees," came thronging in her train, with proffers of "honourable love, and rites of marriage;" and even among the youths of a higher rank, whom the wild levity of Irish blood and high spirits sent to mingle in the festivities of Owen's garden, a jealousy prevailed respecting the favour of the rope-maker's handsome daughter. It was no wonder that attentions paid by individuals so much superior to her ordinary admirers, should render Eily indifferent to the sighs of those plebeian suitors. Dunat O'Leary, the hair-cutter, or Foxy Dunat, as he was named in allusion to his red hair, was cut to the heart by her utter coldness. Myles Murphy, likewise, a good-natured farmer from Killarney, who travelled through the country selling Kerry ponies, and claiming a relationship with every one he met, claimed kindred in vain with Eily, for his claim was not allowed. Lowry Looby, too, the servant of Mr. Daly, a wealthy middleman who lived in the neighbourhood, was suspected by many to entertain delusive hopes of Eily O'Connor's favour—but this report was improbable enough, for Lowry could not but know that he was a very ugly man; and if he were as beautiful as Narcissus, Mihil O'Connor would still have shut the door in his face for being as poor as Timon. So that, though there was no lack of admirers, the lovely Eily, like many celebrated beauties in a higher rank, ran, after all, a fair chance of becoming what Lady Mary Montague has elegantly termed "a lay nun." Even as a book-worm, who will pore over a single volume from morning till night, if turned loose into a library, wanders from shelf to shelf, bewildered amid a host of temptations, and unable to make any selection until he is surprised by twilight, and chagrined to find, that with so much happiness within his grasp, he has spent, nevertheless, an unprofitable day.

But accident saved Eily from a destiny so deeply dreaded and so often lamented as that above alluded to—a condition which people generally agree to look upon as one of utter desolation, and which, notwithstanding, is frequently a state of greater happiness than its opposite. On the eve of the seventeenth of March, a day distinguished in the rope-maker's household, not only as the festival of the national Saint, but as the birthday of the young mistress of the establishment—on this evening Eily and her father were enjoying their customary relaxation at Owen's garden. The jolly proprietor was seated as usual with his rope-twisting friend under the yellow osier, while Myles Murphy, who had brought a number of his wild ponies to be disposed of at the neighbouring fairs, had taken his place at the

end of the table, and was endeavouring to insinuate a distant relationship between the Owens of Kilteery, connections of the person whom he addressed, and the Murphys of Knockfodhra, connections of his own. A party of young men were playing fives at a ball-alley, on the other side of the green; and another, more numerous, and graced with many female figures, were capering away to the tune of the Fox-hunter's Jig on the short grass. Some poor old women, with baskets on their arms, were endeavouring to sell off some *Patrick's crosses* for children, at the low rate of one halfpenny a piece, gilding, paint, and all. Others, fatigued with exertion, were walking under the still leafless trees, some with their hats, some with their coats off, jesting, laughing, and chatting familiarly with their female acquaintances.

Mihil O'Connor, happening to see Lowry Looby among the promenaders, glancing now and then at the dance and whistling Patrick's Day, requested him to call his daughter out of the group, and tell her that he was waiting for her to go home. Lowry went, and returned to say, that Eily was dancing with a strange young gentleman in a boating dress, and that he would not let her go until she had finished the slip jig.

It continued a sufficient time to tire the old man's patience. When Eily did at last make her appearance, he observed there was a flush of mingled weariness and pleasure on her cheek, which showed that the delay was not quite in opposition to her own inclinations. This circumstance might have tempted him to receive her with a little displeasure, but that honest Owen at that moment laid hold on both father and daughter, insisting that they should come in and take supper with his wife and himself.

This narrative of Eily's girlhood being merely introductory, we shall forbear to furnish any detail of the minor incidents of the evening, or the quality of Mrs. Owen's entertainment. They were very merry and happy; so much so, that the Patrick's eve approached its termination before they rose to bid their host and hostess a good night. Owen advised them to walk on rapidly, in order to avoid the "Pathrick's boys," who would promenade the streets after twelve, to welcome in the mighty festival with music and uproar of all kinds. Some of the lads, he said, "might be playin' their tricks upon Miss Eily."

The night was rather dark, and the dim glimmer of the oil-lamps, which were suspended at long intervals over the street doors, tended only in a very feeble degree to qualify the gloom. Mihil O'Connor and his daughter had already performed more than half their journey, and were turning from a narrow lane at the head of Mungret Street, when a loud and tumultuous sound broke with sudden violence upon their hearing. It proceeded from a multitude of people who were moving in confused and noisy procession along the street. An ancient and still honoured custom summons the youthful inhabitants of the city on the night of this anniversary to celebrate the approaching holiday of the patron saint and apostle of the island, by promenading all the streets in succession, playing national airs, and filling up the pauses in the music with shouts of exultation. Such was the procession which the two companions now beheld approaching.

The appearance which it presented was not altogether destitute of interest and amusement. In the midst were a band of musicians who played alternately, "Patrick's Day," and "Garryowen," while a rabble of men and boys pressed round them, thronging the whole breadth and a considerable portion of the length of the street. The men had got sprigs of shamrock in their hats, and several carried in their hands lighted candles, protected from the wasting night-blast by a simple lamp of whited brown paper. The fickle and unequal light which those small torches threw over the faces of the individuals who held them, afforded a lively contrast to the prevailing darkness.

The crowd hurried forward, singing, playing, shouting, laughing, and indulging, to its full extent, all the excitement which was occasioned by the tumult and the motion. Bedroom windows were thrown up as they passed, and the half-dressed inmates thrust their heads into the night air to gaze upon the mob of enthusiasts. All the respectable persons who appeared in the streets as they advanced, turned short into the neighbouring by-ways to avoid the importunities which they would be likely to incur by a contact with the multitude.

But it was too late for our party to adopt this precaution. Before it had entered their minds, the procession (if we may

3

dignify it by a name so sounding) was nearer to them than they were to any turn in the street, and the appearance of flight, with a rabble of men, as with dogs, is a provocation of pursuit. Of this they were aware; and accordingly, instead of attempting a vain retreat, they turned into a recess formed by one of the shop-doors, and quietly awaited the passing away of this noisy torrent. For some moments they were unnoticed; the fellows who moved foremost being too busy in talking, laughing, and shouting, to pay any attention to objects not directly in their way. But they were no sooner espied than the wags assailed them with that species of wit which distinguishes the inhabitants of the back lanes of a city, and forms the terror of all country visitors. These expressions were lavished upon the rope maker and his daughter, until the former, who was as irritable an old fellow as Irishmen generally are, was almost put out of patience.

At length, a young man, observing the lamp shine for a moment on Eily's handsome face, made a chirp with his lips as he passed by, as if he had a mind to kiss her. Not Papirius himself, when vindicating his senatorial dignity against the insulting Gaul, could be more prompt in action than Mihil O'Connor. The young gentleman received, in return for his affectionate greeting, a blow over the temples which was worth five hundred kisses. An uproar immediately commenced, which was likely to end in some serious injury to the old man and his daughter. A number of ferocious faces gathered round them, uttering sounds of harsh rancour and defiance, which Mihil met with equal loudness and energy. Indeed, all that seemed to delay his fate, and hinder him from sharing in the prostration of his victim, was the conduct of Eily, who, flinging herself in bare-armed beauty before her father, defended him for a time against the upraised weapons of his assailants. No one would incur the danger of harming, by an accidental blow, a creature so young, so beautiful, and so affectionate.

They were at length rescued from this precarious condition by the interposition of two young men, in the dress of boatmen, who appeared to possess some influence with the crowd, and who used it for the advantage of the sufferers. Not satisfied with having brought them safely out of all immediate danger, the taller of the two conducted them to their door, saying little on the way, and taking his leave as soon as they were once in perfect safety. All that Mihil could learn from his appearance was, that he was a gentleman, and very young—perhaps not more than nineteen years of age. The old man talked much and loudly in praise of his gallantry, but Eily was altogether silent on the subject.

A few days after, Mihil O'Connor was at work upon the rope-walk, going slowly backward in the sunshine, with a little bundle of hemp between his knees, and singing "Maureen Thierna."* A hunchbacked little fellow, in a boatman's dress, came up, and saluting him in a sharp city brogue, reminded the old rope-maker that he had done him a service a few evenings before. Mihil professed his acknowledgments, and with true Irish warmth of heart, assured the little boatman that all he had in the world was at his service. The hunchback, however, only wanted a few ropes and blocks for his boat, and even for those he was resolute in paying honourably. Neither did he seem anxious to satisfy the curiosity of old Mihil with respect to the name and quality of his companion; for he was inexorable in maintaining that he was a turf-boatman from Scagh, who had come up to town with him to dispose of a cargo of fuel at Charlotte's Quay. Mihil O'Connor referred him to his daughter for the ropes, about which, he said, she could bargain as well as himself, and he was unable to leave his work until the rope he had in hand should be finished. The little deformed, no way displeased at this intelligence, went to find Eily at the shop, where he spent a longer time than Mihil thought necessary for his purpose.

From this time forward, the character of Eily O'Connor seemed to have undergone a second change. Her former gravity returned, but it did not reappear under the same circumstances as before. In her days of religious retirement, it appeared only in her dress and in her choice of amusements. Now, both her recreations and her attire were much gayer than ever, so much so as almost to approach a degree of dissipation, but her cheerfulness of mind was gone, and the sadness which

* Little Mary Tierney.

had settled on her heart, like a black reef under sunny waters, was plainly visible through all her gaiety. Her father was too much occupied in his eternal rope twisting to take particular notice of this change, and, besides, it is notorious that one's constant companions are the last to observe any alteration in one's manner or appearance.

One morning, when Mihil O'Connor left his room, he was surprised to find that the breakfast table was not laid as usual, and that his daughter was not in the house. She made her appearance, however, while he was himself making the necessary arrangements. They exchanged a greeting somewhat colder on the one side, and more embarrassed on the other, than was usual at the morning meetings of the father and daughter. But when she told him, that she had been only to the chapel, the old man was perfectly satisfied, for he knew that Eily would as readily think of telling a falsehood to the priest as she would to her father. And when Mihil O'Connor heard that people were at chapel, he generally concluded (poor old man!) that it was only to pray they went there.

In the meantime Myles Murphy renewed his proposals to Eily, and succeeded in gaining over the father to his interests. The latter was annoyed at his daughter's obstinate rejection of a fine fellow like Myles, with a very comfortable property, and pressed her either to give consent to the match, or a good reason for her refusal. But this request, though reasonable, was not complied with; and the rope-maker, though not so hot as Capulet, was as much displeased at the contumacy of his daughter. Eily, on her part, was so much afflicted at the anger of her only parent, that it is probable her grief would have made away with her if she had not prevented that catastrophe by making away with herself.

On the fair day of Garryowen, after sustaining a long and distressing altercation with her father and her mountain suitor, Eily O'Connor threw her blue cloak over her shoulders, and walked into the air. She did not return to dinner, and her father felt angry at what he thought a token of resentful feeling. Night came; and she did not make her appearance. The poor old man, in an agony of terror, reproached himself for his vehemence, and spent the whole night in recalling, with a feeling of remorse, every intemperate word which he had used in the violence of dispute. In the morning, more like a ghost than a living being, he went from the house of one acquaintance to another, to inquire after his child. No one, however, had seen her, except Foxy Dunat, the hair-cutter, and he had only caught a glimpse of her as she passed his door on the previous evening. It was evident that she was not to return. Her father was distracted. Her young admirers feared that she had got privately married, and run away with some shabby fellow. Her female friends insinuated that the case might be still worse, and some pious old people shook their heads when the report reached them, and said they knew what was likely to come of it, when Eily O'Connor left off attending her daily mass in the morning, and went to the dance at Garryowen.

CHAPTER III:

HOW MR. DALY, THE MIDDLEMAN, SAT DOWN TO BREAKFAST.

THE Dalys (a very respectable family in middle life) occupied, at the time of which we write, a handsome cottage on the Shannon side, a few miles from the suburban district above mentioned.

They had assembled, on the morning of Eily's disappearance, a healthy and blooming household of all sizes, in the principal sitting-room, for a purpose no less important than that of dispatching breakfast. It was a favourable moment for any one who might be desirous of sketching a family picture. The windows of the room, which were thrown up for the purpose of admitting the fresh morning air, opened upon a trim and sloping meadow, that looked sunny and cheerful with the bright green after-grass of the season. The broad and sheety river washed the very margin of the little field, and bore upon its quiet bosom (which was only ruffled by the circling eddies that encountered the advancing tide) a variety of craft, such as might be supposed to indicate the approach to a large commercial city. Majestic vessels, floating idly on the basined flood, with sails half furled, in keeping with the languid beauty of the scene—lighters, burdened to the water's edge with bricks or sand—large rafts of timber, borne onward towards the neighbouring quays under the guidance of a shipman's boat-hook—pleasure-boats, with gaudy pennons hanging at peak and top-mast—or turf-boats, with their unpicturesque and ungraceful lading, moving sluggishly forward, while their black sails seemed gasping for a breath to fill them; such were the incidents that gave a gentle animation to the prospect immediately before the eyes of the cottage dwellers. On the farther side of the river arose the Cratloe hills, shadowed in various places by a broken cloud, and rendered beautiful by the chequered appearance of the ripening tillage, and the variety of hues that were observable along their wooded sides. At intervals, the front of a handsome mansion brightened up in a passing gleam of sunshine, while the wreaths of blue smoke, ascending at various distances from amongst the trees, tended to relieve the idea of extreme solitude which it would otherwise have presented.

The interior of the cottage was not less interesting to contemplate than the landscape which lay before it. The principal breakfast-table (for there were two spread in the room) was placed before the window, the neat and snow white damask cloth covered with fare that spoke satisfactorily for the circumstances of the proprietor, and for the housewifery of his helpmate. The former, a fair, pleasant faced old gentleman, in a huge buckled cravat and square-toed shoes, somewhat distrustful of the meagre beverage which fumed out of Mrs. Daly's lofty and shining coffee-pot, had taken his position before a cold ham and fowl which decorated the lower end of the table. His lady, a courteous old personage, with a face no less fair and happy than her husband's, and with eyes sparkling with good nature and intelligence, did the honours of the board at the farther end. On the opposite side, leaning over the back of his chair with clasped hands, in an attitude which had a mixture of abstraction and anxiety, sat Mr. Kyrle Daly, the first pledge of connubial affection that was born to this comely pair. He was a young man already initiated in the rudiments of the legal profession; of a handsome figure, and in manner—but something now pressed upon his spirits, which rendered this an unfavourable occasion for describing him.

A second table was laid in a more retired portion of the room, for the accommodation of the younger part of the family. Several well-burnished goblets, or porringers, of thick milk, flanked the sides of this board, while a large dish of smooth-coated potatoes reeked up in the centre. A number of blooming boys and girls, between the ages of four and twelve, were seated at this simple repast eating and drinking away with all the happy eagerness of youthful appetite. Not, however, that this employment occupied their exclusive attention, for the prattle which circulated round the table frequently became so boisterous as to drown the conversation of the older people, and to call forth the angry rebuke of the master of the family.

The furniture of the apartment was in accordance with the appearance and manners of its inhabitants. The floor was handsomely carpeted, a lofty green fender fortified the fireplace, and supplied Mr. Daly in his facetious moments with occasions for the frequent repetition of a favourite conundrum—"Why is that fender like Westminster Abbey?"—a problem with which he never failed to try the wit of any stranger who happened to spend a night beneath his roof. The wainscoted walls were ornamented with several of the popular prints of the day, such as Hogarth's Roast Beef, Prince Eugene, Schomberg at the Boyne, Mr. Betterton playing Cato in all the glory of

"Full wig, flower'd gown, and lacker'd chair;"

of the royal Mandane, in the person of Mrs. Mountain, strutting among the arbours of her Persian palace in a lofty tête and hooped petticoat. There were also some family drawings done by Mrs. Daly in her school days, of which we feel no inclination to say more than that they were prettily framed. In justice to the fair artist, it should also be mentioned that, contrary to the established practice, her sketches were never retouched by the hand of her master, a fact which Mr. Daly was fond of insinuating, and which no one who saw the pictures was tempted to call in question. A small book-case, with the edges of the shelves handsomely gilded, was suspended in one corner of the room, and, on examination, might be found to contain a considerable number of works on Irish history, for which study Mr. Daly had a national predilection, a circumstance much deplored by all the impatient listeners in his neighbourhood, and (some people hinted) in his own household; some religious books, and

a few volumes on cookery and farming. The space over the lofty chimney-piece was assigned to some ornaments of a more startling description. A gun rack, on which were suspended a long shore gun, a brass-barrelled blunderbuss, a cutlass, and a case of horse pistols, manifested Mr. Daly's determination to maintain, if necessary, by force of arms, his claim to the fair possessions which his honest industry had acquired.

"Kyrle," said Mr. Daly, putting his fork into a breast of cold goose, and looking at his son—"you had better let me put a little goose (with an emphasis) on your plate. You know you are going a wooing to-day."

The young gentleman appeared not to hear him. Mrs. Daly, who understood more intimately the nature of her son's reflections, deprecated, by a significant look at her husband, the continuance of any raillery upon so delicate a subject.

"Kyrle, some coffee?" said the lady of the house, but without being more successful in awakening the attention of the young gentleman.

Mr. Daly winked at his wife.

"Kyrle!" he called aloud, in a tone against which even a lover's absence was not proof, "do you hear what your mother says?"

"I ask pardon, sir—I was absent—I—what were you saying, mother?"

"She was saying," continued Mr. Daly, with a smile, "that you were manufacturing a fine speech for Anna Chute, and that you were just meditating whether you should deliver it on your knees, or out of brief, as if you were addressing the Bench in the Four Courts."

"For shame, my dear! Never mind him, Kyrle, I said no such thing; I wonder how you can say that, my dear, and the children listening."

"Pooh! the little angels are too busy and too innocent to pay us any attention," said Mr. Daly, lowering his voice, however. "But, speaking seriously, my boy, you take this affair too deeply to heart; and whether it be in our pursuit of wealth, or fame, or even in love itself, an extreme solicitude to be successful is the surest means of defeating its own object. Besides, it argues an unquiet and unresigned condition. I have had a little experience, you know, in affairs of this kind," he added, smiling and glancing at his fair helpmate, who blushed with the simplicity of a young girl.

"Ah, sir," said Kyrle, as he drew nearer to the breakfast-table, with a magnanimous affectation of cheerfulness, "I fear I have not so good a ground for hope as you may have had. It is very easy, sir, for one to be resigned to disappointment, when he is certain of success."

"Why, I was not bidden to despair, indeed," said Mr. Daly, extending his hand to his wife, while they exchanged a quiet smile, which had in it an expression of tenderness and of melancholy remembrance.

"I have, I believe, been more fortunate than more deserving persons. I have never been vexed with useless fears in my wooing days, nor with vain regrets when those days were ended. I do not know, my dear lad, what hopes you have formed, what prospects you may have shaped out of the future, but I will not wish you a better fortune, than that you may as nearly approach to their accomplishment as I have done, and that Time may deal as fairly with you as he has done with your father." After saying this, Mr. Daly leaned forward on the table, with his temple supported by one finger, and glanced alternately from his children to his wife, while he sang in a low tone the following verse of a popular song:—

"How should I love the pretty creatures,
    While round my knees they fondly clung—
To see them look their mother's features,
    To hear them lisp their mother's tongue!
And when with envy Time, transported,
    Shall think to rob us of our joys,
You'll in your girls again be courted,
    And I"——

with a glance at Kyrle—

"And I go wooing with the boys."

"And this," thought young Kyrle, in the affectionate pause that ensued, "this is the question which I go to decide upon this morning—whether my old age shall resemble the picture which I see before me, or whether I shall be doomed to creep into the winter of my life, a lonely, selfish, cheerless, money-hunting old bachelor. Is not this enough to make a little solicitude excusable, or pardonable at least?"

"It is a long time now," resumed Mr. Daly, "since I have had the pleasure of meeting Mrs. Chute. She was a very beautiful, but a very wild girl when I knew her. Nothing has ever been more inexplicable to me than the choice she made of a second husband. You never saw Anne's step-father, Tom Chute, or you would be equally astonished. You saw him, my love—did you not?"

Mrs. Daly laughed, and answered in the affirmative.

"It showed, indeed, a singular taste," said Mr. Daly. "They tell a curious story, too, about the manner of their courtship."

"What was that, sir?" asked Kyrle, who felt a strong sympathetic interest in all stories connected with wooers and wooing.

"I have it, I confess, upon questionable authority; but you shall hear it, such as it is. Now, look at that young thief!" he added, laughing, and directing Kyrle's attention to one of the children, a chubby young fellow, who, having deserted the potato-eating corps at the side-table, was taking advantage of the deep interest excited by the conversation, to make a sudden descent upon the contents of the japanned bread-basket. Perceiving that he was detected, the little fellow relaxed his fingers, and drew back a little, glancing, from beneath his eyelashes, a half dismayed and bashful look at the laughing countenance of his parent.

"Charles is not well to-day," said the mother, in a compassionate tone, cutting him a large wedge of her best home-made bread, which the lad began to demolish with a degree of rapidity that scarcely corroborated the assertion.

"But the story, sir?" said Kyrle.

"But the story. Well, little Tom Chute (he might have been better called little Tom-tit, only that he was not half so sprightly) was a very extraordinary man, for although he was small and fat, he was not merry nor talkative. You would have pitied him to see him walking about a ball-room, with ruffles that looked like small buckles, and a queue half as long as himself, reminding one of the handle of a pump when the sucker is up—with the most forlorn aspect in the world, as if he were looking for a runaway wife. It was a curious anomaly in his character, that although he—(Silence, there! My dear, will you speak to those children?) that although he always looked miserable in the midst of society, he really was so when out of it, as if the continued embarrassment and mortification which he experienced were a stimulus which he could not do without. Round, fat, shy, awkward, and oily, as he was, however, he tumbled his little rotund figure into the heart of Mrs. Trenchard, who was at that time, though a widow, one of the leading belles in Munster. A fair friend was the first to disclose this rapturous secret to poor Tom, for he might have known Mrs. Trenchard for a century without being able to make it out himself. He did not know whether he should be most frightened or pleased at the intelligence; but certain it is that, in the warmth of his first feelings, he made a tender of his hand to the lady, and was instantly accepted. A dashing, handsome fellow, who had been rejected by her some time before, and who knew Chute's irresolute temper, resolved to indemnify himself for the mortification he had received, by throwing some embarrassment in the way of the nuptials, and effected it simply enough. It seems the lady's accomplishments were of a very general description, for besides playing the harpsichord to admiration, she could manage a horse with any hero of the County Club, and was known to join their hunting parties, and even to ride a steeple chase with éclat. Indeed it was generally admitted that she possessed more spirit than might have answered her purposes, or her husband's either. What fancy she could have taken to Tom Chute I cannot for my life conceive. Well, this fellow met Tom going to her house one evening, as spruce as a water-wagtail, with his queue poking up behind, like the flag-staff in the stern of a privateer. They got into conversation about the widow. 'Beautiful creature, isn't she?' simpered Tom, blushing up to the eyes, for it was another funny foible of Tom's to redden up like a rose whenever there was any discourse of ladies, even when nobody dreamed of anything like raillery. 'Beautiful creature, isn't she?' says Tom. 'Beautiful, indeed,' replied the other. And Tom stood on his toes, threw out his right elbow, and took snuff. 'And accomplished, I think?' 'And very sensible,' says the other. 'And lively,' says Tom. 'And high spirited,' says the other, 'so, they say, her late husband found, poor man, to his cost.' Tom dropped his jaw a little, and looked inquisitive. But the other, who saw that his business was done, declined all explanation, and hurried off with a concluding remark, that 'the lady was unquestionably a capital whip.' Well, Tom got a sudden attack of—I don't know what complaint—went home that night, and sent an apology to the widow. He was not seen near her house for a fortnight after, and a report reached her ears that he had some notion of quitting the country. But if he had, she put a stop to it. One morning when Tom was looking over his books, he was startled by the apparition of a tall woman in a riding-dress, with a horsewhip in one hand, and a case of duelling pistols in the other. She nodded to Tom. 'I understand,' said she——"

At this moment a potato-peel, flung from the side-table, whisked past Mr. Daly's nose, and with happier aim, lighted on that of Prince Eugene in the print before mentioned. The venerable but too little venerated story-teller, who had been for the last few minutes endeavouring to raise his voice so as to make it audible above the increasing uproar of the young people, now turned round at this unparalleled and violent aggression, and confronted the daring group in awful silence. Satisfied, however, with the sudden hush of terror which this action occasioned, and willing to reserve the burst of wrath for a future transgression, he turned again in silence, and directing the servant girl, who was in the room, to take the potato-peel off Prince Eugene's nose, he resumed the thread of his narrative.

"'I understand,' said Mrs. Trenchard—for it was no other than the widow—'that you intend leaving Ireland?' Tom stammered and hesitated. 'If my brother were living,' continued the lady, 'he would horsewhip you; but although he is not, Hetty Trenchard is able to fight her own way. Come, sir, my carriage is at the door below; either step into it with me this minute, or take one of these pistols, and stand at the other end of the room.' Well, Tom looked as like a fool as any man in Ireland. He wouldn't fight, and he wouldn't be horsewhipped; so the business ended in his going into the carriage, and marrying the lady. Some persons, indeed, insinuated that Tom was observed in the course of the day to chafe his shoulders two or three times with an expression of pain, as if his change of condition had been the result of a still harsher mode of reasoning than I have mentioned; but this part of the story is without foundation."

"What a bold creature!" said the gentle Mrs. Daly.

"And is it possible, sir," asked Kyrle, "that this Amazon is the kind old lady whom Anne Chute attends with so much affection and tenderness in her infirmity?"

"Ah ha! Kyrle, I see the nature of the bolt that has wounded you, and I like you the better for it, my boy. A good face is a pippin that grows on every hedge; but a good heart—that is to say, a well-regulated one—is the apple of the Hesperides, worth even the risk of ease and life itself."

Kyrle assented to this sagacious aphorism with a deep sigh.

"Are the Cregans and they on terms now?" asked Mrs. Daly.

"As much on terms as two families of such opposite habits can be. The Chutes invite the Cregans to a family dinner once or twice in the year, and the Cregans ask the Chutes to their Killarney cottage, both of which invitations are taken as French compliments, and never accepted. Cregan himself hates going to Castle Chute, because he has nobody there to make jovial the night with him, and young Hardress (your friend, Kyrle) is too wild a lad to confine himself to mere drawing-room society. Apropos, talk of—'Tis a vulgar proverb, and let it pass; but there goes his trim pleasure-boat, the Nora Creina, flying down the river, and there sits the youth himself, tiller in hand as usual. Patcy, bring me the telescope; I think I see a female dress on board."

The telescope was brought and adjusted to the proper focus, while a dozen eager faces were collected about the small window, one over another, in the manner of those groups in painting called "Studies of Heads."

"That is he, indeed," continued Mr. Daly, resting the glass on the window frame, and directing it towards the object of their attention—"there is no mistaking that dark and handsome face, buried up as it is in the huge oiled penthouse hat, and there is his hunchbacked boatman, Danny Mann, or Danny the Lord, as the people call him since his misfortune, tending the foresheet in the bow. But that female—there is a female there unquestionably in a blue mantle, with the hood brought low over her eyes, sitting on the ballast. Who can she be?"

"Perhaps Danny Mann's cousin, Cotch Coonerty," said Mrs. Daly.

"Or some western dealing woman, who has come up to Limerick to purchase a reinforcement of pins, needles, whiskey, and reading-made-easys for her village counter, and is getting a free passage home from young Master Hardress."

"Like enough, like enough; it is just his way. Hillo! the fellow is going to run down that fishing cot, I believe!"

A hoarse cry of "Bear away!—hold up your hand!" was heard from the water, and reiterated with the addition of a few expletives, which those who know the energy of a boatman's dialect will understand without our transcribing them here. The pleasure-boat, however, heedless of those rough remonstrances, and apparently indisposed to yield any portion of her way, still held her bowsprit close to the wind, and sailed on, paying no more regard to the peril of the plebeian craft, than a French aristocrat of the *vieille cour* might be supposed to exhibit for that of a *sans culottes*, about to be trodden down by his leaders in the Rue St. Honoré. The fishermen, with many curses, backed water, and put about as rapidly as possible, but without being able to avoid the shock of the Nora Creina, who touched their stern with sufficient force to make the cot dart forward nearly an oar's length through the water, and to lay the rowers sprawling on their backs in the bottom. Fortunately the wind, which had sprung up with the returning tide, was not sufficiently strong to render the concussion more dangerous.

"Like his proud mother in every feature," said Mr. Daly. "Is it not singular that while we were speaking of the characters of the family, he could not pass our window without furnishing us with a slight specimen of his own? See how stately the fellow turns round and contemplates the confusion he has occasioned. There is his mother's grandeur, blended with the hair-brained wildness and idle spirit of his father."

"Hardress Cregan's is the handsomest boat in the river," said Patcy, a stout, sunburnt boy. "She'd beat all the Galway hookers from this to Beale. What a nice green hull!—and white sails, and beautiful green colours flying over her peak and gaff-topsail! Oh! how I'd like to be steering her."

Mr. Daly winked at his wife, and whispered her that he had known rear-admirals come of smaller beginnings. Mrs. Daly, with a little shudder, replied that she should not wish to see him a rear-admiral, the navy was so dangerous a service. Her husband, in order to soothe her, observed that the danger was not very near at hand.

In the meantime, Hardress Cregan became a subject of vehement debate at the side-table, to which the juvenile squadron had returned. One fair-haired little girl declared that she was his "pet." A second claimed that distinction for herself.

"He gave me an O'Dell-cake when he was last here," said one.

"And me a stick of peppermint."

"He gave me a—" in a whisper—"a kiss."

"And me two."

"He didn't."

"He did."

"I'll tell dadda it was you threw the potato-peel while ago."

"Ah ha, tattler, tell-tale!"

"Silence there!—fie! fie!—what words are these?" said Mrs. Daly. "Come, kiss and be friends, now both of you, and let me hear no more."

The young combatants complied with her injunction, and, as the duelling paragraphs say, "the affair terminated amicably."

"But I was speaking," Mr. Daly resumed, "of the family pride of the Cregans. It was once manifested by Hardress's father in a manner that might make an Englishman smile. When their little Killarney property was left to the Cregans, amongst many other additional pieces of display that were made on the occasion, it behoved Mr. Barny Cregan to erect a family vault and monument in his parish churchyard. He had scarcely, however, given directions for its construction, when he fell ill of a fever, and was very near enjoying the honour of *hanselling* the new cemetery himself. But he got over the fit, and made it one of his first cares to saunter out as far as the church and inspect the mansion which had been prepared for his reception. It was a handsome Gothic monument, occupying a retired corner of the churchyard, and shadowed over by a fine old sycamore.

But Barny, who had no taste for the picturesque, was deeply mortified at finding his piece of sepulchral finery thrown so much into the shade. 'What did I or my people do,' he said to the architect, 'that we should be sent skulking into that corner? I paid my money, and I'll have my own value for it.' The monument was accordingly got rid of, and a sporting, flashy one erected opposite the gateway, with the Cregan crest and shield (in what herald's office it was picked up I cannot take upon me to say) emblazoned on the frontispiece. Here, it is to be hoped, the aspiring Barnaby and his posterity may one day rest in peace."

"That would be a vain hope, I fear," said Kyrle, "at least so far as Mr. Cregan is concerned, if it were true, as our peasantry believe, that the churchyard is frequently made a scene of midnight mirth and revel, by those whose earthly carousals are long concluded. But what relationship is there between that family and Mrs. Chute?"

"She is step-sister to Mrs. Cregan."

"Indeed! So near?"

"Most veritable; therefore, look to it. They tell a story—" But the talkative old gentleman was interrupted in his anecdotical career by the entrance of a new actor on the scene.

CHAPTER IV.

HOW MR. DALY, THE MIDDLEMAN, ROSE UP FROM BREAKFAST.

BUT what pen less gifted than his of Chios, or his of Avon, the delineator of Vulcan or of Grumio, can suffice to convey to the reader any idea of the mental and bodily proportions of this new comer, who thrust his small and shining head in upon the family party, to awaken their curiosity, and to rob Mr. Daly of so many attentive listeners as he numbered around him at this moment?

The person who opened the door acted as a kind of herdsman or out-door servant to the family, and was a man of a rather singular appearance. The nether parts of his frame were of a size considerably out of proportion with the trunk and head which they supported. His feet were broad and flat like those of a duck; his legs long and clumsy, with knees and ankles like the knobs on one of those grotesque walking-sticks which were in fashion among the fine gentlemen of our own day, some time since; his joints hung loosely like those of a pasteboard Merry Andrew; his body was very small; his chest narrow; and his head so diminutive as to be even too little for his herring shoulders. It seemed as if nature, like an extravagant projector, had laid the foundation of a giant, but, running short of material as the structure proceeded, had been compelled to terminate her undertaking within the dimensions of a dwarf. So far was this economy pursued, that the head, small as it was, was very scantily furnished with hair, and the nose with which the face was garnished might be compared for its flatness to that of a young kid. "It looked," as the owner of this mournful piece of journey-work himself facetiously observed, "as if his head was not thought worth a roof, nor his countenance worth a handle." His hands and arms were likewise of a smallness which was much to be admired, when contrasted with the hugeness of the lower members, and brought to mind the fore-paws of a kangaroo, or the fins of a seal, the latter similitude prevailing when the body was put in motion, on which occasions they dabbled about in a very extraordinary manner. But there was one feature in which a corresponding prodigality had been manifested, namely, the ears, which were as long as those of Riquet with the Tuft, or of any ass in the barony.

The costume which enveloped this singular frame was no less anomalous than was the nature of its own construction. A huge *riding coat* of grey frieze hung lazily from his shoulders, and gave to view in front a waistcoat of calf-skin, with the hairy side outwards; a shirt, of a texture almost as coarse as sail cloth, made from the refuse of flax, and a pair of corduroy nether garments, with two bright new patches upon the knees. Grey worsted stockings, with dog-skin brogues well paved in the sole, and greased until they shone again, completed the personal adornments of this unaspiring personage. On the whole, his appearance might have brought to the recollection of a modern beholder one of those architectural edifices, so fashionable in our time, in which the artist, with an admirable ambition, seeks to unite all that is excellent in the Tuscan, Doric, Corinthian, and Ionic order in one *coup d'œil*.

7

The expression of the figure, though it varied with circumstances, was for the most part thoughtful and deliberative; the effect, in a great measure, of habitual penury and dependence. At the time of Lord Halifax's administration, Lowry Looby, then a very young man, held a *spot of ground* in the neighbourhood of Limerick, and was *well to do* in the world, but the scarcity which prevailed in England at the time, and which occasioned a sudden rise in the price of beer, butter, and other produce of grazing land in Ireland, threw all the agriculturists out of their little holdings, and occasioned a general destitution, similar to that produced by the anti-cottier system in the present day. Lowry was among the sufferers. He was saved, however, from the necessity of adopting one of the three ultimata of Irish misery—begging, enlisting, or emigrating—by the kindness of Mr. Daly, who took him into his service as a kind of runner between his farms; an office for which Lowry, by his long and muscular legs, and the lightness of the body that encumbered them, was qualified in an eminent degree. His excelling honesty, one of the characteristics of his country, which he was known to possess, rendered him a still more valuable acquisition to the family than had been at first anticipated. He had, moreover, the national talent for adroit flattery, a quality which made him more acceptable to his patron than the latter would willingly admit, and every emulsion of this kind was applied under the disguise of a simpleness which gave it a wonderful efficacy.

"Ha! Lowry," said Mr. Daly. "Well, have you made your fortune since you have agreed with the post-master?"

Lowry put his hands behind his back, looked successively at the four corners of the room, then round the cornice, then cast his eyes down at his feet, turned up the soles a little, and finally straightening his person, and gazing on his master, replied, "To lose it I did, sir, for a place."

"To lose what?"

"The place of postman, sir, through the country westwards. Sure there I was a gentleman for life if it wasn't my luck."

"I do not understand you, Lowry."

"I'll tell you how it was, masther. After the last postman died, sir, I took your recommendation to the post-masther, an' axed him for the place. 'I'm used to thravellin', sir,' says I. 'for Mister Daly, over, and——' 'Ay,' says he, takin' me up short, 'an' you have a good long pair o' legs, I see.' 'Middlin', sir,' says I (he's a very pleasant gentleman); 'it's equal to me any day, winther or summer, whether I go ten miles or twenty, so as I have the nourishment.' 'Twould be hard if you didn't get that, anyway,' says he. 'Well, I think I may as well give you the place, for I don't know any gentleman that I'd sooner take his ricommendation than Misther Daly's, or one that I'd sooner pay him a compliment, if I could.'"

"Well, and what was your agreement?"

"Ten pounds a year, sir," answered Lowry, opening his eyes, as if he announced something of wonderful importance, and speaking in a loud voice, to suit the magnitude of the sum, "besides my clothing and shoes throughout the year."

"'Twas very handsome, Lowry."

"Handsome, master? 'Twas wages for a prince, sir. Sure there I was, a made gentleman all my days, if it wasn't my luck, as I said before."

"Well, and how did you lose it?"

"I'll tell you, sir," answered Lowry: "I was going over to the post-masther yesterday, to get the Thralee mail from him, and to start off with myself on my first journey. Well an' good, of all the world, who should I meet, above upon the road, just at the turn down to the Post-office, but that red-headed woman that sells the freestone in the sthreets! So I turned back."

"Turned back! for what?"

"Sure the world knows, masther, that it isn't lucky to meet a red-haired woman, and you going of a journey."

"And you never went for the mail-bags?"

"Faiks, I'm sure I didn't that day."

"Well, and the next morning?"

"The next morning, that's this morning, when I went, I found they had engaged another boy in my place."

"And you lost the situation?"

"For this turn, sir, anyway. 'Tis luck that does it all. Sure I thought I was cock sure of it, an' I having the post-masther's word. But, indeed, if I meet that freestone crathur again, I'll knock her red head against the wall."

8

"Well, Lowry, this ought to show you the folly of your superstition. If you had not minded that woman when you met her, you might have had your sitnation now."

"'Twas she was in fault still, begging your pardon, sir," said Lowry, "for sure if I didn't meet her at all, this wouldn't have happened me."

"Oh," said Mr. Daly, laughing, "I see you are well provided against all argument. I have no more to say, Lowry."

The man now walked slowly towards Kyrle, and bending down with a look of solemn importance, as if he had some weighty intelligence to communicate, he said, "The horse, sir, is ready this way, at the doore abroad."

"Very well, Lowry. I shall set out this instant."

Lowry raised himself erect again, turned slowly round, and walked to the door, with his eyes on the ground, and his hand raised to his temple, as if endeavouring to recollect something farther which he had intended to say.

"Lowry!" said Mr. Daly, as the handle of the door was turned a second time. Lowry looked round.

"Lowry, tell me, did you see Eily O'Connor, the rope-maker's daughter, at the fair of Garryowen yesterday?"

"Ah, you're welcome to your game, masther."

"'Pon my word, then, Eily is a very pretty girl, Lowry, and I'm told the old father can give her something besides her pretty face."

Lowry opened his huge mouth (we forgot to mention that it *was* a huge one), and gave vent to a few explosions of laughter which much more nearly resembled the braying of an ass. "You are welcome to your game, masther," he repeated; "long life to your honour."

"But is it true, Lowry, as I have heard it insinuated, that old Mihil O'Connor used, and still does, twist ropes for the use of the county jail?"

Lowry closed his lips hard, while the blood rushed into his face at this unworthy allegation. Treating it, however, as a new piece of "the masther's game," he laughed, and tossed his head.

"Folly * on, sir—folly on."

"Because, if that were the case, Lowry, I should expect to find you a fellow of too much spirit to become connected, even by affinity, with such a calling. A rope-maker!—a manufacturer of rogues' last neckcloths—an understrapper to the gallows—a species of collateral hangman!"

"Ah, then, missiz, do you hear this? and all rising out of a little ould fable of a story that happened as good as five years ago, because Moriarty, the crooked hangman (the thief!) stepped into little Mihil's place of a night, and nobody knowin' of him, an' bought a couple o' pen'orth o' whip-cord for some vagary or other of his own. And there's all the call Mihil O'Connor had ever to gallowses or hangmen in his life. That's the whole toto o' their *insiniwaytions*."

"Never mind your master, Lowry," said Mrs. Daly; "he is only amusing himself with you."

"Oh, ha! I'm sure I know it, ma'am; long life to him, and 'tis he that's welcome to his joke."

"But, Lowry——"

"Ah, Heaven bless you now, masther, an' let me alone. I'll say nothing to you."

"Nay, nay, I only wanted to ask you what sort of a fair it was at Garryowen yesterday."

"Middling, sir, like the small *piatees*, they tell me," said Lowry, suddenly changing his manner to an appearance of serious occupation; "but 'tis hard to make out what sort a fair is when one has nothing to sell himself. I met a huckster, an' she told me 'twas a bad fair, because she could not sell her piggins; an' I met a pig-jobber, an' he told me 'twas a dear fair, pork ran so high; an' I met another little meagre creatur, a neighbour that has a cabin on the road above, an' he said 'twas the best fair that ever came out o' the sky, because he got a power for his pig. But Mr. Hardress Cregan was there, an' if he didn't make it a dear fair to some of 'em, you may call me an honest man."

"A very notable undertaking that would be, Lowry. But how was it?"

"Some o' them boys—them Garryowen lads—sir, to get about Danny Mann, the Lord, Mr. Hardress's boatman, as he was comin' down from Mihil's with a new rope for some part o' the

* Follow.

KYRLE DALY PAYS FORFEIT FOR GOING A COURTING.

at, and to begin *reflecting* on him in regard o' the hump on is back, poor creatur! Well, if they did, Master Hardress aerd 'em; and he having a stout blackthorn in his hand, this way, ad he made up to the foremost of 'em. 'What's that you're tying, you scoundrel?' says he. 'What would you give to now?' says the other, mighty impudent. Master Hardress ade no more, only up with the stick, and without saying this : that, or by your leave, or how do you do, he stretched him. 'ell, such a scuffle as began among 'em was never seen. They I fell upon Master Hardress, but faix they had only the half : it, for he made his way through the thick of 'em without as uch as a mark. Aw, indeed; it isn't a goose or a duck they had , do with when they came across Mr. Cregan, for all."

"And where were you all this while, Lowry?"

"Above in Mihil's door, standin' and lookin' about the fair r myself."

"And Eily?"

"Ah, hear to this again, now! I'll run away out o' the place itirely from you, masther, that's what I'll do;" and suiting the tion to the phrase, exit Lowry Looby.

No. 2.

"Well, Kyrle," said Mr. Daly, as the latter rose and laid aside his chair, "I suppose we are not to expect you back to-night?"

"Likely not, sir. If I have any good news to tell, I shall send an answer by Lowry, who goes with me; and if "—something seemed to stick in his throat, and he tried to laugh it out—"if I should be unsuccessful, I will ride on to the dairy-farm at Gurtenaspig, where Hardress Cregan promised to meet me."

Mr. Daly wished him better fortune than he seemed to hope for, and repeated an old proverb about a faint heart and a fair lady. The affectionate mother, who felt the feverishness of the young lover's hand, as he placed it in hers, and probably in secret participated in his apprehensions, followed him to the steps of the hall door. He was already on horseback.

"Kyrle," said Mrs. Daly, smiling, while she looked up in his face, and shaded her own with her hand—"remember, Kyrle, if Anne Chute should play the tyrant with you, that there is many a prettier girl in Munster."

Kyrle seemed about to reply, but his young horse became restive, and as the gentleman felt rather at a loss, he made the

9

impatience of the animal an apology for his silence. He waved his hand to the kind old lady, and rode away.

"And if she *should* play the tyrant with you, Kyrle," Mrs. Daly continued in soliloquy, while she saw his handsome and graceful figure diminish in the distance, "Anne Chute is not of my mind."

So said the mother as she returned to the parlour, and so would many younger ladies have said, had they known Kyrle Daly as well as she did.

While Mrs. Daly, who was the empress of all housekeepers, superintended the removal of the breakfast-table, not disdaining with her own fair hands to restore the plate and china to their former neatness, the old gentleman called all his children around him, to undergo a customary examination. They came flocking to his knees, the boys with their satchels thrown over their shoulders, and the girls with their gloves and bonnets on, ready for school. Occasionally, as they stood before the patriarchal sire, their eyes wandered from his face towards a lofty pile of sliced bread and butter, and a bowl of white sugar which stood near his elbow.

"North-east!" Mr. Daly began, addressing the eldest.

It should be premised that this singular name was given to the child in compliance with a popular superstition; for, sensible as the Dalys were accounted in their daily affairs, they were not wholly exempt from the prevailing weakness of their countrymen. Three of Mrs. Daly's children died at nurse, and it was suggested to the unhappy parents that if the next little stranger were baptized by the name of North-east, the curse would be removed from their household. Mrs. Daly acceded to the proposition, adding to it at the same time the slight precaution of changing her nurses. With what success this ingenious remedy was attended, the flourishing state of Mr. Daly's nursery thenceforward sufficiently testified.

"North-east," said the old gentleman, "when was Ireland first peopled?"

"By Bartholanus, sir, in anno mundi 1056, the great-great-great-great-great-grandson of Noah."

"Six greats. Right, my boy, although the Cluan-Mac-Nois makes it 1969. But a difference of a few years, at a distance of nearly four thousand, is not a matter to be quarrelled with. Stay, I have not done with you yet. Mr. Tickleback tells me you are a great Latinist. What part of Ovid are you reading now?"

"The Metamorphoses, sir, book the thirteenth."

"Ah, poor Ajax! he's an example and a warning for all Irishmen. Well, North-east, Ulysses ought to supply you with Latin enough to answer me one question. Give me the construction of this: *Mater mea sus est mala.*"

The boy hesitated a moment, laughed, reddened a little, and looked at his mother. "That's a queer thing, sir," he said at last.

"Come, construe, construe."

"*My mother is a bad sow,*" said North-east, laughing; "that's the only English I can find for it."

"Ah, North-east, do you call me names, my lad?" said Mrs. Daly, while she laid aside the china in a cupboard.

"'Tis dadda you should blame, ma'am; 'twas he said it. I only told him the English of it."

This affair produced much more laughter and merriment than it was worth. At length Mr. Daly condescended to explain.

"You gave me one construction of it," said he, "but not the right one. However, these things cannot be learned all in a day, and your translation was correct, North-east, in point of grammar, at all events. But (he continued with a look of learned wisdom) the true meaning of the sentence is this: *Mater*, mother, *mea*, hasten, *sus*, the sow, *est*, eats up (*edere*, my boy, not *esse*), *mala*, the apples."

"Oh, it's a *cran*, I see," said the boy with some indignation of tone. "One isn't obliged to know *crans*. I'd soon puzzle you if I was to put you all the *crans* I know."

"Not so easily as you suppose, perhaps," said his father in dignified alarm, lest his reputation should suffer in the eyes of his wife, who really thought him a profound linguist. "But you are a good boy. Go to school, North-east. Here, open your satchel."

The satchel was opened, a huge slice of bread from the top of the pile above mentioned was dropped into it, and North-east set off south-south-west out of the house.

10

"Charles, who is the finest fellow in Ireland?"

"Henry Grattan, sir."

"Why so, sir?"

"Because he says we must have a free trade, sir."

"You shall have a lump of sugar with your bread for that. Open your satchel. There; run away now to school. Patcy!"

"Sir?"

"Patcy tell me, who was the first Lord Lieutenant of Ireland in the present reign?"

Patcy, an idle young rogue, stood glancing alternately at the pile of bread and at his father's face, and shifting from one foot to another like a foundering nag. At last he said stoutly—

"Julius Cæsar, sir."

"That's a good boy. Ah, you young villain, if I had asked you who won the last boat-race, or how many hookers went by this morning, you'd give me a better answer than that. Was it Julius Cæsar sailed round the revenue cutter, near Tarbert, the other day?"

"No, sir, it was Larry Kett."

"I'll engage you know that. Well, tell me this, and I'll forgive you! Who was the bravest seaman you ever heard of, always excepting Hardress Cregan?"

"Brown, sir, the man that brought the Bilboa ship into Youghal, after making prisoners of nine Frenchmen: the fellows, dadda"—the boy continued, warming with his subject—"were sent to take the vessel into France, and Brown had only three men and a boy with him, and they retook the ship, and brought her into Youghal. But sure one Irishman was more than a match for two Frenchmen."

"Well, I perceive you have some knowledge in physics and comparative physiology. There's some hope of you. Go to school." And the pile of bread appeared a few inches lower.

The remainder was distributed amongst the girls, to whom the happy father put questions in history, geography, catechism, &c., proportioned to the capacity of each. At length he descended to the youngest, a little cherub, with roses of three years' growth in her cheeks.

"Well, Sally, my pet, what stands for sugar?"

"I, dadda."

"Ah, Sally's a wag, I see. You do stand for it, indeed, and you shall get it. We must not expect to force nature," he added, looking at his wife, and tossing his head. "Every beginning is weak, and Sam Johnson himself was as indifferent a philologist once in his day. And now, to school at once, darlings, and bring home good judgments. Nelly will go for you at three o'clock."

The little flock of innocents, who were matched in size like the reeds of a pandean pipe, each under each, having left the scene, Mr. Daly proceeded to dispatch his own affairs, and possessed himself of his hat and cane.

"I'll step over to the meadow, my dear, and see how the hay gets on. And give me that pamphlet of Hutchinson's—Commercial Restraints—I promised to lend it to Father Malachy. And let the stranger's room be got ready, my love, and the sheets aired, for I expect Mr. Windfall, the tax-gatherer, to sleep here to-night. And Sally, if Ready should come about his pigs that I put in pound last night, let him have them free of cost, but not without giving the fellow a fright about them; and above all, insist upon having rings in their noses before night. My little lawn is like a fallow-field with them. I'll be back at five."

Saying this, and often turning his head as some new commission arose to his memory, the Munster "Middleman" sallied out of his house, and walked along the gravelled avenue, humming as he went a verse of the popular old song:—

> "And when I at last must throw off this frail covering,
> Which I have worn for threescore years and ten,
> On the brink of the grave I'll not seek to keep hovering,
> Nor my thread wish to spin o'er again.
> My face in the glass I'll serenely survey,
> And with smiles count each wrinkle and furrow,
> For this old worn-out stuff that is threadbare to-day
> May become everlasting to-morrow!
> To-morrow! to-morrow!
> May become everlasting to-morrow!"

Such, in happier days than ours, was the life of a Munster farmer. Indeed, the word is ill adapted to convey to an English reader an idea of the class of persons whom it is intended to designate, for they were, and are, in mind and education, far superior to the persons who occupy that rank in most other countries. Opprobrious as the term "middleman" has been rendered in our own time, it is certain that the original formation of the sept was both natural and beneficial. When the country was deserted by its gentry, a general promotion of one grade took place among those who remained at home. The farmers became gentlemen, and the labourers became farmers, the former assuming, together with the station and influence, the quick and honourable spirit, the love of pleasure, and the feudal authority, which distinguished their aristocratic archetypes, while the humbler classes looked up to them for advice and assistance, with the same feeling of respect and of dependence which they had once entertained for the actual proprietors of the soil. The covetousness of landlords themselves, in selling leases to the highest bidder, without any inquiry into his character or fortune, first tended to throw imputations on this respectable and useful body of men, which, in progress of time, swelled into a popular outcry, and ended in an act of the legislature for their gradual extirpation. There are few now in that class as prosperous, many as intelligent and high-principled, as Mr. Daly.

CHAPTER V.

HOW KYRLE DALY RODE OUT TO WOO, AND HOW LOWRY LOOBY TOLD HIM SOME STORIES ON THE WAY.

KYRLE DALY had even better grounds than he was willing to insist upon for doubting his success with Anne Chute. He had been introduced to her for the first time, in the course of the preceding spring, at an assize ball, and thought her, with justice, the finest girl in the room: he danced two sets of country-dances (ah! ces beaux jours!) with her, and was ravished with her manners; he saw her home at night, and left his heart behind him when he bade her farewell.

The conquest of his affections might not have been so permanent as to disturb his quiet, had it not been quickly followed by that of his reason likewise. His subsequent acquaintance with the young lady produced a confirmation of his first impressions, from which he neither sought nor hoped to be delivered. The approbation of his parents fixed the closing rivet in the chain which bound him. Mrs. Daly loved Anne Chute for her filial tenderness and devotion, and Mr. Daly, with whom portionless virtue would have met but a tardy and calm acceptance, was struck motionless when he heard that she was to have the mansion and demesne of Castle Chute, which he knew had been held by her father's family at a peppercorn rent, insomuch that Kyrle might have said with Lubin in the French comedy, "Il ne tiendra qu'à elle que nous ne soyons mariés ensemble."

Nothing, however, in the demeanour of the young lady led him to believe that their acquaintance would be likely to terminate in such a catastrophe. It was true she liked him, for Kyrle was a popular character amongst all his fair acquaintances. He had, in addition to his handsome appearance, that frank and cheerful manner, not unmingled with a certain degree of tenderness and delicacy, which is said to be most successful in opening the female heart. Good nature spoke in his eyes, in his voice, and in "the laughter of his teeth," and he carried around him a certain air of ease and freedom, governed by that happy and instinctive discretion which those who affect the quality in vain attempt to exercise, and always overstep. But he could not avoid seeing that it was as a mere acquaintance he was esteemed by Miss Chute—an intimate, familiar, and, he sometimes flattered himself, a valued one, but still a mere acquaintance. She had even received some of his attentions with a coldness intentionally marked; but as an elegant coldness formed a part of her general manner, the lover, with a lover's willing blindness, would not receive those intimations as he at first thought they were intended.

When the affections are once deeply impressed with the image of beauty, everything in nature that is beautiful to the eyes, musical to the ears, or pleasing to any of the senses, awakens a sympathetic interest within the heart, and strengthens the impression under which it languishes. The loveliness of the day, and of the scenes through which he passed, occasioned a deep access of passion in the breast of our fearful wooer. The sky was mottled over with those small bright clouds which sailors, who look on them as ominous of bad weather, term mackerel; large masses of vapour lay piled above the horizon, and the deep blue openings overhead, which were visible at intervals,

appeared streaked with a thin and drifted mist which remained motionless, while the clouds underneath were driven fast across by a wind that was yet unfelt on earth.

The wooded point of land which formed the site of Castle Chute projected considerably into the broad river, at a distance of many miles from the road on which he now travelled, and formed a point of view on which the eye, after traversing the extent of water which lay between, reposed with much delight. Several small green islands and rocks, black with seaweed, and noisy with the unceasing cry of sea-fowl, diversified the surface of the stream, while the shores were clothed in that graceful variety of shade, and light, and hue, which is peculiar to the season. As Kyrle, with the fidelity of a lover's eye, fixed his gaze on the point of land above mentioned, and on the tall castle which overtopped the elms, and was reflected in the smooth and shining waters underneath, he saw a white-sailed pleasure-boat glide under its walls, and stand out again into the bed of the river. A sudden flash shot from her bow, and after the lapse of a few seconds the report of a gun struck upon his ear. At the same moment, the green flag which hung at the peak of the boat was lowered in token of courtesy, and soon after hoisted again to its former position. Kyrle, who recognised the Nora Creina, felt a sudden hurry in his spirits at the sight of this telegraphic communion with the family of his beloved. The picture instantly rushed into his mind of the effects produced by this incident in the interior of Castle Chute; Anne Chute looking up, and starting from her work-table; her mother leaning on her gold-headed cane, and rising with difficulty from her easy chair, to move towards the window; the cross old steward, Dan Dawley, casting a grum side glance from his desk through the hall window; the housemaid, Syl Carney, pausing, brush in hand, and standing like an evoked spirit, in a cloud of dust, to gape in admiration of the little pageant; the lifting of the sash, and the waving of a white handkerchief, in answer to the greeting from the water. But could it be visible at that distance? He put spurs to his horse, and rode forward at a brisker rate.

The figure of Lowry Looby, moving forward at a sling trot on the road before him, was the first object that directed his attention from the last-mentioned incident, and turned his thoughts into a merrier channel. The Mercury of the cabins, with a hazel stick for his *herpe*, and a pair of well-paved brogues for his *talaria*, jogged forward at a rate which obliged his master to trot at the summit of his speed in order to overtake him. He carried the skirts of his great frieze "riding-coat" under his arm, and moved—or more properly, sprang—forward, throwing out his loose-jointed legs forcibly, and with such a careless freedom, that it seemed as if, when once he lifted his foot from the ground, he could not tell where it would descend again. His hat hung so far back on his head that the disc of the crown was fully visible to his followers, while his head was so much in the rear of his shoulders, and moved from side to side with such a jaunty air, that it seemed at times as if the owner had a mind to leave it behind him altogether. In his right hand, fairly balanced in the centre, he held the hazel stick before alluded to, while he half hummed, half sung aloud, a verse of a popular ballad:—

> "Bryan O'Lynn had no small-clothes to wear,
> He cut up a sheep-skin to make him a pair,
> With the skinny side out and the woolly side in—
> ''Tis pleasant and cool,' says Bryan O'Lynn."

"Lowry!" shouted Kyrle Daly.

"Going, sir!"

"Going! I think you *are* going, and at a pretty brisk rate, too. You travel merrily, Lowry."

"Middlen, sir, middlen—as the world goes. I sing for company, ever and always, when I go a long road by myself; an' I find it a dale pleasanter and lighter on me. Equal to the lark, that the louder he sings the higher he mounts, it 's the way with me, an' I travellin'—the lighter my heart, the faster the road slips from under me.

> 'I am a bold bachelor, airy and free,
> Both cities and counties are equal to me;
> Among the fair females of every degree
> I care not how long I do tarry.' "

"Lowry, what do you think of the day?"

"What do I think of it, sir? I'm thinkin' 'twill rain, an' I'm sorry for it, an' the master's hay out yet. There 's signs o'

11

wind an' rain. The forty days ar'n't out yet, and there was a sight o' rain the last Saint Sweeten." And he again resumed his melody, suffering it to sink and swell in a manner alternately distinct and inarticulate, wih a slight mixture of that species of enunciation which Italians term the voice of the head :—

> " I never will marry while youth 's at my side,
> For my heart it is light and the world is wide ;
> I 'll ne'er be a slave to a haughty old bride,
> To curb me and keep me uneasy."

" And why should last St. Swithin have anything to do with this day ? "

" Oyeh, then, sure enough, sir. But they tell an ould fable about Saint Sweeten when he was first buried——"

" Why, was he buried more than once, Lowry ? "

" Oyeh, hear to this! Well, well—'tis makin' a hand o' me your honour is, fairly, kind father for you! He *was*, then, buried more than once, if you go to that of it. He was a great saint living, an' had a long *berrin* when he died; an' when they had the grave dug, and were for puttin' him into it, the sky opened, an' it kep' powerin', powerin' rain for the bare life, an' stop' so for forty days an' nights."

" And they couldn't bury him ? "

" An' they couldn't bury him till the forty days were over——"

" He had a long wake, Lowry."

" Believe it, sir. But ever since that, they remark, whatever way Saint Sweeten's day is, it is the same for forty days after. You don't b'lieve that, sir, now ? "

" Indeed, I am rather doubtful."

" See that, why! Why, then, I seen a schoolmaster westwards, that had as much Latin an' English as if he swallowed a dictionary, an' he 'd outface the world, that it was as true as you 're going the road this minute. But the *quollity* doesn't give in to them things at all. Heaven be with ould times! There is nothin' at all there as it used to be, Master Kyrle. There isn't the same weather there, nor the same peace, nor comfort, nor as much money, nor as strong whiskey, nor as good *piatees*, nor the gentlemen isn't so pleasant in themselves, nor the poor people so quiet, nor the boys so divartin', nor the girls so coaxin', nor nothin' at all is there as it used to be formerly. Hardly, I think, the sun shines as bright in the day; an' nothin' shows itself now by night, neither spirits nor good people. In them days a man couldn't go a lonesome road at night without meetin' things that would make the hair of his head stiffen equal to bristles. Now you might ride from this to Dingle without seeing anything uglier than yourself on the way. But what help for it ?

> ' Once in fair England my Blackbird did flourish,
> He was the chief flower that in it did spring ;
> Prime ladies of honour his person did nourish,
> Because that he was the true son of a king.
> But this false fortune,
> Which still is uncertain,
> Has caused this long parting between him and me,
> His name I'll advance
> In Spain an' in France,
> An' seek out my Blackbird, wherever he be.'

An' you wouldn't believe, now, Master Kyrle, that anything does be showin' itself at night at all? or used to be of ould?"

" It must be a very long while since, Lowry."

" Why, then, see this, sir. The whole country will tell you that after Mr. Chute died, the ould man of all, Mr. Tom's father —you heerd of him ? "

" I recollect to have heard of a fat man, that——"

" Fat !" exclaimed Lowry, in a voice of surprise—" you may say fat. There isn't that door on hinges that he 'd pass in, walkin' with a fair front, widout he turned sideways, or skamed in one way or other. You an' I, an' another along wid us, might be made out of the one half of him aisy. His body-coat, when he died, *med* a whole shoot for Dan Dawley, the steward, besides a jacket for his little boy ; an' Dan was no fishing-rod that time, I tell *you*. But anyway, fat or lain, he was buried, an' all the world will tell you that he was seen rising a fortnight after by Dan Dawley, in the shape of a drove o' young pigs."

" A whole drove ? "

" A whole drove. An' 'tisn't lain, lanky carcaishes o' store pigs either, only fat, fit for bacon. He was passin' the forge, near the ould gate, an' the moon shinin' as bright as silver, when he seen him comin' again' him on the road. Sure he isn't the same man ever since."

12

" Dan Dawley is not easily caught by appearances. What a sharp eye he must have had, Lowry, to recognise his master under such a disguise !"

" Oyeh, he knew well what was there. 'Tisn't the first time with Dan Dawley seein' things o' the kind. Didn't you ever hear what happened Dan in regard of his first wife, sir ? "

" No."

" Well, aisy, an' I'll tell you. Dan was married to a girl o' the Hayeses, a very inthricate little creatur, that led him a mighty uneasy life from the day they married out. Well, it was Dan's luck, she got a stitch, an' died one mornin', an' if she did, Dan made a *pilliloo* an' a *lavo* over her, as if he lost all belongin' to him. They buried her, for all, an' Dan was sittin' in his own doore, an' he twistin' a gad, to hang a little taste o' bacon he had, an' he singin' the *Rovin' Journeyman* for himself, when, tundher alive! who should walk in the doore to him only his dead wife, an' she livin' as well as ever! Take it from me, he didn't stay long where he was. 'Eh! is that you, Cauth?' says he. 'The very one,' says she. 'How does the world use you, Dan?' 'Wisha middlin', says Dan again. 'I didn't think we'd see you any more, Cauth,' says he. 'Nor you wouldn't either,' says she, 'only for yourself.' 'Do you tell me so?' says Dan Dawley. 'How was that?' 'There are two dogs,' says she, 'that are sleeping on the road I was goin' in the other world, an' the noise you made cryin' over me wakened 'em, an' they *riz* again me, and wouldn't let me pass.' 'See that, why!' says Dan, grinning; 'warn't they the conthrairy pair?' Well, after another twelvemonth Cauth died the second time; but I'll be your bail, it was long from Dan Dawley to cry over her this turn as he did at first. 'Twas all his trouble to see would he keep the women at the wake from *keening* over the dead corpse, or doing anything in life that would waken the dogs. Signs on, she passed 'em, for he got neither tale nor tidin's of her from that day to this. 'Poor Cauth,' says Dan, 'why should I cry, to have them dogs tearin' her maybe?'"

" Dan Dawley was a lucky man," said Kyrle. " Neither Orpheus nor Theseus had so much to say for himself as he had.

" I never hear talks o' them gentlemen, sir. Wor they o' these parts ? "

" Not exactly. One of them was from the county of Attica, and the other from the county of Thrace."

" I never heard o' 'em ; I partly guess they wor strangers," Lowry continued with much simplicity ; " but anyway, Dan Dawley was a match for the best of 'em, an' a luckier man than I told you yet, moreover—that's in the first beginnin' of his days."

At this moment a number of smart young fellows, dressed out in new felt hats, clean shoes and stockings, with ribbons flying at the knees, passed them on the road. They touched their hats respectfully to Mr. Daly, while they recognised his attendant by a nod, a smile, and a familiar " Is that the way, Lowry?"

" The very way, then, lads," said Lowry, casting a longing look after them. " Goin' to Garryowen they are now, divartin' for the night," he added in a half-envious tone, after which he threw the skirt of his coat from the left to the right arm, looked down at his feet, struck the ground with the end of his stick, and trotted on, singing—

> " I 'm noted for dancin' a jig in good order,
> A min'et I'd march, an' I'd foot a good reel :
> In a country-dance I'd still be the leading partner ;
> I ne'er faltered yet from a crack on the heel.

" My heart is wid ye, boys, this night. But I was tellin' you, Master Kyrle, about Dan Dawley's luck. Listen hether."

He dried his face, which was glistening with moisture and flushed with exercise, in his frieze coat, and commenced his story:—

" 'Tis not in Castle Chute the family lived always, sir, only in ould Mr. Chute's time ; he built it, an' left the Fort above, an' I'll tell you for what raison. The ould man of all, that had the Fort before him, used to be showing himself there at night, himself an' his wife, an' his two daughters, an' a son, an' there were the strangest noises ever you hear going on above stairs. The master had six or seven sarvints, one after another, stopping up to watch him, but there isn't one of 'em but was killed by the spirit. Well, he was forced to quit at last on the 'count of it, an' it is then he built Castle Chute—the new part of it, where Miss Anne an' the ould lady lives now. Well an' good, if he did, he was standin' one mornin' oppozit his own gate on the road-side, out, an' the sun shining, an' the birds singing for themselves in the bushes, when who should he see only Dan Dawley, an' he a little gaffer the same time, serenadin' down the road for the bare life. 'Where to now, lad?' says Mr. Chute (he was a mighty pleasant man). 'Looking for a master, then,' says Dan Dawley. 'Why, then, never go past this gate for him,' says Mr. Chute, 'if you 'll do what I bid you,' says he. 'What 's that, sir?' says the boy. So he up an' told him the whole story about the Fort, an' how something used to be showin' itself there, constant, in the dead hour o' the night. An' have you the courage,' says he, 'to sit up a night, an' watch it?' 'What would I get by it?' says Dan, looking him up in the face. 'I 'll give you twenty guineas in the mornin', an' a table, an' a chair, an' a pint o' whiskey, an' a fire, an' a candle, an' your dinner before you,' says Mr. Chute. 'Never say it again,' says the gossoon; ''tis high wages for one night's work, an' I never yet done,' says he, 'anything that would make me in dread o' the living or the dead, or afraid to trust myself into the hands o' the Almighty.' 'Very well, away with you,' says the gentleman, 'an' I 'll have your life if you tell me a word of a lie in the mornin',' says he. 'I will not, sir,' says the boy, 'for what?' Well, he went there, an' he drew the table a-near the fire for himself, an' got his candle, an' began readin' his book. 'Tis the lonesomest place you ever seen. Well, that was well an' good, till he heerd the greatest racket that ever was goin' on above stairs, as if all the slates on the roof were fallin'. 'I'm in dread,' says Dan, 'that these people will do me some bad hurt,' says he; an' hardly he said the word, when the doore opened, and in they all walked, the ould gentleman with a great big wig on him, an' the wife, an' the two daughters, an' the son. Well, they all put elbows upon themselves, an' stood lookin' at him out in the middle o' the floore. He said nothin', and they said nothin', an' at last, when they were tired o' lookin', they went out, an' walked the whole house, an' went upstairs again. The gentleman came in the mornin' early. 'Good morrow, good boy,' says he. 'Good morrow, sir,' says the boy. 'I had a dale o' fine company here last night,' says he, 'ladies an' gentlemen.' 'It's a lie you're tellin' me,' says Mr. Chute. ''Tis not a word of a lie, sir,' says Dan; 'there was an ould gentleman with a big wig, an' an ould lady, an' two young ones, an' a young gentleman,' says he. 'True for you,' says Mr. Chute, puttin' a hand in his pocket, and reaching him *twenty* guineas. 'Will you stay there another night?' says he. 'I will, sir,' says Dan. Well, he went walkin' about the fields for himself, and when night comes——"

"You may pass over the adventures of the second night, Lowry," said Kyrle, "for I suspect that nothing was effected until the third."

"Why, then, you just guessed it, sir. Well, the third night he said to himself, 'Escape how I can,' says he, 'I 'll speak to that ould man with the wig, that does be puttin' an elbow on himself, an' looking at me!' Well, the ould man, an' all o' them, came and stood oppozit him with elbows on 'em as before. Dan got frightened, seeing 'em stop so long in the one place, and the ould man lookin' so wicked (he was after killin' six or seven in the same Fort), an' he went down on his two knees, an' he put his hands together, an' says he——"

A familiar incident of Irish pastoral life occasioned an interruption in this part of the legend. Two blooming country girls, their hair confined with a simple black ribbon, their cotton gowns pinned up in front, so as to disclose the greater portion of the blue stuff petticoat underneath, and their countenances bright with health and laughter, ran out from a *cottage* door, and intercepted the progress of the travellers. The prettier of the two skipped across the road, holding between her fingers a worsted thread, while the other retained between her hands the large ball from which it had been unwound. Kyrle paused, too well acquainted with the country customs to break through the slender impediment.

"Pay your *footing* now, Master Kyrle Daly, before you go farther," said one.

"Don't overlook the wheel, sir," added the girl who remained next the door.

Kyrle searched his pocket for a shilling, while Lowry, with a half-smiling, half-censuring face, murmured—

"Why, then, Heaven send ye sense, as it is it ye want this mornin'."

"And you manners, Mr. Looby. Single your freedom, and double your distance, I beg o' you. Sure your purse, if you have one, is safe in your pocket. Long life an' a good wife to you, Master Kyrle, an' I wisht I had a better hould than this o' you. I wisht you were in *looze*, an' that I had the finding o' you this mornin'."

So saying, while she smiled merrily on Kyrle, and darting a scornful glance at Lowry Looby, she returned to her woollen wheel, singing, as she twirled it round—

"I want no lectures from a learned master;
  He may bestow 'em on his silly train;
  I'd sooner walk through my blooming garden,
  An' hear the whistle of my jolly swain."

To which Lowry, who received the lines, as they were probably intended, in a satirical sense, replied, as he trotted forwards, in the same strain:—

"Those dressy and smooth-faced young maidens,
  Who now looks at present so gay,
  Has borrowed some words o' good English,
  An' knows not one half what they say.
  No female is fit to be married,
  Nor fancied by no man at all,
  But those who can sport a drab mantle,
  An' likewise a cassimere shawl."

Hoop-whishk! Why, then, she 's a clean-made little girl for all, isn't she, Master Kyrle? But I was tellin' you—where 's this I was? Iss, just. Dan Dawley going on his knees an' talking to the *sperrit*. Well, he raised his two hands this way, an' 'The Almighty be betune you an' me this night!' says he. 'Ah! that 's my good boy,' says the ould man. 'I was waiting these three nights to have you speak first, an' if you hadn't that time, I 'd have your life equal to all the others,' says he. 'But come with me now, an' I 'll make a gentleman o' you, for you 're the best boy that ever I see,' says he. Well, the boy got a tremblin', an' he couldn't folly him. 'Don't be one bit afeerd o' me,' says the ould gentleman, 'for I won't do you a ha'porth o' hurt.' Well, he carried Dan after him through the house, and he showed him three crocks o' goold buried behind a doore, an' 'D'ye hear to me now?' says he. 'Tell my son to give one o' these crocks to my daughter, an' another to you, an' to keep the third himself, an' then I won't show myself this way any more,' says he, 'for it is the goold that does be always troubling us in the ground. An' tell him, if he lives,' says he, 'to give you my daughter in marriage, an' this Fort along with her.' 'Alilu! me tell him!' cries Dan Dawley. 'I'm sure I wouldn't take him such a message for the world.' 'Do, ayeh,' says the ould man, 'an' show him this ring for a token, an' tell him I 'll be showing myself be day an' be night to him until he 'll give her to you.' So he vanished in the greatest tundher ever you hear. That was well an' good. Well, the next mornin' Mr. Chute come, an' if he did, 'Good morrow, good boy,' says he. 'Good morrow, sir,' says Dan. 'Have you any news for me after the night?' says he. 'I have very good news,' says Dan. 'I have three crocks o' goold for you, I got from the ould gentleman,' says he, an' he up an' tould him all about it, an' showed him the goold. 'It's a lie you 're telling me,' says Mr. Chute, 'an' I 'll have your life,' says he—'you went rootin' au' found these yourself.' So Dan put a hand in his pocket, an' pulled out the ring and gave it into his hand. It was the ring, sir, his father wore the day he was buried. 'I give it into you,' says Mr. Chute; 'you did see them surely. What else did he say to you?' Well, Dan begin lookin' down an' up, an' this way, an' that way, an' didn't know what to say. 'Tell me at once,' says Mr. Chute, 'an' fear nothing.' Very well. He did. 'Sir,' says he, 'the ould gentleman told me, an' sure 'tis a thing I don't expect—but he said I should get Miss Anne, your sister, in marriage.' Well, Mr. Chute stood lookin' at Dan as if he had three heads on him. 'Give you my sister, you *keowt* of a *geocogh!*' says he; 'you flog Europe for bouldness—get out of my sight,' says he, 'this minute, or I 'll give you a kick that will raise you from poverty to the highest pitch of affluence.' 'An' won't I get the crock o' goold, sir?' says Dan. 'Away out o' that with you,' says the gentleman; ''tis to rob me you want, I believe, you notorious delinquent.' Well, Dan was forced to cut, but in a while after the ould man sent for him, an' made him a compliment o' something handsome, and put him over his business as he is to-day with the present people, an' an honest creatur as could be. There 's more people says that it was all a fable, an' that Dan Dawley *dremt* of it, but this was his own story. An' sure *I* might as well be draming too," he added, casting a side glance at

Kyrle, "for it's little attention you are paying to me or my story." In this assertion Lowry was perfectly correct, for his young master's thoughts at that moment were occupied by a far more interesting subject.

CHAPTER VI.

HOW KYRLE DALY WAS MORE PUZZLED BY A PIECE OF PAPER THAN THE ABOLISHERS OF THE SMALL-NOTE CURRENCY THEMSELVES.

In taking out of his pocket the piece of silver which he wanted to bestow on the cottage Omphale, he drew forth with it a little paper, containing a copy of verses which he had taken from one of Anne Chute's music books. They were written in a boyish hand, and signed with the letters H. C.; and Kyrle was taxing his memory to recapitulate all the bachelors in the county who bore those initials. There was, in the first place, Hyland Creagh, commonly called Fireball Creagh, a great *sweater* and *pinker*—a notorious duellist, who had been concerned, either on behalf of himself or his friends, in more than one hundred "affairs of honour," a member of the Hell-Fire Club, a society constituted on principles similar to those of the Mohocks, which flourished in London about half a century before Kyrle's time, and whose rules and orders the reader may peruse at full length in the manifesto of their Emperor Taw Waw Eben Zan Kaladar, as set forth in Mr. Addison's amusing journal. Of the provincial branch of this society above mentioned (it is a name that we are loath to repeat oftener than is necessary), Mr. Hyland Fireball Creagh had been a member in his early days, and was still fond of recounting their customs and adventures with greater minuteness than always accorded with the inclinations of his hearers. There were some qualities in the composition of this gentleman which made it probable enough that he might write verses in a lady's music book. He was as gallant as any unmarried Irishman of his day, and he had a *fighting name*, a reputation which was at that time in much higher repute than it is in our own. He had *conversation* (an essential talent in a man of gallantry)—he dressed well, though with a certain antiquated air—and he had a little poodle dog, which shut the door when you said "*Baithershin*," and chucked a crust of bread from his nose into his mouth at the word "Fire!" And Mr. Creagh, whenever his canine follower was called on to perform those feats, was careful to make the ladies observe that Pincher never ventured to snap at the word "Make ready!" or "Present!" while if you whispered "Fire!" in ever so gentle a tone—pop! the bread vanished in an instant. But then there were some objections, which were likely to neutralise these accomplishments of Fireball and his dog, and to render it unlikely, after all, that he (that is, the former) had been the perpetrator of the verses. He had run through his property, and reduced himself to the mean estate of a needy guest at other men's tables, and a drinker of other men's wine, or rather whiskey, for that was the fundamental ingredient of his customary beverage. This circumstance laid him under the necessity of overlooking a greater number of unhandsome speeches than was consistent with his early fame. And there was one other objection, which rendered it still more improbable that Anne Chute would think any of his effusions worth preserving. He was just turned of sixty-five.

It could not, therefore, be Mr. Hyland Fireball Creagh. H. C.?—Who was it? Hepton Connolly?

Now, reader, judge for yourself what a wise conjecture was this of Mr. Kyrle Daly's. Mr. Hepton Connolly was a still more objectionable swain than the Irish diner-out above described; indeed, he had no single qualification to recommend him as a social companion, except that of being able to contain a prodigious quantity of whiskey-punch at a sitting—a virtue in which a six-gallon jar might have excelled him. Nor do I find that there was any part of Anne Chute's demeanour which could lead Kyrle Daly to suppose that this circumstance would take a powerful hold of her affections, although it secured him an envied place in those of her uncle, Mr. Barnaby Cregan, of Roaring Hall. For the rest, Mr. Hepton Connolly was one individual of a species which is now happily extinct among Irish gentlemen. He just retained enough of a once flourishing patrimony to enable him to keep a hunter, a racer, and an insolent groom. He was the terror of all the pettifogging lawyers, the three-and-ninepenny attorneys, bailiffs, and process servers in the county. Against these last, in particular, he had

carried his indignation to such a length as to maim one of them for life by a shot from his hall window. And he told fifty anecdotes, which made it appear astonishing that he had escaped the gallows so long. But he relied strongly (and in those days not without reason) on the fact, that there could not be a jury empanelled against him on which he might not number a majority of his own relations. It was not, indeed, that he calculated much on their personal regard or affection for himself, but the stain upon their own name was such, he knew, as they would not willingly incur. His reliance upon this nicely of honour in his friends was so complete, that he never suffered any uneasiness upon those occasions when it became necessary for him to plead to an indictment, however irresistible the evidence by which it was supported; and the only symptoms of anxiety which he ever manifested consisted in a frequent reference to his watch, and a whisper to the under-turnkey, to know whether he had left directions at the jail to keep his dinner hot. One amusing effect produced by Mr. Connolly's repeated collisions with judicial authorities was, that he acquired a gradual fondness for the law itself, and became knowing upon the *rights of persons* and the *rights of things*, in proportion to the practical liberties which he was in the habit of taking with the one and the other. While he made little account of breaking a man's head at a second word, he would prosecute, to the rigour of the law, a poor half-naked mountaineer, for stealing a basket of turf from his ricks, or cutting a faggot in one of his hedges. To do him justice, however, it should be mentioned that he never was known to pursue matters to extremity in the instance of punishment, and was always satisfied with displaying his own legal skill before the petty sessions. Nay, he had even been frequently known to add considerably to his own loss in those cases, by making a gift to the culprit of many times the amount of the pilfered property. If Anne Chute could receive this single trait of good feeling as a counterpoise for much bad principle—if she could love to see her house filled with jockeys, horseriders, grooms, and drunken gentlemen—if she could cherish a fondness for dogs and unlicensed whiskey—if, in a word, she could be the happy wife of a mere sportsman—then it was possible that Mr. Hepton Connolly might be the transcriber (author was out of the question) of the little effusion that had excited Kyrle Daly's curiosity.

Who was it? The question still remained without solution. Ha! Her cousin and his college friend, Mr. Hardress Cregan? The conjecture at first made the blood fly into his face, while his nerves were thrilled by a horrid sensation of mingled fear, grief, and anger. But a moment's reflection was sufficient to restore quiet to his mind, and to smile down the spirit of jealousy at its first motion within his breast. Hardress Cregan was perfectly indifferent to the lady; he seldom spoke of her, and scarcely ever visited at Castle Chute. It could not be Hardress. He was a great deal too shy and timid to carry on a lengthened interchange of raillery with any young lady, and if it were more than raillery, he knew the intensity of his friend's character too well to suppose that he would refrain from pursuing his fortunes. It could not be Hardress. He was perfectly aware of Kyrle Daly's secret—he had repeatedly expressed the warmest wishes for his success; and Hardress Cregan was no hypocrite. They had been friends, attached friends, at college, and although their intercourse had been much interrupted since their return home, by difference of pursuits and of tastes or habits, still their early friendship remained unchanged, and they never met but with the warmth and the affection of brothers. It was true he had heard Hardress speak of her with much esteem, on his first introduction to college, and when he was yet a very young lad; but a little raillery was abundantly sufficient to strike him dumb for ever on the subject; and he had not taken many lounges among the beauties of Capel Street and the Phœnix Park, when he appeared to have lost all recollections of his boyish attachment. Kyrle Daly had penetration enough to be aware that he could not, with certainty, calculate on a character at once so profound and so unsettled as that of his young friend, who had always, even in his mere boyhood, been unapproachable by his most intimate acquaintances, and whom he suspected to be capable of one day wielding a mightier influence in society than he seemed himself to hope or aspire to. But Hardress was no hypocrite. That was a sufficient security that, if there were a rival in the case, he was not the man; and if Kyrle needed a more positive argument, it might be found in the fact

14

of a new attachment, which had of late been intimated to him by his young friend himself.

The love which Kyrle entertained for this lady was so singular, so rational, and regulated by so fine a principle of judgment, that the warmest, the wisest, and the best of men might condescend to take an interest in its success. Naturally gifted with the gentlest qualities of heart, and educated by a mother who taught him the use of that mind by which they were to be directed, it would not be easy to discover a more estimable character among the circles in which he moved. He was the more fortunate, too, that his goodness was the result of natural feeling rather than that of principle alone; for it is a strange and a pitiable peculiarity in our nature, that if a man, by mere strength of reason and perseverance, have made himself master of all the social virtues, he shall not be as much loved in the world as another who has inherited them from nature, although, in the latter instance, they may be obscured by many hideous vices. It may appear presumptuous to hazard an opinion upon a subject of so much gravity; but, perhaps, the reader will not charge us with having caught the paradoxical air of the day, if we venture to intimate, that the true source of the preference may be referred to the common principle of self-preservation. A character that is naturally, and by necessity, generous, may be calculated upon with more certainty than that which is formed by education only, as long as men's opinions shall be found more variable than their feelings. Otherwise, why should we bestow more affection on that character which is really the less admirable of the two?. But the reader may receive or reject this conjecture as he pleases. We proceed with our history.

For this, or for some better reason, it was, that Kyrle Daly, though highly popular among his inferiors and dependents, had only a second place in their affection, compared with his friend Hardress. A generosity utterly reckless and unreasoning is a quality that in all seasons has wrought most powerfully upon the inclinations of the Irish peasantry, who are themselves more distinguished for quick and kindly feeling, than for a just perception of moral excellence. Because, therefore, the flow of generosity in Hardress Cregan, was never checked nor governed by motives of prudence nor of justice, while good sense and reason regulated that of Kyrle Daly, the estimation in which they were held was proportionably unequal. The latter was spoken of amongst the people as "a good master;" but Hardress was their darling. His unbounded profusion made them entertain for him that natural tenderness which we are apt to feel towards any object that seems to require protection. "His heart," they observed, "was in the right place." "It would be well for him if he had some of Master Kyrle's sense, poor fellow." "Master Kyrle would buy and sell him at any fair in Munster."

It was only, therefore, among those who were thoroughly intimate with his character, that Kyrle Daly was fully understood and appreciated; and it is not saying a little in his praise, to remark that his warmest admirers, as well as his best lovers, were to be found within the circle of his own family.

It is impossible that such a mind as we have described could give a tranquil entertainment to any serious passion. Few could suppose from the general gaiety and cheerfulness of his demeanour, and the governed and rational turn of his discourse, that he held a heart so acutely susceptible of passion, and so obnoxious to disappointment. It is true, that, in the present instance, he was in some degree guarded by his own doubts and fears against the latter contingency; but he had also cherished hope sufficient to insure him, in case of rejection, a grievous load of misery. He had weighed well the lady's worth before he fixed his affections upon her; and when he did so, every faculty of his mind and feeling of his heart subscribed to the conviction, that with her, and her alone, he could be earthly happy.

The sun had passed the meridian before Kyrle Daly again beheld the small and wooded peninsula which formed the site of Castle Chute. The languor of heart that always accompanies the passion in its hours of comparative inaction, that luxurious feeling of mingled pensiveness and joy, which fills up the breast, and constitutes in itself an Elysium even to the doubting lover, were aided in their influence by the sunny calmness of the day, and the beauty of the landscape, which every step unfolded to his view. The fever of suspense became more tormenting in proportion as he drew nearer to the solution of his doubts, and the last few miles of his journey seemed incomparably the most tedious. His horse, however, who was not in love, and had not broken fast since morning, began, at sight of a familiar baiting-place, to show symptoms of inanition, to remedy which his considerate master drew up, and alighted at the inn-door.

CHAPTER VII.

HOW KYRLE DALY DISCOVERS THAT ALL THE SORROW UNDER THE SUN DOES NOT REST UPON HIS SHOULDERS ALONE.

HE left Lowry Looby standing by the trough to see justice done to the dumb creature, while he strolled onwards in the sunshine, unwilling to disturb the current of his own thoughts by any conversation with the people of the inn.

The owner of this place of "entertainment" also filled the dignified post of pound-keeper to the neighbouring village, and his roofless bastile was situated at no great distance farther on the roadside. As Kyrle walked by the iron gate he was surprised to see it crowded by a number of Kerry ponies, such as may be discerned along the mountain sides from the Upper Lake of Killarney. They were of various colours, bright, bay, dun, and cream; but the shagginess of their coats, and the diminutiveness of their size, rendered them but a little more respectable in appearance than the same number of donkeys. Several of these half-starved creatures had their heads thrust out over the low pound wall, as if to solicit the interference of passengers, while others, resigned to their fate, stood in drooping postures in the centre of the inclosure, quite chop-fallen. Kyrle Daly's curiosity was sufficiently excited to induce him to turn once more upon his path, and make some inquiry at the inn concerning the owner of the herd.

He found the landlord at the door, a small, withered old man, with an air of mingled moroseness and good nature in his countenance—the former the effect of his office, the latter of his natural disposition. He was standing on a three-foot stool, and occupied in taking down a sign-board, for the purpose of transmitting it to a scene of rural festivity which was going forward in the neighbourhood.

He suspended his labours, and was about to enter into an ample exposition of the history of the ponies, when his wife, a blooming, middle-aged woman, in a tête, and glossy green petticoat, came to the door, and looked out to know what made the hammering cease. The glance of her eye was enough for the innkeeper, who recommenced his work with fresh diligence, while his watchful helpmate undertook to satisfy the curiosity of our traveller.

The ponies, she told him, were the property of a mountaineer from Killarney, who was making a "tower" of the country, to try and sell them at the fairs and patterns. He had come to their neighbourhood last night, and turned his ponies out on the common; but finding that it furnished only short commons for them, the poor things had made their way into the improvements of Castle Chute, and were apprehended by Mr. Dan. Dawley in the act of trespass. That inexorable functionary had issued an order for their immediate committal to pound; and Myles Murphy, the owner, was now gone off to make interest with Miss Anne, "the young mistress," for their release.

"He'll be a lucky boy," she continued, "if he overtakes her at home this way, for herself and a deal o' quality are to be at the sands below, to see the races and doings there."

"Races?" repeated Kyrle. "I never heard of races in this quarter."

"Oyeh, what races!" exclaimed her husband. "A parcel of ould staggeens, sir, that's running for a saddle; that's all the races they'll have."

"So itself, what hurt," returned the wife. "The whole European world will be there to look at 'em; and I'll be bound they'll drink as hearty as if Jerry Sneak an' Sappho were on the coorse. An' 'tis there you ought to be an hour ago in your tent, instead of crusheening here about Myles Murphy an' his ponies."

"Miles Murphy!—Myles-na-Coppaleen!—Miles of the Ponies, is it?" said Lowry Looby, who just then led Kyrle Daly's horse to the door. "Is he in these parts now?"

"Do you know Myles, croo?" was the truly Irish reply.

"Know Myles-na-Coppaleen? Wisha, an' 'tis I that do, an' that well! O murther! an' are them poor Myles's ponies I see in the pound over? Poor boy! I declare I'm sorry for his trouble."

"If you be as you say," the old innkeeper muttered with a distrustful smile, "put a hand in your pocket, an' give me four-and-eightpence, an' you may take the fourteen of 'em after him."

"Why, then, see; I'm blest, if I had it, but I wouldn't break your word this day, or more than that, if it was in my power, for poor Myles. There isn't a better son nor brother this moment goin' the road than what he is."

"It's true for you, by all accounts," said the pound-keeper, as he counted over Kyrle Daly's change; "but people must do their duty for all."

"Surely, surely," said Lowry, turning off.

Mrs. Normal, the hostess, here made her re-appearance at the door, with a foaming pot of Fermoy ale in her hand, to which she directed Lowry's attention.

"Ah, then, what's that you're doin'?" he said with a look of rough remonstrance, while he fixed, nevertheless, a steady and wistful eye upon the draught.

"Drink it off, I tell you."

"Sorrow a drop."

"You must, again."

"I won't, I tell you."

"Do you refuse my *hansel*,* an' I goin' to the races? Be said by me, I tell you. The day is *drouthy*."

Lowry offered no further objection, but made his own of the ale, observing, as he returned the vessel, with closed and watery eyes, that it was "murtherin' sthrong." The colloquy above detailed was carried on with so much roughness of accent and violence of gesture, that a person at a little distance might have supposed the parties were on the eve of coming to blows in an actual quarrel. But it was all politeness.

Kyrle Daly obtained from his attendant, as they proceeded on their way, an account of the individual in whom he had expressed so deep an interest. Myles Murphy, or, as he was more generally called, Myles of the Ponies, was the occupier of a tract of land on one of the Killarney mountains, comprising about seven hundred acres. For this extensive holding he paid a rent of fifteen pounds sterling in the year; and if there were a market for gray limestone in the neighbourhood, Myles would be one of the wealthiest men in Kerry. But as the agricultural taste of the vicinity ran chiefly in favour of mud, his property in mineral was left as an heir-loom upon his hands. Of the whole seven hundred acres, there was no more under tillage than sufficed to furnish potatoes for the consumption of his own family. The vast remainder was stocked with numerous herds of wild ponies, who found scanty pasturage between the fissures of the crags, and yet were multiplied to such a degree, that Myles could not estimate the amount of his own stud.

"His own goodness it was," continued Lowry, "that got that for him. He was left, poor fellow, after his father dying of *the sickness*,† with a houseful o' childther—fourteen sons an' two daughters, besides himself to provide for, an' his ould mother. He supported 'em all be the labour of his two hands, till Lord K—— hear talk of him of a day, an' give him a lease o' that farm, an' behaved a good landlord to him since. Still an' all, Myles do be poor, for he never knew how to keep a hoult o' the money. He provided for all his brothers—had one *priested*, an' another bound to a brogue-maker, an' another settled as a school-master in the place, an' more listed from him, an' two went to *say*, an' I don't know what he done with the rest, but they're all very well off; an' left poor Myles with an empty pocket in the latter end."

Lowry went on to inform our traveller that this said Myles was a giant in stature, measuring six feet four inches "in his vamps;" that he never yet met "that man that could give him a stroke, and he having a stick in his hand;" that he was a clean-made boy as ever "walked the ground," and such a master of his weapon, that himself and Luke Kennedy, the Killarney boatman, used to be two hours "oppozite" one another, without a single blow being received on either side. On one occasion, indeed, he was fortunate enough to "get a vacancy at Kennedy," of which he made so forcible a use, that the stick which was in the hand of the latter flew over Ross Castle into the lower lake, merely from a successful tip on the elbow.

"But," Lowry added, "there's a change come in poor Myles of late. It was his *luck* to meet Eily O'Connor, the rope-maker's daughter, of a day, an' he selling his ponies, an' 'tis a new story

* It is considered not lucky to refuse a hansel.   † Typhus fever.
16

with him since. He's mad, sir—mad in love. He isn't good for anything. He says she gave him powders one day in an apple at Owen's garden, where they had a *benefit*, but I wouldn't give into such a story as that at all, for Eily is as delicate and tender in herself as a lady."

They were interrupted at this juncture by a startling incident. A mounted countryman galloped up to them, dressed in a complete suit of frieze, made from the undyed wool of black sheep, such as formed the texture of the *phalang* in the days of Gerald Barry. His face was pale and moist, and grimed with dust. A smooth, yellow wig was pushed away upon his temples, disclosing a mass of gray hair that was damp and matted with the effects of violent exercise. He looked alternately at both the travellers with an expression of mingled wildness and grief in his countenance; and again clapping spurs to his horse, rode off, and disappeared at a short turn in the road.

"I'm blest but that flogs Europe!" exclaimed Lowry Looby, in a tone of utter surprise and concern—"There's something great happened, surely."

"Who is he, Lowry? I think I ought to know his face."

"Mihil O'Connor, sir, father to the girl we were just talking of. He looks to be in trouble. Easy! Here's little Foxy Dunat, the hair-cutter, trottin' after him, an' he'll tell us."

The person whom he named, a small, red-haired man, rode up at the same moment, appearing to keep his seat on horseback with much difficulty. The animal he rode, though lean, was of great size, and presented a circumference much too extensive to be embraced by the short legs of the hair-cutter. His feet, for greater security, were stuck between the stirrup-leathers, while the empty irons remained dangling underneath. For the purpose of making assurance doubly sure, he had grasped fast with one hand the lofty pommel of the saddle, while the other was entwined in the long and undressed mane.

"Pru-h! Pru-h! Stop her, Lowry, *eroo*! Stop her, an' heavens bless you. I'm fairly flayed alive from her, that's what I am, jowltin', jowltin', for the bare life. Your sarvent, Mr. Daly—I'm not worth lookin' at. See my wig"—he pulled one out of his pocket, and held it up to view. "I was obleeged to take it off an' put it in my pocket, 'twas so tossed from the shakin' I got. I never was a-horseback before, but once at Molly Mac's funeral, an' I never'll be a-horseback again, till I'm going to my own. O murther! murther! I have a pain in the small o' my back that would kill the Danes. Well, Mr. Daly, I hope the master liked his new wig? I kep' it a long time from him, surely. I never'll be the better o' this day's ridin'. Did you see Mihil-na-thiadrucha* go by this way? I'm kilt an' spoiled, that's what I am."

"I did see him," said Lowry; "what's the matter with him?"

"Eily, his daughter, is gone from him, or spirited away."

"Erra, you don't tell me so?"

"She is, I tell you, an' he's like a wild man about it. Here he's back himself."

O'Connor again appeared at the turn of the road, and galloped roughly back upon the group. He looked ferociously at Lowry, and pointing his stick into his face, while his frame trembled with rage, he roared out: "Tell me, did you see her, this minute, or I'll thrust my stick down your throat? Tell me, do you know anything of her, I advise you."

"I don't," said Lowry, with equal fierceness. Then, as if ashamed of resenting a speech uttered by the poor old man, under so terrible an occasion of excitement, he changed his tone, and repeated more gently, "I don't, Mihil, an' I don't know what cause I ever gave you to speak to me *in that strain*."

The old ropemaker dropped the bridle, his clasped hands fell on the pommel of the saddle, and he drooped his head, while he seemed to gasp for utterance: "Lowry," he said, "heavens guide you, an' tell me do you know, or could you put me in a way of hearing anything of her?"

"Of who, ayeh?"

"Eily, my daughter! Oh, Lowry, *a'ra gal*, my daughter! My poor girl!"

"What of her, Mihil?"

"What of her? Gone! lost! Gone from her ould father, an' no account of her."

* Michael of the ropes. This practice of naming individuals from their professions (in which the great proportion of surnames are said to have originated), is quite general among the Irish peasantry. So far is the humour sometimes carried, that a poor widow in our own village has been nicknamed *Vauria n'thau Llanuv*, i.e., *Mary of the Two Children.*

HARDRESS CREGAN CARRIES OFF THE COLLEEN BAWN.

"Erra, no!"

"Yes, I tell you!" He threw a ghastly look around. "She is stolen or she strayed. If she is stolen, may the Almighty forgive them that took her from me; an' if she strayed of her own liking, may my curse——"

"Howl! howl!* I tell you, man," cried Lowry, in a loud voice; "don't curse your daughter without knowin' what you do. Don't I know her, do you think? An' don't I know that she wouldn't be the girl you say for her apronful of goold?"

"You're a good boy, Lowry; you're a good boy," said the old man, wringing his hands; "but she's gone. I had none but her, an' they took her from me. Her mother is dead these three years, an' all her brothers an' sisters died young, an' I reared her like a lady, an' this is the way she left me now. But what hurt? Let her go."

"The M'Mahons were at the fair of Garryowen yesterday," said Lowry, musing. "I wonder could it be them at all. I tell

    * Hold.

you there are bad boys among them. There was one of 'em hanged for spiriting away a girl o' the Hayeses before."

"If I thought it was one o' them," O'Connor exclaimed, stretching his arm to its full length, and shaking his clenched hand with great passion; 'an' if I knew the one that robbed me, I'd find him out, if he was as cunning as a rabbit, an' I'd tear him between my two hands if he was as strong as a horse. They think to play their game on me because my hair is grey. But I can match the villains yet. If steel, or fire, or pikes, or powder, can match 'em, I'll do it. Let go my horse's bridle, an' don't be holding me here when I should be flying like the wind behind 'em."

Here he caught the eye of Kyrle Daly, as the latter asked him whether he "had not laid informations before magistrates."

Instead of answering, the old man, who now recognised Daly for the first time, took off his hat with a smile in which grief and anger were mingled with native courtesy, and said, "Mr.

Daly, a *stoir*,* I ask your pardon for not knowing you; I meant no offence to you, or to your father's son. I couldn't do it. How are you, sir? How is the masther an' the misthress? The Lord direct 'em, an' spare 'em their children!" Here the old man's eyes grew watery, and the words were broken in his throat. "Lay informations?" he continued, taking up Kyrle Daly's question. "No, no, sir. My *back*† isn't so poor in the country that I need to do so mean a thing as that."

"And what other course would you take to obtain justice?"

"I'll tell you the justice I'd want," said O'Connor, griping his stick hard, and knitting his brows together, while the very beard bristled upon his chin for anger. "To plant him over-right me in the heart o' Garryowen fair, or where else he'd like, an' give him a stick, an' let me pick justice out of his four bones!" Here he indulged himself with one rapid flourish of the blackthorn stick above his head, which considerably endangered that of the young gentleman to whom he addressed himself.

At the same moment a neighbour of O'Connor's galloped up to them and exclaimed, "Well, Mihil, agra, any tidings of her yet?"

"Sorrow tale or tidings."

"An' is it here you're stoppin' talkin', an' them villains spiriting your daughter away through the country? Wisha, but you're a droll man this day!"

Not Hamlet, in that exquisitely natural burst of passion over the tomb of "the fair Ophelia," where he becomes incensed against the affectionate Laertes for the "bravery of his grief," and treats it as an infringement on his own prerogative of sorrow—not Hamlet the Dane, in that moment of "towering passion," could throw more loftiness of rebuke into his glance than did Mihil O'Connor, as he gazed upon the daring clansman who had thus presumed to call his fatherly affection to account. More temperate, however, than the Danish Prince, he did not let his anger loose, but compressed his teeth, and puffed it forth between them. Touching his hat to Kyrle, and bidding Lowry "stand his friend," he put spurs to his horse, and rode forwards, followed by his friend; while Lowry laid his hand on the hair-cutter's arm, and asked him for an account of the particulars.

"Sonuher‡ to me if I know the half of it," said the foe of unshaven chins, speaking in a shrill, professional accent; "but I was standing in my little place above, shaving a boy o' the Downeses against the *benefit* at Batt Coonerty's, an' being delayed a good while (for the Downeses have all very strong hair—I'd as lieve be shaving a horse as one of 'em), I was sthrappin' my razhor (for the twentieth turn), and lookin' out into the fair, when who should I see going by only Eily O'Connor, an' she dressed in a blue mantle with the hood over her head, an' her hair curling down about her neck like strings of gould. (Oh, the beauty o' that girl!) Well, 'It's a late walk you're taking, Eily,' says I. She made me no answer, only passed on, an' I thought no more about it till this morning, when her father walked in to me. I thought, at first, 'tis to be shaved he was coming, for, dear knows, he wanted it, when all at once he opened upon me in regard of his daughter. Poor girl, I'm sure sorrow call had I to her goin' or stayin' more than I had to curl the Princess Royal's front—a job that'll never trouble me, I'm thinking."

"Wisha, but it's a droll business!" ejaculated Lowry, letting go the stirrup-leather, which he had held fast during the foregoing narrative. "Ride on after him, Dunat, or you won't catch him before night. Oh, vo! vo! Eily, *a stoir*. Oh, wirra, Eily! this is the black day to your ould father!"

"An' the black an' blue day to me, I'm sure," squeaked out the hair-cutter, trotting forwards, and groaning aloud at every motion, as he was now thrown on the pommel, now on the hind-bow of the saddle; those grievances telling the more severely as he was a lean little man, and but scantily furnished by nature with that material which is best able to resist concussion.

The misfortune of the poor rope-maker indisposed Lowry (who had once been a respectful and distant admirer of the lovely Eily) from proceeding with the conversation; and his young master had ample leisure for the indulgence of his own luxurious reveries, until they reached the entrance to the fair demesne of Castle Chute.

* My dear. † Faction. ‡ A good wife.

CHAPTER VIII.

HOW THE READER, CONTRARY TO THE DECLARED INTENTION OF THE HISTORIAN, OBTAINS A DESCRIPTION OF CASTLE CHUTE.

AN old portress, talking Irish, with a huge bunch of keys at her girdle—a rusty gate-lock—piers, lofty, and surmounted by a pair of broken marble vases, while their shafts, far from exhibiting that appearance of solidity so much admired in the relics of Grecian architecture, were adorned in all their fissures by tufts of long grass—an avenue, with rows of elms, forming a vista to the river—a sudden turn, revealing a broad and sunny lawn—haycocks—mowers at work—a winding gravel-walk lost in a grove—the house appearing above the trees—the narrow-paned windows glittering amongst the boughs—the old ivied castle, contrasted in so singular a manner with the more modern addition to the building—the daws cawing about the chimneys—the stately herons settling on the castellated turrets, or winging their majestic way through the peaceful kingdom of the winds—the screaming of a peacock in the recesses of the wood—a green hill, appearing sunny bright against a clouded horizon—the heavy Norman archway—the shattered sculpture—the close and fragrant shrubbery—the noisy farmyard and out-offices (built, as was then the fashion, quite near the dwelling-house)—the bowering monthly rose, embracing the simple pediment over the hall-door—the ponderous knocker—the lofty gable—the pieces of broken sculpture and tender foliage, that presented to the mind the images of youth and age, of ruined grandeur and of rising beauty, blended and wreathed together under the most pleasing form.

Such were the principal features of the scenery through which Kyrle Daly passed into the dwelling of his beloved. The necessities of our narrative forbid us to dwell at a more ample length on the mere description of a landscape.

To his surprise, and, in some degree, to his disappointment, he found the castle more crowded with company than he had expected. He was admitted by a richly-ornamented Gothic archway, while Lowry remained walking his horse under the shade of the trees. A handsome, though rather ill-used curricle, which appeared to have been lately driven, was drawn up on the gravel plat; and a servant in tarnished livery was employed in cooling two horses on the slope which shelved downward to the river side. The foam that flecked their shining necks, and covered the curbs and branches, showed that they had been ridden a considerable distance, and by no sparing masters.

"Oh, murther, Master Kyrle, is this you?" exclaimed Falvey, the servant-boy; as he looked into the harrow hall and recognised the young "collegian." "*Ma yrine three hu!* it's an opening to the heart to see you!"

"Thank you, Pat. Are the ladies at home?"

"They are, sir. Oh, murther, murther! are you come at last, sir?" he repeated, with an air of smiling wonder; then suddenly changing his manner, and nodding with great freedom and cunning, "Oh, the ladies?—they are at home, sir, *both* of 'em."

"And well?"

"And well. I give praise—*both* of 'em well. Where is the horse, sir?"

"Lowry is walking him near the shrubbery."

"An' is Lowry come too? Oh, murther, murther!" He ran to the door and looked out, nodded, and raised his hand in courtesy, and then hastened back to Kyrle. "Gi' me the hat, sir, an' I'll hang it up—poof, it's full o' dust—come in here, Masther Kyrle, an' I'll give you a touch before you go up-stairs; there's a power o' quollity in the drawin'-room, an'"—here he again cast down his head with a knowing smile—"there's reasons for doin's; the ladies must be plaised surely. An' how is Mr. Daly an' herself an' all of 'em, sir? Oh, murther, murther!"

"They are all well, Pat, thank you."

"The Lord keep 'em so! There's a sight above stairs in the new house. Mr. Cregan, of Roaring Hall (ah, that's a *rale* sporting gettleman), an' Mr. Creagh, an' Pincher, an' Doctor Lake, an' the officer, westwards;" then, with another familiar wink, "There's the drollest cratur in life in the servants' hall abroad, the officer's *sarrent-boy*, a Londoner, afeerd o' the world that he'll have his throat cut be the Whiteboys before he quits the country. Poor cratur, he makes me laugh the way he talks of Ireland, as if he was a marked man among us, the little sprissawneen, that nobody ever would trouble their heads about—coming!"—a bell rang. "That's for the luncheon; I must smarten myself, or Miss Anne will kill me. They're all going off, after they take something, to the races near the point below, where they're to have the greatest divarsion ever you hear. An' so the master is well eastwards? Why, then, I'm glad to hear it. That's a good gentleman as ever sat down to his own table"—the bell rang again. "Oh, murther! there's the bell again; I'll be kilt entirely! There now, Master Kyrle, you're purty well, I think; they're all upstairs in the drawin'-room in the new house. I need not tell you the way. Syl Carney will open the doore for you, an' I'll wait aisy a minute, for it wouldn't look seemly for me to be takin' in the thray and things close behind you."

While this communicative retainer slipped away, napkin in hand, to the pantry, Kyrle Daly ascended a corkscrew flight of narrow stone steps, at the head of which he was met by the blooming handmaiden above named. Here he had as many "Masther Kyrles" and pretty smiles, and officious, though kindly meant, attentions to undergo as in the narrow hall. These he repaid in the usual manner, by complimenting Syl on her good looks, wondering she had not got married, and reminding her that Shrovetide would be shortly coming round again; in return for which the pretty Syl repeatedly told him that he was "a funny gentleman" and "a great play-boy."

They passed through an old banqueting-room which had once formed the scene of a council of the Munster chieftains in the days of Elizabeth, and descending a flight of a few wooden steps, stood in the centre of a lobby of much more modern architecture. Here Kyrle Daly felt his heart beat a little wildly, as he heard voices and laughter in the adjoining room. Modestly conscious, however, of his graceful person, and aware of the importance of displaying to some advantage in the eyes of his mistress, he adjusted his ruffles, and, with something like the feeling of a young *débutant* conscious of merit, yet afraid of censure, made his entrance on the little domestic scene.

The company all rose and received him with that pompous display of affability and attention which our fathers mistook for politeness, but which their wiser descendants have discovered to be the exact contrary, and discarded from the drawing-room as unbefitting the ease and sincerity of social life. Mrs. Chute was unable to rise, but her greeting was at once cordial and dignified. Anne gave him her hand with the air of an affectionate relative; Mr. Hyland Creagh placed his heels together, adjusted his ample shirt frills, and bowed until the queue of his powdered wig culminated to the zenith; while Pincher wagged his tail, looked up at his master as if to inquire the nature of his movements, and finally coiled himself up on the carpet and slept; Mr. Barnaby Cregan griped his hand until the bones cracked, expressing, in very concise language, a wish that his soul might be doomed to everlasting misery in the next world if he were not rejoiced to see him; Dr. Leake tendered him a finger, which Kyrle grasped hard, and (in revenge, perhaps, for the punishment inflicted on him by Cregan) shook with so lively an expression of regard, that the worthy physician was tempted to repent his condescension. To the young officer, an Englishman, Kyrle was introduced by the formal course of— "Captain Gibson, Mr. Daly—Mr. Daly, Captain Gibson," on which they bowed as coldly and stiffly as the figures in a clock-maker's window in Holborn, and all resumed their places.

After the usual inquiries into the condition of both families had been made and answered, Kyrle Daly indulged himself in a brief perusal of the personal appearance of the individuals in whose society he was placed. The information which he derived from the few glances that happened to fall wide of Miss Chute shall here be laid before the reader.

Mrs. Chute, the venerable lady of the mansion, was seated in a richly-carved arm-chair, near an ebony work-table, on which were placed a pair of silver spectacles and the last racing calendar. A gold-headed cane rested against her chair, and a small spaniel, in the attitude which heralds term *conchant*, lay at her side, burlesquing the lion of Britannia in the popular emblem. In her more youthful days, indeed, Mrs. Chute might have assumed her part in the latter without exciting any ludicrous association; and even in this decay and mouldering of her womanly attractions there was a grace, a dignity, a softened fire, and even a beauty, to be traced, which awakened the spec-

tator's respect, and sometimes warmed it into admiration. Old age, while it took nothing away from her dignity, had imparted to her manner that air of feminine dependence in which she was said to have been somewhat too deficient in her youth, and replaced in tenderness and interest the beauty which it had removed.

Her daughter, who bore a very perceptible resemblance to the old lady in the cast of her features, as well as in their expression, looked at this moment exceedingly beautiful- A dark blue riding-dress displayed her figure to such advantage, that if a young sculptor could have taken it as a model for a study of Minerva, and could likewise afford a lobster and a bottle of sherry to a critic in the "Fine Arts," there is little doubt that he would make his fortune. Her hair, which was shining black, cut short, and curled so gracefully that it might vie with the finest head in Mr. Hope's book of costumes, crept out from beneath her small round hat, and shaded a countenance that glowed at this moment with a sweet and fascinating cheerfulness. The common herd of mankind frequently exhibit personal anomalies of so curious a description as to remind one of Quevedo's fanciful vision of the general resurrection, where one man, in his hurry, claps his neighbour's head upon his own shoulders, and the upper portion of a turtle-fed alderman is borne along by the trembling shanks of a starveling magazine poet. But nothing of this incongruity was observable in the charming person of the heiress of Castle Chute. Her countenance was exquisitely adapted, both in form and character, to the rest of her frame; and she might be justly admired as a piece of workmanship not intrusted by Nature, as in a pin manufactory, to the hands of nine journeymen, but wrought out and polished by that great adept herself as a sample of womankind for the inspection of customers.

It was, indeed, remarked, by those who enjoyed only a visiting acquaintance with Anne Chute, that her general manner was cold and distant, and that there was, in the wintry lustre of her large black eyes and the noble carriage of her fine person, a loftiness which repelled in the spectator's breast that enthusiasm which her beauty was calculated to awaken, and induced him to stop short at the feeling of simple admiration. Hardress Cregan, who, with all his shyness, had the reputation of being a fine critic on these subjects, had been heard to say of her, on his return from college, that "she was perfect." Her form and face were absolutely faultless, and a connoisseur might, with a better taste, pretend to discover a fault in the proportions of the Temple of Theseus. But there," he added, "I must terminate the eulogy; for I could no sooner think of loving such a piece of frost-work than of flinging my arms in ecstasy around one of the Doric pillars of the old edifice itself."

But Hardress Cregan had been only once, and for a few minutes, in the lady's company, when he pronounced this judgment. Neither was he an impartial observer, for the embarrassment which he experienced, in consequence of her unconscious dignity, made him throw more asperity into his criticism than the occasion actually required. Those who enjoyed a longer and a nearer intimacy with Miss Chute found an additional fascination in that very coldness which kept ordinary acquaintances at a distance, and which for them was so cheerfully and so winningly removed. In proportion to the awe which it inspired on a first introduction was the delight occasioned by its subsequent dissipation; and it gave to her whole character that effect of surprise which is dangerous or available to the influence of the fair possessor, according as the changes which it reveals are attractive or otherwise. The feelings which accompanied a growing intimacy with this lovely girl resembled those of one who endeavours, by a feeble light, to discover the graces of a landscape which he knows to be beautiful, but which he is unable to appreciate until the morning light streams in upon the picture, and brings it forth in all its exquisite reality before his eyes.

The remainder of the company are not so interesting as to claim an equal portion of the reader's notice. Mr. Barnaby Cregan, a stout, top-booted old gentleman, with a nose that told tales of many a rousing night, was seated close to Mrs. Chute, and deeply engaged in a discussion upon cocks and cockerels, sparring, setting, impounding, the long law, the short law, and every other law that had any connection with his reigning passion. The rosy and red-coated Captain Gibson, who was a person of talent and industry in his profession, was listening with much interest to Dr. Lucas Leake, who possessed some little antiquarian skill in Irish remains, and who was at this moment unfolding the difference which existed between the tactics of King Lugh-Lamb-Fada and those issued from his late most gracious Majesty's War Office; between one of King Malachy's hobblers and a life-guardsman; between an English halberd and a stone-headed gai-bulg; and between his own commission of lieutenant and the Fear Comhlan Caoguid of the Fion Erin.

Mr. Hyland Creagh, who, as before mentioned, notwithstanding the perfect maturity of his years, still continued to affect the man of gallantry, was standing near Miss Chute, and looking with a half-puzzled, half-smiling air over a drawing which she had placed in his hands. Now and then, as he held the picture to the light, he looked askance, and with a forbidding expression, at Kyrle, who was carelessly sauntering towards the fair object of his attentions, and yet endeavouring to give his approximation rather the appearance of accident than of design. Mr. Creagh's experience in society had long since made him aware that youth was a quality which contributed materially to success with the ladies, and the consequence of this discovery was a hearty detestation—a term more qualified would not express the feeling—of every gentleman who was younger than himself. "Puppies!" he would exclaim, "they assume the air and port of men, when they should be confined to bibs and frills, and bestride a blood-horse, when their highest corvet should be made in the hall on their grandfather's walking-cane." But he had the mortification to find that his sentiments on this head were adopted by no unmarried ladies, except those whose wisdom and experience were equal to his own; and about *their* opinions, unhappily, Mr. Creagh was as indifferent as the young coxcombs whom he censured.

"I profess my ignorance," he said, after contemplating the picture for several minutes. "The drawing is admirable; the colouring has a depth and softness of tone that I have seen rarely produced by water-colours; and the whole design bears the stamp of reality upon it; but I profess my ignorance of the place which you say it is intended to represent."

"Indeed!" said Anne, affecting a disappointed tone, and pleased to put the old gentleman's gallantry to the torture; "then I must have made a sad failure, for the scene ought to be quite familiar to you."

"I am the worst person in the world at tracing a resemblance," said Mr. Creagh, looking puzzled. "Perhaps it is meant for Ballylin Point?"

"Oh, Mr. Creagh, can you find any resemblance? What a wretched bungler you must think me! You did well to say *meant for*—that expression indicates so exactly the degree of relation between my sketches and the originals."

"'Pon my honour, Miss Chute—'pon my honour, as a gentleman—"

"Mr. Daly!" Kyrle flew to her side. "Perhaps you could restore me to my self-esteem. Do you know that Mr. Creagh has mistaken this for a sketch of Ballylin Point! Try if you can restore my credit, for it is sinking very fast, even in my own estimation."

"Ballylin Point!" exclaimed Kyrle, taking the drawing into his hands. "I do not see the least resemblance." Mr. Creagh's eyes flashed fire at this unceremonious declaration; but he checked his resentment, and congratulated Miss Chute on this proof that the fault lay in his want of observation, not in her want of skill.

"And do you recognise the scene?" continued Miss Chute, who was well aware of the old *servente's* foible, and loved to toy with it for her amusement. "Let me hear if I have been indeed so very unsuccessful."

Her lover delayed answering, not because he shared the difficulty of Mr. Creagh, but that he was rapt in admiration of the drawing. It was an interesting landscape, and finished with more taste and fineness of touch than are usually to be traced in the efforts of accomplished young ladies. The foreground of the picture exhibited a grassy slope, which formed a kind of peninsular in a magnificent sheet of water, running a little to the left, and terminating at what artists term the middle distance in a gracefully-wooded point. The remains of an old castle appeared among the trees, the gloom and majesty of which were exhibited, in a striking degree, by a brilliant effect of sunshine on the water and on the green slope above mentioned. Two small islands, affording an anchorage to some open boats, broke the expanse of water on the right; while the small bay, formed by the point before described on the left, was graced by the figures of fishermen in the act of casting their nets. The waters were bounded in the distance by a range of blue hills, some of which projected into rocky or wooded headlands; while the whole was softened by that deep and rich blue tint which is peculiar to the moist atmosphere of the climate, and, by imparting at once distinctness sand softness to the landscape, is far better adapted to the scenes of rural solitude than even the lonely splendour of a Tuscan sun.

"Ballylin!" echoed Mr. Cregan, who had walked over to look at the drawing. "'Tis as like Ballylin as Roaring Hall is to Dublin Castle. 'Tis Castle Chute, and right well touched off too, by jingo." To this observation he added, in language which the altered customs of society prevent our copying *verbatim*, that he wished the spiritual foe of the human race might lay hold of him if it were not an admirable resemblance.

Mr. Creagh had his own reasons for not taking offence at any opinion that was urged by his good friend and frequent host, Mr. Cregan; but he did not forget the difference of opinion that was hazarded by his young acquaintance. To the fair artist's raillery he replied, with a bow and an air of old-fashioned politeness, that, "frequently as he had the honour of visiting Castle Chute, he was yet unfamiliar with the scenery, for his thoughts on approaching it were exclusively occupied by *one object*."

"And even though they were at liberty," added Kyrle, "it is more than probable Mr. Creagh has never seen Castle Chute at this point of view, so that it could hardly be expected to remain on his recollection." Then moving closer to Anne, and speaking in a lower tone of voice, he said, "This is the very scene of which I told you Hardress Cregan was so enthusiastic an admirer. You have drawn it since?"

Miss Chute answered in the affirmative, and, turning quickly away, replaced the sketch in her portfolio. Then, turning to Creagh, she told him that he would be very shortly qualified to give an opinion as to the fidelity of her design, for they would pass the spot in question on their way to the little race-course. There was some further conversation, not worth detailing, on the subject of Hardress Cregan's salute; and some conjectures were hazarded concerning the female in the blue cloak, none of which, however, threw any certain light upon that mystery.

CHAPTER IX.

HOW MYLES MURPHY IS HEARD ON BEHALF OF HIS PONIES.

Pat Falvey, supposing that he had remained a sufficient time without to prevent the suspicion of any private understanding between him and Mr. Daly, now made his appearance with luncheon. A collared head, cream cheese, honey, a decanter of gooseberry wine, and some garden fruit, were speedily arranged on the table, and the visitors, no way loath, were pressed to make a liberal use of the little banquet; for the time had not yet gone by when people imagined that they could not display their regard for a friend more effectually than by cramming him up to the throat with food and strong drink. Kyrle Daly was in the act of taking wine with Mrs. Chute, when he observed Falvey stoop to his young mistress's ear, and whisper something with a face of much seriousness.

"A boy wanting to speak to me?" said Miss Chute. "Has he got letters? Let him send up his message."

"He says he must see yourself, Miss. 'Tis in regard of some ponies of his that were impounded be Mr. Dawley for trespassing above here last night. He hasn't the mains of releasing 'em, poor craythur, an' he's far from home. I'm sure he's an honest boy. He says he'd have a good friend in Mr. Cregan, if he knew he was below."

"Me?" said Mr. Cregan. "Why, what's the fellow's name?"

"Myles Murphy, sir, from Killarney, westwards."

"Oh, Myles-na-Coppaleen! Poor fellow, is he in tribulation? We must have his ponies out by all means."

"It requires more courage than I can always command," said Miss Chute, "to revoke any command of Dawley's. He is an old man, and whether that he was crossed in love, or from a natural peevishness of disposition, he is such a morose creature that I am quite afraid of him. But I will hear this Myles at all events."

She was moving to the door when her uncle's voice made her turn.

"Stay, Anne," said Mr. Cregan; "let him come up. 'Twill be as good as a play to hear him and the steward *pro* and *con.* Kyrle Daly here, who is intended for the bar, will be our assessor, to decide on the points of law. I can tell you, Kyrle, that Myles will give you a lesson in the art of pleading that may be of use to you on circuit at one time or another."

Anne laughed, and looked to Mrs. Chute, who, with a smile of tolerating condescension, said, while she cleared with a silken kerchief the glasses of her spectacles, "If your uncle desires it, my love, I can see no objection. Those mountaineers are amusing creatures."

Anne returned to her seat, and the conversation proceeded, while Falvey, with an air of great and perplexed importance, went to summon Myles upstairs.

"Mountaineers!" exclaimed Captain Gibson. "You call every upland a mountain here in Ireland, and every one that lives out of sight of the sea a mountaineer."

"But this fellow is a genuine mountaineer," cried Mr. Cregan, "with a cabin two thousand feet above the level of the sea. If you are in the country next week, and will come down and see us at the Lakes, along with our friends here, I promise to show you as sturdy a race of mountaineers as any in Europe. Dr. Leake can give you a history of 'em up to Noah's flood, some time when you are alone together—when the country was first peopled by one Parable or Sparable."

"Paralon," said Dr. Leake; "Paralon, or Migdonia, as the Psalter sings:—

'On the fourteenth day, being Tuesday,
    They brought their bold ships to anchor
In the blue fair port with beauteous shore,
    Of well-defended Inver Sceine.'

In the rest of Munster, where——"

"Yes—well, you'll see 'em all, as the doctor says, if you come to Killarney," resumed Mr. Cregan, interrupting the latter, to whose discourse a country residence, a national turn of character, and a limited course of reading, had given a tinge of pedantry; and who was, moreover, a firm believer in all the ancient Shanachus, from the yellow book of Moling to the black book of Molega. "And if you like to listen to him, he'll explain to you every action that ever befell, on land or water, from Ross Castle up to Carrigaline."

Kyrle, who felt both surprise and concern at learning that Miss Chute was leaving home so soon, and without having thought it worth her while to make him aware of her intention, was about to address her on the subject, when the clatter of a pair of heavy and well-paved brogues on the small flight of stairs in the lobby produced a sudden hush of expectation amongst the company. They heard Pat Falvey urging some instructions in a low and smothered tone, to which a strong and not unmusical voice replied, in that complaining accent which distinguishes the dialect of the more western descendants of Heber, "Ah, lay me alone, you foolish boy; do you think did I never speak to *quollily* in my life before?"

The door opened, and the uncommissioned master of horse made his appearance. His appearance was at once strikingly majestic and prepossessing, and the natural ease and dignity with which he entered the room might almost have become a peer of the realm coming to solicit the *interest* of the family for an electioneering candidate. A broad and sunny forehead, light and wavy hair, a blue cheerful eye, a nose that in Persia might have won him a throne, healthful cheeks, a mouth that was full of character, and a well-knit and almost gigantic person, constituted his external claims to attention, of which his lofty and confident, although most unassuming carriage showed him to be in some degree conscious. He wore a complete suit of brown frieze, with a gay-coloured cotton handkerchief around his neck, blue worsted stockings, and brogues carefully greased, while he held in his right hand an immaculate felt hat, the purchase of the preceding day's fair. In the left he held a straight-handled whip and a wooden rattle, which he used for the purpose of collecting his ponies when they happened to straggle. An involuntary murmur of admiration ran amongst the guests at his entrance. Dr. Leake was heard to pronounce him a true Gadelian, and Captain Gibson thought he would cut a splendid figure in a helmet and cuirass, under one of the arches in the Horse Guards.

Before he had spoken, and while the door yet remained open,

Hyland Creagh roused Pincher with a chirping noise, and gave him the well-known countersign of "Baithershin!"

Pincher waddled towards the door, raised himself on his hind legs, closed it fast, and then trotted back to his master's feet, followed by the staring and bewildered gaze of the mountaineer.

"Well," he exclaimed, "that flogs cock-fighting! I never thought I'd live to have a dog taich me manners, any way. '*Baithershin,*' says he, an' he shets the dooro like a Christian."

The mountaineer now commenced a series of most profound obeisances to every individual of the company, beginning with the ladies, and ending with the officer; after which he remained glancing from one to another with a smile of mingled sadness and courtesy, as if waiting, like an evoked spirit, the spell-word of the enchantress who had called him up. "'Tisn't manners to speak first before quollity," was the answer he would have been prepared to render, in case any one had inquired the motive of his conduct.

"Well, Myles, what wind has brought you to this part of the country?" said Mr. Barney Cregan.

"The ould wind always then, Mr. Cregan," said Myles, with another deep obeisance, "seeing would I get a *feow* o' the ponies off. Long life to you, sir; I was proud to hear you wor above stairs, for it isn't the first time you stood my friend in trouble. My father (the heavens be his bed this day!) was a fosterer o' your uncle Mick's, an' a first an' second cousin, be the mother's side, to ould Mrs. O'Leary, your honour's aunt, westward. So 'tis kind for your honour to have a leanin' towards uz."

"A clear case, Myles; but what have you to say to Mrs. Chute about the trespass?"

"What have I to say to her? Why, then, a deal. It's a long while since I see her now, an' she wears finely, the Lord bless her! Ah, Miss Anne!—Oyeh, murther! murther! Sure I'd know that face all over the world—your own livin'image, ma'am" (turning to Mrs. Chute), "an' a little dawney touch o' the master (heaven rest his soul!) about the chin, you'd think. My grandmother an' himself wor third cousins. Oh, vo! vo!"[*]

"He has made out three relations in the company already," said Anne to Kyrle. "Could any courtier make interest more skilfully?"

"Well, Myles, about the ponies."

"Poor craturs, true for you, sir. There's Mr. Creagh there (long life to him!) knows how well I airn 'em for ponies. You seen what trouble I had with 'em, Mr. Creagh, the day you fought the *jewel* with young M'Farlane from the north. They went skelping like mad over the hills down to Glena when they heerd the shot. Ah, indeed, Mr. Creagh, you *cowed* the north countryman that morning fairly. 'My honour is satisfied,' says he, 'if Mr. Creagh will apologise.' 'I didn't come to the ground to apologise,' says Mr. Creagh; 'it's what I never done to any man,' says he, 'and it'll be long from me to do it to you.' 'Well, my honour is satisfied any way,' says the other, when he heerd the pistols cocking for a second shot. I thought I'd split laughing."

"Pooh, pooh! nonsense, man!" said Creagh, endeavouring to hide a smile of gratified vanity. "Your unfortunate ponies will starve while you stay inventing wild stories."

"If he has gained another friend since," whispered Miss Chute.

"Invent!" echoed the mountaineer. "There's Docthor Leake was on the spot, an' he knows if I invent. An' *you* did a good job too that time, docthor," he continued, turning to the latter. "Old Keys, the piper, gives it up to you, of all the docthors going, for curing his eyesight. An' he has a great leaning to you, moreover, you're such a fine *Irishian*."[†]

"Another," said Miss Chute apart. .

"Yourself an' ould Mr. Daly," he continued. "I hope the master is well in his health, sir?" (turning to Kyrle with another profound *congé.*) "May the Lord fasten the life in you an' him! That's a gentleman that wouldn't see a poor boy in want of his supper or a bed to sleep in, an' he far from his own people, nor persecute him in regard of a little trespass that was done *unknown.*"

"This fellow is irresistible," said Kyrle; "a perfect Ulysses."

"And have you nothing to say to the captain, Myles? Is he no relation of yours?"

"The captain, Mr. Cregan? Except in so far as we are all

---

[*] Equivalent to the French *Helas!* the Italian *Oime!* and the Spanish *Ag de mi!* etc.

[†] One skilled in Irish antiquities, language, etc.

servants of the Almighty and children of Adam, I know of none. But I have a *feeling* for the red coat, for all. I have three brothers in the army, serving in America; one of 'em was made a corporal, or an admiral, or some *ral* or another, for behavin' well at Quaybee, the time of Woulf's death. The English showed themselves a great people that day, surely."

Having thus secured to himself what lawyers call "the ear of the court," the mountaineer proceeded to plead the cause of his ponies with much force and pathos, dwelling on their distance from home, their wild habits of life, which left them ignorant of the common rules of boundaries, inclosures, and field-gates, setting forth with equal emphasis the length of road they had travelled, their hungry condition, and the barrenness of the common on which they had been turned out; and finally urged, in mitigation of penalty, the circumstances of this being a first offence, and the improbability of its being ever renewed in future.

The surly old steward, Dan Dawley, was accordingly summoned for the purpose of ordering the discharge of the prisoners, a commission which he received with a face as black as winter. Miss Anne might "folly her liking," he said, "but it was the last time he'd ever trouble himself about damage or trespass any more. What affair was it of his if all the horses in the barony were turned loose into the kitchen-garden itself?"

"*Horses*, do you call 'em?" exclaimed Myles, bending on the old man a frown of dark remonstrance—"a parcel of little ponies not the height o' that chair."

"What signify is it?" snarled the steward—"they'd eat as much, an' more than a racer."

"Is it they, the craturs? They'd hardly injure a plate of stirabout if it was put before 'em."

"Ayeh! hugh!"

"An' 'tisn't what I'd expect from you, Mr. Dawley, to be going again a relation o' your own in this manner."

"A relation o' mine!" growled Dawley, scarcely deigning to cast a glance back over his shoulder as he hobbled out of the room.

"Yes, then, o' yours."

Dawley paused at the door and looked back.

"Will you deny it o' me if you can," continued Myles, fixing his eye on him, "that Biddy Nale, your own gossip, an' Larry Foley wor second cousins? Deny that o' me, if you can."

"For what would I deny it?"

"Well, why! An' Larry Foley was uncle to my father's first wife—(the angels spread her bed this night!) An' I tell you another thing, the Dawleys would cut a poor figure in many a fair westwards, if they hadn't the Murphys to back 'em, so they would; but what hurt? Sure you can folly your own pleasure."

The old steward muttered something which nobody could hear, and left the room. Myles of the Ponies, after many profound bows to all his relations, and a profusion of thanks to the ladies, followed him, and was observed in a few minutes after on the avenue talking with much earnestness and apparent agitation to Lowry Looby. Kyrle Daly, who remembered the story of the mountaineer's misfortune at Owen's garden, concluded that Lowry was making him aware of the abduction of the beautiful Eily, and felt a pang of sympathetic affliction for the poor fellow, in which probably no one else in the room would have participated; at least not altogether so deeply.

CHAPTER X.
HOW KYRLE DALY SPED IN HIS WOOING.

THE sun was in the west when the party arrived at the bridle-road that turned off to the race-ground. To Kyrle Daly's great delight, Mr. Cregan had taken his horse, resigning to him the agreeable office of driving Anne Chute in the curricle, while he rode forward with the gentlemen. Seldom indeed, I believe, did the wheels of that vehicle enter so many ruts, or come in contact with so many obstacles, as in this short drive—a circumstance rather to be attributed to the perplexity of the driver's mind than to any deficiency of skill or practice in his hand.

None of the company knew, or indeed cared to be informed, what the nature was of the conversation which had passed between Miss Chute and her young escort on the road. They observed, however, when the curricle drew up, that Kyrle looked pale and flurried, and that his manner was absent; while that of his fair companion was marked by an unusual degree of seriousness, not unmingled with confusion.

"What!" exclaimed Cregan, "you look as ruffled as if you had been sparring. Get your hutts in order, then, for you must be set again before you come to the ground. You have a quarter of a mile through the fields to travel yet."

"Why, uncle, does not the road sweep by it?"

"No nearer than I tell you, and the curricle can go no further. Come, Creagh, give my niece her little hunter, and walk with me across the fields. Mr. Daly, I resign your seat to you once more. A pretty stepping thing this is of yours. I'd like to see her tried with ten or twelve stone weight at a steeple-chase."

"Do not," said Kyrle, in a low and earnest tone, addressing Anne Chute, "do not, I entreat of you, deprive me of this last opportunity. I would give the whole world for a minute's conversation."

"I believe I shall walk, uncle," said the young lady, with some hesitation, "and Mr. Daly is kind enough to say he will accompany me on foot."

"With all my heart," cried the cock-fighter. "I remember the time, Daly, when I would not have given up a walk through the fields with a fine girl, on a sunshiny evening, for all the races in Munster. If Hepton Connolly be on the ground, as his insolent groom tells me he is, I will make him keep the *staggeens* at the starting-post until you come up."

So saying, he rode on with the *ci-devant* sweater, to overtake the doctor and captain, who, he observed, had grown as *thick* as two pickpockets since morning.

"I am afraid," said Kyrle, with a mixture of dignity and disappointment in his manner, "I am afraid, Miss Chute, that you will think this importunate, after what you have already told me. But that rejection was so sudden—I will not say so unexpected—that I cannot avoid entering more at length into the subject. Besides, it may, it *must* be a long time before we shall meet again."

"I am sorry you should think that necessary, Mr. Daly," said Anne; "I always liked you as a friend, and there is not a person I know whose society, in that light, I could prize more highly; but if you think it necessary to your own peace of mind to remain away from us, it would be very unreasonable in me to murmur. Yet I think and hope," she added, affecting a smiling air as she looked round upon him, "that it will not be long before we shall see you again with altered sentiments, and a mind as much at ease as ever."

"You do me wrong, Anne!" said Kyrle, with sudden passion. "I am not so ignorant of my own character as to suppose that possible. No, Miss Chute; this is not with me a boyish fancy—a predilection suddenly formed, and capable of being just as suddenly laid aside. If you had said this last summer—a few weeks after I first saw you—the remark, perhaps, might have been made with justice. I knew little of you then besides your beauty, your talents, and your accomplishments; and I will say, in justice to myself, that those qualities in any woman never could so deeply fix or interest me as to produce any lasting disquiet in my mind. But our acquaintance has been since too much prolonged; I have seen you too often; I have known you too well; I have loved you too deeply and too sincerely, to feel this disappointment as anything less than a dreadful stroke. Let me entreat you," he continued with increasing warmth, and disregarding the efforts which Miss Chute made to interrupt him, "let me implore you to recall that hasty negative. You said you were unprepared—that you did not expect such a proposal from me. I do not press you to answer at this moment; the torture of suspense itself is preferable to absolute despair. Say you will think of it; say anything rather than at once decide on my—destruction; I cannot but call it."

"I must not, I will not, act with so much injustice," said Anne, who was considerably distressed by the depth of feeling that was evident in her lover's voice and manner. "I should be treating you most unfairly, Mr. Daly, if I did so. It is true that I did not expect such a declaration as you have made—not in the least; but my decision is taken notwithstanding. It is impossible I can ever give you any other answer than you have already received. Do not, I will entreat of you in my turn, give way to any groundless expectations—any idea of a change in my sentiments on this subject. It is as impossible we should ever be united as if we lived in two separate planets."

The unhappy suitor looked the very image of pale and ghastly despair itself. His eye wandered, his cheek grew wan, and every muscle in his face quivered with passion. His words, for several moments, were so broken as to approach a degree of incoherency, and his knees trembled with a sickly faintness. He continued, nevertheless, to urge his addresses. Might he not be favoured with Miss Chute's reasons? Was there anything in his own conduct—anything that might be altered? The dejection that was in his accents, as well as his appearance, touched and almost terrified his obdurate mistress, and she took some pains to alleviate his extreme despondency, without, however, affording the slightest ground for a hope which she felt could never be accomplished. The consolations which she employed were drawn rather from the probability of a change in his sentiments than her own.

"You are not in a condition," she said, "to judge of the state of your own mind. Believe me, this depression will not continue, as you seem to fear. The Almighty is too just to interweave any passion with our nature which is not in the power of our reason to subdue."

"Ay, Anne," said Kyrle; "but there are some persons for whose happiness the struggle is quite sufficient. I am not so ignorant as you suppose of the effect of a disappointment like this. I know that it will not be at all times as violent and oppressive as I feel it at this moment; but I know, too, that it will be as lasting as life itself. I have often experienced a feeling of regret that amounted to actual pain, in looking back to years that have been distinguished by little beyond the customary enjoyments of boyhood. Imagine, then, if you can, whether I shall sit alone in the evening, and think of the time that was spent in your society."

Miss Chute heard this speech with a feeling of deep and even sympathetic emotion. As Kyrle ventured to glance at her countenance, and observed the peculiar expression of her sorrow, the idea of a rival, which till that moment had not once occurred to him, now flashed upon his mind, and changed the current of his feelings to a new direction. The sensation of jealousy was almost a useful stimulant in the excessive dejection under which he laboured.

"Will you forgive me," he said, "and take the present state of my feelings as an apology, if there should be anything offensive in the question I am about to ask you? There can be only one reason for my rejection which would save my pride the mortification of believing myself altogether unworthy. I should feel some consolation in knowing that my own misery was instrumental to your happiness; indeed, I should not think of breathing another word upon the subject, if I thought that your affections had been already engaged."

The agitation seemed now to have passed over to the lady's side. Her brow became dark red, and then returned to more than its accustomed whiteness. "I have no other engagement," she said, after a pause. "If I had, I should think it hardly fair to press such an inquiry; but, I assure you, I have none. And since you have spoken of my own views of life, I will be more explicit, and confess to you that I do not at present think it is likely I shall ever contract any. I love my mother; and her society is all that I desire or hope to enjoy at present. Let me now entreat you as a friend, for my sake, as well as your own, never again to renew any conversation on this subject."

This was said in a tone of such decision that Kyrle saw it would be impossible, without hazarding the loss of the young lady's friendship, to add another word of remonstrance or of argument. Both, therefore, continued their walk in silence, nor did they exchange even an indifferent observation until they reached the summit of the little slope from which the course was visible.

Their thoughts, however, were not subjected to the same restriction, and the train of reflection in either case was not calculated to awaken envy.

"She received my question with embarrassment," thought Kyrle, "and she evaded a reply. I have a rival, it is evident, and a favoured, at least, if not a declared one. Well, if she is to be happy, I am content; but unquestionably the most miserable contented man upon the earth."

The lady's meditation also turned upon the same crisis in the conversation. "All that I desire?" she mentally repeated, quoting her own words to her rejected suitor. "And have I so far conquered my own feelings as to be capable, with perfect sincerity, of making an assertion such as that? or, if it be sincere, am I sure that I run no risk of disqualifying myself for retaining the same liberty of mind by accepting my uncle's invitation? But it is not possible, surely, that my peace should be endangered in the society of one who treats me with something more, and colder, than indifference itself; and if it were, my part is already taken, and it is now too late to retract. Poor Kyrle! he wastes his eloquence in exciting my commiseration for a state of mind with which I have been long and painfully conversant. If he knew how powerful a sympathy my own experience had awakened for him, he need not use an effort to increase it."

A loud shout of welcome, sent forth in honour of the heiress of Castle Chute, and the lady-patroness of the day's amusements, broke in upon these sombre meditations, and called the attention of that lady and of her downcast escort to a novel scene and new performers.

> "Clamoren immensum tollit, quo pontus et omnes
> Intremuere undæ, penitusque exterrita tellus
> Momoniæ."

The sounds of greeting then sank into a babbling murmur, and at last into a hush of expectation, similar to that with which Pasta is welcomed at the Italian Opera when she comes forward to stop the mouths of the unintelligible chorus, and to thrill the bright assembly with the frantic sorrows of Medea.

The spot selected for the occasion was the shore of a small bay, which was composed of a fine hard sand, that afforded a very fair and level course for the horses. At the farther end was a lofty pole, on the top of which was suspended by the stirrup a new saddle, the destined guerdon of the conqueror. A red handkerchief, stripped from the neck of Dan Hourigan, the house carpenter, was hoisted overhead, and a crowd of country people dressed, notwithstanding the fineness of the day, in their heavy frieze great coats, stood round the winning-post, each faction being resolved to see justice done to its own representative in the match. A number of tents, composed of old sheets, bags, and blankets, with a pole at the entrance, and a sheaf of reed, a broken bottle, or a sod of turf, erected for a sign, were discernible among the multitude that thronged the side of the little rising ground before mentioned. High above the rest Mick Normal's sign-board waved in the rising wind. Busy was the look of that lean old man as he bustled to and fro among his pigs, kegs, mugs, pots, and porringers. A motley mass of felt hats, white muslin caps and ribbons, scarlet cloaks, and blue riding-jocks filled up the spaces between the tents, and moved in a continual series of involutions, whirls, and eddies, like those which are observable on the surface of a fountain newly filled. The horses were to start from the end of the bay, opposite to the winning-post, go round Mick Normal's tent, and the cowel on the hill side, and returning to the place from whence they came, run straight along the sand for the saddle. This was to be the victor's prize.

> "Hic, qui forte velint rapido contendere cursu,
> Invitat pretiis animos, et premia ponit."

The solatia victo were to be had at the rate of fourpence a tumbler at Mick Normal's tent.

A rejected lover can hardly be supposed to have any predilection for the grotesque. Kyrle Daly, however, observing that Miss Chute made an effort to appear disembarrassed, and feeling, in the sincerity of his affection, a sentiment of grief for the uneasiness he had occasioned her, compelled himself to assume the appearance of his usual good humour, and entered with some animation into the spirit of the scene. Captain Gibson, who now approached them on foot, could not, with the recollections of Ascot and Doncaster fresh in his mind, refrain from a roar of laughter at almost every object he beheld: at the condition of the horses; the serious and important look of the riders; the Teniers appearance of the whole course; the band, consisting of a blind fiddler, with a piece of listing about his waist and another about his old hat; the self-importance of the stewards, Tim Welsh, the baker, and Batt Kennedy, the poet or janius of the village, as they went in a jog trot round the course, collecting shilling subscriptions to the saddle from all who appeared on horseback.

"Well, Anne," said Mr. Cregan, riding up to the group, "we have lost three of our company. Hepton Connolly is gone off to fight a duel with some fellow from the mountains that called him a scoundrel, and taken Creagh with him for a second. That's the lad that 'll see them properly set. Dr. Leake has followed for the purpose of stopping up any holes they may happen to make in one another, so we have all the fun to ourselves. If the doctor had stayed we should have had so many accounts of the sports of Tailten, and all that. He is a very learned little man, the doctor; I don't suppose there's so long a head in the county; but he talks too much. Captain, I see you laugh a great deal, but you mustn't laugh at our girls, though; there are some pretty bits o' muslin here, I can tell you."

"I like them uncommonly," said the captain; "their dress, in particular, I think very becoming. The muslin cap, with a ribbon tied under the chin and a pretty knot above, is a very simple and rural head-dress; and the scarlet cloak and hood, which seems to be a favourite article of costume, gives a gay and flashy air to their rustic assemblies. Look at that girl, now, with the black eyes, on the bank—what a pretty modest dress that is! A handkerchief pinned across the bosom, a neat figured gown, and check apron; but what demon whispered her to case her little feet in black worsted stockings and brogues?"

"They are better than the clouted shoes of the continent," said Anne, "and durability must sometimes be preferred to appearance."

"Why, that's Syl Carney, Anne," exclaimed Cregan.

"It is, sir. She has seen her *beau* somewhere on the course, I will venture to say."

A roar of laughter from Captain Gibson here attracted their attention.

"Look at that comical fellow on horseback!" he cried. "Did you ever see such a pair of long legs with so small a head? A fire-tongs would sit a horse as well. And observe the jaunty way he carries the little head, and his nods and winks at the girls. That's an excruciating fellow! And the arms—the short arms! How the fellow gathers up the bridle, and makes the lean animal hold up his head, and jog anily forward. Is that fellow really going to run for the stake?"

Kyrle Daly turned his eyes in the same direction, and suffered them to dilate with an expression of astonishment, when he beheld his own saucy squire seated upon the hair-cutter's mare, and endeavouring to screen himself from his master's observation by keeping close to the side of Batt Kennedy, the *janius*; while the latter recited aloud a violent satire which he had made upon a rival versifier in the neighbourhood. In fact, Lowry Looby, understanding that Syl Carney was to be at the course, and wishing to cut a figure in her eyes, had coaxed Foxy Dunat "out of the loand of his mare for one hate," while that indifferent equestrian refreshed his galled person with a "soft sate" on the green sod in Mick Normal's tent.

Mr. Cregan here left the party with the view of assuming his place as judge of the course at the winning-post; while the *staggeens* with their riders moved forward, surrounded by a dense and noisy crowd, to the starting-post, near the elevation that was occupied by our three friends.

"We are at a loss here," said Miss Chute, "for—*List of this day's running horses, the colour of the rider, and the rider's name.*" (Here she imitated, with some liveliness, the accent of the boys who sell those bills at more regular fêtes of the kind.) "But you, Captain Gibson, seem to take an interest in the proceeding; and I am acquainted not only with the character of the heroes who hold the reins, but with all the secret machinery of intrigue which is expected to interfere with the fair dealing of the day. I will, therefore, if you please, let you into the most amusing parts of their history as they pass."

Captain Gibson, with a fresh burst of laughter, protested that "he would give the world for a peep into the social policy of an Irish village."

"Well, then," said Anne, assuming a mock Ossianic manner, "the first whom you see advancing on that poor half-starved black mare, with the great lump on her knee, and the hay-rope for a saddle-girth, is Jerry Cooley, our village nailer, famed alike for his dexterity in shaping the heads of his brads and demolishing those of his acquaintance. Renowned in war is Jerry, I can tell you—Gurtenaspig and Derrygortnaclogby re-echo with his fame. Next to him, on that spavined grey horse, rides John O'Reilly, our blacksmith, not less estimated in arms, or rather in cudgels. Not silent, Captain Gibson, are the walks of Garryowen on the deeds of John O'Reilly, and the bogs of Ballinvoric quake when his name is mentioned. A strength of arm, the result of their habitual occupations, has

rendered both these heroes formidable among the belligerent factions of the village, but the nailer is allowed a precedence. He is the great Achilles; O'Reilly, the Telemon Ajax of the neighbourhood. And, to follow up my Homeric parallels, close behind him, on that long-backed, ungroomed creature, with the unnameable colour, rides the crafty Ulysses of the assemblage, Dan Hogan, the process-server. You may read something of his vocation in the sidelong glance of his eye, and in the paltry, deprecating air of his whole demeanour. He starts, as if afraid of a blow, whenever any one addresses him. As he is going to be married to Dooley's sister, it is apprehended by the O'Reillys that he will attempt to cross the blacksmith's mare; but the smoky Achilles, who gets drunk with him every Saturday night, has a full reliance on his friendship. Whether, however, Cupid or Bacchus will have the more powerful influence upon the process-server is a question that I believe yet remains a mystery even to himself; and I suspect he will adopt the neutral part of doing all he can to win the saddle for himself. The two who ride abreast behind Hogan are mountaineers, of whose motives or intentions I am not aware. The sixth and last is Lowry Looby, a retainer of my friend Mr. Daly's, and the man whose appearance made you laugh so heartily a little while since. He is the only romantic individual of the match. He rides for love, and it is to the chatty disposition of the lady of his affections, our own housemaid, that I am indebted for all this information."

One would have thought the English officer was about to die with laughter several times during the course of this speech. He leaned, in the excess of his mirth, upon the shoulder of Kyrle Daly, who, in spite of his depression, was compelled to join him, and placing his hand against his forehead—

> "Laughed, sans intermission,
> An hour by the dial."

The mere force of sympathy compelled the lady and gentleman to lay aside for the moment their more serious reflections, and adapt their spirits to the scene before them. It seemed curious to Kyrle Daly that, slightly as he esteemed this new military acquaintance, he felt jealous for the moment of the influence thus exercised by the latter on the temper of Anne Chute, and wished at the time that it were in his power to laugh as heartily as Captain Gibson. But a huge diaphragm though a useful possession in general society, is not one that is most likely to win the affections of a fine girl. In affairs of the heart your mere laugher is a fool to your thinker and sentimentalist.

Before the captain could sufficiently recover himself to make his acknowledgments for the entertainment which Miss Chute had afforded him, a cry of "Clear the coorse! clear the coorse!" resounded along the sand, and the two stewards, the baker and the poet, came galloping round at a furious rate, laying about them stoutly with their cord-whips, while the horses scattered the sand and pebbles in all directions with their hoofs, and the stragglers were seen running off to the main body of the spectators to avoid a fate similar to that sustained by the victims of Juggernaut, in that pious procession to which his majesty's non-emancipating government so largely and so liberally contribute. "Clear the coorse!" shouted the baker, with an accent as if he were King Pharaoh's own royal dough-kneader. "Clear the coorse!" sung the melodious Batt Kennedy, the favourite of the muses, as he spurred his broken-winded Pegasus after the man of loaves; and, of course, the course was cleared and kept clear, less perhaps by the violence of Tim Welsh than the amenity of Batt Kennedy, who, though not a baker, was the more pithy and flowery orator of the two.

CHAPTER XI.

HOW KYRLE DALY HAS THE GOOD LUCK TO SEE A STAGGEEN RACE.

THE signal was given, and the six horsemen started in good order, and with more zeal and eagerness in their faces than were to be found in the limbs of the animals which they bestrode. For a few moments the strife seemed doubtful, and victory hovered, with an indecisive wing, now over one helmet, and now over another. The crowd of spectators, huddling together on a heap, with faces that glowed, and eyes that sparkled with intense interest, encouraged the riders with shouts and exclamations of hoarse and vehement applause. "Success! success, Jerry!" "It's done; a half-pint wit you, Dan Hogan wins!"

THE LAST "TALLY-HO!"

"I depend my life upon John O'Reilly." "Give her a loose, Lowry!" and other expressions of a similar nature.

But ere they again came round the winning-post the position of the horses was altered. O'Reilly rode in front, lashing his horse in the flank with as much force as if he were pounding on his own anvil. Dooley, the nailer, came close behind, drubbing his black mare's lean ribs with the calves of his legs, as if designing to beat the poor beast out of the last remnant of her wind. The others followed, lashing their horses and one another, each abusing his neighbour in the grossest terms, all except Lowry Looby, who prudently kept out of harm's way, keeping a loose rein in his hand, and giving the hair-cutter's mare the advantage of what jockeys term a *sob*—a relief, indeed, of which the poor creature stood in the utmost need. He was thus prepared to profit by the accident which followed. The blacksmith's grey horse started at a heap of seaweed, and suffered the nailer's mare to come down like a thunderbolt upon his haunches. Both steeds fell, and the process-server, who rode on their heels, falling foul of them as they lay kicking on the sand, was compelled to share in their prostration. This accident produced among the fallen heroes a series of kicks and bruises, in which the horses were not idle. O'Reilly, clenching his hand, hit the nailer a straightforward blow between the eyes, which so effectually interfered with the exercise of those organs, that he returned the favour with a powerful thrust in the abdomen of his own prostrate steed. For this good office he was rewarded by the indignant quadruped with a kick over the right ear, which made it unnecessary to inflict a second, and the quarrel remained between the process-server and the black-smith, who pummelled one another as if they were pounding flax, and with as much satisfaction as if they had never got drunk together in their lives. They were at length separated and borne from the ground, all covered with blood and sand, while their horses with much difficulty were set upright on their legs, and led off to the neighbouring slope.

In the mean time our party observed Lowry Looby returning from the winning-post, under the protection of Mr. Cregan, with the saddle torn to fritters between his hands, and his person exhibiting tokens of severe ill-usage. He had contrived to out-strip the mountaineers, and had obtained the prize; but the adverse factions, irritated at beholding their laurels flourishing on a stranger's brow, had collected around, and dragged him from his horse, alleging that it was an unfair heat, and that there should be a second trial. Mr. Cregan, however, with some exertion, succeeded in rescuing Lowry from their hands; but not until every man in the crowd had put a mark upon him by which he might be easily distinguished at any future meeting.

Tired of the deafening uproar that surrounded him, and longing for retirement, that he might brood at leisure over his disappointment, Kyrle Daly now left the course, notwithstanding the invitation of Anne Chute that he would return and dine at the castle. His intention was to spend the night at the cottage on one of his father's dairy-farms, which lay at the distance of a few miles lower on the river-side, and where one neat room was always kept in order for his use, whenever he joined Hardress Cregan in a shooting excursion towards the mouth of the stream. Hardress had promised to visit him at this cottage a few weeks before, and as he knew that his young friend must have come to an anchor in waiting for the tide, he judged it not unlikely that he might see him this very night. He had now an additional reason for desiring to hold conversation with Hardress, in order that he might receive the consolations of his friendship under his own disappointment, and, if possible, obtain some knowledge of the true condition of his mistress's affections.

Lowry Looby, once more reduced to his legs, followed him at a distance somewhat more considerable than that recommended by Dean Swift as proper to be observed by gentlemen's gentlemen. He lingered only to restore the mare to Foxy Dunat, presenting him at the same time with the mutilated saddle, and obstinately declining the hair-cutter's proposal of "traiting him to the best that the Cat an' Bagpipes could afford." After which conversation the two friends threw their arms about each other's neck, and kissed, as in France, and separated.

The night had fallen before Kyrle alighted at the cottage door. Mrs. Frawley, the dairy-woman, had been provident enough to light a fire in the little yellow room, and to place beside it the arm-chair and small painted table, with the volume of Blackstone which her young master was accustomed to look into in the evening. The night, she observed, "was smart enough to make an air o' the fire no unpleasant thing; and even if it were not cold a fire was company when one would be alone that way." With equal foresight she had prepared the materials for a tolerable dinner, such as a hungry man might not contemn without trial. Whether it were the mere effect of custom, or an indication of actual and unromantic appetite, the eye of our desponding lover was not displeased, on entering the little parlour, to see the table decorated with a snow-white damask cloth, a cooler of the sweetest butter, a small cold ham, and an empty space which he knew to be destined for a roast duck or chickens. There is no time at which the heart is more disposed to estimate in a proper light the comforts of home and a quiet fireside than when it has experienced some severe rejection in society; and it was with the feeling of one who, after much and harassing annoyance, encounters a sudden refuge, that our drooping traveller flung himself into the chair, and exclaimed in the words of Oriana,—

"Though but a shadow, but a sliding,
Let me know some little joy.
We that suffer long annoy
Are contented with a thought,
Through an idle fancy wrought.
Oh, let my joys have some abiding!"

While Mrs. Frawley superintended the dressing of the fowl in the kitchen, much wondering at the forlorn and absent air with which her officious attentions were received by the young collegian, that meditative gentleman was endeavouring to concentrate his attention on the pages of the learned work that lay before him. His eyes wandered over the concise and lucid detail of the reciprocal rights of baron and feme; but what purpose could this answer, except to remind him that he could never claim the lovely Anne Chute as his feme, nor would the lovely Anne Chute consent to acknowledge him as her baron? He closed the volume, and laying it on the little chimney-piece, resumed his mood of settled meditation by the fire.

The silence of the place was favourable to that sort of drowsy musing in which the mind delights to repose its energies after any strong and passionate excitement. There was no effort made to invite or pursue a particular train of reflection; but those thoughts which lay nearest to the heart—those memories, hopes, fears, and wishes, with which they were most intimately associated, passed in long and still procession before his mind. It was a dreary and funereal train to witness, but yet the lover found a luxurious indulgence in its contemplation. He remained gazing on the fire, with his hand supporting his temple, until every crackling turf and faggot became blended in his thoughts with the figures which his memory called up from the past, or his fancy created for the future.

While he leaned thus silent in his chair, he overheard in the adjoining kitchen a conversation which for the moment diverted his attention from the condition of his own fortunes.

"Where to are you running in such a hurry, Mary?" said Mrs. Frawley. "One would think it was for the seed o' the fire you come. Sit down again."

"Oh, wisha," said a strange voice, "I'm tired from sitting. Is it to look after the butter Mr. Kyrle is come down to ye?"

"Oych, no. He doesn't meddle in them things at all. If he did we'd have a bad story to tell him. You'll burn that duck, Nelly, if you don't mind it."

"Why, so—a bad story, Mrs. Frawley?"

"I'll tell you, Mary. I don't know what the reason of it is, but our butter is going from us this two months now. I'd almost take the vestment* of it that Mr. Enright's dairyman, Bill Noonan, made a pishog,† and took away our butter."

"Oyeh!"

"What else, what would become of it? Sure Bill himself told me they had double their complement last week, at a time when, if we were to break our hearts churning from this till doomsday, we could get nothing but the buttermilk in the latter end."

"Did you watch your cows last May-eve, to see that nobody milked 'em from ye?"

"I did to be sure. I sat up until twelve o'clock to have the first milk myself; for Shaun Lauther, the fairy doctor, told me that if another milked 'em that night, she'd have their butter the whole year round. And what good was it for me? I wouldn't wonder if old Moll Noonan had a hand in it."

"Nor I neither. They say she's a witch. Did I ever tell you what Davy Neal's wife did to her of a time?"

"Not as I know."

"The same way as with yourself, the butter—no, 'tisn't the butter, but the milk itself was going from Katty Neal, although her little cow was a kind Kerry, and had the best of grazing. Well, she went, as you done, to Shaun Lauther, the knowledge-able man, and put a half-a-crown into his hand, and asked his advice. 'Well, tell me,' says Shaun, 'were you at Moll Noonan's yesterday?' 'I was,' says Kate. 'And did you see a hair spancel hanging over the chimney?' says he. 'I did see that, too,' says Kate. 'Well,' says Shaun, ''tis out of that spancel that Moll do be milking your cows every night, by her own chimney corner, and you breaking your heart at a dry udder the same time.' 'And what am I to do?' says Kate. 'I'll tell you,' says he. 'Go home, and redden this horseshoe in the fire, and observe when you're milking that a grey cat will sit by you on the lawn. Just strike her with the red shoe, and your business will be done.' Well, she did his bidding. She saw the grey cat, and burnt her with the shoe, till she flew screeching over the hedge."

"Oh, murther, hadn't she the courage!"

"She had. Well, the next day she went to Moll Noonan's, and found her keeping her bed, with a great scald she said she got from a pot of boiling water she had down for scalding the keelers. 'Ayeh,' thought Kate, 'I know what ails you well, my

---

* Swear by the priest's vestment.

† A mystic rite, by which one person is enabled to make a supernatural transfer of his neighbour's butter into his own churns. The failure and diminution of butter at different times, from the poverty of the cream, appear so unaccountable that the country people can only attribute it to witchcraft; and these dairy superstitions have prevailed to a similar degree in the country parts of England. In The Devil is an Ass his Satanic Majesty is thus made to jest on the petty mischief of his imp, Pug, who seeks a month's furlough to the Earth :—

"You have some plot now,
Upon a tunning of ale, to stale the yest,
Or keep the churn so that the butter come not,
Spite of the housewife's cord and her hot spit."

old lady.' But she said nothing, and I'll engage she had the fine can o' milk from her cows next morning."

"Well, she was a great girl."

"Ah, what should ail her?" said Nelly, the servant wench, who was employed in turning the duck. "I remember Jug Flanigan, the cooper's wife, above, was in the same way, losin' all her butter, an' she got it again by puttin' a taste o' the last year's butter into the churn, before churnin', along with the crame, and into every keeler in the house. Here, Mrs. Frawley, will you have an eye to the spit a minute while I go look at them hens in the *coob* abroad? Master Kyrle might like a fresh egg for his *tay*, an' I hear them clockin'."

"Do, then, Nell, *a'ra gal*, and, as you're going, turn in the turkeys, for the wind is rising, and I'm in dread it will be a bad night."

A loud knocking at the door was the next sound that invaded the ear of Kyrle Daly. The bolt flew back, and a stranger rushed in, while, at the same moment, a gust of wind and rain dashed the door with violence against the wall, and caused a cloud of smoke and ashes to penetrate even to the room in which he sat.

"Shut out the doore! shut out the doore!" screamed Mrs. Frawley, "the duck will be all destroyed from the ashes. Ah, Lowry, what kep' you till now?"

"Oh, let me alone, woman," exclaimed Lowry, in a loud and agitated voice. "Where's Masther Kyrle?"

"Sitting in the parlour within. What's the matter, eroo?"

Without making any reply, Lowry Looby presented himself at the parlour door, and waving his hand with much force, exclaimed, "Come out! come out, Master Kyrle! There's the Nora Creina abroad just goin' down, and every soul aboard of her. She never will reach the shore. Oh, vo! vo! 'tis frightful to see the swell that's round her. The Lord in his mercy stretch out his hand upon the wathers this fearful night!"

Kyrle started up in alarm, snatched his hat, and rushed out of the room, not paying any attention to the recommendation of Mrs. Frawley that he would throw the frieze riding-coat over his shoulders before he went out in the rain. Lowry Looby, with many ejaculations of terror and of compassion, followed his master to the shore, within a gun-shot of which the cottage was situated. They arrested their steps on a rocky point, which, jutting far into the river, commanded a wide prospect on either side. It was covered with wet seaweed and shell-fish, and afforded a slippery footing to the young collegian and his squire. A small fishing-boat lay at anchor on the leeward side of the point, and her crew, consisting of a swarthy old man and a youth, were standing on the shore, and watching the pleasure-boat with much interest.

CHAPTER XII.

HOW FORTUNE BRINGS TWO OLD FRIENDS TOGETHER.

THE situation of the little vessel was in reality terrific. A fierce westerly wind, encountering the receding tide, occasioned a prodigious swell in the centre of the channel; and even near the shore the waves lashed themselves with so much fury against the rocky headland before mentioned, that Kyrle and his servant were covered with spray and foam. There was yet sufficient twilight in the sky to enable them to discern objects on the river, and the full autumnal moon, which ever and anon shot, like a flying ghost, from one dark mass of vapour to another, revealed them at intervals with a distinctness scarcely inferior to that of day. The object of the pleasure-boat seemed to be that of reaching the anchorage above alluded to; and, with this view, the helmsman held her head as close to the wind as a reefed mainsail and heavy swell would allow him. The white canvas, as the boat came foaming and roaring towards the spectators, appeared half drenched in brine from the breaking of the sea against the windward bow.

The appearance of the vessel was such as to draw frequent ejaculations of compassion from Lowry and the boatman, and to make Kyrle Daly's heart sink low with fear and anxiety. At one time she was seen on the ridge of a broken wave, showing her keel to the moonlight, and bending her white and glistening sails over the dark gulf upon her lee.

At another the liquid mountain rolled away, and left her buried in the trough, while her vane alone was visible to the landsmen; and the surges, leaping and whitening in the moon-

shine, seemed hurrying to overwhelm and engulf their victim. Again, however, suddenly emerging into the light, she seemed to ride the waters in derision, and left the angry monsters roaring in her wake.

"She never'll do it, I'm in dread," said Lowry, bending an inquisitive glance on the boatman. The latter was viewing intently, and with a grim smile, the gallant battle made by the little vessel against the elements.

"'Tis a good boy that has the rudder in his hand," he said; "and as for their lives, 'tis the same Lord that is on the water as on the land. When their hour is come, on sea or shore, 'tis all the same to 'em. I wouldn't wondher if he done it yet. Ah, that swell put him off of it. He must make another tack. 'Tis a good boy that houlds the rudder."

"What!" exclaimed Kyrle, "do you think it will be necessary for them to put out into the tide again?"

"Indeed, I don't say she'll ever do without it," said the old boatman, still keeping his eyes fixed on the Nora Creina. "There she comes round. She spins about like a top, God bless her!" Then putting his huge chapped hands at either side of his mouth, so as to form a kind of speaking-trumpet, he cried out, in a voice as loud and hoarse as that of the surges that rolled between them, "Ahoy! ahoy! Have an oar out in the bow, or she'll mis stay in the swell."

"Thank you, thank you, it is done already," shouted the helmsman in answer. "Kyrle, my boy, how are you? Kyrle, have a good fire for us when we go in. This is cold work."

"Cold work!" repeated Lowry Looby. "Dear knows, it's true for you. Ah, then, isn't it little he makes of it, after all, God bless him! an' it blowin' a perfect *harico*."

Notwithstanding the vigour and confidence which spoke in the accents of the hardy helmsman, Kyrle Daly, when he saw the vessel once more shoot out into the deep, felt as if he had been listening to the last farewell of his friend. He could not return his gallant greeting, and remained with his head leaning forward and his arm outstretched, and trembling, while his eyes followed the track of the pleasure-boat. Close behind him stood Lowry, his shoulders raised against the wind, and his hand placed over that ear on which it blew, clacking his tongue against his palate for pity, and indulging in many sentiments of commiseration for "Master Hardress" and "the family," not forgetting "Danny the Lord," and his sister, "Fighting Poll of the Reeks."

We shall follow the vessel in her brief but daring course. The young helmsman has been already slightly introduced to the reader in the second chapter of this history; but the change which circumstances had since effected in his appearance rendered it well worthy of our pains to describe his person and bearing with more accuracy and distinctness. His figure was tall, and distinguished by that muscularity and firmness of set which characterise the inhabitants of the south-west of Europe. His attitude, as he kept one hand on the rudder, and his eye fixed upon the foresail, was such as displayed his form to extreme advantage. It was erect, composed, and manly. Every movement seemed to be dictated by a judgment perfectly at ease, and a will that, far from being depressed, had caught a degree of fire and excitement from the imminent dangers with which it had to struggle. The warm and heroic flush upon his cheek could not be discovered in the pale and unequal light that shone upon him; but the settled and steady lustre of his large dark eye, over which not even the slightest contraction of the arched brow could be discerned, the perfect calmness of his manner, and the half-smiling expression of his mouth (that feature which, of all others, is most traitorous to the dissembling coward), bespoke a mind and heart that were pleased to encounter danger, and well calculated to surmount it. It was such a figure as would have at once awakened associations in the beholder's mind of camps and actions, of states confounded in their councils, and nations overrun by sudden conquest. His features were brightened by a lofty and confident enthusiasm, such as the imagination might ascribe to the Royal Adventurer of Sweden, as he drew his sword on his beleaguerers at Belgrade. His forehead was ample and intellectual in its character; his hair "coal-black" and curling; his complexion of that rich, deep, gipsy yellow, which, showing as it did the healthy bloom beneath, was far nobler in its character than the feminine white and red. The lower portion of his physiognomy was finely and delicately turned; and a set of teeth as white as

27

those of a young beagle gave infinite vivacity to the expression of his lips. The countenance was such a one as men seldom look upon, but when once beheld can never be forgotten.

On a seat at the weather-side sat a young girl, her slight person wrapped in a blue cloak, while her eyes were raised to the cheerful face of the helmsman, as if from him she derived all her hope and her security. The wind had blown back the hood from her shoulders, and the head and countenance which thus "unmasked their beauty to the moon" were turned with a sylph-like grace and lightness. The mass of curly hair which was blown over her left temple seemed of a pale gold, that harmonised well with the excelling fairness and purity of her complexion; and the expression of her countenance was tender, affectionate, and confiding.

In the bow sat a being who did not share the beauty of his companions. He bore a prodigious hunch upon his shoulders, which, however, did not prevent his using his limbs with agility, and even strength, as he tended the foresail, and bustled from side to side with an air of the utmost coolness and indifference. His features were not disagreeable, and were distinguished by that look of pert shrewdness which marks the low inhabitant of a city, and vents itself in vulgar cant and in ridicule of the honest and wondering ignorance of rustic simplicity.

Such were the individuals whom the spirit of the tempest appeared at this moment to hold environed by his hundred perils; and such was the manner in which they prepared to encounter their destiny.

"Mind your hand, Mr. Hardress," said the boatman, in a careless tone; "we are in the tide."

It required the hand of an experienced helmsman to bring the little vessel through the danger which he thus announced. An immense overtopping billow, capped in foam, came thundering downward like an avalanche upon her side. In spite of the precautions of Hardress, and the practised skill with which he timed the motion of the wave, as one would take a ball upon the bound or a hunter on the rise, the bowsprit dipped and cracked like a withered sapling; a whole ton of water was flung over the stern, drenching the crew as completely as if they had been drawn through the river. The boat seemed to stagger and lose her way like a stricken hart, and lay for a moment weltering in the gloomy chasm in which the wasted wave had left her. A low and smothered scream was breaking from the female, when her eye again met that of Hardress Cregan, and her lip, though pale and quivering, was silent.

"That was right well done, sir," said Danny Mann, as the boat once more cleft the breakers on the landward course. "A minute sooner or a minute later up with the hand would put it all into her."

"A second would have done it," said Hardress, "but all is well now. A charming night this would be," he continued, smiling on the girl, "for beaver and feathers."

This jest produced a short hysteric laugh in answer, which was rather startling than agreeable to the person who addressed her. In a few minutes after, and without any considerable disaster, the vessel dropped her peak, and ran alongside the rocks on which Kyrle Daly was expecting them.

"Remain in the boat," said Hardress, addressing the girl, while he fastened the hood over her head; "I see that talkative fellow, Looby, above on the rocks. I will procure you an unoccupied room, if possible, in the cottage, as a neighbour and relative of Danny Man. Endeavour to conceal your countenance, and speak as little as possible. We are ruined if I should be seen paying you any attention."

"And am I not to see you to-night again?" said the girl, in a broken and affectionate accent.

"My own love, I would not go to rest without taking leave of you for all the world. Be satisfied," he added, pressing her hand tenderly, and patting her upturned cheek. "You are a noble girl. Go, pray—pray, and return thanks for your husband's life, as he shall do for yours. I thought we should have supped in heaven. Dan!" he continued aloud, calling to the boatman, "take care of your sister."

"His sisther!" echoed Lowry Looby on the rocks. "Oh, murther! is Fighting Poll of the Reeks aboord to? Why, then, he needn't bid Danny to take care of her, for she is well able to do that job for herself."

Hardress leaped out upon the shore, and was received by Kyrle Daly with a warmth and delight proportioned to the anxiety which he had previously experienced.

"My dear fellow, I thought I should never have seen you on your feet again. A thousand and a hundred thousand welcomes! Lowry, run to the house, and get dinner hastened. Stay! Hardress, have you any things on board?"

"Only a small trunk and my gun. You would for ever oblige me, Kyrle, by procuring a comfortable lodging, if you have no room to spare, for this poor fellow of mine and his sister. He is sickly, and you know he is my foster-brother."

"He shall be taken care of: I have a room. Come along; you are dripping wet. Lowry, take up Mr. Cregan's trunk and gun to the cottage. Come along, Hardress, you will catch your death of cold. Pooh! are you afraid Fighting Poll will break her tender limbs, that you look back and watch her so closely?"

"No, no, my dear Daly; but I am afraid that fellow—Booby—Looby—(what's his stupid name?)—will break my trunk; he is watching the woman and peering about her, instead of minding what he is doing. But come along! Well, Kyrle, how are you? I saw you all in the window to-day when I was sailing by."

"Yes; you edified my mother with that little feat you performed at the expense of the fishermen."

"Ah, no! was she looking at that, though? I shall not be able to show my face to her this month to come. Hollo! you sir, Booby, Looby, come along! Do you remain long in the west, Kyrle?"

"As long as you will take a bed in the cottage with me. But we will talk of this when you have changed your dress and dined. You came on the very point of time. *Rem acu tetigisti*, as our old college tutor, Doyle, would say. Mrs. Frawley was just preparing to dish me a roast duck. I bless the wind, all boisterous as it was, that blew you on these shores, for I thought I should have spent a lonesome evening, with the recollections of merry old times, like so many evil familiars, to dine, and sup, and sleep with me. But now that we are met again, farewell the past! The present and the future shall furnish our entertainment—after we have done with the roast duck."

"The fume of which salutes my senses at this moment with no disagreeable odour," said Hardress, following his friend into the little hall of the cottage. "Mrs. Frawley, as fat, and fair, and rosy as ever! Well, Mrs. Frawley, how do you and the cows get on? Has any villanous imp been making *pishogs* over your keelers? Does the cream mount? Does the butter break? Have you got the devil well out of your churn?"

"Oh, fie, Masther Cregan, to go spake of such a thing at all. Oh, vo, a vich-o, you're drownded wet, an' that's what you are. Nelly, eroo, bring hether the candle. Oh, sir, you never will get over it."

"Never mind, Mrs. Frawley, I'll be stout enough to dance at your wedding yet."

"My wedding, ma vourneen!" returned the buxom dairy-woman, in a gentle scream of surprise, not unqualified, however, by a gracious smile. "Oyeh, if you never fut a mooneen till then! Make haste hether with the candle, Nelly, eroo; what are you doing?"

Nelly, not altogether *point device* in her attire, at length appeared with a light to conduct the gentlemen to their chamber, while Mrs. Frawley returned to the kitchen. This accident of the stranger's arrival was of fatal consequence to three individuals in the cottage; namely, two fat chickens and a turkey-poult, upon whom sentence of death was immediately pronounced and executed, without more form of law than might go to the hanging of a croppy. Mrs. Frawley, meantime, fulfilled the office of sheriff on the occasion, ejaculating, out of a smiling reverie, while she gazed listlessly on the blood of the innocent victims, "Why, then, I declare that Mr. Hardress is a mighty pleasant gentleman."

In the mean time Lowry Looby was executing the commission he had received with regard to Mr. Cregan's trunk. Lowry, who was just as fond of obtaining or communicating strange intelligence, had his own good reason for standing in awe of the far-famed Fighting Poll of the Reeks, who was renowned in all the western fairs as a fearless, whiskey-drinking, virago, over six feet in her stocking vamps, and standing no more in awe of the gallows than she might of her mother's arms. It may at once be seen that a character of this description was the very last that could have been personated with any success by the lovely young creature who accompanied Hardress; and, indeed, her only chance of escaping detection consisted in the unobtrusiveness of the attempt she made, and the care she used in concealing her features. The first circumstance that excited the astonishment of Lowry, as he stood bowing with his hat off upon the rocks, while Danny the Lord assisted her to land, was the comparative diminutiveness of her stature, and the apparent slightness of her form.

"Your sarvent, Mrs. Naughten," he said in a most insinuating accent. "I hope I see you well in your health, ma'am. You wouldn't remember a boy of the Loobys at all, you met of a time at Nelly Hewsan's wake, westwards (Heaven rest her soul this night!) That was the place where the great giving-out was, surely."

To his gentle remembrance of old merry times the female in the blue cloak only answered by a slight, short courtesy, while she drew the hood closer about her face, and began, though with a feeble and tottering step, to ascend the rocks.

"Bread, an'—beef, an'—tay, an'—whiskey, an'—turkeys, an'—cakes, an' everything that the heart could like," the officious Lowry continued, following the pseudo-Amazon among the stones and seaweed, and marvelling not a little at her unaccustomed taciturnity. "The Hewsans could well afford it; they were strong, snug farmers—relations o' your own, I'm thinking, ma'am. Oh, vo! sure I forgot the thrunk, and there's Mr. Hardress calling to me. Larry Kett," he continued, addressing the old boatman before mentioned, "will show Mrs. Naughten the way to the house, while I'm getting the thrunk out o' the boat; an' if you want a fire o' turf, or a *gwal* o' piatees, Mrs. Frawley will let you have 'em an' welcome."

The old boatman willingly came into terms so easy and advantageous; and the fair counterfeit hurried on, well pleased at the exchange of companions. Lowry, in the mean time, returned to the boat, and stole into conversation with Danny the Lord, whom, in fear of his sneering satirical temper, he always treated with nearly as much respect as if his title were not so purely a thing of courtesy. Danny Mann, on the other hand, received his attentions with but little complaisance; for he looked on Lowry as a foolish, troublesome fellow, whose property in words (like the estate of many a young absentee) far overbalanced his discretion and ability in their employment. He had often told Looby in confidence "that it would be well for him he had a bigger head and a smaller mouth"—alluding to that peculiar conformation of Lowry's upper man, with which the reader has been already made acquainted. The country people (who are never at a loss for a simile), when they saw this long-legged fellow following the sharp-faced little hunchback from place to place, used to lean on their spades, and call the attention of their companions to "the wran an' the cuckoo goin' the road."

The "cuckoo" now found the "wran" employed in coiling up a wet cable on the forecastle, while he sang, in a voice that more nearly resembled the grunting of a pig at the approach of rain than the melody of the sweet songstress of the hedges above named,—

> "An' of all de meat dat ever was hung,
> A cheek o' pork is my fancy—
> 'Tis sweet an' toothsome when 'tis young;
> Fait, dat 's no lie, says Nancy.
> 'Twill boil in less dan half an hour,
> Den with your nail you may try it,
> 'Twill taste like any cauliflower—
> 'Tis better do dat dan to fry it.
> Sing re-rig-i-dig-i-dum-derom-dum.

"How does the world use Misther Mann this evening?" was the form of Lowry's first greeting, as he bent over the gunwale of the stern, and laid his huge paws on the small trunk.

"As you see me, Lowry," was the reply.

"A smart evening ye had of it."

"Purty fair, for de matter o' dat."

"Dear knows, it's a wondther ye wor'n't drownded. 'Twas blowin' a *harico*. An' you singin' now, as if you wor comin' from a jig-house, or a wake, or a weddin'. Ah, tell me, now, Misther Mann, wasn't it your thought, when you were abroad that time, how long it was since you were with the priest before?"

"I dought o' dat first, Lowry, an' I tried to say a prayer; but it was so long from me since I did de like before, dat I might

as well try to talk Latin, or any oder book-larning. But sure if I dought o' myself rightly, dere wasn't de laste fear of us, for I had a book o' St. Margaret's confession in me buzzum, an as long as I'd have dat, I knew dat if de boat was to go down under me itself, she'd come up again."

"Erra, no!"

"Iss, dear knows."

"I wisht I had one of 'em," said Lowry. "I do be often goin' in boats across to Cratloe, an' them places."

"You'd have no business of it, Lowry. Dem dat's born for one death has no reason to be afeerd of anoder."

"Gondoutha! You're welcome to your joke this evening. Well, if I was to put my eyes upon sticks, Misther Mann, I never would know your sister again."

"She grew a dale, I b'lieve."

"Grew?—if she did, it's like the cow's tail, downwards. Why, she isn't to say taller than myself now, in place o' bein' the head an' two shoulders above me. An' she isn't at all the rattlin' girl she was of ould. She didn't spake a word."

"An' dat's a failing dat's new to both o' ye," said his lordship; "but Poll made a vow again' talkin' of a Tursday, bekeys it was of a Tursday her first child died, an' dey said he was hoist away be de good people, while Poll was gossiping wid Ned Hayes over a glass at de public."

"And that's her raison?"

"Dat's her raison."

"An' in regard o' the drink?"

"Oh, she's greatly altered dat way, too, dough 'twas greatly again' natur. A lime-burner's bag was notten to her for soakin' formerly, but now she'd take no more than a wet sponge."

"That's great, surely. An' about the cursin' an' swearin'?"

"Cursin'! You'd no more find a curse after her dan you would after de clargy. An' 'tisn't dat itself, but you wouldn't get a crooked word outside her lips from year's end to year's end."

"Why, then, it was long from her to be so mealy-mouthed when I knew her. An' does she lift a hand at the fair at all now? Oyeh, what a terrible 'oman she was, comin' again' a man with her stockin' off, an' a stone in the foot of it!"

"She was. Well, she wouldn't raise her hand to a chicken now."

"That flogs cock-fighting."

"Only, I'll tell you in one case. She's apt to be contrary to any one dat would be comin' discoorsin' her of a Tursday at all, or peepin' or spyin' about her, she's so vexed in herself not to be able to make 'em an answer. It used to be a word an' a blow wid her; but now, as she can't have de word, 'tis de blow comes mostly first, an' she didn't make e'er a vow again' dat."

"Shasthone!" exclaimed Lowry, who laid up this hint for his own edification. "Great changes, surely. Well, Misther Mann, an' will you tell me now, if you plase, is your masther goin' westwards in the boat to-morrow?"

"I don't know, an'—not makin' you a short answer, Lowry—I don't care. And a word more on de back o' dat again: aldough I have a sort of a rattlin' regard for you, still an' all, I'd rader be takin' a noggin o' whiskey, to warm de heart in me dis cold night, dan listenin' to your talkin' dere. Dat I may be happy but I would, an' dat's as good as if I was after takin' all de books in Ireland of it."

This hint put an end to the conversation for the present, and Danny the Lord (who exercised over Lowry Looby an influence somewhat similar to that which tied Master Matthew to the heels of Bobadil) adjourned with that loquacious person to the comforts of Mrs. Frawley's fireside.

CHAPTER XIII.

HOW THE TWO FRIENDS HOLD A LONGER CONVERSATION TOGETHER THAN THE READER MAY PROBABLY APPROVE.

THE female in the blue cloak withstood all the recommendations and entreaties of the good-natured dairy-woman that she would "step in, and take an air of the kitchen fire." She pleaded extreme fatigue, and requested that she might be permitted to occupy at once the chamber in which she was to pass the night. Finding her resolute, Mrs. Frawley insisted on having a cheerful fire lighted up in the little room outside her own dormitory, which was appropriated to the fair stranger's use. It was impossible to maintain her close disguise in the presence of this officious and hospitable woman, whose regard for her guest was in no degree diminished by a view of her person and dress. Her hair was wringing wet, but her cloak had in a great measure preserved the remainder of her attire, which was just a shade too elegant for a mere *paysanne*, and too modest for a person claiming the rank of a gentlewoman. The material, also, which was a pretty flowered cotton—" a dawny pattern," as Mrs. Frawley declared—proclaimed a pocket altogether at ease, and led the dairy-woman to the conclusion that "the Naughtens were decent, *credible* people, that knew how to industher, and turn and stretch a penny as far as more would a shilling."

Having supplied the counterfeit Poll with everything necessary for her immediate uses, Mrs. Frawley left her to make what changes she pleased in her dress, and went to look after the young gentlemen's dinner, as well as to prepare some refreshment for the weary Mrs. Naughten herself.

Scarcely had Mrs. Frawley departed when a soft tapping at the room door announced the approach of another visitor. The lovely *inconnue*, who was employed at the moment in arranging and drying her hair, felt her heart beat somewhat quickly and strongly at the sound. She threw back from her temples the wavy masses of gold that hung around them, and ran to the door with lips apart, and a flushed and eager cheek. "It is he!" she exclaimed to her own breast as she undid the bolt.

It was not *he*. The weather-worn, freckled face of the little hunchback was the first object that met her eyes. Between his hands he held a small trunk, the lid of which was studded with brass nails, forming the letters E. O'C.

"By a dale to do, Miss, I laid hoult o' dis," said Danny. "Lowry said de letters didn't stand for Mr. Hardress at all, only one of 'em."

"Thank you, Danny. Where is your master?"

"Aten his dinner in de parlour wid Mr. Daly before a tunderin' big fire."

"Was Lowry speaking to you?"

"Did anybody ever see him oderwise? I'll bail he was so."

"But does he know——?"

"I didn't hear him say a word about it," replied the little lord; "an' I tink, if he knew, he'd tell."

"Well, Danny, will you find an opportunity of speaking to your master without being observed, and tell him that I wish to see him very much indeed? I am very uneasy; and he has not told me how long we are to stay here, or where we are to go next, or anything. I feel quite lonesome, Danny, for it is the first evening I have ever spent alone in my life, I think." Here the poor young creature's lip quivered a little, and the water started into her eye.

"Never fear, ma gra hu! ma grein chree hu!" said Danny in a soothing tone; "I'll speak a word in his ear, an' he'll come to you. Dat I may never die in a frost if I wouldn't go from dis to Dublin to sarve you, next to Mr. Hardress himself."

He was as good as his word, and took an opportunity, while Hardress was giving him some directions about the boat, to mention the request of their gentle companion in the storm. The young gentleman inquired the situation of her room, and bade his servant say that he would not fail to visit her, if only for a few minutes, before he retired to rest. It was necessary that the utmost caution should be observed, to avoid awakening suspicion.

Kyrle Daly, in the mean time, was employed in manufacturing a capacious bowl of whiskey-punch by the parlour fireside. Instead of the humble but capacious tumbler, or still more modern small stone-china jug, over which you, good Irish reader, are probably accustomed to solace your honest heart on a winter's evening, two glasses, more than a foot in height, were displayed upon the board, and seemed intended to meet the lips without the necessity of any assistance from the hand.

By one of those inconsistencies in our nature on which it is idle to speculate, Kyrle Daly found a difficulty in getting into conversation with his friend upon the very subject on which, a few minutes before, he had longed for his advice and assistance. Hardress appeared to be in high, noisy, and even exulting spirits, the sound of which rang jarringly and harsh upon the ear of the disappointed lover. The uproar of his happy heart offended the languor of his young companion's mind, as

the bustle of the city noon sounds strange and unfamiliar on a sick man's hearing.

Neither, perhaps, is there any subject to which young men of equal pretensions have a greater distaste than that of love-confidences one with another. If the tale be of a past and unhappy attachment, it is wearisome and annoying; and if it relate to a present and successful passion, a sentiment of jealousy is apt to invade the heart of the listener, while he is made to contemplate a picture of happiness which, perhaps, the sternness of his own destiny has allowed him to contemplate as a picture only. A better test could scarcely be adopted to distinguish a sincere and disinterested friendship from one of mere convenience than a trial of patience on such a topic. It is true, indeed, that the incidents lately recorded afford reason to believe that Hardress Cregan was not one of those forlorn beings who are made

" To love, and not be loved again;"

but it is certain, nevertheless, that when Kyrle Daly first mentioned his having been at Castle Chute, and driving Anne to the race-course, his manner was rather reserved and discouraging than otherwise.

"The longer I live," Kyrle said at length, with some hesitation in his manner—" the longer I live in this luckless condition, and the oftener I think of that excellent girl, the more deep and settled is the hold which she has taken of my imagination. I wonder, Hardress, how you can be so indifferent to her acquaintance. Placing my own unfortunate affection altogether out of view, I can scarcely imagine an enjoyment more desirable than that of cultivating the society of so amiable a creature."

Here he drew a long sigh, and replenished the void thus occasioned by having recourse to the bowl and ladle.

"I am not of the same opinion, Kyrle," said Hardress. "Anne Chute is unquestionably a very fine girl, but she is too highly educated for me."

"Too highly educated!"

"Echo me not. The words are mine. Yes, Kyrle, I hold that this system of polishing girls, *ad unguem*, is likely to be the destruction of all that is sincere, and natural, and unaffected in the sex. It is giving the mind an unwholesome preponderance over the heart, occasioning what an astronomer would call an *occultation* of feeling, by the intervention of reason."

"I cannot imagine a case," said Kyrle, "in which the exercise of reason can ever become excessive; and there are sneerers under the sun, Hardress, who will tell you that this danger is least of all to be apprehended among the lovely beings of whom you are speaking."

"I think otherwise. As I prefer the works of nature to the works of man, the fresh river breeze to the dusty and smoky zephyr of Capel Street, the bloom on a cottage cheek to the crimson japan that blazes at the Earl of Buckinghamshire's drawing-rooms; as I love a plain beef-steak before a grilled attorney,* this excellent whiskey-punch before my mother's confounded currant wine, and anything else that is pure and natural before anything else that is adulterated and artificial; so do I love the wild hedge-flower, simplicity, before the cold and sapless exotic, fashion; so do I love the voice of affection and of nature before that of finesse and affectation."

"Your terms are a little too hard, I think," said Kyrle; "elegance of manner is not finesse, nor at all the opposite of simplicity; it is merely simplicity made perfect. I grant you that few, very few, are successful in acquiring it; and I dislike its ape, affectation, as heartily as you do. But we find something that is conventional in all classes, and I like affectation better than vulgarity, after all."

"Vulgarity of manner," said Hardress, "is more tolerable than vulgarity of mind."

"One is only offensive as the indication of the other, and I think it not more tolerable, because I prefer ugliness masked to ugliness exposed."

"Why, now, Daly, I will meet you on tangible ground. There is our friend Anne Chute, acknowledged to be the loveliest girl

* It is notorious that the drumstick of a goose or turkey, grilled and highly spiced, was called a *devil*. Some elegant persons, however, who deemed that term too strong for "ears polite," were at the pains of looking for a synonyme of a milder sound, and discovered a happy substitute in the word *attorney*, which conveys all the original force, without the coarse cacophony of the other phrase.

in her circle, and one whom I remember a charming, good-natured little hoyden in her childhood. And see what high education has done for her. She is cold and distant, even to absolute frigidity, merely because she has been taught that insensibility is allied to elegance. What was habit has become nature with her; the frost which she suffered to lie so long upon the surface has at length penetrated to her affections, and killed every germ of mirth, and love, and kindness, that might have made her a treasure to her friends and an ornament to society."

"Believe me, Hardress, believe me, my dear Hardress, you do her wrong," exclaimed Kyrle with exceeding warmth. "It is not that I love Anne Chute I speak, but because I know and esteem her. If you knew her but for three days, instead of one hour, you never would again pronounce so harsh a sentence. All that is virtuous, all that is tender and affectionate, all that is amiable and high-principled, may be met with in that admirable woman. Take the pains to know her, visit her, speak of her to her friends—her dependents—to her aged mother—to any one that has observed her conduct, and you will be undeceived. Why will you not strive to know her better?"

"Why, you must consider that it is not many months since I returned from Dublin; and, to say a truth, the single visit I paid at Castle Chute was not calculated to tempt me to a second. Considering that I was an old playfellow and a kind of cousin, I thought Anne Chute need not have received me as if I were a tax-gatherer or a travelling dancing-master."

"Why, what would you have her do? Throw her arms about your neck, and kiss you, I suppose?"

"Not exactly. You know the class of people of whom little Flaccus said, *Quum vitia vitant in contraria currunt ;* and, after all, I think Anne Chute is not one of those. Her education is little worth if it could not enable her to see a medium between two courses so much at variance."

"But will you allow a friend to remind you, Hardress, that you are a little overapt to take exception in matters of this kind? And, notwithstanding all you have been saying against the polite world, I will venture to prophesy this, that when circumstances shall more frequently thrust you forward on the stage, and custom shall make you blind to the slight and formal insincerities that grieve you at present, your ideas on fashion, and elegance, and education will undergo a change. I know you, Hardress: you are not yet of age. The shadow of a repulse is now to you a sentence of banishment from any circle in which you suppose it is offered; but when you shall be courted, when mothers shall dress their daughters at you, and daughters shall shower down smiles upon your path; when fathers shall praise your drinking, and sons shall eulogise your horses, then, Hardress, look to it. You will then be as loud and talkative before the whole world as now in presence of your humble friend. You will smile, and smile a hundred times over, at your young philosophy."

"Oh, 'never shall sun that morrow see!' cried Hardress, throwing himself back in his chair, and raising his hands in seeming deprecation. "I perceive what you are hitting at, Kyrle," he continued, reddening a little; "you allude to my—my—timidity—bashfulness—what you will—my social cowardice. But I disclaim the petty, paltry failing. The feeling that unnerves me in society is as widely different from that base consciousness of inferiority, or servile veneration of wealth, rank, or power, as the anger of Achilles from the spite of Thersites. You may laugh, and call me self-conceited; but, upon my simple honour, I speak in pure sincerity. My feeling is this, my dear Kyrle. New as I was to the world after leaving college (where you know I studied pretty hard), the customs of society appeared to wear a strangeness in my sight, that made me a perfect and competent judge of their value. Their hollowness disgusted, and their insipidity provoked me. I could not join with any ease in the solemn folly of bows, and becks, and wreathed smiles, that can be put on or off at pleasure. The motive of the simplest forms of society stared me in the face when I saw them acted before me, and if I attempted to play a part among the hypocrites myself, I supposed that every eye around me was equally clear-sighted, saw through the hollow assumption, and despised it as sincerely in me as I had done in others. The consciousness of guilt was evident in my manner, and I received the mortification which ensued as the just punishment of my meanness and hypocrisy."

"You *do* express yourself in sufficiently forcible terms when you go about it," said Daly, smiling. "What great hypocrisy or meanness there can be in remarking that it is a fine day, or asking after the family of an acquaintance, even though he should know that the first was merely intended to draw on a conversation, and the second to show him a mark of regard?"

"Which I did not feel."

"Granted. Let him perceive that never so clearly, there is still an attention implied in your putting the questions at all with which he cannot be disobliged. It is flattering to acknowledge the necessity of such a deference. And, my dear Hardress, if you were never to admit of ceremony as the deputy of natural and real feeling, what would become of the whole social system? How soon the mighty vessel would become a wreck ! how silent would be the rich man's banquet! how solitary the great man's chambers! how few would bow before the throne! how lonely and how desolate would be the temples of religion!"

"You are the more bitter satirist of the two," said Hardress.

"No, no," exclaimed Kyrle. "I merely remind you of an acknowledged fact, that when you enroll your name on the social list, you pledge yourself to endure as well as to enjoy. As long as ever you live, Hardress, take my word for it, you will never make nor look upon a perfect world. It is such philosophy as yours that goes to the making of misanthropes. The next time you go into society, resolve to accept any mortifications you shall endure as a punishment for your sins, and so think no more of them. This indifference will become habitual, and while it does so, those necessary hypocrisies of which you speak will grow familiar and inoffensive."

"I see no occasion," said Hardress, "to make the trial. Plain human nature is enough for me. If I were to choose a companion for life, I should rather hope to cull the sweet fruit of conjugal happiness in the wild orchard of nature than from the bark-beds and hot walls of society."

"I advise you, however," said Kyrle, "not to make the choice until you have greater opportunities of observing both sides of the question. Trust not to the permanence of your present feelings, nor to the practical correctness of your curious theories. It would be too late, after you had linked yourself to—to—simplicity, I shall call it, to discover that elegance was a good thing after all."

Hardress did not appear to relish this speech, and the conversation, in consequence, was discontinued for some minutes. Young Cregan was, indeed, as incapable of calculating on his future character as Kyrle Daly asserted. He was in that period of life (the most critical, perhaps, of all) when the energies of the mind, as well as of the frame, begin to develope themselves, and exhibit in irregular outbreaks the approaching vigour and fire of manhood. A host of new ideas at this time crowd in upon the reason, distinguished rather by their originality and genius than by that correctness and goodorder which are derivable from instruction or experience alone ; and it depends upon the circumstances in which the young thinker is placed, whether his future character shall be that of a madman or a sage. It was, perhaps, a knowledge of this inventive pride in youth that made the Stagirite assert that men should not look into philosophical works before the age of five-and-twenty.

Hardress, however, although very sensitive, was not one of those who can brood a long time over an evil feeling. "Well, Daly," he exclaimed, starting from a reverie, "we will each of us pursue our inclinations on this subject. Leave me to the indulgence of my theories, and I will wish you joy of your Anne Chute."

"*My* Anne Chute!" echoed Daly, sipping his punch with a sad face. "I have no lien upon that lady, as the counsellors say. She may sue as a *feme sole* for me in any court in Christendom."

Hardress turned on him a look of extreme surprise, in answer to which Kyrle Daly furnished him with an account of his unsuccessful suit to Anne, as also with his suspicions as to another attachment. The deep feeling of disappointment under which he laboured became apparent, as he proceeded in his discourse, in the warmth and eagerness of his manner, the frequent compression of his lips, and clenching of his trembling hands, the dampness of his forehead, and the sparkling of his moistened eyeballs. The sight of his friend in suffering turned the stream of Hardress Cregan's sympathies into another channel, and he employed all his eloquence and ingenuity in combating the dangerous dejection which was hourly gaining upon his spirit. He declared his disbelief in the idea of another attachment, and recommended perseverance by every argument in his power.

"But the state of her mind," he continued, "shall not remain long a secret to you. They have been both (Anne and her mother) invited to spend a part of the winter with us at Dinis Cottage. My mother is a great secret hunter, and I need only tell her where the game lies to make certain that it will be hunted down. Trust everything to me—for your sake I will take some pains to become better known to this extraordinary girl; and you may depend upon it, if she will suffer me to mount above zero, you shall not suffer in my good report."

When the conversation had reached this juncture the silence which prevailed in the cottage showed that the night was already far advanced. The punch had descended so low as to leave the bowl of the ladle more than half visible; the candles seemed to meditate suicide, while the neglected snuff, gathering to a pall above the flame, threw a gloomy and flickering shadow on the ceiling; the turfen fire was little more than a heap of pale ashes, before which the drowsy household cat, in her sphynx-like attitude, sat winking and purring her monotonous song of pleasure; the abated storm (like a true Irish storm) seemed to mourn with repentant howlings over the desolating effects of its recent fury; the dog lay dreaming on the hearth; the adjoining farmyard was silent, all but the fowl-house, where some gurrulous dame partlet, with female pertinacity, still maintained a kind of drowsy clucking on her roost; the natural hour of repose seemed to have produced its effect upon the battling elements themselves; the tempest had folded his black wings upon the ocean, and the waters broke upon the shore with a murmur of expiring passion. Within doors, or without, there was no sight nor sound that did not convey a hint of bed-time to the watchers.

To make this hint the stronger Mrs. Frawley showed the disk of her full-blown countenance at the door, as round as the autumnal moon, and, like that satellite, illuminated by a borrowed light, namely, the last inch of a dipped candle which burned in her hand. "Masther Kyrle, darlin'," she exclaimed, in a tone of tender remonstrance, "won't you go to bed to-night, child? 'Tis near mornin', dear knows."

"Is Lowry Looby in bed?"

"No, sir, he's waitin' to know have you any commands to Cork; he's going to guide the car in the mornin' with the firkins."

Lowry here introduced his person before that of the dairy-woman, causing, however, rather a transit than an eclipse of the moon of womanhood.

"Or Misther Cregan?" he exclaimed. "Maybe he'd have some commands westwards? Because, if he had, I could lave 'em at the forge at the cross, above, with directions to have 'em sent down to the house."

"I have no commands," said Hardress, "except to say that I will be at home on next Friday."

"And I have none whatever," said Kyrle Daly, rising and taking one of the candles. "Hardress, mind you don't give me the counterfeit, the slip, in the morning."

This caution produced a hospitable battle, which ended in Hardress Cregan's maintaining his purpose of departing with the dawn of day. The friends then shook hands, and separated for the night.

CHAPTER XIV.

HOW LOWRY BECOMES PHILOSOPHICAL.

As Lowry Looby returned to the kitchen he was met by Nelly, the housemaid, who reminded him that he would be obliged to start before the potatoes could be boiled in the morning, and recommended, as a preparatory measure, that he should take his breakfast overnight. Secure of his indulging her in so reasonable a request, she had already, under Mrs. Frawley's favour, laid on a little table before the kitchen fire the remains of the ducks (so often commemorated in this narrative), a plate of "re-heaters" (such was Nelly's term for potatoes suffered to cool, and warmed again in the red turf-ashes), as also a piece of pork four inches in depth, and containing no lean that was visible on a cursory inspection. This last was a dish for which Nelly knew Lowry Looby to entertain a fondness worthy of his ancient Irish descent. Indeed, on all occasions Nelly was observed to take an interest in consulting the inclinations of this long-legged person—a kindness upon her part which the ungrateful Lowry seemed little inclined to appreciate.

The present proposal, however, harmonised so sweetly with his own feelings at the moment, that he signified a speedy compliance, and followed the nymph into her culinary retreat. The kitchen presented a scene no less drowsy than the parlour. Mrs. Frawley was saying her prayers by the fireside, with a string of beads that hung down to the ground, now and then venting a deep sigh, then "running her godly race" through a fit of yawning, and anon casting a glance over her shoulder at the proceedings of the two domestics, while every new distraction was followed by a succession of more audible groans, and more vehement assaults with the closed hand upon her bosom. Danny Mann was sleeping heavily on the other side of the fire, with his red woollen comforter drying on his knee. In order to avoid disturbing either the slumbers of the one or the devotions of the other, Nelly and her swain were obliged to carry on their conversation in a low whispering voice, which gave additional effect to the sleepy tone of the entire scene. The shadows of the whole party, like the fame of genius magnified by distance, were thrown in gigantic similitude upon the surrounding walls. There Mrs. Frawley dilated to the dimensions of an ogre's wife, and here Danny Mann's hunch became to the original as Ossa to Knock Patrick. Looby's expanded mouth showed like the opening to Avernus, and the tight little Nelly herself, as she sat opposite, assumed the stature of Mr. Salt's black breccia Memnon, which any reader who is curious about Nelly's personal outline may behold in the ninth room of the British Museum.

While Lowry consoled himself with the greasy pork, swallowing it with as lively a relish as if it were the green fat of a Gallipagos turtle, he gave Nelly a history of the day's adventures, not forgetting his own triumph at the *staggeen* race, and the disappearance of Eily O'Connor. Nelly was the better pleased with his account of these transactions, as he thought fit to abstain, in the first instance, from all mention of Syl Carney; and, in speaking of the rope-maker's daughter, to omit those customary eulogies which he dealt forth whenever her name was brought in question. Emboldened by this circumstance, Nelly did not hesitate to throw out some plain insinuations as to the probable cause of the mystery, which did not much redound to the honour of the charming fugitive, and she became still more impassioned in her invective after Mrs. Frawley had relieved them from the restraint of her presence, and retired to her sleeping-room.

"Often an' often I told you, Lowry, that it wasn't for you to be lookin' afther a girl o' that kind, that thought herself as good as a lady. Great business, indeed, a poor man o' your kind would have of one like her, that would be too grand to put a leg in a *skeogh* * to wash the potatoes, or lay a hand on the pothooks, to sthrain 'em, if they wor broke to tatthers."

"That I may never die in sin if ever I had a thought of her, Nelly, only just divartin' at Batt Coonerty's."

"What a show the house would be with ye," continued Nelly, still following up the matrimonial picture, "an' you a hard-workin' boy, obleest to be up early an' late at other people's biddin'. I'll be bound that isn't the girl that would be up with the lark, an' have a fire made, an' a griddle o' bread down in the mornin' before you, an' you goin' a long road; or have the hearth swep' and your supper ready, an' everythin' nate anon he place for you, when you'd be comin' back at night. But I believe there's a *chimœra* † before the boys' eyes, that they don't know what's good for 'em."

"Look!" exclaimed Lowry, while he broke a potato between his fingers, swallowed one half at a mouthful, and tossed the crisped peel upon the table; "that I may be happy, if she was offered to me this minute, if I'd take her. Sure I know I'd have no more business of such a girl upon my floore than I would of Miss Chute herself. But there's no reason, for all, why I wouldn't be sorry for ould Mihil's throuble. He's gone westwards, Foxy Dunat the hair-cutter tells me, to Castle Island, to his brother, Father Ned, I suppose, to get him to publish her from the altar, or somethin'. They think 'tis westwards she went."

Happening at this moment to cast his eyes upon Danny Mann, Lowry perceived, with a sensation of disagreeable surprise, that

* Basket.   † An optical illusion.

LOWRY LOOBY PREPARES FOR HIS JOURNEY.

he was awake, and peering curiously upon him from below the half-raised lids. The red fire-light which gleamed on the eye-balls gave them a peculiar and equivocal lustre, which added force to their native sharpness of expression. Danny felt the ill effect he had produced, and carried it off with a fit of yawning and stretching, asking Lowry at the same time, with a drowsy air, if he meant to go to bed at all.

"To be sure I do," said Lowry, "when it's pleasin' to the company to part. There's a time for all things, as they say in the Readin'-made-asy."

"Surely, surely," returned Danny, with a yawn. "Dear knows, den, de Readin'-made-asy time is come now, for 'tis a'most mornin'."

"I always mostly smoke a drass before I go to bed of a night," said Lowry, turning towards the fire, and clearing the bowl of his pipe by knocking it gently against the bar of the grate; "I like to be smokin' an' talkin' when the company is agreeable, and I see no rason for bein' in a hurry to-night, above all others. Come, Nelly," he added, while he chopped up

a little tobacco, and pressed it into the bowl with the tip of his finger, "come here, an' sit near me; I want to be talkin' to you."

Saying this, he took a half-burnt sod from the fire, crushed the bowl into the burning portion, and after offering it in vain to Danny, placed it in the corner of his mouth. He then remained for some moments with his eyes half closed, drawing in the fire with his breath, and coaxing it with his finger, until the vapour flowed freely through the narrow tube, and was emitted at intervals, at the opposite corner of his mouth, in a dense and spiry stream.

"An' what do you want to be saying?" said Nell, taking her seat between Lowry and the lord. "I'll engage you have nothin' to say to me afther all."

"Come a little nearer," said Lowry, without changing his position.

"Well, there, why?" returned Nelly, moving her chair a little closer. "Will that do?"

"No, it won't. 'Tis a whisper I have for you. Misther Mann would hear me if I told it to you where you are."

"Oh, a whisper! Well, now I'm close enough, any way," she said, placing her chair in contact with that of Lowry.

The latter took the pipe from his mouth, and advanced his face so close to that of the expectant housemaid, that she feared he was about to snatch a kiss. Perhaps it was in mere curiosity to satisfy herself whether in fact he could possess so much audacity, that Nelly did not avoid that danger by moving her head aside; but, greatly to her surprise, and doubtless likewise to her satisfaction, the honest man proved that he had no such insolent intention. When he had attained a convenient proximity, he merely parted his lips a little, and puffed a whole volume of smoke into her eyes. Nelly uttered a gentle scream, and covered her face with her hands, while Danny and Lowry exchanged a broad grin of satisfaction.

"Well, Lowry," exclaimed the girl with much good humour, "you're the greatest rogue goin', and that's your name this night."

Lowry continued to muse for a few moments, while he continued the enjoyment of his pipe. In a little time he once more took it from his lips, puffed forth the last whiff, and said, "Misther Mann, they may say this and that o' the world, an' of poverty, an' riches, an' humility, an' gentility, an' everythin' else they like, but here's my word, ever: If I was a king upon a throne this minute, an' I wanted to have a smoke for myself by the fireside, why, if I was to do my best, what could I smoke but one pen'orth o' tobacco in the night, afther all? And can't I have that as it is, just as asy? If I was to have a bed with down feathers upon it, what could I do more than sleep there? An' sure I can do that in the settle-bed above. If I was able to buy the whole market out an' out, what could I ate of it more than I did to-night o' that pork upon the table? Do you see, now, Mr. Mann? do you see, Nelly? Unless he could smoke two pipes of a night, instead of one, or sleep more, or ate more without hurt, I don't say what's the advantage a king has over a poor man like myself,"

"Ah, sure, you know that's foolish talk, Lowry. Sure the king could buy and sell you at the fair if he liked."

"He couldn't without the jury," returned Lowry—"the judge an' jury ever. He couldn't lay a wet finger on me without the jury, be course o' law. The round o' the world is as free to me as it is to him, if the world be round in airnest, as they say it is."

"Round, ayeh?" said Nell.

"Iss, to be sure."

Danny Mann looked at him for a moment. "Is it the world we're walkin' on?" he asked in some surprise.

"To be sure, what else?"

"Ah, don't be talkin'," returned Danny, turning his head away in perfect scorn of the hypothesis.

"Faix, I tell you no lie," said Lowry; "'tis printed in all the books in Europe. They say that if it wasn't round we'd soon be done for. We couldn't keep a hoult upon it at all, only to go flyin' through the elements. The Lord save us!"

"Oh, vo, vo!" said Nelly; "well, that bates Ireland."

"Sure there's more says that it isn't the sun above do be movin' at all, only we goin' round it."

"That the sun doesn't stir?"

"Not a peg."

"Well, now, you may bould your tongue after dat," said Danny, "after wantin' to take de eyesight from us. Sure the whole world sees the sun goin', any way."

"I wouldn't b'lieve that," said Nelly, "if they were to put their eyes upon sticks."

"I wouldn't be so," returned Lowry. "What business would a poor boy o' my kind have goin' again' men that are able to write books, let alone readin' 'em? But 'tis the foolishness of the women," he continued, fixing upon Nelly as the least pugnacious opponent; "women are always for foolishness. They'd b'lieve, or not b'lieve, just as they like themselves, equal to Dan Dawley's second wife. Did you ever hear o' that business, Misther Mann?"

"Not as I know."

"Well, stir up the fire, Nelly, an' put down a couple o' sods, an' I'll tell it while I am finishin' my pipe, an' then we'll all be off to bed. Dan Dawley was married a second time to a very nice girl, one Jug Minaham (he's the steward at Castle Chute behind). Well, he was out of a day at work, an' his wife was setten' alone by the fire, a few weeks afther they bein' married.

Now, there was one o' the stones in the chimney (as it might be that stone there), an' it stood out loose from the morthar a dale beyond the rest. Well, she sat lookin' at it for a while, and the thought come in her head, 'If I had a child now,' says she, 'an' he was standin' a-near that stone, maybe 'twould fall out and brain him on me.' An' with the thought o' that she began roarin' and bawlin' equal to anythin' ever you hear.'

"Oh, then, she was a foolish girl!" said Nelly.

"Dear knows, that was her name," said Danny.

"Well, her old mother heered her bawlin,' an' she came in the greatest hurry. 'A! what ails you, Jug?' says she. So Jug up an' tould her her thought about the stone, an' began bawlin' worse than ever. An' if she did, the mother joined her, an' such a pillilu as they raised between 'em was never known. That was well an' good. Well, Dan was abroad in the potato-garden, an' he heard the work goin' on in his house, cryin' equal to a funeral. 'What's this about?' says Dan; 'there's somebody murthered, surely.' So he made for the doore, an' in he walked, an' there he found the pair o' ladies. 'A! what ails you, mother?' said he. 'Jug will tell you, agra,' says the mother. So he looked at Jug. 'Thinkin' I was,' says she, still crying, 'that if the child was born, an' if that stone there fell upon him, 'twould brain him on me.' Well, Dan stood for a while lookin' at her. 'If the sky fell,' says he, 'we'd catch larks. An' is that all that happened to you?' 'Isn't it enough?' says she again. Well, he stopped a long while thinkin' in his mind, and then he reached out his hand to her. 'Well,' says he, 'that's the foolishest thing I ever knew in my life, an' I'll tell you what it is, I never'll take a day with you from this hour, until I'll find a woman,' says he, 'that's foolisher than yourself.' No sooner said than done: out he walked, lavin' 'em after him to do as they plased. Well, there was a long day before him, an' he walked a dale before nightfall, an' he didn't know where he'd turn to his bed and dinner. 'But sure I'm asy about it,' says he; 'sure, while there's fools of women in the place, I'll engage I needn't starve.' Well, he called a gorsoon that was goin' the road. 'Whose farmhouse,' says he, 'is that I see over there?' 'It's belongin' to a widow woman, sir,' said the boy. 'What sort of a man was her husband?' says Dan. 'A small, dark man, an' wearin' top-boots,' says the boy. Well became Dan, he made for the house, an' axed for the lone woman. She was standin' on the lawn lookin' at her cows milkin', when Dan made towards her. 'Well, where do you come from?' says the widow woman. 'From heaven, ma'am,' says Dan, makin' a bow. 'From heaven?' says she, lookin' at him with her eyes open. 'Yes, ma'am,' says he, 'for a little start. An' I seen your husband there too, ma'am.' 'My husband, ivagh?' says she, lookin' at him very knowin'. 'Can you tell me what sort of a man he was?' 'A small dark man, says Dan, 'an' wearin' top-boots.' 'I give into you,' says she, 'that's the man. Come this way, an' tell me what did he say to you, or did he give any message to me?' Well, Dan put no bounds to his tongue, just to thry her. 'He bid me tell you,' says he, 'that he's very badly off for want o' victuals; an' he'd like to have the young grey horse to be ridin' for himself, an' he'd do as much if you could send 'em to him.' 'Why, then, I'll do that,' says the widow, 'for he was a good husband to me when he lived. What time will you be goin' back?' 'To-morrow or afther,' says Dan, 'afther I see my people.' 'Well, stay here to-night,' says she, 'an' I'll give you somethin' to take to him in the mornin'.' Well became her, she brought him in, and treated him like a prince that night with music an' dancing; an' in the mornin' she had the grey horse at the doore with a bag o' flour, an' a crock o' butter, an' a round o' corned beef. Well, Dan mounted the horse, an' away with him home to his wife. 'Well, Jug,' says he, 'I'll take with you all my days; for, bad as you are, there's more that's twice worse, an' I believe if I went farther 'tis worse an' worse I'd be gettin' to the world's end.' So he up an' told 'em the whole business, and they had a merry supper that night, and for weeks afther, on what Dan brought home with him."

"He was a rogue for all," said Nelly, "to keep the poor woman's horse upon her."

"She deserved it," said Danny, "an' worse. I never hear o' such a fool. Well, Lowry, will you go to bed now at last?"

The question was answered in the affirmative; and Danny was at the same time pressed to take a share of the sweets of

* Is it?

the table, which he resolutely refused. Soon after, the careful Nelly, having made Lowry turn his head another way, ascended by a ladder to a pallet on a loft over the parlour; while Lowry and the little lord rolled into the settle-bed together, the one to dream of breakers, raw onions, whiskey, and "Misther Hardress;" the other of Foxy Dunat's mare, and the black eyes of Syl Carney.

CHAPTER XV.

HOW HARDRESS SPENT HIS TIME WHILE KYRLE DALY WAS ASLEEP.

ALL were now asleep except the two strangers, and the silence which reigned throughout the little cottage showed Hardress that no ear was capable of detecting his movements. He opened his room door softly, slipped his shoes from his feet, and leaving the light burning on his table, trusted to the famous sixth sense of the German physiologists, for a chance of finding his way among the chairs and tables in the dark. He reached the door without a stumble, and perceived by the light, which streamed through the keyhole and under the door of his friend's apartment, that she still expected him.

Their meeting, though silent, was impassioned and affectionate. Hardress inquired, with the tender and sedulous attention of a newly-married man, whether she felt any injurious effects from the storm—whether she had changed her dress and taken some refreshment—whether, in fine, her situation was in any way inconvenient to her.

"In no way at all, Mr. Hardress, as to any of these things you mention," she replied in a low voice, for she was fearful of waking Mrs. Frawley in the next room. "But as to the mind—may Heaven never give you the affliction of spending two such hours as I have done since I entered this room!"

"My life! why will you speak so? What other course remained for our adoption? You know your father's temper; he would as soon have died as sanctioned a private marriage, such as ours must be for some time longer. It would be absolute ruin to me if my mother knew of my having contracted such an engagement without consulting her wishes; and my father, as I have before told you, will act exactly as she desires. And why, now, my love, will you indulge those uneasy humours? Are you not my bride, my wife, the chosen of my heart, and the future partner of my fortunes? Do you really think that I would forget my little angel's feelings so far as to omit anything in my power that might set her mind at rest? If you do, I must tell you that I love you more than you imagine."

"Oh, Mr. Hardress! oh, don't say that at all, sir," said the young woman, with frankness and ready warmth of manner. "Only I was just thinking, an' I sitting by the fire, what a heartbreak it would be to my father if anybody put it into his head that the case was worse than it is" (here she hung down her head), "and no more would be wanting but just a little word on a scrap o' paper to let him know that he needn't be uneasy, and that he'd know all in time."

This suggestion seemed to jar against the young gentleman's inclinations. "If you wish," said he, with a little earnestness of voice, "I will return with you to Garryowen to-morrow, and have our marriage made public from the altar of John's Gate chapel. I have no object in seeking to avoid my own ruin, greater than of preventing you from sharing it. But if you will insist upon running the hazard—hazard!—I mean if you are determined on certainly destroying our prospects of happiness, your will shall be dearer to me than fortune or friends either. If you have a father to feel for, you will not forget, my love, that I have a mother whom I love as tenderly, and whose feelings deserve some consideration at my hands."

The gentle girl seemed affected, but not hurt, at this speech. "Don't be angry with me," she said, laying her hand affectionately on his shoulder; "don't be angry with me, Mr. Hardress. I know I have a very bad head, and can't see into everything at once; but one word from you (and it needn't be an angry one either) is enough to open my eyes. Insist, do you say, Mr. Hardress? Indeed, sir, I was never made to insist upon anything. But when a thought, foolish as it is, once comes into my head, I long to speak of it, to know what you will say, to know if it is wrong or right. You wouldn't wish that I should keep it from you, sir?"

"Never, oh, never! Do not think of that."

"I never will practise it long, any way; for such thoughts as those, if I were to hide them, would kill me before a month. But keep always near me, my dear, dear Mr. Hardress, for though you showed me that there is nothing very criminal in what I have done, yet when you leave me alone, the reasons go out of my head, and I only think of what the neighbours are saying about me this day, and of what my father must feel listening to them. Don't think, now, sir, that I am going to question what you tell me (for I trust in you next to Heaven), but if I am not so much to blame, why is it that my mind is not at ease? The storm, sir—oh, that storm! When the waves rose, and the boat rocked, and the wind howled about me, how my feelings changed on a sudden! I strove to look quiet before you, but my heart was leaping for fear within me. When we sank down in the darkness, and rose in the light, when the waves were dashin' in over the side, and the sails were dippin' in the water, I thought of my father's fireside, and I was sure it was the anger of the Almighty hunting the disobedient child over the dark waters. I thought I never would walk the land again; and how will it be, says I, if the boat breaks under us, and my father is told that his daughter was washed ashore a corpse, with a blot upon her name, and no one living that can clear it? But, I give thanks to Heaven!" the poor girl continued, clasping her hands, and looking upward with tears in her eyes, "that judgment has been spared—not for my own merit, I am sure, but for its own mercy."

"And is not that a quieting remembrance, Eily?" said her husband.

"Oh, that is not all," said Eily; "that is not the worst. Every movement that I make seems to bring down the anger of Heaven, since I first thought of deceiving my father. Do you remember the morning of our marriage?" she added with a slight shudder. "I never can put that frightful morning out of my mind. 'Tis always before my eyes—the little room inside the sacristy, and the candles burning on the small table, and the grey dawn just breaking through the window. We did not marry as other people do, in their families, or in the open daylight. We married in secret, like criminals in prison, without preparation, without confession, or communion, or repentance. We chose a priest that was disgraced by his bishop, to give us that great sacrament for money. May Heaven forgive him! How soon and how suddenly he was called to judgment for that act!"

Hardress, who had himself been struck by the circumstance last alluded to, remained silent for a moment, while his eyes were fixed upon the earth.

"Why did you go back to the chapel that time, Eily," he said at length, "after I parted from you at the door?"

"Everything looked bad and disheartening," said the young woman; "I was just going to lift the latch of my father's door, when I found that I had forgot the priest's certificate. I went back to the chapel as fast as I could walk. I passed through the sacristy and into the little room. The certificate was there upon the table, the candles were burning, and the clergyman was sitting upright in his chair—a dead man! Oh, I can no more tell you how I felt that moment than if I was dumb. I thought the world was coming to an end, and that I had no more hold of life than of the wind that was going by me. I ran out into the chapel, and strove to pray, but my blood was boiling out at my fingers' ends. While I was on my knees, I heard the people running to and fro in the sacristy, and I hurried out of the chapel for fear I'd be questioned."

"And did you go home at once?"

"No; I took a walk first to quiet my mind a little, and when I did go home, I found my father was up and getting the breakfast ready before me. Ah, he deserved a better daughter than Eily!"

"Come, come," said her husband kindly, "you will be a good daughter to him yet."

"I hope so, sir," said Eily in a mournful voice. "There's one thing, at all events—he loves me very well, and whenever I return, I'm sure of being easily forgiven."

"And can you find no encouragement in that?" Hardress said, while he took her hand in his, and pressed it in a soothing manner. "You say that you have confidence in me, and the few happy weeks that we have counted since our marriage have furnished me with no occasion for complaint on that subject. Continue yet a little longer to trust in your own Hardress, and the time will shortly come when you shall find that it was not bestowed in vain. Come, now, let me dry those sweet eyes, while I tell you shortly what my plans shall be. You have heard me speak of Danny Mann's sister Naughten, who lives on the side of the Purple Mountain, in the Gap of Dunlough (you don't know those places now; but you'll be enchanted with them by and by). She is a good-natured creature, though somewhat violent; and is, moreover, entirely at my command. I have had two neat rooms fitted up for you in her cottage, where you can have some books to read, a little garden to amuse you, and a Kerry pony to ride over the mountains, and see all that is to be seen about the lakes. In the mean time I will steal a visit now and then to my mother, who spends the autumn in the neighbourhood. She loves me, I know, as well as I love her, and that is very well. I will gradually let her into my secret, and obtain her forgiveness—I am certain she will not withhold it—and my father's will follow as a matter of course, for he has the greatest respect for her opinions." (If Hardress had not been Barney Cregan's son, he would have given this respect another name.) "I shall then present you to my mother—she will commend your modesty and gentleness to my father, who will rap out an exclamation on your beauty; we shall send for *your* father and priest O'Connor to the hauling-home, and then where is the tongue that shall venture to wag against the fame of Eily Cregan? If such a one there be, it shall never sting again, for I will cut the venom out of it with my small-sword."

"Hush, hush, sir! Do not speak so loud," cried the young woman, in some alarm; "there's one asleep in the next room."

"Who is it? Mrs. Frawley?"

"The fat, good old woman that got dinner ready for me."

"Never fear her. She is a hard-working, diligent woman, that always minds the business she has in hand. It was not to lie awake and make use of her ears that she got between the blankets. Hark! there is a clearer proof still that she is asleep. She must be dreaming of a hunt, she imitates the horn of chase so finely. Well, Eily, be ready to start for Ballybunion at sunrise in the morning. You must contrive to slip down to the shore without being seen by Lowry, or anybody else, if possible."

The creaking of the bed which sustained the ponderous Mrs. Frawley here startled the young and passionate, though most ill-sorted pair. After a hurried good night, Hardress returned to his room just in time to escape the observation of the good dairy-woman, who had been awaked out of a dream of pecks and keelers and fresh-prints by the sound of voices in the stranger's room. On opening the door, however, she was a little astonished to observe her lovely guest in the attitude of devotion. Deprived, by this circumstance, of the opportunity of putting any awkward questions, Mrs. Frawley, after yawning once or twice, and shaking her shoulders as often, tumbled into bed again, and speedily resumed the same tune upon the horn which had excited the admiration of Hardress.

Reader, I desire you not to think that this speedy fit of devotion was a manœuvre of the gentle Eily. The sin, assuredly, was not done with reflection. But if the case appears suspicious, go down upon your knees, and pray that as (alas, the while!) it has not been the first, it may be the last, instance in which religion shall be made subservient to human and terrestrial purposes.

There was a slight feeling of chagrin mingled with the happier emotions of the young husband as he prepared for slumber. Gifted as he was with a quick perception and keen feeling of the beautiful and worthy, the passion he had conceived for the gentle Eily had been as sudden as it was violent. The humility of her origin, at a period when pride of birth was more considered in matrimonial alliances than it is at present, might, it is true, have deterred him from contravening the wishes of his friends, if the impression made on his imagination had been less powerful; but his extreme youth, and the excelling beauty of his bride, were two circumstances that operated powerfully in tempting him to overlook all other counsels than those which love suggested. He thought, nevertheless, that he acted towards Eily O'Connor with a generosity which approached a species of magnanimity in preferring her before the whole world and its opinions; and perhaps, too, he entertained a little philosophical vanity in the conceit that he had thus evinced an independent reliance on his own mental resources, and shown a spirit superior to the ordinary prejudices of society. He felt, therefore, a little chagrined at Eily's apparent slowness in

appreciating so noble an effort, for indeed she did him the justice to believe that it was a higher motive than the love of self-adulation which induced him to bestow upon her his hand and his affections. But the reader is yet only partially acquainted with the character of Hardress, and those early circumstances which fashioned it to its present state of irregular and imperfect virtue. We will, therefore, while that fiery heart lies quenched in slumber, employ those hours of inaction in a brief and comprehensive view of the natural qualities and acquirements of our hero.

While Hardress Cregan was yet a child he displayed more symptoms of precocious ability than might have shed a lustre on the boyhood of many a celebrated genius. He obtained, even in his school days, the sobriquet of "Counsellor," from his fondness for discussion, and the childish eloquence which he displayed in maintaining a favourite position. His father liked him for a certain desperation of courage, which he was apt to discover on occasions of very inadequate provocation. His mother, too, doted on him for a mother's own best reason —that he was her child. Indulgent she was, even to a ruinous extent; and proud she was when her sagacious acquaintances, after hearing her relate some wonderful piece of wit in little Hardress, would compress their lips, shake their heads with much emphasis, and prophesy that "that boy would *shine* one day or another." His generosity, too (a quality in which Mrs. Cregan was herself pre-eminent), excited his mother's admiration, and proved, indeed, that Hardress was not an ordinary child.

And yet he was not without the peculiar selfishness of genius —that selfishness which consists not in the love of getting, or the love of keeping—in cupidity or avarice—but in a luxurious indulgence of one's natural inclinations even to an effeminate degree. His very generosity was a species of self-seeking, of that vulgar quality which looks to nothing more than the gratification of a suddenly awaked impulse of compassion, or, perhaps, has a still meaner object for its stimulus—the gratitude of the assisted, and the fame of an open hand. If this failing were in Hardress, as in Charles Surface, the result of habitual thoughtlessness and dissipation, it might challenge a gentler condemnation, and awaken pity rather than dislike; but young Cregan was by no means incapable of appreciating the high merit of a due self-government, even in the exercise of estimable dispositions. He admired in Kyrle Daly that noble and yet unaffected firmness of principle which led him, on many occasions, to impose a harsh restraint upon his own feelings, when their indulgence was not in accordance with his notions of justice. But Hardress Cregan, with an imagination which partook much more largely of the national luxuriance, and with a mind which displayed at intervals bursts of energy which far surpassed the reach of his steady friend, was yet the less estimable character of the two. They were, nevertheless, well calculated for a lasting friendship; for Kyrle Daly liked and valued the surpassing talent of Hardress, and Hardress was pleased with the even temper and easy resolution of his schoolfellow.

Seldom, indeed, it was that esteem formed any portion in the leading motive of Hardress Cregan's attachments. He liked for liking's sake, and as long only as his humour lasted. It required but a spark to set him all on fire; but the flame was often as prone to smoulder and become extinct as it was hasty to kindle. The reader is already aware that he had formed, during his boyhood, a passion for Anne Chute, who was then a mere girl, and on a visit at Dinis Cottage. His mother, who, from his very infancy, had arranged this match within her own mind, was delighted to observe the early attachment of the children, and encouraged it by every means in her power. They studied, played, and walked together; and all his recollections of the magnificent scenery of those romantic mountain lakes were blended with the form, the voice, the look, and manner of his childish love. The long separation, however, which ensued when he was sent to school, and from thence to college, produced a total alteration in his sentiments; and the mortification which his pride experienced on finding himself, as he imagined, utterly forgotten by her, completely banished even the wish to renew their old familiar life. Still, however, the feeling with which he regarded her was one rather of resentment than indifference, and it was not without a secret creeping of the heart that he witnessed what he thought the successful progress of Kyrle Daly's attachment.

It was under these circumstances that he formed his present hasty union with Eily O'Connor. His love for her was deep, sincere, and tender. Her entire and unbounded confidence, her extreme beauty, her simplicity, and timid deference to his wishes, made a soothing compensation to his heart for the coldness of the haughty, though superior beauty, whose inconstancy had raised his indignation.

"Yes," said Hardress to himself, as he gathered the blankets about his shoulders, and disposed himself for sleep ; " her form and disposition are perfect. Would that education had been to her as kind as nature ! Yet she does not want grace nor talent—but that brogue ! Well, well, the materials of refinement are within and around her, and it must be my task and my delight to make the brilliant shine out that is yet dark in the ore. I fear Kyrle Daly is, after all, correct in saying that I am not indifferent to those external allurements." (Here his eyelids drooped.) " The beauties of our mountain residence will make a mighty alteration in her mind, and my society will—will gradually—beautiful—Anne Chute—Poll Naughten—independent——"

The ideas faded on his imagination—a cloud settled on his brain—a delicious languor crept through all his limbs—he fell into a profound repose.

CHAPTER XVI.

HOW THE FRIENDS PARTED.

" Is Fighting Poll up yet, I wonder ? " said Lowry Looby, as he stood cracking his whip in the farmyard, while the morning was just beginning to break, and the dairy people were tying down the firkins on his car. " I 'd like to see her before I 'd go, to know would she have any commands westwards. There 's no hoult upon her to hinder her speaking of a Friday whatever."

" Is who up ? " exclaimed a shrill voice which proceeded from the grated window of the dairy. It was that of the industrious Mrs. Frawley, who, as early, if not as brisk and sprightly, as the lark, was already employed in setting her milk in the keelers.

" Fighting Poll of the Reeks," replied Lowry, turning toward the wire grating, through which he beheld the extensive figure of the dairy-woman, as neat as a bride, employed in the health-giving, life-prolonging avocations.

" Who is she, why ? " said Mrs. Frawley.

" Don't you know the girl that come in the boat with Mr. Cregan, an' slep' in the room outside you ? "

" Oyeh ! I didn't know who you meant. The boatman's handsome little sister ? "

" Handsome, ayeh ? "

" Yes, then, handsome. She has the dawniest little nose I think I ever laid my two eyes upon."

" Why, then, 'tis a new story wid' it for a nose. Formerly, when I knew it, it was more like a button musharoom than anything else, and the colour of a boiled carrot. Good raison it had for that, as the publicans could tell you."

" Hold your tongue, man. Is it to drink you say she used ? "

" A thrifle, I 'm tould."

" Eh, then, I never see one that has less sign of it than what she has."

" She 's altered lately, Danny Mann tells me. Nelly, croo,' he added, changing his tone—" sonohur* to you, now, an' get me a dram, for it's threatenin' to be a moist, foggy mornin', an' I have a long road before me."

Nelly was occupied in liberating a whole regiment of ducks, hens, pouts, chicks, cocks, geese, and turkeys, which all came quacking, clucking, whistling, chirping, crowing, cackling, and gobbling, through the open fowl-house door into the yard, where they remained shaking their wings on tiptoe, stretching their long necks over the little pool, the surface of which was green, and covered with feathers, appearing to congratulate each other on their sudden liberation, and seeming evidently disposed to keep all the conversation to themselves.

" What is it you say, Lowry ? Choke ye for ducks, will ye let nobody spake but yerselves ? What is it, Lowry ? "

Lowry repeated his request, making it more intelligible amid the clamour of the farmyard by using a significant gesture. He imitated the action of one who fills a glass and drinks it.

* A good husband.

He then laid his hand upon his heart and shook his head, as if to intimate the comfort that would be produced about that region by performing in reality what he only mocked at present.

Nelly understood him as well as if he had spoken volumes. Commissioned by Mrs. Frawley, she supplied him with a bottle of spirits and a glass, with the use of which, let us do Lowry the justice to say, there was not a man in the barony better acquainted.

While he dashed from his eyes the tears which were produced by the sharpness of the stimulus, he heard footsteps behind him, and, looking round, beheld Danny the Lord, and the soi-disant Mrs. Naughten, still muffled in her blue cloak and hood, and occupying a retired position near the kitchen door.

" I 'll tell you what it is, Nelly," said Lowry, with a knowing wink to the soubrette. " Poll Naughten lives very convanient on the Cork road, or not far from it, an' I do be often goin' that way of a lonesome night. I 'll make a friend o' Poll before she leaves this, so as that she 'll be glad to see me another time. I 'll go over and offer her a dhram. That I may be blest but I will ! "

So saying, and hiding the bottle and glass under the skirt of his coat, he moved toward the formidable heroine of the mountains with many respectful bows, and a smile of the most winning cordiality.

" A fine moist mornin', Mrs. Naughten. I hope you feel no fatague afther the night, ma'am. Your sarvant, Misther Mann. I hope you didn't feel us in the yard, ma'am ; I sthrove to keep 'em quiet o' purpose. 'Tisn't goen' ye are so airly, Misther Mann ? "

Danny, who felt all the importance of directing Lowry Looby's attention from his fair charge, could find no means so effectual as that of acknowledging the existence of a mystery, and admitting him into a pretended confidence. Advancing, therefore, a few steps to meet him, he put on a most serious countenance, and laid his finger warily along his nose.

" What 's the matther ? " whispered Lowry, bending down in the eagerness of curiosity.

Danny the Lord repeated the action, with the addition of a cautionary frown.

" Can't she talk of a Friday either ? " said Lowry, much amazed. " I understand, Misther Mann. Trust me for the bare life. A nod is as good as a wink to a blind horse."

" Or an ass eider," muttered the hunchback as he turned away.

" But, Misther Mann," cried Lowry, laying his immense claw upon his lordship's shoulder, " listen hether. The mornen' will be smart enough, and maybe I 'd betther offer her a dhram, and she goen' upon the wather ? "

He strode past the lord, and was close to the muffled fair one, when Danny pulled him back by the skirt.

" Didn't I tell you before," said he, " dat Poll never drank ? "

" Iss, of a Thursday, you said."

" Or a Friday, or any day. Oh den, oh den, Lowry ! "

" Well, I meant no harm. Maybe you 'd have no vow yourself on the head of it any way, sir ? " And he displayed the bottle.

" Dere are tree kinds of oats, Lowry," responded Danny Mann, as he twined his bony fingers fondly around the neck of the bottle ; " dere are tree kind of oats dat are forbidden to be tuk as unlawful. Dey are false oats, rash oats, and unjust oats. Now do you see me, Lowry," he continued, as he filled his glass, " if I made a vow o' dat kind, it would be an unjust oat, for it would be traitin' myself very bad, a poor boy dat 's night an' day at sech cold work as mine, an' it would be a rash oat, Lowry, for——" (here he tossed off the spirits)—" I 'm blest but it wouldn't be long before I 'd make it a false oat."

Lowry was greatly shocked at this unprincipled speech. " That 's a nate youth," he said privately to Nelly. " That 's a nice pet, not judging him. If that lad doesn't see the inside of the Stone Jug* for some bad business one time or another, I 'll give my lave to say black is the white of my eye. If the gallows isn't wrote upon his face, there 's no mait in mutton. Well, good mornen' to you, Nelly, I see my load is ready. I have everything now, I suppose, Mrs. Frawley ? Whup, get up here, you old garron ! Good mornen' to you, Mrs. Naughten, an' a fair wind after you. Good mornen', Misther Mann." He cracked his whip, tucked the skirt of his riding-coat under his arm, as usual, threw his little head back, and followed the car out of the yard, singing, in a pleasant, contented key,—

* The jail.

" Don't you remember, the time I gave you my heart,
You solemnly swore from me you never would part?
But your mind's like the ocean,
Each notion
Has now taken flight,
And left me bemoaning the loss of the red-haired man's wife."

Kyrle Daly and his young friend were meanwhile exchanging a farewell upon the little gravel-plot before the front door.

"Come, come, go in out of the air," said Hardess; "you shall not come down to the shore in that slight dress. Remember what I have told you, and sustain your spirits. Before another month shall pass, I pledge myself to become master, for your sake, of Anne Chute's secret."

"And to honour it?" said Kyrle, smiling as he gave him his hand.

"According to its value," replied Hardress, tossing his head. "Good-by; I see Danny Mann and his sister coming round, and we must not lose the morning's tide."

They shook hands and parted.

It was one of those still and heavy mornings which are peculiar to the close of summer in this climate. The surface of the waters was perfectly still, and a light wreath of mist steamed upward from the centre of the channel, so as to veil from their sight the opposite shores of Clare. This mist, ere long, became a dense and blinding fog, that lasted until noon, and, together with the breathless calm that lay upon the land and water, prevented their reaching Ballybunion until sunset. In one of those caverns which are hollowed out of the cliffs on this shore, the traveller may discern the remains of an artificial chamber. It was used, at the period of which we write, as a kind of ware-room for contraband goods—a species of traffic which was freely engaged in by nearly all the middling gentry and small farmers along the coast. A subterraneous passage, faced with dry stonework, opened into the interior of the country; and the chamber itself, from constant use, had become perfectly dry and habitable. In this place Hardress proposed to Eily that they should remain and take some refreshment, while Danny the Lord was dispatched to secure a better lodging for the night at some retired farmhouse in the neighbourhood.

A small canvas-built canoe, summoned from the interior of the cave by a whistle from the lord, was employed to convey them from the pleasure-boat into the gloomy porch of this natural subterrain. Before the fragile skiff had glided into the darkness, Eily turned her head to catch a parting look at the descending sun. The scene which met her gaze would have appeared striking, even to an accustomed eye; and to one like hers, acquainted only with the smoky splendour of a city sunset, it was grand and imposing in the extreme. Before her lay the gigantic portals of the Shannon, through which the mighty river glided forth with a majestic calmness, to mingle with the wide and waveless ocean that spread beyond and around them. On her right arose the clifted shores of Clare, over which the broad ball of day, although some minutes hidden from her sight, seemed yet, by refraction, to hold his golden circlet suspended amid a broken and brilliant mass of vapours. Eily kept her eyes fixed in admiration on the dilated orb, until a turn in the cave concealed the opening from her view, and she could only see the stream of light behind, as it struck on the jagged and broken walls of the orifice, and danced upon the surface of the agitated waters.

The place to her seemed terrible. The hollow sound of the boatman's voice, the loud plash of the oars, and the rippling of the water against the vessel's prow, reverberating through the vaulted chambers, the impenetrable darkness into which they seemed to plunge headlong, and reckless of danger or impediment, all united, constituted a scene so new to the simple Eily, that she grasped close the arm of her husband, and held her breath for some moments, as if in expectation of some sudden and terrific encounter. In a little time the boatman rested on his oars, and a voice from the interior of the cave was heard exclaiming in Irish, " Is it himself?"

" It is," said the boatman, in the same language. " Light up the fire at once, and put down a few of the fresh herrings. The lady is hungry."

" You will join for the first time, Eily," said Hardress, " in a fisherman's supper. Well, Larry, had you much luck last night?"

" Poor enough, masther," said the same oracular voice which

Eily now recognised as that of the man to whose escort she had been intrusted by Lowry Looby on the previous evening. " We left Misther Daly's point as soon as ever the wind fell, and come down as far as Kilcordane, thinking we might come across the skull; but, though we were out all night, we took only five hundhert, more or less. A' why don't you light up the fire, Phaudrigh? And 'twasn't that the herrings didn't come into the river either, for when the moon shone out we saw the skull to the westward, making a curl on the waters, as close an' thick as if you threw a shovelful o' gravel in a pond."

The fire now blazed suddenly upward, revealing the interior of the apartment before alluded to, and the figure of the rough old boatman and his boy. The latter was stooping forward on his hands, and kindling the fire with his breath, while Larry Kett himself was rinsing a small metal pot at the water side. The effect of the smoky and subterraneous light upon uncouth and grisly figures, and on the rude excavation itself, impressed the timid Eily with a new and agitating sensation, too nearly allied to fear to leave her mind at ease.

In a few minutes she was seated on a small keg near the fire, while Hardress hurried the men who were preparing dinner. Larry Kett was not so proficient in the science of gastronomy as the celebrated Louis of Crockford's, and yet it is to be questioned whether the culinary preparations of the latter were ever dispatched with more eagerness and satisfaction. Eily, indeed, only ate a heroine's proportion; but she wondered at the voracity of the boatmen, one of whom, placing a raw onion on an unpeeled potato, swallowed both at a mouthful, almost without employing a single masticatory action.

Danny Mann, in the mean time, was occupied in procuring a more eligible lodging for the night. He returned when they had concluded their unceremonious meal, to say that he had been successful in procuring two rooms in the house of " a little 'oman dat kep' a private bottle between that an' Beale."

" A private bottle!" exclaimed Hardress. " What do you mean by a private bottle?"

" I mean," replied the little lord, " dat she sell as good a drop as if she paid license for it; a ting she never was fool enough to do."

" Where does she live?"

" Close to de road above. She told me"——(here he drew Hardress aside—" when I axed her, dat Myles of de Ponies, an' de master, an' a deal o' gentlemen, went de road westwards yesterday, an' dat Phil Naughten (Poll's Phil) was in Beale waitin' for you dese two days with the horse an' jauntin'-car."

" I am glad to hear it. Step over there to-night, and tell him to be at the door before daybreak to-morrow morning. Tell him I will double his fare if he uses diligence."

" Why, din, indeed," said Danny, " I'll tell him notin' o' de sort. 'Twould be de same case wit him still, for he's a boy dat if you gave him England, Ireland, an' Scotland for an estate, he'd ax de Isle o' Man for a kitchen-garden."

" Well, well, do as you please about it, Danny, but have him on the spot. That fellow," he continued, speaking to Eily, as he conducted her out of the cavern, " that fellow is so impudent sometimes, that nothing but the recollection of his fidelity, and the honesty of his motive, keeps my hand at rest. He is my foster-brother, and you may perceive, with the exception of one deformity, a well-looking man."

" I never observed anything but the hunch," said Eily.

" For which," added Hardress, with a slight change in his countenance, " he has to thank his master."

" You, Mr. Hardress?"

" Even so, Eily. When we were both children that young fellow was my constant companion. Familiarity produced a feeling of equality, on which he presumed so far as to offer a rudeness to a little relative of mine, a Miss Chute, who was on a visit at my mother's. She complained to me, and my vengeance was summary. I met him at the head of the kitchen stairs, and without even the ceremony of a single question or preparatory speech, I seized him by the collar, and hurled him with desperate force to the bottom of the flight. He was unable to rise as soon as I expected, and, on examination, it was discovered that an injury had been done to the spine, which, notwithstanding all the exertions that were employed to repair it, had its result in its present deformity."

" It was shocking," said Eily, with much simplicity of feeling. " No wonder you should be kind to him,"

" If I were a mere block," said Hardress, " I could not but be affected by the good nature and kindly feeling which the poor fellow showed on the occasion, and, indeed, down to the present moment. It seemed to be the sole aim and study of his life to satisfy me that he entertained not even a sentiment of regret for what had happened; and his attachment ever since has been the attachment of a zealot. I know he cannot but feel that his prospects in life have been made dark and lonely by that accident; and yet he is congratulating himself, whenever an opportunity occurs, on his good fortune in being provided with a constant service, as if (poor fellow!) that were any compensation to him. I have been alarmed to observe that he sometimes attaches even a profane importance to his master's wishes, and seems to care but little what laws he may transgress when his object is the gratification of my inclinations. I say I am alarmed on this subject, because I have taken frequent occasion to remark that this injury to his spine has in some degree affected his head, and left him less able to discern the impropriety of such a line of conduct than people of sounder minds."

CHAPTER XVII.

HOW HARDRESS LEARNED A LITTLE SECRET FROM A DYING HUNTSMAN.

NOTWITHSTANDING the message which Hardress Cregan sent by Lowry Looby, it was more than a week before he visited his parents at their Killarney residence. Several days were occupied in seeing Eily pleasantly situated in her wild cottage in the Gap, and a still greater number in enjoying with her the pleasures of an autumnal sojourn amid these scenes of mystery, enchantment, and romance. To a mind that is perfectly at freedom, Killarney forms in itself a congeries of Elysian raptures; but to a fond bride and bridegroom!—the heaven, to which its mountains rear their naked heads in awful reverence, alone can furnish a superior happiness.

After taking an affectionate leave of his beautiful wife, and assuring her that his absence should not be extended beyond the following day, Hardress Cregan mounted one of Phil Naughten's rough-coated ponies, and set off for Dinis Cottage. It is not situated (as its name might seem to import) on the sweet little island which is so called, but far apart, near the ruined Church of Aghado, commanding a distant view of the lower lake and the lofty and wooded Toomies.

The sun had gone down before he left the wild and rocky glen in which was situated the cottage of his bride. It was, as we have already apprised the reader, the first time Hardress had visited the lake since his return from college, and the scenery now, to his matured and well-regulated taste, had not only the effect of novelty, but it was likewise invested with the hallowing and romantic charm of youthful association. The stillness, so characteristic of majesty, which reigned throughout the gigantic labyrinth of mountain, cliff, and valley, through which he rode; the parting gleam of sunshine that brightened the ever-moving mists on the summit of the lofty peaks by which he was surrounded; the solitary appearance of the many nameless lakes that slept in black repose in the centre of the mighty chasm; the echo of his horse's hoofs against the stony road; the voice of a goatherd's boy as he drove homeward, from the summit of a heath-clad mountain, his troublesome and adventurous charge; the lonely twitter of the kirkeen dhu, or little water-hen, as it flew from rock to rock on the margin of the broken stream—these, and other long-forgotten sights and sounds, awakened at the same instant the consciousness of present and the memory of past enjoyments, and gradually lifted his thoughts to that condition of calm enthusiasm and fulness of soul which constitutes one of the highest pleasures of a meditative mind. He did not fail to recall at this moment the memory of his childish attachment, and could not avoid a feeling of regret at the unpleasing change that education had produced in the character of his first, though not his dearest love.

This feeling became still more deep and oppressive as he approached the cottage of his father. Every object that he beheld—the lawn, the grove, the stream, the hedge, the stile—all brought to mind some sweet remembrance of his boyhood. The childish form of Anne Chute still seemed to meet him, with her bright and careless smile, at every turn in the path, or to fly before him over the shorn meadow, as of old; while the wild and merry peal of infant laughter seemed still to ring upon his hearing. "Dear little being!" he exclaimed, as he rode into the cottage avenue, " the burning springs of Gluver, I thought, might sooner have been frozen than the current of that once warm and kindly heart; but, like those burning springs, it is only in the season of coldness and neglect that tountain can resume its native warmth. It is the fervour of universal homage and adulation that strikes it cold and pulseless in its channels."

The window of the dining-parlour alone was lighted up, and Hardress was informed, in answer to his inquiries, that the ladies, Mrs. Cregan and Miss Chute, were gone to a grand ball in the neighbourhood. Mr. Cregan and two other gentlemen were drinking in the dining-room, and, as he might gather from the tumultuous nature of their conversation, and the occasional shouts of ecstatic enjoyment, and bursts of laughter which rang through the house, already pretty far advanced in the bacchanalian ceremonies of the night. The voices he recognised, besides his father's, were those of Hepton Connolly and Mr. Creagh the duellist.

Feeling no inclination to join the revellers, Hardress ordered candles in the drawing-room, and prepared to spend a quiet evening by himself. He had scarcely, however, taken his seat on the straight-backed sofa, when his retirement was invaded by old Nancy, the kitchen-maid, who came to tell him that poor Dalton, the huntsman, was " a'most off," in the little green room, and that when he heard Mr. Hardress had arrived, he begged of all things to see him before he'd go. "He never was himself rightly, a'ra gal," said old Nancy, wiping a tear from the corner of her eye, " since the masther sold the hounds and took to the cock-fighting."

Hardress started up and followed her. " Poor fellow!" he exclaimed as he went along, " poor Dalton! And is that breath, that wound so many merry blasts upon the mountain, so soon to be extinguished? I remember the time when I thought a monarch on his throne a less enviable being than our stout huntsman, seated on his keen-eyed steed, in his scarlet frock and cap, with his hounds, like painted courtiers, thronging and baying round his horse's hoofs, and his horn hanging silent at his waist. Poor fellow! Every beagle in the pack was his familiar acquaintance, and was as jealous of his chirp or his whistle as my cousin Anne's admirers might be of a smile or secret whisper. How often has he carried me before him on his saddle-bow, and taught me the true fox-hunting cry! How often at evening has he held me between his knees, and excited my young ambition with tales of hunts hard run, and neck-or-nothing leaps; of double ditches cleared by an almost miraculous dexterity; of drawing, yearning, challenging, hunting mute, hunting change, and hunting counter! And now the poor fellow must wind his last recheat, and carry his own old bones to earth at length! never again to awaken the echoes of the mountain lakes—never again beneath the shadow of those immemorial woods that clothe their lofty shores—

' Ære ciere viros, Martemque accendere cantu!'

The fox may come from kennel, and the red-deer slumber on his lair, for their mighty enemy is now himself at bay."

While these reflections passed through the mind of Hardress, old Nancy conducted him as far as the door of the huntsman's room, where he paused for a moment on hearing the voice of one singing inside. It was that of the worn-out huntsman himself, who was humming over a few verses of a favourite ballad. The lines which caught the ear of Hardress were the following:—

" Ah, huntsman dear, I'll be your friend,
    If you let me go till morning;
Don't call your hounds for one half hour,
    Nor neither sound your horn;
For indeed I'm tired from yesterday's hunt,
    I can neither run nor walk well,
Till I go to Rock-hill amongst my friends,
    Where I was bred and born.
            Tally-ho the fox!
            Tally-ho the fox!
Tally-ho the fox, a coilauneen,
            Tally-ho the fox!
    Over hills and rocks,
And chase him on till morning."

" He cannot be so very ill," said Hardress, looking at the old woman, " when his spirits will permit him to sing so merrily."

"Oyeh, Heaven help you, agra!" replied Nancy: "I believe if he was at death's doore this moment, he'd have that song on his tongue still."

"Hush! hush!" said Hardress, raising his hand, "he is beginning again."

The ballad was taken up, after a heavy fit of coughing, in the same strain:—

> "I lock'd him up an' I fed him well,
> An' I gave him victuals of all kinds;
> But I declare to you, sir, when he got loose,
> He ate a fat goose in the morning.
> So now kneel down and say your prayers,
> For you'll surely die this morning.
> 'Ah, sir,' says the fox, 'I never pray,
> For my father he bred me a Quaker.'
> Tally-ho the fox!
> Tally-ho the——"

Hardress here opened the door, and cut short the *refrain*.

The huntsman turned his face to the door as he heard the handle turn. It was that of a middle-aged man in the very last stage of pulmonary consumption. A red nightcap was pushed back from his wasted and sunken temples, and a flush like the bloom of a withered pippin played in the hollow of his fleshless cheek.

"Cead millia fealtha! My heart warms to see you, my own Masther Hardress!" exclaimed the huntsman, reaching him a skeleton hand from beneath the brown quilt. "I can die in peace now, as I see you again in health. These ten days back they're telling me you're coming an' coming, until I began to think at last that you wouldn't come until I was gone."

"I am sorry to see you in this condition, Dalton. How did you get the attack?"

"Out of a could I think I got it first, sir. When the masther sold the hounds—(ah, Masther Hardress! to think of his parting them dogs, an' giving up that fine, manly exercise for a paltry parcel o' cocks and hens!)—but when he sold them an' took to the cock-fighting, my heart felt as low an' as lonesome as if I lost all belonging to me! To please the masther, I turned my hand to the cocks, an' used to go every morning to the hounds' kennel, where the birds were kept, to give 'em food and water; but I could *never warm* to the birds. Ah, what is a cock-fight, Masther Hardress, in comparison of a well-rode hunt among the mountains, with your horse flying under you like a fairy, an' the cry o' the hounds like an organ out before you, an' the ground fleeting like a dream on all sides o' you, an'——? Ah! what's the use o' talking?" Here he lay back on his pillow with a look of sudden pain and sorrow that cut Hardress to the heart.

After a few moments he again turned a ghastly eye on Hardress, and said in a faint voice, "I used to go down by the lake in the evening to hear the stags belling in the wood; an' in the morning I'd be up with the first light to blow a call on the top o' the hill, an' I used to do to comfort the dogs; an' then I'd miss their cry, an' I'd stop listenin' to the aychoes o' the horn among the mountains, till my heart would sink as low as my ould boots. An' bad boots they wor, too; signs on, I got wet in 'em; an' themselves an' the could morning air, and the want o' the horse exercise, I believe, an' everything, brought on this fit. Is the misthress at home, sir?" he added, after struggling through a severe fit of oppression.

"No, she is at a ball with Miss Chute."

"Good *luck* to them both, wherever they are! That's the way o' the world. Some in health, an' some in sickness; some dancing, and more dying."

Here he raised himself on his elbow, and after casting a haggard glance around, as if to be assured that what he had to say could not be overheard, he leaned forward towards Hardress, and whispered, "I know one in this house, Masther Hardress, that loves you well."

The young gentleman looked a little surprised.

"Indeed I do," continued the dying huntsman, "one, too, that deserves a better fortune than to love any one without a return—one that was kind to me in my sickness, and that I'd like to see happy before I'd leave the world, if it was Heaven's will."

During this conversation both speakers had been frequently rendered inaudible by occasional bursts of laughter and shouts of bacchanalian mirth from the dining-room. At this moment, and before the young gentleman could select any mode of inquiry into the particulars of the singular communication above mentioned, the door was opened, and the face of old Nancy appeared, bearing on its smoke-dried features a mingled expression of perplexity and sorrow.

"Dalton, a'ra gal!" she exclaimed, "don't blame me for what I'm going to say to you, for it is my tongue, an' not my wish nor my heart, that speaks it. The masther and the gentlemen sent me in to you, an' bid me tell you, for the sake of old times, to give them one fox-huntin' screech before you go."

The old huntsman fixed his brilliant but sickly eyes on the messenger, while a flush that might have been the indication of anger or of grief, flickered like a decaying light upon his brow. At length he said, "An' did the masther send that message by you, Nancy?"

"He did, Dalton, indeed. Ayeh, the gentlemen must be excused."

"True for you, Nancy," said the huntsman after a long pause; then, raising his head with a smile of seeming pleasure, he continued, "Why, then, I'm glad to see the masther hasn't forgot the dogs entirely. Go to him, Nancy, an' tell him that I'm glad to hear that he has so much o' the sport left in him still; and that it is kind father for him to have a feeling for his huntsman, an' I thank him. Tell him, Nancy, to send me in one good glass o' parliament punch, an' I'll give him such a cry as he never heard in a cock-pit, any way."

The punch was brought, and, in spite of the remonstrances of Hardress, drained to the bottom. The old huntsman then sat erect in the bed, and letting his head back, indulged in one prolonged "hoicks!" that made the phials jingle on the table, and frightened the sparrows from their roosts beneath the thatch. It was echoed by the jolly company in the dining-parlour, chorused by a howling from all the dogs in the yard, and answered by a general clamour from the fowl-house. "Another! another! Hoicks!" resounded through the house. But the poor consumptive was not in a condition to gratify the revellers. When Hardress looked down upon him next, the pillow appeared dark with blood, and the cheek of the sufferer had lost even the unhealthy bloom that had so long masked the miner Death in his work of snug destruction. A singular brilliancy fixed itself upon his eyeballs, his lips were dragged backward, blue and cold, and with an expression of dull and general pain—his teeth—But wherefore linger on such a picture? It is better to let the curtain fall.

Hardress Cregan felt less indignation at this circumstance than he might have done if it had occurred at the present day; but yet he *was* indignant. He entered the dining-parlour to remonstrate, with a frame that trembled with passion.

"And pray, Hardress," said Hepton Connolly, as he emptied the ladle into his glass, and turned on him an eye whose steadiness, to say the least, was equivocal; "pray, now, Hardress, is poor Dalton really dead?"

"He is, sir. I have already said it."

"No offence, my boy. I only asked, because if he be, it is a sure sign"—(here he sipped his punch and winked at Cregan with the confident air of one who is about to say a *right good thing*)—"it is a sign that he never will die again."

There was a loud laugh at Hardress, which confused him as much as if he had been discomfited by a far superior wit. So true it is that the influence, and not the capacity, of an opponent renders him chiefly formidable, and that at least a fair half of the sum of human motive may be placed to the account of vanity.

Hardress could think of nothing that was very witty to say in reply, and as the occasion hardly warranted a slap on the face, his proud spirit was compelled to remain passive. Unwilling, however, to leave the company while the laugh continued against him, he called for a glass and sat down amongst them.

CHAPTER XVIII.

HOW THE GENTLEMEN SPENT THE EVENING, WHICH PROVED RATHER WARMER THAN HARDRESS EXPECTED.

"PEACE!" said Hepton Connolly, with a face of drunken seriousness, "peace to the manes of poor Dalton!"

"Amen, with all my heart!" exclaimed Mr. Cregan, "although the cocks are well rid of him; but a better horseman never backed a hunter."

HARDRESS CREGAN OVERCOMES THE TEMPTER.

"I drink him," said Hyland Creagh, "although I seldom care to toast a man who dies in his bed."

"That's all trash and braggery, Creagh," cried Connolly; "we'll have you yet upon the flat of your back, and roaring for a priest into the bargain."

"Upon my honour as a gentleman, I am serious," said Creagh. "They may talk of the field of battle and bloody breaches, forlorn hopes and hollow squares, and such stuff, but what is the glory of a soldier after all? To drag through the fatigues of a whole campaign, with its concomitants of night-watches, marches in marshes, and bivouacs in rainy weather, and with no brighter prospect at the year's end than that of making one among half a million of fighting fellows who are shot on a heap like larks; and even then you meet, not hand to hand, but cloud to cloud, moving about in a flock, and waiting your turn to take your allowance of cold lead, and fill a pit with your neighbours. Glory! What glory is there in figuring in small types among a list of killed and wounded?—the utmost distinction that a poor sub can ever hope for. Why, a coward is no

more ball-proof than a gallant fellow, and both may often shine together upon the same list. No—my ambition should have a higher aim. While I live, let my life be that of a fearless fellow; and when I die, let my epitaph be found in a handsome paragraph, under the head of 'Domestic Intelligence.' in the county journal. 'Affair of Honour.—Yesterday morning at five o'clock—meeting took place—Hyland Creagh, Esquire, attended by Blank, Esquire—and Captain Blank, attended by Blank, Esquire—regret to state—Mr. Creagh—third fire—mortally wounded—borne from the ground. The affair, we understand, originated in a dispute respecting a lovely and accomplished young lady, celebrated as a reigning toast in that quarter.'"

"And grand-niece, we understand," added Hardress, laughing, "to the unhappy gentleman whose fate we have just recorded."

There was a laugh at Creagh.

"Nay, my young friend," he said, adjusting his ruffles with the air of a Chesterfield, "the journal that shall mention that circumstance must be dated many years hence."

"Adad, not so far off, neither, Creagh," exclaimed Mr. Cregan;

"and if you were to go out to-morrow morning, I should not like to see you go posting to the devil upon such a mission as that."

"Talking of the devil," said Hepton Connolly, "did you hear, Creagh, that the priest is to have us all upon the altar next Sunday, on account of that little squib we had in the mountains the day of the races?"

"It may be," said Creagh, with a supercilious smile; "mais ce n'est pas mon affaire. I have not the honour to belong to his communion."

"Oh," cried Mr. Cregan, "true enough. You belong to the genteel religion."

"There you have the whip hand of me," said Connolly, "for I am a Papist. Well, Creagh, not meaning to impugn your gallantry now, I say this: a Papist, to fight a duel, requires and possesses the courage of a Protestant ten times over."

"Pray will you oblige me with a reason for that pleasant speech?"

"'Tis as clear as this glass. A Protestant is allowed a wide discretionary range on most ethical, as well as theological, points of opinion. A poor Papist has none. The Council of Trent, in its twenty-fifth session (I have it from the bishop), excommunicates all duellists, and calls the practice an invention of the devil. And what can I say against it? I know something of the common law, and the rights of things, persons, and so forth, but the canonical code to me is a fountain sealed. 'Tis something deeper than a cause before the petty sessions. 'Tis easier to come at Blackstone, or even Coke upon Littleton himself, than at Manochius or St. Augustine."

"Well, but how you run on! You were talking about the courage of a Protestant and Catholic."

"I say a Papist must be the braver man; for, in addition to his chance of being shot through the brains on a frosty morning in this world (a cool prospect), it is no joke to be damned everlastingly in the next."

"That never struck me before," exclaimed Cregan.

"And if it had," said Creagh, "I confess I do not see what great disadvantage the reflection could have produced to our friend Connolly, for he knew that, whether he was to be shot yesterday in a duel, or physicked out of the world twenty years hence, that little matter of the other life will be arranged in precisely the same manner."

"As much as to say," replied Connolly, "that, now or then, the devil is sure of his bargain."

"My idea precisely, but infinitely better expressed."

"Very good, Creagh. I suppose it was out of a filial affection for the sooty old gentleman you took so much pains to send me to him the other morning."

"You placed your honour in my hands, and I would have seen you raked fore and aft fifty times rather than let the pledge be tarnished. If you did go to the devil, it was my business to see that you met him with clean hands."

"I feel indebted to you, Creagh."

"I have seen a dozen shots exchanged on a lighter quarrel. I was present myself at the duel between Hickman and Leake, on a somewhat similar dispute. They fired fourteen shots each, and when their ammunition was exhausted, actually remained on the ground until the seconds could fetch a new supply from the nearest market town."

"And what use did they make of it when it came?"

"Give me time, and you shall hear. 'Twas Hickman's fire, and he put his lead an inch above Leake's right hip (as pretty a shot as ever I saw in my life). Leake was not killed, though, and he stood to his ground like a man. I never will forget the ghastly look he gave me (I was his second), when he asked whether the laws of the duello would allow a wounded man a chair. I was confident they did, so long as he kept his feet upon the sod, and I said so. Well, the chair was brought. He took his seat somewhat in this manner, grasping the orifice of the wound closely with his disengaged hand." (Here the speaker moved his chair some feet from the table, in order to enact the scene with greater freedom.) "There was a fatal steadiness in every motion. I saw Hickman's eye wink, and not without a cause. It winked again, and never opened after. The roof of his skull was literally blown away."

"And the other fellow?"

"The other gentleman fell from his chair a corpse at the same moment, after uttering a sentiment of savage satisfaction too horrible, too blasphemous to think of, much less to repeat."

"They were a murderous pair of ruffians," said Hardress, "and ought to have been impaled upon a cross-road."

"One of them," observed Hyland Creagh, sipping his punch, "one of them was a cousin of mine."

"Oh! and therefore utterly blameless, of course," said Hardress, with an ironical laugh.

"I don't know," said Creagh. "I confess I think it a hard word to apply to a gentleman who is unfortunate enough to die in defence of his honour."

"Honour!" exclaimed Hardress, with indignant zeal; for though he was no great devotee, he had yet some gleams of a half-religious virtue shining through his character. "Call you that honour? I say a duellist is a murderer, and worthy of the gallows, and I will prove it. The question lies in the justice or injustice of the mode of reparation. That cannot be a just one which subjects the aggressor and aggrieved to precisely the same punishment. If the duellist be the injured party, he is a suicide; and if the inflicter of the wrong, he is a murderer."

"Ay, Hardress," said his father; "but there are cases——"

"Oh, I know what you mean, sir. Fine, delicate, thin-spun modes of insult, that draw on heavier assaults, and leave both parties labouring under the sense of injury. But they are murderers still. If I filled a seat in the legislature, do you think I would give my voice in favour of a law that made it a capital offence to call a man a scoundrel in punishment? And shall I dare to inflict with my own hand in the streets that which I would shudder to see committed by the hangman?"

"But if public war be justifiable," said Connolly, "why should not private?" *

"Ay," exclaimed Hardress, "I see you have got that aphorism of Johnson's, the fat moralist, to support you; but I say shame upon the recreant, for as mean and guilty a compliance with the prejudices of the world as ever parasite betrayed. I stigmatise it as a wilful sin, for how can I esteem the author of 'Rasselas' a fool?"

"Very hardly," said Creagh; "and pray what is your counter-argument?"

"This: public war is never (when justifiable) a quarrel for sounds and convental notions of honour; public war is at best a social evil, and cannot be embraced without the full concurrence of society, expressed by its constituted authorities, and obtained only in obedience to the necessity of the case. But to private war society has given no formal sanction, nor does it derive any advantage from the practice."

"Upon my word," said Creagh, "you have some very curious ideas."

"Well, Hardress," exclaimed Connolly, "if you have a mind to carry those notions into practice, I should recommend you to try it in some other country besides Ireland; you will never go through with it in this."

"In every company, and on every soil," said Hardress, "I will avow my sentiments. I never will fight a duel; and I will proclaim my purpose in the ears of all the duellists on earth."

"But society, young gentleman——"

"I bid society defiance—at least that reckless, godless, heartless crew, to whom you wrongfully apply the term. The greater portion of those who bow down before this bloody error is composed of slaves and cowards, who are afraid to make their own conviction the guide of their conduct,—

'Letting I dare not wait upon I would,
Like the poor cat i' the adage.'"

"I am sure," said Creagh, "I had rather shoot a man for doubting my word than for taking my purse."

"Because you are as proud as Lucifer," exclaimed Hardress. "Who but the great father of all injustice would say that he deserved to be shot for calling you a (it is an unpleasant word, to be sure)—a liar?"

"But he does more; he actually does strike at my life and property, for I lose both friends and fair repute, if I suffer such an insult to pass unnoticed."

In answer to this plea Hardress made a speech, of which (as the newspapers say) we regret that our space does not allow us to offer more than a mere outline. He contended that no consequences could justify a man in sacrificing his own persuasion of what was right to the error of his friends. The more general

* I am sorry the author of "Guy Mannering" should have thought proper to adopt the same mode of reasoning. Will posterity remove that bar-sinister from his literary escutcheon?

this error was, the more criminal it became to increase the number of its victims. The question was not, whether society would disown or receive the passive gentleman, but whether society was in the wrong or in the right; and if the former, then he was bound to adopt the cause of justice at every hazard. He drew the usual distinction between moral and animal courage, and painted with force and feeling the heroism of a brave man encountering alone the torrent of general opinion, and taking more wounds upon his spirit than ever Horatius Cocles risked upon his person. He quoted the celebrated passage of the faithful seraph in Milton, alluded to the Athenian manners, and told the well-known story of Lucian Anacharsis, all which tended considerably more to exhaust the patience than to convince the understanding of his hearers.

"Finally," said he, "I denounce the system of private war, because it is the offspring of a barbarous pride. It was a barbarous pride that first suggested the expedient, and it is an intolerable pride that still sustains it. Talk of public war! The world could not exist, if nation were to take up the sword against nation upon a point of honour, such as will call out for blood between man and man. The very word means pride. It is a measureless, bloody pride that demands a reparation so excessive for every slight offence. Take any single quarrel of them all, and dissect its motive, and you will find every portion of it stained with pride, the child of selfishness—pride, the sin of the first devil—pride, the poor pitiful creature of folly and ignorance—pride, the——"

"Oh, trash and stuff, man!" exclaimed Connolly, losing patience. "If you are going to preach a sermon, choose another time for it. Come, Creagh, send the bowl this way, and let us drink. Here, young gentleman, stop spouting, and give us a toast. You'll make a fool of yourself, Hardress, if you talk in that manner among gentlemen."

Without making any answer to this speech (which, however, he felt a little difficulty in digesting), Hardress proposed the health and future fame of young Kyrle Daly.

"With all my heart," exclaimed both his father and Connolly.

"I'll not drink it," said Creagh, putting from him his glass.

Hardress was just as proud (to borrow his own simile) as Lucifer himself, and probably it was on this account he held the quality so cheap. It must be admitted, likewise, that his ambitious love of singularity formed but too considerable a part of his motive in the line of argument which he had followed up; and he was by no means prepared to perform the heroic part which he had described with so much enthusiasm. Least of all could he be expected to do so at the present moment; for while he was speaking he had also been drinking, and the warmth of dispute, increased by the excitement of strong drink, left his reason still less at freedom than it might have been under the dominion of an ordinary passion. He insisted upon Creagh's drinking his toast.

"I shall not drink it," said Creagh; "I consider him as an impertinent puppy."

"He is my friend," said Hardress.

"Oh, then, of course," said Fireball, with an ironical smile, evidently intended as a retort, "he is utterly blameless."

To use a vulgar but forcible expression, the blood of Hardress was now completely up. He set his teeth for a moment, and then discharged the contents of his own glass at the face of the offender. The fire-eater, who, from long experience, was able to anticipate this proceeding, evaded by a rapid motion the degrading missile, and then quietly resuming his seat, "Be prepared, sir," he said, "to answer this in the morning."

"I am ready now," exclaimed Hardress. "Connolly, lend me your sword, and be my friend. Father, do you second that gentleman, and you will oblige me."

Mr. Barnaby Cregan rose to interfere; but in doing so, he betrayed a secret which had till that moment lain with himself; he was the first who fell.

"No, no swords," said Connolly; "there are a pretty pair of pistols over the chimney-piece. Let them decide the quarrel."

It was so agreed. Hardress and Creagh took their places in the two corners of the room, upon the understanding that both were to approach step by step, and fire when they pleased. Hepton Connolly took his place out of harm's way in a distant corner, while Cregan crept along the floor, muttering, in an indistinct tone. "Drunk? Ay, but not dead drunk. I call no man dead drunk while he lies on the high road, with sense

enough to roll out of the way when a carriage is driving towards him."

Hardress fired after having made two paces. Creagh, who was unhurt, reserved his shot until he put the pistol up to the head of his opponent. Hardress never flinched, although he really believed that Creagh was about to shoot him.

"Come," said he loudly, "fire your shot, and have done with it. I would have met you at the end of a handkerchief upon my friend's quarrel."

Hyland Creagh, after enjoying for a moment the advantage he possessed, uncocked his pistol, and laid it on the table.

"Hardress," said he, "you are a brave fellow. I believe I was wrong. I ask your pardon, and am ready to drink your toast."

"Oh, well," said Hardress, with a laugh, "if that be the case, I cannot, of course, think of pursuing the affair any further." And he reached his hand to his opponent with the air of one who was exercising rather than receiving a kindness.

The company once more resumed their places at the table, somewhat sobered by this incident, which, though not unusual at the period, was yet calculated to excite a little serious feeling. It was not long, however, before they made amends for what was lost in the way of intoxication. The immense blue jug, which stood inside the fender, was replenished to the brim, and the bowl flew round more rapidly than ever. Creagh told stories of the Hell-fire Club in the sweating and pinking days. Connolly overflowed with anecdotes of attorneys outdone, of plates well won, of bailiffs maimed and beaten; and Cregan, whose tongue was the last member of his frame that became accessory to the sin of intoxication, filled up his share in the conversation with accounts of cocks and of ghosts, in the appearance of which last he was a firm though not a fearful believer. Hardress remained with the company until the sound of a vehicle drawing up at the hall-door announced the return of his mother and cousin. He then left the room and hurried to his own apartment, in order to avoid meeting them under circumstances which he well supposed were not calculated to create any impression in his own favour.

We cannot better illustrate the habits of the period than by transcribing an observation made in Mr. Cregan's kitchen at the moment of the dispute above detailed. Old Nancy was preparing the mould candles for poor Dalton's wake when she heard the shot fired in the dining-parlour.

"Run in to the gentlemen, Mike, eroo," she exclaimed, without even laying aside the candle, which she was paring with a knife, in order to make it fit the socket more exactly. "I lay my life the gentlemen are fighting a *jewel*."

"It can't be a *jewel*," said Mike, the servant boy, who was courting slumber in a low chair before the blazing fire; "it can't be a *jewel*, when there was only one shot."

"But it isn't far from 'em, I'll be bail, till they'll fire another, if they do not be hindered; for 'tis shot for shot with 'em. Run in, eroo."

The servant boy stretched his limbs out lazily, and rubbed his eyes. "Well," said he, "fair play all the world over. If one fired, you wouldn't have the other put up with it, without havin' his fair revenge?"

"But maybe one of 'em is kilt already," observed Nancy.

"E'then, d'ye hear this? Sure you know well that if there was anybody shot, the master would ring the bell."

This observation was conclusive. Old Nancy proceeded with her gloomy toil in silence, and the persuasive Mike, letting his head hang back from his shoulders, and crossing his hands upon his lap, slept soundly on, undisturbed by any idle conjectures on the cause of the noise which they had heard.

CHAPTER XIX.

HOW HARDRESS MET AN OLD FRIEND AND MADE A NEW ONE.

FANCY restored the dreaming Hardress to the society of his beloved Eily. He sat by her side once more, quieting, with the caresses of a boyish fondness, her still recurring anxieties, and comforting her apprehensions by endeavouring to make her share his own steady anticipation of his mother's favour and forgiveness. This hope, on his own part, it must be acknowledged, was much stronger in his sleeping than his waking moments; for it was extraordinary how different his feeling on that subject became after he had reached his home, and when the moment of disclosure drew near. His extreme youth, all ruined as he was by over-indulgence, made him regard his mother with a degree of reverence that approached to fear; and as he seldom loved to submit when once aroused to contest, so he was usually careful to avoid, as much as possible, any occasion for the exercise of his hereditary perseverance. The influence of his parent, however, consisted not so much in her parental authority, as in the mastery which she held over his filial affections, which partook of the intensity that distinguished his entire character. Mrs. Cregan governed both her husband and her son; but the means which she employed in moulding each to her own wishes were widely different. In her arguments with the former it was her usual practice to begin with an entreaty and end with a command. On the contrary, when she sought to work upon the inclinations of Hardress, she opened with a command and closed with an entreaty. It was, indeed, as Hardress had frequently experienced, a difficult task to withstand her instances, when she had recourse to the latter expedient. Mrs. Cregan possessed all the national warmth of temperament and liveliness of feeling. Like all naturally generous people, whose virtue is rather the offspring of a kindly heart than a well-regulated understanding, Mrs. Cregan was not more boundless in her bounty than in her exaction of gratitude. She not only looked for gratitude from those whom she had obliged, but was so exorbitant as to imagine that all those, likewise, whom she really wished to serve should return her an equal degree of kindness, and actually evince as lively a sense of obligation as if her wishes in their favour had been deeds. Alas! in this selfish world we are told that real benefits are frequently forgotten by the receiver, and sometimes repaid by cold unkindness or monstrous hostility. It is no wonder, then, that Mrs. Cregan should have sometimes found people slow to appreciate the value of her vain desires.

While Hardress was still murmuring some sentiment of passionate admiration in the ear of his visionary bride, he was awakened by the pressure of a light finger on his shoulder. He looked up and beheld a lady in a broad-leafed beaver hat and ball dress standing by his bedside, and smiling down upon him with an air of affection and reproof. Her countenance, though it had already acquired, in a slight degree, that hardness of outline which marks the approach of the first matronly years, was striking and even beautiful in its character. The forehead was high and commanding, the eye of a dark hazel, well opened, and tender and rapid in its expression. The entire face had that length of feature which painters employ in their representation of the tragic muse, and the character of the individual had given to this natural conformation a depth of feeling which was calculated to make a strong and even a gloomy impression on the imagination of the beholder. Her person likewise partook of this imposing character, and was displayed to some advantage by her dress, the richness of which was perfectly adapted to her lofty and regal air. It consisted of a beautiful poplin, a stomacher set off with small brilliants, and a rich figured silk petticoat, which was fully displayed in front. The skirt of the gown parted and fell back from either side, while a small hoop occupying the position of the modern Vestris, imparted to this interesting portion of the figure a degree of fashionable slimness and elegance. An amber necklace, some enormous brooches, and rings containing locks of hair, the bequests of three preceding generations, completed the decorations of her person.

"You are a pretty truant," she said, "to absent yourself for a whole fortnight together, and at a time, too, when I had brought a charming friend to make your acquaintance. You are a pretty truant! And immediately on your return, instead of showing any affectionate anxiety to compensate for your in-attention, you run off to your sleeping-chamber, and oblige your foolish mother to come and seek you."

"My trim, mother, would have hardly become your drawing-room."

"Or looked to advantage in the eyes of my lovely visitor?"

"Upon my word, mother, I had not a thought of her. I should feel as little inclined to appear wanting in respect to you as to any visitor to whom you could introduce me."

"Respect!" echoed Mrs. Cregan, while she laid the light away upon the dressing-table, in such a position that it could shine full and bright upon the features of her son, and took a chair near his bedside. "Respect is fond of going well

dressed, I grant you; but there is another feeling, Hardress, that is far more sensitive and exquisite on points of this nature, a feeling much more lively and anxious than any that a poor fond mother can expect. Do not interrupt me; I am not so unreasonable as to desire that the course of human nature should be inverted for my sake. But I have a question to ask you. Have you any engagement during the next month that will prevent your spending it with us? If you have, and if it be not a very weighty one, break it off as politely as you can. You owe some little attention to your cousin, and I think you ought to pay it."

Hardress looked displeased at this, and muttered something about his inability to see in what way this obligation had been laid upon him.

"If you feel no disposition to show a kindness to your old playfellow," said his mother, endeavouring to suppress her vexation, "you are, of course, at liberty to act as you please. You, Hardress, in your own person, owe nothing to the Chutes, unless you except their general claim as near relatives of mine."

"They could not, my dear mother, possess a stronger. But this is a sudden change. While I was in Dublin, I thought that both you and my father had broken off the intercourse that subsisted between the families, and lived altogether within yourselves."

"It was a foolish coldness that had arisen between your aunt and myself, on account of some free, some very free, expressions she had used with regard to your father. But when she fell ill, and my poor darling Anne was left to struggle, unassisted, beneath the weight of occupation that was thrown thus suddenly upon her hands, my self-respect gave way to my love for them both. I drove to Castle Chute, and divided with Anne the cares of nurse-tending and housekeeping, until my dear Hetty's health was in some degree restored. About a fortnight since, by the force of incessant letter-writing, and the employment of her mother's influence, I obtained Anne's very reluctant consent to spend a month at Killarney. Now, my dear Hardress, you must do me a kindness. I have no female friend of your cousin's age, whose society might afford her a constant source of enjoyment, and, in spite of all my efforts to procure her amusement, I cannot but observe that she has been more frequently dull than merry since her arrival. Now, you can prevent this if you please. You must remain at home while she is with us, entertain her while I am occupied, walk with her, dance with her, be her *beau*. If she were a stranger, hospitality alone would call for those attentions, and I think, under the circumstances, your own good feeling will teach you that she ought not to be neglected."

"My dear mother, do not say another word upon the subject. It will be necessary for me to go from home sometimes; but I can engage to spend a great portion of the month as you desire. Send for a dancing-master to-morrow morning. I am but an awkward fellow at best, but I will do all that is in my power."

"You will breakfast with us, then, to-morrow morning, and come on a laking party? It was for the purpose of making you promise, I disturbed your rest at this hour; for I knew there was no calculating in what part of Munster one might find you after sunrise."

"How far do you go?"

"Only to Innisfallen."

"Ah! dear, dear Innisfallen! I will be with you, certainly, mother. Ah, dear Innisfallen! Mother, do you think that Anne remembers the time when Lady K—— invited us to take a cold dinner in St. Finian's oratory? It is one of the sweetest days that ever brightened my recollection. I think I can still see that excellent lady laying her hand upon Anne Chute's shoulder, and telling her that she should be the little princess of this little fairy isle. Dear Innisfallen! If I were but to tell you, mother, how many a mournful hour that single happy one has cost me!"

"Tell me of no such thing, my boy. Look forward, and not back. Reserve the enjoyment of your recollections until you are no longer capable of present and actual happiness. And do not think, Hardress, that you make so extraordinary a sacrifice in undertaking this pretty office. There is many a fine gentleman in Killarney who would gladly forego a whole season's sport for the privilege of acting such a part for a single day. I cannot describe to you the sensation that your cousin has produced since her arrival. Her beauty, her talents, her elegance, and her accomplishments are the subject of conversation in every circle. You will acquire a greater brilliance as the satellite of such a planet than if you were to move for ages in your own solitary orbit. But if I were to say all that I desire you would not sleep to-night, so I shall reserve it to a moment of greater leisure. Good night, Hardress, and sleep soundly, for the cockswain is to be at the door before nine."

Mrs. Cregan was well acquainted with the character of her son. The distinction of attending on so celebrated a beauty as his cousin was one to which his vanity could never be indifferent, and nothing could be more agreeable to his pride than to find it thus forced upon him, without any effort of his own to seek it. To be thus, out of pure kindness, and much against his own declared wishes, placed in a situation which was so generally envied—to obtain, likewise (and these were the only motives that Hardress would acknowledge to his own mind), to obtain an opportunity of softening his mother's prejudices against the time of avowal, and of forwarding the interests of his friend Kyrle Daly in another quarter; all these advantages were sufficient to compensate to his pride for the chance of some mortifying awkwardness, which might occur through his long neglect of, and contempt for, the habitual forms of society.

"And of all the places in the world," thought Hardress, "Killarney is the scene for such a *début* as this. There is such an everlasting fund of conversation. The very store of commonplace remarks is inexhaustible. If it rains, one can talk of the Killarney showers, and tell the story of Mr. Fox; and if the sun shines, it must shine upon more wonders than a hundred tongues, as nimble as those of Fame herself, could tell—the teasing of the guides, the lies of the boatmen, the legends of the lakes, the English arrivals, the echoes, the optical illusions, the mists, the mountains. If I were as dull as Otter,* I could be as talkative as the barber in the 'Arabian Nights' on such a subject, and yet without the necessity of burdening my tongue with more than a sentence at a time."

Notwithstanding these encouraging reflections, Hardress next morning experienced many a struggle with his false shame before he left his chamber to encounter his mother's charming visitor. What was peculiar in the social timidity of this young gentleman lay in the circumstance that it could scarcely ever be perceived in society. His excessive pride prevented his often incurring the danger of a mortifying repression, and it could hardly be inferred from his reserved, and at the same time dignified demeanour, whether his silence were the effect of ill-temper, stupidity, or bashfulness. Few, indeed, ever thought of attributing it to that lofty philosophical principle to which he himself pretended; and there was but one in addition to Kyrle Daly, of all his acquaintances, on whom it did not produce an unfavourable impression.

After having been summoned half a dozen times to the breakfast parlour, and delaying each time to indulge in a fresh peep at the mirror to adjust his hair, which had now too much and now too little powder; to alter the disposition of his shirt frill, and consummate the tying of his cravat, Hardress descended to the parlour, where, to his surprise, he found his cousin seated alone. She was simply dressed, and her hair, according to the fashion of unmarried ladies at the period, fell down in black and shining ringlets on her neck. A plain necklace of the famous black oak of the lakes, and a Maltese cross formed from the hoof of the red deer, constituted the principal decorations of her person. There was a consciousness and even a distress in the manner of their meeting. A womanly reserve and delicacy made Anne unwilling to affect an intimacy that might not be met as she could desire; and his never-failing pride prevented Hardress from seeming to desire a favour that he had reason to suppose might not be granted him.

Accordingly, the great store of conversation which he had been preparing the night before, now, to his astonishment, utterly deserted him, and he discovered that subject is an acquisition of little use, while it is unassisted by mutual confidence and good-will among the interlocutors. Nothing was effective, nothing told; and when Mrs. Cregan entered the parlour she lifted her hands in wonder to see her fair visitor seated by the fire, and reading some silly novel of the day (which happened to lie near her), while Hardress affected to amuse himself with Creagh's dog Pincher at the window, and

* A character in Ben Jonson's "Epicœne."

said repeatedly within his own heart, "Ah, Eily! you are worth this fine lady a hundred times over."

"Anne! Hardress! My lady and my gentleman! Upon my word, Hardress, you ought to be proud of your gallantry. On the very first morning of your return, I find you seated at the distance of half a room from your old playfellow, and allowing her to look for entertainment in a stupid book! But perhaps you do not know each other. Oh! then it is *my* duty to apologise for being out of the way. Miss Chute, this is Mr. Hardress Cregan; Mr. Hardress Cregan, this is Miss Chute." And she went through a mock introduction in the formal manner of the day.

The lady and gentleman each muttered something in reply. "We *have* spoken, ma'am," said Hardress. "We have spoken, ma'am!" echoed Mrs. Cregan. "Sir, your most obedient servant! You have made a wonderful effort, and shown a great deal of condescension! You *have* spoken! You have done everything that a gentleman of so much dignity and consequence was called upon to do, and you will not move a single footstep farther. But perhaps," she added, glancing at Anne, "perhaps I am dealing unjustly here. Perhaps the will to hear, and not the will to say, was wanted. If the fault lay with the listener, Hardress, speak. It is the only defence that I will think of admitting."

"Except that the listener might not be worth the trial," said Anne, in the same tone of liveliness, not unmingled with pique, "I don't know how he can enter such a plea as that."

"Oh, Hardress! Oh, fie, Hardress! There's a charge from a lady."

"I can assure you," said Hardress, a little confused, yet not displeased with the manner in which his cousin took up the subject, "I am not conscious of having deserved any such accusation. If you call upon me for a defence, I can only find it in a simple recrimination. Anne has been so distant to me ever since my return from Dublin, that I was afraid I had offended her!"

"Very fair, sir; a very reasonable plea indeed. Well, Miss Chute," continued Mrs. Cregan, turning round with an air of mock gravity to her young visitor, "why have you been so distant to my son since his return, as to make him suppose he had offended you?" And she stood with her hands expanded before her, in the attitude of one who looks for an explanation.

"Offended me!" said Anne. "I must have been exceedingly unreasonable indeed if I had quarrelled with anything that was said or done by Hardress, for I am sure he never once allowed me the opportunity."

"Oh! oh!" exclaimed Mrs. Cregan, clasping her hands, and bursting into a fit of laugher; "you grow more severe. If I were a young gentleman, I should sink down with shame after such an imputation as that."

Hardress found himself suddenly entrapped in a scene of coquetry. "Might not one do better, mother," he said, running lightly across the room, and taking a seat close by the side of his cousin—"might not one do better by endeavouring to amend?"

"But it is too late, sir," said Anne, affecting to move away; "my aunt Cregan is right, and I *am* offended with you. Don't sit so near, if you please. The truth is, I have made up my mind not to like you at all, and I never will change it, you may be certain."

"That is too hard, Anne. We are old friends, you should remember. What can I have done to make you so inveterate?"

"That's right, Hardress," said Mrs. Cregan, who had now taken her place at the breakfast-table; "do not be discouraged by her. Give her no peace until she is your friend. But in the mean time come to breakfast. The cockswain has been waiting this half hour."

The same scene of coquetry was continued during the morning. Hardress, who was no less delighted than surprised at this change of manner in his lovely cousin, assumed the part of a duteous knight, endeavouring, by the most assiduous attentions, to conciliate the favour of his offended "ladye;" and Anne maintained with a playful dignity the inexorable coldness and reserve which were the prerogative of the sex in those days of chivalry and sound sense. "We hate those," says Bruyère, "who treat us with pride; but a smile is sufficient to reconcile us." In proportion to the chagrin which the fancied coldness of his fair cousin had occasioned to the quick-hearted Hardress, was the pleasure which he received from this unexpected and intimate turn of manner. And now it was, moreover, that he became capable of doing justice to the real character of the young lady. No longer embarrassed by the feeling of strangeness and apprehension which had kept her spirits back on their first meeting, Anne now assumed to him that ease and liveliness of manner with which she was accustomed to fascinate her more familiar acquaintances. He was astonished, even to a degree of consternation, at the extent both of her talents and her knowledge. On general subjects he found, with extreme and almost humiliating surprise, that her information very nearly approached his own; and in a graceful and unostentatious application of that knowledge to familiar subjects she possessed the customary female superiority.

We will not intrude so far upon the peculiar province of the guide-books as to furnish any detail of the enchanting scenery through which our party travelled in the course of the forenoon. Every new sight that he beheld, every new hour that he spent in the society of his cousin, assisted in disabusing his mind of the prejudice which he had conceived against her, and supplying its place by a feeling of strong kindness It happened, likewise, that in the course of the day, many circumstances occurred to render him well satisfied with the company of his new associates. The disposition to please and be pleased was general amongst them; and Hardress was flattered by the degree of attention which he received, not only from his own party, but from his mother's fashionable acquaintances, to whom he was introduced in passing. Life, spirit, courtliness of manner, and kindness of feeling, governed the tone of conversation throughout the day; and Hardress bore his part, in quality of host, with a degree of success and effect that was a matter of astonishment to himself. One or two of the younger ladies only were heard to say that Mr. Cregan was a little inattentive, and that he seemed to imagine there was not another lady of the party besides Miss Chute; but it is suspected that even those pretty murmurers were by no means the least sensible of the merit of the person whom they censured. When the evening drew near, and the party left the island for home, Hardress was once more surprised to find, that although he had been speaking for nearly half the day, he had not once found it necessary to make allusion to the Killarney showers, the optical deceptions, or the story of Charles James Fox.

When he parted from the merry circle, in order to fulfil his promise to Eily, a feeling of blank regret fell suddenly upon his heart, like that which is experienced by a boy when the curtain falls at the close of the first theatrical spectacle which he has ever witnessed. His mother, who knew him too well to press any inquiry into the nature of his present engagement, had found no great difficulty in making him promise to return on the next day, in order to be present at a ball which she was about to give at the cottage. The regret which Anne manifested at his departure (to her an unexpected movement), and the cordial pleasure with which she heard of his intention to return on the next morning, inspired him with a feeling of happiness which he had not hitherto experienced since his childhood.

The next time he thought of Anne and Eily at the same moment the conjunction was not so unfavourable to the former as it had been in the morning. "There is no estimating the advantage," he said within his own mind, "which the society of so accomplished a girl as that must produce on the mind and habits of my dear little Eily. I wish they were already friends. My poor little love! how much she has to learn before she can assume with comfort to herself the place for which I have designed her! But women are imitative creatures. They can more readily adapt themselves to the tone of any new society than we, who boast a firmer and less ductile nature; and Eily will find an additional facility in the good nature and active kindness of Anne Chute. I wish from my heart they were already friends."

As he finished this reflection he turned his pony off the Gap road, upon the crags which led to the cottage of Phil Naughten.

CHAPTER XX.

HOW HARDRESS HAD A STRANGE DREAM OF EILY.

THE burst of rapture and affection with which he was received by Eily banished for the moment every other feeling from the mind of the young husband. Her eyes sparkled, and her countenance brightened at his entrance, with the innocent delight of a child. Her colour changed, and her whole frame was agitated by a passion of joy, which Hardress could scarcely have anticipated if his absence had been prolonged to a much more considerable time. He could not avoid feeling that Eily was as far beyond his cousin in gentleness of feeling, in ready confidence, and winning simplicity of manner, as she was excelled by the latter in dignity of mind and of demeanour, in elegant knowledge, and in correctness of taste.

They stood at the open door, Eily being yet encircled by the arm of her husband, and gazing on his face, while the expression of rapture that had illumined the countenance of both faded gradually away into a look of calm and settled joy. On a sudden their ears were startled by a hoarse, husky, and yet piercing voice, which seemed to proceed from a crag that sheltered the cottage on the left side. Looking upward, Hardress beheld a woman standing on the turf, whose gesture and appearance showed her to be one of a race of viragos who are now less numerous in the country parts of Ireland than they were some twenty years since. Her face and hair announced a Spanish origin; her dress consisted of a brown stuff garment, fastened up the back with a row of brass buttons, and a muslin cap and ribbon, considerably injured by the effect of long possession. An old drab jock, soiled and stained by many a roll in the puddle of the mountain fairs, was superadded, and in her right hand she grasped a short heavy oak stick, which, if one might judge by the constant use she made of it in enforcing her gestures, was as necessary to her discourse as the famous thread of Lord Chesterfield's orator. Her eyes were bloodshot from watching and intemperance; and the same causes, joined to an habitual violence of temper, had given to her thin, red, and streaky countenance a sudden and formidable turn of expression.

"Ha! ha! my children! my two fine, clever children, are ye there? Oh, the luck o' me, that it wasn't a lad like you I married; a clever boy, with the red blood running under his yellow skin, like that sun over behind the clouds, instead of the mane, withered disciple that calls my house his home this day. Look at the beauty of him! Look at the beauty of him! I might have been a lady if I liked. Oh, the luck o' me! the luck o' me! Five tall young men, every one of 'em a patthern for a faction, and all, all dead in their graves, down, down; an' no one left but that picthur o' misery that calls himself my husband. If it wasn't for the whiskey," she added, while she came down the crags, and stood before the pair, "my heart would break with the thoughts of it. Five tall young men, brothers every one, an' they to die, an' he to live! Wouldn't it kill the Danes to think of it? Five tall young men! Gi' me the price o' the whiskey."

"Indeed I will not, Poll. You have had enough already."

"No, nor half!" shouted the amazon. "A dhram is enough, but two dhrams isn't half enough, an' I had only two. Coax him, *ma chree, ma lanuv*, to gi' me the price o' the whiskey."

Eily, who stood in great terror of this virago, turned a supplicating glance on Hardress.

"Your young mistress," said the latter, "would not become a participator in the sin of your drunkenness."

"*My* misthress! The rope-maker's daughter! *My* misthress! Eily-na-thiadarucha! Welcome from Gallows Green, my misthress! The poor silly crathur! Is it because I call you, with the blood of all your fathers in your veins, a gentleman, my masther, that I'd call her a lady, and my misthress? Gi' me the price o' the whiskey."

"I shall not, Poll. Go back."

"Gi' me the price o' the whiskey, or I 'll tear the crooked eyes out o' your yellow face! Gi' me it, I tell you, or I 'll give my misthress more kicks than ha'pence the next time I catch her alone in the house, an' you away coortin' and divartin' at Killarney."

"Cool yourself, Poll, or I 'll make you cool."

"You a gentleman! There isn't a noggin o' genteel blood in the veins o' your whole seed, breed, an' generation. You have a heart! you stingy, bone-polishing, tawny-faced, beggarly, mane-spirited mohawk, that hadn't the spirit to choose between poverty an' dignity! You a gentleman! The highest and the finest in the land was open to you, an' you hadn't the courage to stand up for your fortune. You a heart! Except a lady was to come an' coort you of herself, sorrow chance she'd ever have o' you, or you of her. An' signs on, see what a misthress you brought over us! I wondher you had the courage to spake to her itself. While others looked up, you looked down. I often seen a worm turn to a butterfly, but I never heard of a butterfly turning to a worm in my life before. You a heart! I'll lay a noggin, if the docthors open you when ye die, they won't find such a thing as a heart in your whole yellow carcass, only a could gizzard, like the turkeys."

Hardress turned pale with anger at this coarse but bitter satire. "Do stop her mouth, my dear Hardress," murmured Eily, whose total want of pride rendered her almost incapable of resentment. "Do silence her. That woman makes me afraid for my very life."

"Never entertain the least apprehension on that subject, Eily. There is one key to the good-will of Fighting Poll, by which you may be always certain of keeping your place in her affections. It is whiskey. Keep her in whiskey, and you keep her faithful. Nor need you ever fear to be out-purchased; for Poll has just good principle enough to prefer a little whiskey with honesty to a great deal obtained as the wages of treason. Well, Poll," he continued, turning to that amazon, "you are too many for me. Here is half-a-crown to drink my health, and be a good girl."

"Half-a-crown!" shouted the woman, catching the glittering coin as Hardress sent it twirling through the air. "I knew you were your father's son for all! I knew 'tis o' purpose you were. I knew you had the nature in you, after all! Ha! here comes Phil and Danny at last. Come, sthrip, now, Phil! Sthrip off the coat at once, an' let us see if M'Donough laid the horsewhip over your shoulders to-day."

The man only returned her a surly glance in answer to this speech.

"What M'Donough is this, Phil?" said Hardress; "what horse-whipping do you speak of, Poll?"

"I'll tell you, sir," returned Phil. "He is our landlord, and the owner of all the land about you, as far as you can see, an' farther. He lives about a mile away from us, an' is noted for being a good landlord to all, far an' near. Only there's one fashion he has, and that's a throublesome one to some of his people. As he gives all manner of lases at a raisonable rent himself, he wishes that his land should be sub-let raisonable also, which makes him very conthrary whenever there does be any complaints of hard usage from the under tenants. I'll tell you his plan when he finds anything o' the sort afther his head tenants. He doesn't drive 'em nor be hard upon them, nor ax for the arrears, nor one ha'porth, only sends his sarvant boy down to their house with a little whip-handle, about so big, that's as well known upon his estate as the landlord's own face. Well, the sarvant boy comes in, as it might be to my cabin there (if he had anything again' me), an' without ever saying one word, he walks into the middle o' the floore, an' lays the whip-handle upon the table, an' walks out again without ever sayin' one word. Very well; the tenant knows, when he sees the whip, that he must carry it up to his landlord next morning, as sure as he has a head upon his shoulders; an' take it from me, there's many lads among 'em have no great welcome for the sight of it. Well, up they go to the great house, an' there they ax for the masther, an' they carry the whip-handle into his parlour, where he locks the door upon 'em, an' if they can't well account for what they done, he makes 'em sthrip, and begins flaking 'em with a horsewhip until their backs is all one grishkin; an' then he tells 'em to go about their business, an' let him hear no more complaints in future. I thought it was a ghost I seen myself last night when I found the whip-handle on my own table. But I made all clear when I seen the masther."

"That is pushing his authority to a feudal extent," said Hardress.

"A what, sir?" asked Phil, looking puzzled.

"Nothing, Phil, nothing. Poll, go in now, and get supper ready in your mistress's room."

"Let Phil get it," returned the amazon; "I want to step over to the *sthreet* * for a pound o' candles."

"A pound o' candles!" echoed her helpmate, with sneering emphasis.

"Iss, what else?" exclaimed Poll, grasping her baton, and looking back on him with a menacing gesture.

"You know best what else yourself," said the husband. "We all know what sort o' candles it is you're going for. I lay my

* Village.

life you're afther gettin' money from the masther. But away with you—don't think I want to stop you. Your absence is better company than your presence any day in the year." So saying, he preceded our hero and heroine into the cottage, muttering, in a low voice, a popular distich :—

" Joy be with you, if you never come back,
   Dead or alive, or o' horseback."

In the course of this evening Eily remarked that her husband, though affectionate as she could desire, was more silent and abstracted than she had ever seen him, and that he more frequently spoke in correction of some little breach of etiquette, or nelegance of manner, than in those terms of eloquent praise and fondness which he was accustomed to lavish upon her. One advantage, however, of Eily's want of penetration was, that the demon of suspicion never disturbed the quiet of her soul; and it required the utmost and the most convincing evidence of falsehood to shake the generous and illimitable confidence which she reposed in any person who was once established in her affections. While she felt, therefore, some little pain on her husband's account, she never experienced the slightest trouble on her own. She endeavoured with cheerfulness to adapt herself to his wishes, and though in this she could not become immediately successful, he would have owned a rigid temper indeed if it had not been softened by the submissive sweetness of her demeanour.

And Hardress *was* softened, though not satisfied by her gentle efforts. He observed on this evening a much more considerable number of those unpleasing blemishes than he had on any other, and the memory of them pursued him even into his midnight slumbers, where fancy, as usual, augmented their effects upon his mind. He dreamed that the hour had come in which he was to introduce his bride to his rich and fashionable acquaintances, and that a large company had assembled at his mother's cottage to honour the occasion. Nothing, however, could exceed the bashfulness, the awkwardness, and the homeliness of speech and accent, with which the rope-maker's daughter received their compliments; and to complete the climax of his chagrin, on happening to look round upon her during dinner, he saw her in the act of peeling a potato with her fingers! This phantom haunted him for half the night. He dreamed, moreover, that when he reasoned with her on this subject, she answered him with a degree of pert vulgarity and impatience which was in "discordant harmony" with her shyness before strangers, and which made him angry at heart and miserable in mind.

The dreams of passion are always vivid, distinct, and deeply impressive. The feeling of anger and annoyance remained on the mind of Hardress even after he awoke, and although he never failed to correct and dispel the sensation whenever it arose, yet, throughout the whole of the following morning, a strong and disagreeable association was awakened whenever he looked upon Eily.

Before he again left her, Hardress explained the nature of his present position with respect to his mother, and informed his wife of the necessity which existed for spending a considerable portion of the month which was to come at his father's cottage. Eily heard this announcement with pain and grief, but without remonstrance. She cried like a child at parting with him; and after he had ridden away, remained leaning against the jamb of the door, with her moistened handkerchief placed against her cheek, in an attitude of musing sorrow. He had promised to return on the second day after, but how was she to live over the long, long interval? A lonesomeness of heart, that was in mournful accordance with the mighty solitudes in which she dwelt, fell down and abode upon her spirit.

On that night Hardress was one of the gayest revellers at his mother's ball. Anne Chute, who was, beyond all competition, the star of the evening, favoured him with a marked and cordial distinction. The flattering deference with which he was received by all with whom he entered into conversation during the night surprised him into ease and fluency; and the success of his own eloquence made him in love with his auditory. When it is considered that this was the very first ball he had ever witnessed since his boyhood, and that his life, in the interim, had been the life of a recluse, its effect upon his mind will cease to be a matter of surprise. The richness of the dresses—the liveliness of the music—the beauty of the fair dancers—the gaiety of their young partners—the air of elegant mirth that filled the whole apartment—produced a new and delicious sensation of happiness in the susceptible temper of Hardress. Our feelings are so much under the government of our habits,' that a modern English family in the same rank might have denied the praise of *comfort* to that which, in the unaccustomed eyes of Hardress, wore the warmer hue of luxury; for he lived at a time when Irish gentlemen fostered a more substantial pride than at present; when appearances were comparatively but little consulted, and the master of a mansion cared not how rude was the interior, or how ruinous the exterior of his dwelling, provided he could always maintain a loaded larder and a noisy board. The scene around him was not less enervating to the mind of our hero because the chairs which the company used were of plain oak, and the light from the large glass lustre fell upon the coarse, unpapered walls, whose only ornament consisted of the cross-barred lines drawn with the trowel in the rough grey mortar. Many of those who are accustomed to scenes of elegant dissipation might not readily give credence to the effect which was wrought upon his feelings by circumstances of comparatively little import. The perfumed air of the room, the loftiness of the ceiling, the festooning of the drapery above the windows, the occasional pauses and changes in the music, all contributed to raise his mind into a condition of peculiar and exquisite enthusiasm, which made it susceptible of deep, dangerous, and indelible impressions. The wisdom of religion, in prescribing a strict and constant government of the senses, could not be more apparent than on an occasion like this, when their influence upon the reason became almost as potent and absorbing as that of an internal passion.

In the midst of this gaiety of heart and topping fulness of mind, a circumstance occurred to throw it into a more disturbed and serious, but scarcely less delightful condition. The intervals in the dancing were filled up by songs from the company, and Anne Chute, in her turn, was called on for her contribution of melody. Hardress was leaning over her chair, and looking at the music-book, which she was turning over leaf after leaf, as if in search of some suitable piece for the occasion.

"Ah, this will do, I think," said Anne, pausing at a manuscript song, which was adapted to an old air, and running a rapid prelude along the keys of the instrument. The letters H. C. were written at the top of the page, and Hardress felt a glow like fire upon his brow the instant he beheld them. He drew back a little out of the light, and listened with an almost painful emotion to the song, which the fair performer executed with an ease and feeling that gave to the words an effect beyond that to which they might themselves have pretended. They were the following:—

I.
"A place in thy memory, dearest,
  Is all that I claim;
To pause and look back when thou hearest
  The sound of my name.
Another may woo thee, nearer,
  Another may win and wear;
I care not though he be dearer,
  If I am remembered there.

II.
"Remember me—not as a lover
  Whose hope was cross'd,
Whose bosom can never recover
  The light it has lost:
As the young bride remembers the mother
  She loves, though she never may see—
As a sister remembers a brother,
  Oh, dearest! remember me.

III.
"Could I be thy true lover, dearest,
  Couldst thou smile on me,
I would be the fondest and nearest
  That ever loved thee!
But a cloud on my pathway is glooming,
  That never must burst upon thine,
And Heaven, that made thee all blooming,
  Ne'er made thee to wither on mine.

IV.
"Remember me, then! Oh, remember
  My calm, light love!
Though bleak as the blasts of November
  My life may prove,
That life will, though lonely, be sweet,
  If its brightest enjoyment should be
A smile and kind word when we meet,
  And a place in thy memory."

CHAPTER XXII.

HOW HARDRESS MET A STRANGE TRIAL.

"MOTHER, can you tell me why Anne Chute appears so abstracted and so reserved in her manner these few days past? Is she ill? Is she out of spirits? Is she annoyed at anything?"

Hardress Cregan, who spoke this speech, was resting with his arm on the sash of one of the cottage windows. Mrs. Cregan was standing at a table in the centre of the room, arranging several small packages of plate, glass, and china, which had been borrowed from various neighbours on occasion of the ball. At a little distance stood old Nancy in her blue cloak and hood, awaiting the commands of her mistress, who, as she proceeded with her occupation, glanced at intervals a sharp and inquiring eye at her son.

"Here, Nancy, take this china to Mrs. Geogheghan, with my compliments, and tell her that I'm very much obliged to her; and for your life, you horrible old creature, take care and not break them."

"Oyeh, murther! is it I? Fake 'em sure that I won't, so."

"And tell Mike, as you are going downstairs, to come hither. I want to send him with those spoons to Miss Macarthy."

"Mike isn't come back yet, ma'am, since he wint over with the three-branch candlestick to Mrs. Crasbie."

"He is a very long time away, then."

"Can you tell me, mother," said Hardress, after in vain expecting an answer to his former queries—"can you tell me, mother, if Anne Chute has had any unpleasing news from home lately?"

"Well, Nancy," continued Mrs. Cregan, appearing not to have heard her son, "run away with your parcel, and deliver your message as you have been told, and hurry back again, for I have three more places to send you to before dinner."

"Allilu! my ould bones will be fairly wore from undher me with the dint of thrallivantin," muttered Nancy as she left the room.

"I beg your pardon, Hardress, my dear—were you not speaking? My attention is so occupied by these affairs that I have not a head for anything besides. This is one of the annoyances produced by your father's improvidence. He will not purchase those things, and I am obliged to borrow them, and to invite their owners into the bargain. I should not mind the borrowing but for that, as they are, generally speaking, very inferior in quality to the article they lend me. In my thoughts the latter always occupy so much more important a place than their possessors, that in sending a note of invitation to Mrs. Croshie (or Crasbie, as Nancy calls her), the other day, I was on the point of writing, 'Mrs. Cregan presents her compliments to the three-branched candlestick.' But were you not speaking to me?"

"I merely asked you, mother, if you knew the cause of the change which has lately appeared in Anne Chute's manner, and which I have observed more especially since the night of the ball."

"I do," said Mrs. Cregan.

Hardress turned his face round, and looked as if he expected to hear more.

"But before I inform you," continued Mrs. Cregan, "you must answer me one question. What do you think of Anne Chute?"

"Think of her, mother!"

"Think of her, mother! You echo me, like Iago in the play. I hope it is not that you have got any such monster in your thoughts as may not meet the light."

Hardress shook his head with a smile of deep meaning. "Indeed, mother," he said, "it is far otherwise. I am ashamed to trust my lips with my opinion of Anne Chute. She is, in truth, a fascinating girl. If I were to tell you, in the simplest language, all that I think and all that I feel in her favour, you would say that you had found out a mad son in Hardress. She is indeed an incomparable young woman."

"A girl," said his mother, who heard this speech with evident satisfaction—"a girl who is far too amiable to become the victim of disappointed feelings."

"Of disappointed feelings!"

"Another echo! Why, you seem to have caught the mocking spirit from the lakes. I tell you she is within the danger of such an event."

HARDRESS AND DANNY TAKING A GLASS IN COMFORT.

"How is that, mother?"

"Close the door, and I will tell you. I see you have remarked the increasing alteration in her manner. If I should intrust you with a lady's secret, do you think you know how to venerate it?"

"Why so, mother?"

"Ah! that's a safe answer. Well, I think I may trust you without requiring a pledge. Anne Chute has met with the usual fate of young ladies at her age; she is deep in love."

Hardress felt the hot blood gather upon his breath when he heard these words. "You are jesting, mother," he said at length, and with a forced smile.

"It is a sad jest for poor Anne, however," said Mrs. Cregan, with much seriousness. "She is completely caught, indeed. I never saw a girl so much in love in my life."

"He is a happy fellow," said Hardress, after a pause, and in a deep voice; "he is either a very stupid or a very happy fellow whom Anne Chute distinguishes with her regard. And

happy he must be, for a stupid lover could never press so wearily upon the remembrance of such a girl. He is a very happy fellow."

"And yet, to look at him, you would suppose he was neither the one nor the other," said his mother.

"What is his name?"

"Can you not guess?"

The name of Kyrle Daly rose to the lips of Hardress, but from some undefinable cause he was unable to pronounce it. "Guess?" he repeated; "not I. Captain Gibson?"

"Pooh! what an opinion you have formed of Anne, if you suppose her to be one of those susceptible misses to whom the proximity of a red coat in country quarters is an affair of fatal consequence."

"Kyrle Daly, then?"

"Poor Kyrle—no. But that I think she has already chosen better, I could wish it were he, poor fellow! But you do not seem inclined to pay your cousin a compliment this morning. Do you not think you guess a little below her worth?"

"Not in Kyrle Daly. He is a lover for a queen; he is my true friend."

"That," said his mother with emphasis, "might be some recommendation."

Hardress gazed on her, as if altogether at a loss.

"Well, have you already come to a stand?" said Mrs. Cregan. "Then I believe I shall not insist on you exposing your own dulness any longer. Come hither, Hardress, and sit near me."

The young gentleman took a chair at his mother's side, and awaited her further speech with increasing interest.

"Hardress," she said, "I have a claim, independent of my natural right, to your obedience, and I must insist, in this one instance at least, on its not being contested. Listen to me. I have now an object in view, to the accomplishment of which I look forward with a passionate interest, for it has no other aim than the completion of your happiness—a concern, my beloved boy, which has always sat closest to my heart, even from your childhood. I have no child but you. My other little babes are with their Maker. I have none left but you; and I think I feel my heart yearn towards you with all the love which, if those angels had not flown from me, would have been divided amongst them."

She paused, affected; and Hardress lowered his face in deep and grateful emotion.

"It is, I think, but reasonable, therefore," Mrs. Cregan continued, "to desire your concurrence in a project which has your own happiness only for its object. Are you really so dull of perception as not to be aware of the impression you have made on the affections of Anne Chute?"

"That I—I have made?" exclaimed Hardress, with a confusion and even a wildness in his manner which looked like a compound of joy and terror. "That I—did you say, mother?"

"That you have made," repeated his mother. "It is true, indeed, Hardress. She loves you. This fascinating girl loves you long and deeply. This incomparable young woman, with whose praises you dare not trust your tongue, is pining for your love in the silence of her chamber. This beautiful and gifted creature, who is the wonder of all who see and the love of all who know her, is ready to pour forth her spirit at your feet in a murmur of expiring fondness. Use your fortunes. The world smiles brightly on you. I say again, Anne Chute is long, deeply, and devotedly your own."

Hardress drank in every accent of this poisonous speech with that fatal relish which is felt by the infatuated Eastern for his draught of stilling tincture. While he lay back in his chair, however, to enjoy the full and swelling rapture of his triumph, a horrid remembrance suddenly darted through his brain, and made him start from his chair as if he had received a blow.

"Mother," said he, "you are deceived in this. It is not, it cannot be, the fact. I see the object of which you speak, and I am sure your own anxiety for its accomplishment has led you to miscalculate. My own surmises are not in unison with yours."

"My dear child," replied his mother, "I have a far better authority than surmise for what I say. Do you think, my love, that I would run the hazard of disturbing your peace, without an absolute assurance of the truth of my statement? I have an authority that ought to satisfy the most distrustful lover; and I will be guilty of a breach of confidence, in order to set your mind at rest, for I am certain of your honour. It is the confession, the reluctant and hardly-won confession, of my darling Anne herself."

Again a revulsion of frightful rapture rushed through the frame of the listener, and made him resume his chair in silence.

"When she came here first," continued Mrs. Cregan, "I could perceive that there was a secret, although I was far from suspecting its nature. The first glimpse of light that broke upon the mystery was produced by accident. You remember poor Dalton, our old huntsman? I happened to speak to Anne of his attachment to you, and could at once observe that her interest for the man was ardently awakened."

"I remember, I remember like a dream," said Hardress, raising his finger in the manner of one endeavouring to strengthen an indistinct recollection. "Poor Dalton told me Anne had been kind to him. Anne! No, no," he added, with much confusion, "he named no one. He said a person in this house had been kind to him. I was prevented from inquiring farther."

"That person," said Mrs. Cregan, "was Anne Chute. From the moment of that conversation my eyes were opened, and I felt like one who has suddenly discovered the principle of an intricate and complicated system. I saw it in her silence while your arrival was delayed—I saw it on the morning of your meeting—I saw it throughout that day—I saw it in her dissembled grief, in her dissembled joy. Poor dear girl! I saw it in the almost childlike happiness that sparkled in her eyes when you came near us, and in the sudden gloom that followed your departure. For shame, my child! Why are you so dull of perception? Have you eyes? Have you ears? Have you a brain to comprehend, or a heart to estimate your good fortune? It should have been your part, not mine, to draw that dear acknowledgment from the lips of Anne last night."

To this observation Hardress replied only by a low moan, which had in it an expression of deep pain. "How, mother," he at length asked in a hoarse tone, "by what management did you draw this secret from her?"

"By a simple process. By making it worth her while to give me her confidence; by telling her what I have long since perceived, though it may possibly have escaped your own observation, that her passion was not unrequited—that you were as deeply in love with her as she with you."

"Me! me in love! You could not, you would not, surely, mother, speak with so much rashness?" exclaimed Hardress, in evident alarm.

"Why? Do you not love her, then?"

"Love her, mother!"

"I see you have not yet done with the echoes."

"I love her as a cousin should love a cousin—nothing more."

"Ay, but she is no cousin of yours. Come, it must be either more or less. What shall I say?"

"Neither. It is in that light I have always looked upon Anne. I could not love her less. I would not, dare not, love her more."

"Dare not! You have got a strange vocabulary for a lover. What do you mean by 'dare not?' What mighty daring is requisite to enable a young man to fall in love with a young lady, of whose affection he is already certain? The daring that is necessary for wedlock is an old bachelor's sneer, which should never be heard on lips that are ruddy with the blood of less than forty summers. Why dare you not love Anne Chute?"

"Because, by doing so, I should break my faith to another."

Mrs. Cregan fixed her eyes on him, as if somewhat stunned. "What do you say, Hardress?" she murmured, just above her breath.

"I say, mother, that my heart and faith are both already pledged to another, and that I must not break my engagement."

"Do you speak seriously?"

"I could not jest on this subject if I were so inclined."

"And dare you tell me this?" Mrs. Cregan exclaimed, starting up from her seat, with a sudden fierceness of manner. "You have no daring! You dare not love the love that I have chosen for you, and you dare tell me to my face of such a boldness as this! But dare me not too far, I warn you, Hardress. You will not find it safe."

"I dare tell the truth when I am called on," replied Hardress, who never respected his mother so little as in her moments of passion and authority, "in all places, and at all hazards, even including that of incurring my mother's displeasure."

"Listen to me, Hardress," said his mother, returning to her seat, and endeavouring to suppress her anger; "it is better we should fully understand each other."

"It is, mother; and I cannot choose a better time to be explicit than the present. I was wrong, very wrong, in not taking an earlier opportunity of explaining to you the circumstances in which I stand; but it is better even now than later. Mother," he continued, moving near to her, and taking her hand between his with a deprecating tenderness of manner, "forgive your own Hardress! I have already fixed my affections, and pledged myself to another."

Mrs. Cregan pressed her handkerchief against her face, and leaned forward on the table, which position she maintained during the dialogue which followed.

"And who is that other?" she asked with a calmness that astonished her son. "Is she superior to Anne Chute in rank or fortune?"

"Far otherwise, mother."

"In talent, then, or manner?"

"Still far beneath my cousin."

"In what, then, consists the motive of preference, for I am at a loss?"

"In everything that relates to acquirement," said Hardress, "she is not even to be compared to Anne Chute. It is in virtue alone, and in gentleness of disposition, that she can pretend to an equality. I once believed her lovelier, but I was prejudiced."

Mrs. Cregan now raised her head, and showed, by the change in her appearance, what passionate struggles she had been endeavouring to overcome. The veins had started out upon her forehead, a dull fire shone in her eyes, and one dark tress of hair, uncurled by dampness and agitation, was swept across her temples. "Poor, low-born, silly, and vulgar!" she repeated, with an air of perplexity and suppressed anger. Then, assuming an attitude of easy dignity, and forcing a smile, she said, "Oh, my dear Hardress, you must be jesting, for I am sure you could not make such a choice as you describe."

"If it is a misfortune," replied Hardress, "I must only summon up all my philosophy, mother, for there is no escaping it."

Mrs. Cregan again pressed her hand upon her brow for some moments, and then said, "Well, Hardress, let us conduct this discussion calmly. I have got a violent shooting in my head, and cannot say so much as I desire. But listen to me as I have done to you. My honour is pledged to your cousin for the truth of what I have told her. I have made her certain that her wishes shall be accomplished, and I will not have my child's heart broken. If you are serious, Hardress, you have acted a most dishonourable part. Your conduct to Anne Chute would have deceived—it has deceived—the most unbiassed amongst your acquaintances. You have paid her attentions which no honourable man could offer, while he entertained only a feeling of indifference towards their object."

"Mother! mother! how can you make such a charge as that? Was it not entirely, and reluctantly, in compliance with your own injunctions, that I did so?"

"Ay," replied Mrs. Cregan, a little struck, "but I was not then aware of your position. Why did you not then inform me of all this? Let the consequences, sir, of your duplicity fall on your own head, not on my poor girl's, nor mine. I could not have believed you capable of such a meanness. Had you then discovered all, it would have been in time for the safety of your cousin's happiness and for my own honour; for that, too, is staked in the issue. What, sir! is your vanity so egregious that, for its gratification merely, you would interfere with a young girl's prospects in life, by filling up the place at her side to which others, equal in merit and more sincere in their intentions, might have aspired? Is not that consideration alone, putting aside the keener disappointment to which you have subjected her, enough to make your conduct appear hideous?"

The truth and justice of this speech left Hardress without a word.

"You are already contracted at every fireside in Kerry and Limerick also," continued his mother; "and I am determined that there shall be no whispering about my own sweet Anne. You must perform the promise that your conduct has given."

"And my engagement?"

"Break it off!" exclaimed Mrs. Cregan, with a burst of anger, scarcely modified by her feeling of decorum. "If you have been base enough to make a double pledge, and if there must be a victim, I am resolved it shall not be Anne Chute. I must not have to reproach myself with having bound her for the sacrifice. Now, take your choice. I tell you I had rather die—nay, I had rather see you in your coffin than matched below your rank. You are yet unable to cater for your own happiness, and you would assuredly lay up a fund of misery for all your coming years. Now take your choice. If you wed as I desire, you shall have all the happiness that rank, and wealth, and honour, and domestic affection can secure you. If against my wish—if you resist me, enjoy your vulgar taste, and add to it all the wretchedness that extreme poverty can furnish; for, whether I live or die (as, indeed, I shall be careless on that subject henceforward), you never shall possess a guinea of your inheritance. So take your choice."

"It is already made," said Hardress, rising with a mournful dignity, and moving towards the door. "My fortunes are already decided, whatever way my inclinations move. Farewell, then, mother. I am grateful to you for all your former kindness, but it is impossible that I can please you in this. As to the poverty with which you intend to punish me, I can face that consequence without much anxiety, after I have ventured to incur the hazard of your anger."

He was already at the door, when his mother recalled him with a softened voice. "Hardress," she said, with tears in her eyes, "I mistake my heart entirely. It cannot afford to lose a son so easily. Come hither, and sit by me, my own beloved boy. You know not, Hardress, how I have loved and love you. Why will you anger me, my child? I never angered you; even when you were an infant at my bosom. I never denied you anything in all my life. I never gave you a hard word or look since you were a child in my arms. What have I done to you, Hardress? Even supposing that I have acted with any rashness in this, why will you insist on my suffering for it?"

"My dear mother——"

"If you knew how I have loved you, Hardress—but you can never know it, for it was shown most frequently and fondly when you were incapable of acknowledging or appreciating it—if you knew how disinterestedly I have watched and laboured for your happiness, even from your boyhood, you would not so calmly resign your mind to the idea of such a separation. Come, Hardress, we must yet be friends. I do not press you for an immediate answer; but tell me you will think of it, and think more kindly. Bid me but smile on Anne when I meet her next. Nay, don't look troubled: I shall not speak to her until I have your answer; I will only smile upon her. That's my darling Hardress!"

"But, mother——"

"Not one word more. At least, Hardress, my wishes are worth a little consideration. Look there!" she suddenly exclaimed, laying her hand on the arm of her son, and pointing through the open window; "is that not worth a little consideration?"

Hardress looked in that direction, and beheld a sight which might have proved dangerous to the resolution of a more self-regulated spirit. It was the figure of his cousin standing under the shade of a lofty arbutus, a tree which acknowledges Killarney alone, of all our northern possessions, for its natal region. A few streaks of the golden sunshine streamed in upon her figure through the boughs, and quivered over the involutions of her drapery. She was without a bonnet, and her short black ringlets, blown loose about her rather pale and careful countenance, gave it somewhat of the character of an Ariadne or a Penthesilea. She walked towards the house, and every motion of her frame seemed instinct with a natural intelligence. Hardress could not, without a nobler effort than he would use, remove his eyes from this beautiful vision, until a turn in the gravel-walk concealed it from his view, and it disappeared among the foliage, as a lustrous star is lost in a mass of autumnal clouds.

"Mother," said Hardress, "I will think on what you have said. May Heaven defend and guide me! I am a miserable wretch, but I will think of it. Oh, mother, my dear mother, if I had confided in you, or you in me! Why have we been thus secret to each other? But pardon me! It is I alone that am deserving of that reproach, for you were contriving for my happiness only. Happiness! What a vain word that is! I never shall be happy more. Never, indeed! I have destroyed my fortunes."

"Hush, boy! I hear Anne's foot upon the lobby. I told her you would walk with her to-day."

"Me walk with her!" said Hardress, with a shudder. "No, no, I cannot, mother; it would be wrong—I dare not, indeed."

"Dare not again," said Mrs. Cregan, smiling. "Come, come, forget this conversation for the present, and consider it again at your leisure."

"I will think of it," repeated the young man, with some wildness of manner. "May Heaven defend and guide me! I am a wretch already."

"Hush! hush!" said his mother, who did not attach too much importance to these exclamations of mental distress; "you must not let your mistress hear you praying in that way, or she will suppose she has frightened you."

"My mistress, mother!"

"Pooh, pooh! your cousin, then. Don't look so terrified. Well, Hardress, I am obliged to you."

"Ay, mother, but don't be misled by——"

"Oh! be in no pain for that. I understand you perfectly. Remain here, and I will send your cousin to you in a few minutes."

It would have at once put an end to all discussion on this subject if Hardress had informed his mother that he was in fact already married. He was aware of this, and yet he could not tell her that it was so. It was not that he feared her anger, for that he had already dared. He knew that he was called on, in honour, in justice, and in conscience, to make his parent aware of the full extent of his position, and yet he shunned the avowal as he would have done a sentence of despair.

CHAPTER XXII.
HOW THE TEMPTATION OF HARDRESS PROCEEDED.

DURING the few weeks that followed the conversation just detailed, Eily perceived a rapid and fearful change in the temper and appearance of her husband. His visits were fewer and shorter than before, and when he did come, his manner was restrained and cautious in an extraordinary degree. His eye looked troubled; his voice was deep and broken; his cheek grew pale and fleshless; and a gloomy air, which might be supposed the mingled result of discontent and dissipation, appeared in all his person. He no longer conversed with that noisy frankness and gaiety in which he was accustomed to indulge in all societies where he felt perfectly at ease. To Eily he spoke sometimes with coldness and impatience, and very often with a wild affection that had in it as much of grief as of tenderness. To the other inmates of the cottage he was altogether reserved and haughty, and even his own boatman seldom cared to tempt him into a conversation. Sometimes Eily was inclined to think that he had escaped from some unpleasing scenes at home, his demeanour during the evening was so abstracted and so full of care. On other occasions, when he came to her cottage late at night, she was shocked to discover about him the appearance of a riotous indulgence. Born and educated as she was in the Ireland of the eighteenth century, this circumstance would not have much disturbed the mind of our heroine, but that it became gradually more frequent of occurrence, and seemed rather to indicate a voluntary habit than that necessity to which even sober people were often subjected, when they mingled in the society of Irish country gentlemen of that period. Eily thus experienced, for the first time, and with an aching spirit, one of the keenest anxieties of married life.

"Hardress," she said to him one morning when he was preparing to depart, after an interval of gloomy silence, long unbroken, "I won't let you go among those fine ladies any more, if you be thinking of them always when you come to me again."

Her husband started like one conscience-struck, and looked sharply round upon her.

"What do you mean?" he said, with a slight contraction of the brows.

"Just what I say, then," said Eily, smiling and nodding her head with a pretty affectation of authority. "Those fine ladies mustn't take you from Eily. And I'll tell you another thing, Hardress. Whisper." She laid her hand on his shoulder, raised herself on tiptoe, and murmured in his ear, "I'll not let you among the fine gentlemen either, if that's the teaching they give you."

"What teaching?"

"Oh! you know yourself," Eily continued, nodding and smiling; "it is a teaching that you would never learn from Eily, if you spent the evenings with her as you used to do in the beginning. Do you know is there e'er a priest living in this neighbourhood?"

"Why do you ask?"

"Because I have something to tell him that lies upon my conscience."

"And would you not confess your failings to an affectionate friend, Eily, as well as to a holier director?"

"I would," said Eily, bending on him a look of piercing sweetness, "if I thought he would forgive me afterwards as readily."

"Provided always that you are a true penitent," returned Hardress, reaching her his hand.

"There is little fear of that," said Eily. "It would be well for me, Hardress, if I could as easily be penitent for heavier sins."

After a moment's deep thought, Eily resumed her playful manner, and placing both her hands in the still expanded one of her husband, she continued: "Well, then, sir, I'll tell you what's troubling me: I'm afraid I'm going wrong entirely this time back. I got married, sir, a couple o' months ago, to one Mr. Hardress Cregan, a very nice gentleman, that I'm very fond of."

"Too fond, perhaps."

"I'm afraid so, rightly speaking, although I hope *he* doesn't think so. But he told me, when he brought me down to Killarney, that he was going to speak to his friends" (the brow of the listener darkened), "and to ask their forgiveness for himself and Eily. And there's nearly two months now since I came, and what I have to charge myself with, sir, is, that I am too fond of my husband, and that I don't like to vex him by speaking about it, as maybe it would be my duty to do. And besides, I don't keep my husband to proper order at all. I let him stop out sometimes for many days together, and then I'm very angry with him; but when he comes, I'm so foolish and so glad to see him, that I can't look cross, or speak a hard word, if I was to get all Ireland for it. And more than that, again, I'm not at all sure how he spends his time while he is out, and I don't ever question him properly about it. I know there are a great many handsome young ladies where he goes to, and a deal of gentlemen that are very pleasant company after dinner; for indeed my husband is often more merry than wise, when he comes home to me late at night, and still Eily says nothing. And, besides all this, I think my husband has something weighing upon his mind, and I don't make him tell it to me, as a good wife ought to do; and I like to have a friend's advice, as you're good enough to offer it, sir, to know what I'd do. What do you think about him, sir? Do you think any of the ladies has taken his fancy? Or do you think he's growing tired of Eily? Or that he doesn't think so much of her now that he knows her better? What would you advise me to do?"

"I am rather at a loss," said Hardress, with some bitterness in his accent; "it is so difficult to advise a *jealous* person."

"Jealous!" exclaimed Eily, with a slight blush. "Ah, now I'm sorry I came to you at all, for I see you know nothing about me, since you think that's the way. I see now that you don't know how to advise me at all, and I'll leave you there. What would I be jealous of?"

"Why, of those handsome young ladies that your husband visits."

"Ah, if I was jealous that way," said Eily, with a keen and serious smile, "that isn't the way I'd show it."

"How, then, Eily?"

"Why, first of all, I wouldn't as much as think of such a thing without the greatest reason in the world, without being downright sure of it; and if I got that reason, nobody would ever know of it, for I wouldn't say a word, only walk into that room there, and stretch upon the bed and die."

"Why, that's what many a brutal husband, in such a case, would exactly desire."

"So itself," said Eily, with a flushed and kindling cheek; "so itself. I wouldn't be long in his way, I'll engage."

"Well, then," Hardress said, rising and addressing her, with a severe solemnity of manner, "my advice to you is this. As long as you live, never presume to inquire into your husband's secrets, nor affect an influence which he never will admit. And if you wish to avoid that great reason for jealousy, of which you stand in fear, avoid suffering the slightest suspicions to appear; for men are stubborn beings, and when such suspicions are wantonly set afloat, they find the temptation to furnish them with a cause almost irresistible."

"Well, Hardress," said Eily, "you are angry with me, after all. Didn't you say you would forgive me? Oh, then, I'll engage I'd be very sorry to say anything if I thought you'd be this way."

"I am not angry," said Hardress, in a tone of vexation. "I *do* forgive you," he added, in an accent of sharp reproof; "I spoke entirely for your own sake."

"And wouldn't Hardress allow his own Eily her little joke?"

"Joke!" exclaimed Hardress, bursting into a sudden fit of passion, which made his eyes water, and his limbs shake as if they would have sunk beneath him. "Am I become the subject of your mirth? Day after day my brain is verging nearer and nearer to utter madness, and do you jest on that? Do you see this cheek? You count more hollows there than when I met you first, and does that make you merry? Give me your hand! Do you feel how that heart beats? Is that a subject, Eily, for joke or jest? Do you think this face turns thin and yellow for nothing? There are a thousand and a thousand horrid thoughts and temptations burning within me daily, and eating my flesh away by inches. The devil is laughing at me, and Eily joins him."

"Oh, Hardress, Hardress!"

"Yes, you have the best right to laugh, for you are the gainer. Curse on you! Curse on your beauty—curse on my own folly—for I have been undone by both! Let go my knees! Let go my arm! I hate you! Take the truth; I'll not be poisoned with it. I am sick of you—you have disgusted me! I will ease my heart by telling you the whole. If I seek the society of other women, it is because I find not among them your meanness and vulgarity. If I get drunk and make myself the beast you say, it is in the hope to forget the iron chain that binds me to you."

"Oh, Hardress!" shrieked the affrighted girl, "you are not in earnest now?"

"I am; *I do not* joke!" her husband exclaimed with a hoarse vehemence. "Let go my knees! you are sure enough of me. I am bound to you too firmly."

"Oh, my dear Hardress! Oh, my own husband, listen to me! Hear your own Eily for one moment! Oh, my poor father!"

"Ha!"

"It slipped from me! Forgive me! I know I am to blame, I am greatly to blame, dear Hardress; but forgive me! I left my home and all for you. Oh, do not cast me off! I will do anything to please you—I never will open my lips again—only say you did not mean all that! O Heaven!" she continued, throwing her head back, and looking upward with expanded mouth and eyes, while she maintained her kneeling posture and clasped her husband's feet; "merciful Heaven, direct him! Oh, Hardress, think how far I am from home! Think of all you promised me, and how I believed you! Stay with me for a while at any rate! Do not——"

On a sudden, while Hardress was still struggling to free himself from her arms without doing her violence, Eily felt a swimming in her head and a cloud upon her sight. The next instant she was motionless.

The first face she beheld, on recovering from her insensibility, was that of Poll Naughten, who was seated in a low chair, and supporting Eily's head against her knees, while she was striking her in the open palm with a prodigious violence.

"Ah! there she dhraws the breath," said Fighting Poll. "Oh, wirra missiz! what brought you out on your face and hands on the middle of the floore, that way?"

Eily muttered some unmeaning answer, and remained for some minutes struggling with the consciousness of some undefined horror. Looking around at length, and missing the figure of Hardress, she lay back once more, and burst into a fit of hysterical weeping. Phil Naughten, who was smoking a short pipe by the fireside, said something in Irish to his wife, to which the latter replied in the same language, and then turning to Eily, said, "Will you take a dhrop of anything, a-chree?"

Eily raised her hand in dissent.

"Will you come in and take a stretch on the bed, then?"

To this Eily answered in the affirmative, and walked, with the assistance of her hostess, into her sleeping chamber Here she lay during the remainder of the day, the curtain suffered to fall so as to keep the broad sunshine from her aching eyes and head. Her reflections, however, on the frightful and sudden alteration which had taken place in her condition, were cut short, ere long, by a sleep of that sound and dreamless nature which usually supervenes after an excess of passionate excitement or anxiety.

In the mean time Hardress hurried along the Gap Road with the speed of one who desires to counteract, by extreme bodily exertion, the turbulence of an uneasy spirit. As he passed the lonely little bridge which crosses the stream above the Black Lake, his attention was suddenly arrested by the sound of a familiar voice, which appeared to reach him from the clouds. Looking over his shoulder to the summit of the Purple Mountain, he beheld Danny Mann, nearly a thousand feet above him, moving towards the immense pile of loose stones (from the hue

of which the mountain has derived its name), and driving before him a small herd of goats, the property of his brother-in-law. Turning off the road, Hardress commenced the ascent of this toilsome eminence, partly because the difficulty afforded a relief to his spirits, and partly because he wished to converse with his dependent.

Although the day was fine, and sometimes cheered with sunshine near the base of the mountain, its summit was wrapped in mist, and wet with incessant showers. The scenery around was solitary, gigantic, and sternly barren. The figure of some wonder-hunting tourist, with a guide-boy bearing his portfolio and umbrella, appeared at long intervals among the lesser undulations of the mountain-side, and the long road which traversed the gloomy valley dwindled to the width of a meadow footpath. On the opposite side of the enormous ravine the grey and misty Reeks still raised their crumbling summits far above him. Masses of white mist gathered in sullen congress between their peaks, and, sometimes floating upward in large volumes, were borne majestically onward, catching a thousand tints of gold and purple from the declining sun. Sometimes a trailing shower of mingled mist and rain would sweep across the intervening chasm, like the sheeted spectre of a giant, and present to the eye of the spectator that appearance which supplied the imagination of Ossian with its romantic images. The mighty gorge itself, at one end, appeared to be lost and divided amid a host of mountains, tossed together in provoking gloom and misery. Lower down it opened upon a wide and cultivated champaign, which at this altitude presented the resemblance of a rich mosaic of a thousand colours, and afforded a bright contrast to the barren, shrubless gloom of the solitary vale itself. As Hardress approached the summit, this scene of grandeur and of beauty was shut out from his view by the intervening mist, which left nothing visible but the peak on which he stood, and which looked like a barren islet in a sea of vapour. Above him was a blue sky, broken up with masses of cloud, against which the rays of the sun were refracted with various effect, according to their degrees of density and altitude. Occasionally, as Hardress pressed onward through the heath, a heavy grouse would spring up at his feet, challenge, and wheel to the other side of the mountain. Sometimes, also, as he looked downward, a passing gust of wind would draw aside the misty veil that lay between him and the world, and cause the picture once more to open on his sight.

His attendant now met and greeted him as usual. "It's well for you, Masther Hardress, dat hasn't a flock o' goats to be huntin' after dis mornin'; my heart is broke from 'em, dat's what it is. We turn 'em out in the mornin', an' dough dey have plenty to ait below dere, dey never stop till dey go to the top o' the mountain—nothin' less would do for 'em. Like many o' the Christians demselves, they'll be mountin' always, even when 'tis no good for 'em."

"I have no remedy," said Hardress, musing, "and yet the thought of enduring such a fate is intolerable."

"What a fine day this would be for the water, master!" continued his servant. "You don't ever care to take a sail now, sir."

"Oh, Kyrle, Kyrle Daly, what a prophetic truth was in your words! Giddy, headlong wretch that I have been!—I wish that my feet had grown to my mother's hearth when I first thought of evading her control, and marrying without her sanction." He paused in a mood of bitter retrospection. "I'll not endure it," he again exclaimed, starting from his reverie; "it shall not be without recall. I will not, because I cannot! Monster! monster that I am! Wed one, and woo another! Both now are cheated! Which shall be the victim?"

The devil was at his ear, and whispered, "Be not uneasy; hundreds have done the same before you."

"Firm as dat mountain stands, an' as it stood dis hundred, ay, dis tousand year, maybe," continued Danny Mann, "still an' all, to look up dat way at dem great loose stones, dat look as if dey were shovelled up above us by some joyants or great people of ould, a body would tink it hardly safe to stand here under 'em, in dread dey'd come tumblin' down, maybe, an' make *smidereens* of him, bless the mark! Wouldn't he now, Master Hardress?"

The person thus addressed turned his eyes mechanically in the same direction. A kind of desperate satisfaction was visible on his features, as the idea of insecurity which his servant suggested became impressed upon his mind. The latter perceived and understood its expression on the instant.

"Dere's something troublin' you, Master Hardress; dat I see plain enough. An' 'tisn't now, nor to-day, nor 'isterday, I seen it aider. Is dere anyting Danny Mann can do to sarve you? If dere be, say de word dis moment, an' I'll be bail he'll do it before long."

"Danny," said Hardress, after a pause, "I *am* troubled. I was a fool, Danny, when I refused to listen to your advice upon one occasion."

"An' dat was de time when I tould you not to go again' de missiz, an' to have no call to Eily O'Connor."

"It was."

"I tought it would be dis way. I tought all along dat Eily was no wife for you, Master Hardress. It was not in nature she could be—a poor man's daughter, widout money, or manners, or book-larnen', or one ha'port.' I told you dat, Master Hardress, but you wouldn't hear me by any means, an' dis is de way of it now."

"Well, well, 'tis done, 'tis done," said Hardress, with sullen impatience. "I was to blame, and I am suffering for it."

"Does she know herself de trouble she is to you?"

"I could not keep it from her. I did not know myself how utterly my dislike had prevailed within me until the occasion arose for giving it utterance, and then it came forth at once like a torrent. I told her what I felt; that I hated, that I was sick of her. I could not stop my tongue. My heart struck me for the base unkindness, the ungrateful ruffianism of my speech, and yet I could not stop my tongue. I have made her miserable, and I am myself accursed. What is there to be done? Have you only skill to prevent mischief? Have you none to remedy?"

Danny took thought for a moment. "Sorrow trouble would I ever give myself about her," he said at last, "only send her home packin' to her fader, an' give her no tanks."

"And with what face should I appear before my honourable friends, when that old rope-maker should come to demand redress for his insulted child, and to claim her husband's promise? Should I send Eily home to earn for myself the reputation of a faithless villain?"

"I never tought o' dat," said Danny, nodding his head. "Dat's a horse of anoder colour. Why, then, I'll tell you what I'd do. Pay her passage out to Quabec, and put her aboord of a three-master, widout ever sayin' a word to anybody. I'll tell you what it is, Master Hardress. Do by her as you do by dat glove you have on your hand. Make it come off as it come on, and if it fits too tight take de knife to it."

"What do you mean?"

"Only gi' me de word, as I said before, and I'll engage Eily O'Connor will never trouble you any more. Don't ax me any questions at all, only, if you're agreeable, take off dat glove an' give it to me for a token. Dat'll be enough; lave de rest to Danny."

A doubtful, horrible sensation of fear and anxiety gathered upon the heart of the listener, and held him for a minute fixed in breathless agitation. He gazed upon the face of his servant with an expression of gaping terror, as if he stood in the presence of the arch-tempter himself. At length, walking up to him, he laid his open hand upon his neck, and then drawing his fingers close, until the fellow's face was purple with blood, he shook him as if he would have shaken his joints out of their sockets.

"Villain!" he exclaimed, with a hoarseness and vehemence of tone which gave an appalling depth to his expressions; "dangerous villain and tempter! if you ever dare again to utter a word, or meditate a thought of violence towards that unhappy creature, I will tear you limb from limb between my hands."

"Oh, murder, Master Hardress! Dat the hands may stick to me, sir, if I tought a ha'port' o' harm!"

"Do you mark me well, now? I am quite in earnest. Respect her as you would the highest lady in the land. Do as she commands you without murmuring. If I hear her say (and I will question her upon it), that you have leered one glance of those blood-longing eyes upon her, it shall be their last look in this world."

"Oh, vo! Dat I may never die in sin Master Hardress, if——"

"Begone! I am glad you have opened my eyes. I tread more safely now. My heart is lighter. Yet that I should have endured to be so tempted! Fellow, I doubt you for worse than

you appear. We are here alone; the world, the busy world, is hid beneath us, and we stand here alone in the eye of the open Heaven, and without roof or wall to screen us, even in fancy, from the downright reproach of the beholding angels. None but the haughty and insulting Lucifer himself could think of daring Providence upon the threshold of His own region. But be you fiend or mortal, I defy and dare you; I repel your bloody temptation. I tell you, fiend or mortal, that my soul abhors your speech and gesture, both. I may be wretched and impious; I may send up to heaven a cry of discontent and murmuring; the cry of blood shall never leave this earth for me. Blood! *Whose* blood? Hers? Great Heaven! Great Heaven, defend me!" He covered his face with his hands, and bent down for a moment in dreadful agitation; then suddenly starting up, and waving his hand rapidly, he continued,—"Away, away at once, and quit my sight. I have chosen my doom. My heart may burn for years within my breast, if I can find no other way to soothe it. I know how to endure. I am wholly ignorant of guilt like this. Once more," he added, clenching his fist, and shaking it towards his startled dependent, "once more I warn you, mark my words and obey them."

So saying, he hurried down the hill, and was hid in the ascending mist, while his affrighted servant remained gaping after him, and muttering mechanically such asseverations as, "Dat I may never sin, Master Hardress! dat de head may go to de grave wid me! dat I may be happy! dat de hands may stick to me, if I tought any harm!"

More than half of the frantic speech of Hardress, it may be readily imagined, was wholly unintelligible to Danny, who followed him down the mountain, half crazy with terror, and not a little choked into the bargain.

CHAPTER XXIII.

HOW AN UNEXPECTED VISITOR ARRIVED IN EILY'S COTTAGE.

TOWARDS nightfall Eily awoke with that confused and strange feeling which a person experiences who has slept at an unaccustomed hour. The sun had already set; but the red and faintly lustrous shadow of the window, which was thrown on the opposite wall, showed that his refracted light was yet strong and bright on the horizon. While she lay back, endeavouring to recall the circumstances which brought her into her present situation, a voice assailed her ear which made her start in sudden alarm from her reclining posture. It was that of a person singing in a low voice, outside her window, the following words:—

> "As I roved out on a fine summer morning,
>   A speculating most curiously,
> To my surprise, I soon espied
>   A charming fair one approaching me.
> I stood a while——"

Here the melodist knocked gently at the door of the cottage.

> "I stood a while in deep meditation,
>   Contemplating what I should do;
> Till at length, recruiting all my sensation,
>   I thus accosted the fair Colleen rue." *

At the close of the verse, which was prolonged by the customary nasal twang, the singer knocked a little more loudly with the knuckle of his fore-finger:—

> "Oh, was I Hecthor, that noble viethor,
>   Who died a victim to the Grecian skill;
> Or was I a Paris, whose deeds were vaarious,
>   As an arbithraantor on Ida's hill,
> I'd roam through Asia, likewise Arabia,
>   Or Pennsylvania——"

Here he knocked again.

> "Or Pennsylvania, looking for you,
> Through the burning ragions, like famed Orphesus,
>   For one embrace of you, Colleen rue."

"I am ruined! I am undone!" thought Eily, as she listened in deep distress and fear. "My father has found me out, and they are all come to look for me. Oh, Hardress, Hardress!"

"They're all dead or dhraming here, I believe," said the singer. "I'm in fine luck if I have to go down the ould Gap again afther nightfall." Stimulated by this reflection, he turned his back to the door, and began kicking against it with his heel, while he continued his song:—

* Red-haired girl.

"And are you Aurora, or the goddess Flora,
 Or Eutherpasia, or fair Vanus bright,
 Or Helen fair, beyond compare,
 Whoam Paris stole from the Grecian's sight?
Thou fairest creature, how you 've enslaved me!
 I 'm intoxicated by Cupid's clue,
Whoase golden notes and infatuations
 Have deranged my ideas for you, Colleen rue."

Here the same air was taken up by a shrill and broken female voice, at a little distance from the house, and in the words which follow:—

"Sir, I pray be aisy, and do not tease me
 With your false praises most jeatingly;
Your golden notes and insiniwayshuns
 Are vaunting speeches, desaiving me.
I am not Aurora, nor the goddess Flora,
 But a rural female to all men's view,
Who 's here condoling my situation,
 And my appellation is the Colleen rue."

"You 're not Aurora!" muttered the first voice. "Wisha, dear knows, it isn't aisy to conthradict you. They 'd be the dhroll Auroras an' Floras, if that 's the figure they cut. Ah, Mrs. Naughten!" he added, raising and changing his voice as the shadow of the female figure crossed the window of Eily's apartment, "how are you this evening, ma'am? I hope you got well over your voyage that morning?"

"What voyage? Who is it I have there at all?" said Poll, in a tone of surprise. "Oh, Lowry Looby! Oh, ma-gra-hu! how is every inch of you, Lowry? It raises the very cockles o' my heart to see you."

"Purty well, indeed, as for the health, Mrs. Naughten, we 're obleest to you."

"Oh, vo, vo! An' what brought you into this part of the world, Lowry? It 's a long time since you an' I met."

"'Tis as good as two months, a'most, I b'lieve."

"Two months, eroo? 'Tis six years if it 's a day."

"Oh, iss, for good; but I mane the time we met in the cottage behind at the dairy-farm, the night o' the great storm, when ye were near being all lost in the boat, if it wasn't the will o' Heaven."

"The dairy-farm! lost in the boat! I don't know what is it you 're talkin' about at all, man. But come in, come in, Lowry, and take a sate. Stop, here 's Phil. Phil, eroo, this is Lowry Looby, that you heerd me talk of being a friend o' the Hewsans formerly."

Thus introduced, Phil and Lowry both took off their hats, and bowed repeatedly with a most courteous profundity of obeisance. The door was then opened, and a polite contest arose as to the right of precedence between the gentlemen, which was finally decided in favour of Lowry, as the visitor.

"Well, Lowry, what news eastwards?" was the next question.

"Oh, then, nothing sthrange, Mrs. Naughten. I was twice by this way since I seen you that night. Coming from Cork I was to-day, when I thought I 'd step over and see how you wor afther the voyage. I left the horse an' car over in Mr. Cregan's yard."

"I believe you 're lost with the hunger. Phil, stir yourself, an' put down something for supper."

"Don't hurry yourself on my account," said Lowry, affecting an indifference which he did not feel; "I took something at Mr. Cregan's. I saw Masther Hardress there in the parlour windee, playin' chests (I think it is they called it), with Miss Anne Chute. Oh, murder, that 's a darling, a beautiful lady! Her laugh is like music. O dear! O dear! To see the smile of her, though, an' she looking at him! It flogged the world! Mike, the boy they have there, an' old Nancy told me she 's greatly taken with the young masther."

"Why, then, she may as well throw her cap at him."

"Why so, eroo?"

"Oh, for raisons."

"There 's one thing Mike told me, an' I 'm sure I wondher I never heerd a word of it before—that there was some talks of herself and my young masther, Mr. Kyrle Daly. I know he used to be going there of an odd time, but I never heard anything that way. There 's a dale that 's looking afther her, Mike tells me. Whoever gets her, they say, he 'll have as much jewels to fight as will keep him going for the first quarther, any way."

"Tha go bragh," said Phil, tossing his head; "that 's what bothers the gentlemen. Jewels, jewels, always."

"Jewels always, then, just as you say, Misther Naughten," said Lowry. "It 's what ruins 'em, body and soul. At every hand's turn, nothing but a jewel! Let there be a conthrairy look, and pistols is the word at once."

"An' if a poor boy is reflected upon, an' goes to a fair to thry it out with an innocent little kippen, 'Oh, the savages!' the gentlemen cry at once; 'oh, the blood-thirsty villyans!' And they 'll go themselves and shoot one another like dogs, for less raison."

"It 's thrue for you," returned Lowry. "Sure 'twould be a blessing for a man to be aiting a dhry piatie from morning till night, an' to have quietness. I 'll tell you what it is, Misther Naughten, I spake for myself: of all things going, I wouldn't like to be a born gentleman. They 're never out o' trouble, this way or that way. If they 're not fighting, they have more things upon their mind than would bother a dozen poor men; an' if they go divarting, ten to one they have a jewel before the day is over. Sure, if it was a thing two gentlemen axed a lady to dance, an' she gave in to one of 'em, the other should challenge him for to go fighting! Sure that flogs Europe! And they have so much books to read to be able to converse genteel before the ladies. I 'm told a gentleman isn't fit to show his face in company till he reads as much books as would stretch from this to the doore over. And then to be watching yourself, an' spake Englified, an' not to ate half your 'nough at dinner, an' to have 'em all looking at you if you took too big a bit or done anything again' manners, and never to have your own fling, an' let you do what you liked yourself! I wouldn't lade such a life if I got Europe. A snug stool by the fireside, a boiled piatee in one hand, a piggin o' milk in the other, and one (that I won't name now), smiling overright me, that 's all the gentility I 'd ever ax for in this world, any way. I 'd a'most as lieve be born a female as a gentleman, maning no offence to the ladies, Mrs. Naughten."

"Every one to his taste, Lowry. Many men have many minds. Phil, will you go out now and help Danny to put up them goats, not to have them strayin' over on Myles Murphy's ground as they wor o' Cheusday week? I see Danny coming down the mountain."

The obedient husband did as he was commanded, and Lowry took advantage of his absence to enter into a more confidential communication with his formidable hostess.

"Well, Mrs. Naughten, if I was to hear a person swear this upon a book, I 'd say 'twas a lie he was telling me, if I didn't see it with my own eyes."

"What is it you see?"

"Oh! then, nothing but what I 'm well pleased to see. Well, I thought that one that once gave themselves a bad habit could never be broke of it again, no more than a horse could be broke of starting."

At this the virago fixed upon him a kindling and suspicious eye.

"And tell me now, Mrs. Naughten," continued Lowry, not perceiving the indication of incipient wrath, "how did it come on you first, when you dhropt the cursing that way entirely? I think I 'd feel a great loss for the first week or fortnight."

"Folly on, Misther Looby, folly on! You 're welcome to your sport this evening."

"Sport? Faiks, it 's no sport to me, only an admiration. All the people that I ever heerd of making a vow o' the kind wor sure to break it again, if they didn't get inside of it one way or another by shkaming. Sure there was, to my knowledge, John O'Reilly, the blacksmith, near Castle Chute, made as many vows as I have fingers an' toes again' the dhrink, and there isn't one of 'em but what he got the advantage of. First he med a vow he wouldn't dhrink a dhrop for six months to come, any way, either in a house or out of a house. An' sure 'tis where I found him the fortnight afther, was at Mike Normile's, an' he dhrinking as if it was for bets, an' sitting in a chair upon the threshold o' the doore, with a leg at this side and a leg at that. 'Is that the way you 're keeping your vow, Misther O'Reilly?' says I, when I see him. ''Tis,' says he: 'what else? Sure I can dhrink here,' says he, 'an' no thanks, while I 'm neither in the house nor out it.' An' sure 'twas thrue for him. Well, there 's no use in talking, but some people would live where a fox would starve. Sure, of another time, he med a vow he wouldn't drink upon Ireland ground, an' where do you think did I get him afther, only sitting cross-legs upon a branch o' the big beech tree near Normile's, an' he still at the ould work, dhrinking away! 'Wisha, long life to you,' says I, 'if that's the way; a purty fruit the tree bears in you,' says I, 'this morning.' People o' that kind, Mrs. Naughten, has no business making vows at all again' the dhrink or the cursing either."

"I'm hearing to you, Lowry," said Fighting Poll, with an ominous sharpness in her accent.

"An' do you hold to the same plan still, ma'am?"

"What plan do you mane?"

"The same plan as when I met you that night at the Dairy Cottage. Not to be talking, nor drinking, nor cursing, nor swearing, nor fighting, nor—— Oh, murther, Mrs. Naughten! sure you 're not going to sthrike me inside your own doore?"

"To be sure I would, when I see you daar make a hand o' me!"

"Me make a hand o' you, woman! What hand am I makin'?"

"Every hand!" exclaimed the Penthesilea, raising her voice. So saying, and with the accustomed yell of onset, she flourished her short stick, and discharged a blow at Lowry's little head, which, if it had not been warded off by a dexterous interposition of the chair on which he had been sitting, would have left him something to think of for a week to come.

The scuffle waxed hot, and would doubtless have terminated in some serious bodily injury to the party assailed, but that the sudden re-entrance of Phil, with his brother-in-law, Danny Mann, brought it to a premature termination.

"Poll! Poll, ayeh! Misther Looby! What's the matter? Worn't ye as thick as cousins this moment?"

"Ah, Lowry, is dat you? What's all dis about?"

"Don't hould me, Phil, an' I'll bate him while bating is good for him; an' that 's from this till morning."

"Here 's usage, Mr. Naughten! Mr. Mann, here 's thratement! Gi' me my ould hat an' let me be off; I was a fool to come at all! And after my civility eastwards, when you come dhripping wet into the cottage! Well, it's all one."

"Whist, eroo!" said Danny Mann, in a conciliating tone, "come dis way, Lowry, I want to talk to you." And he led him out of the cottage.

Eily, who was perfectly aware of the cause of this misconception, had listened to the whole scene, at one time with intense and painful anxiety, and at another with an inclination to laugh, in spite of all the difficulties and dangers by which she was surrounded. Before long, however, an idea entered her mind, which wholly detached her attention from the *mêlée* in the kitchen. She resolved to write to her father by Lowry, to make him aware at least, of her safety, and of her hope to meet him again in honour, if not in happiness. This would at least remove one great load from her mind, and prepare him for her return. While she arranged her writing materials at the small table, the thoughts of home came crowding on her so thick and fast, that she found a difficulty in proceeding with her task. It was a humble home, to be sure, but yet it *was* her home. He was a humble father, but he *was* her father. She painted a little picture, unconsciously to her own mind, of that forsaken dwelling. She saw her father sitting by the turf fire, leaning forward with his elbow resting on his knee, a finger beneath his temple, and his grey watery eye fixed on her accustomed chair, which stood empty, on the opposite side. His hair had received another shower of silver since they parted. She scarcely dared to breathe aloud, lest she should disturb the imagined loneliness of his condition. On a sudden she figured to herself the latched door put gently back, and the form of Lowry Looby entering with her letter in his hand. She marked the air of cold and sad indifference with which the old man recognised him and received the letter. He looked at the direction—started—tore off the seal, and looked within, while his whole frame trembled until the grey hairs were shaken loose upon his temples; she saw the passion struggling in his throat, and her own eyes were blinded by tears. The picture here became too vivid for her feelings, and pushing the little desk aside, she sank down into her chair in a violent fit of sobbing.

While she remained in this condition, Poll Naughten entered the room, arranging her disordered head-dress, and bearing still upon her countenance the traces of the vanished storm. Its expression, however, was completely altered when she observed the situation of Eily.

"What ails you, a'ra gal?" she asked in a softened voice. "Arn't you betther afther the sleep at all?"

"Poll, do you know that man who is in the kitchen?"

"Is it Lowry Looby? Ah ha! the scoundhril! 'tis I that do, an' I'll make him he 'll know me, too, before I part him."

"Hush, Poll; come hither. I want you to do me a service. I know this man too."

"Why, then, he's little credit to you or any one else."

"I want to caution you against saying a word of my name while he is in the house. It would be ruinous both to your master and myself."

"Faiks, I 'll engage he won't be a bit the wiser of it for Poll Naughten."

"And I wish, besides, that you would give him, if he intends going to Limerick, a letter which I will have for you in a few minutes. You need not tell him from whom it comes; do not even let him know that it is from a person in the house. And now, Poll, will you light me one of those candles, and close the window-shutters?"

This was done, and Eily commenced her letter. Before she proceeded far, however, it occurred to her that the superscription might awaken the suspicions of Lowry; and besides, she felt a very accountable difficulty about the manner of addressing her offended parent. Finally, she decided on forwarding a brief and decorous note to "Mr. Dunat O'Leary, Hair-cutter, Garryowen;" in which she requested him to communicate to his old neighbour the circumstances of which she desired the latter should be made aware.

Whilst she folded the letter she heard the cottage door once more open, and two persons enter the kitchen. A stillness ensued, which was broken by the voice of Danny Mann.

"I was spaking to dis boy here, Poll," he said, "an' I see 'tis all rising out of a mistake betune de two o' ye. He didn't mane anything by it, he tells me. Eh, Lowry?"

"It would be long from me, Mrs. Naughten, to say anything offensive to you, or any o' your people. Misther Mann, here, explained to me the nature of the matther. I own I didn't mane a ha'porth."

"Well, that's enough, that 's enough. Give him the hand now, Poll," said her husband, "and let us ate our little supper in pace."

Eily heard no more, and the clatter of knives and forks, soon after, informed her that the most perfect harmony had been re-established amongst the parties. Nothing further occurred to disturb the good understanding which was thus fortunately restored, or to endanger the secret of our heroine, although Lowry was not without making many inquiries as to the name and quality of the lodger in the inner room. It was a long time, too, before he had ceased to speculate on the nature of the letter to Foxy Dunat. On this his hostess would give him no information, although he threw out several hints of his anxiety to obtain it, and made many conjectures of his own, which he invariably ended by tossing the head, and declaring that "it flogged the world."

CHAPTER XXIV.

HOW EILY UNDERTAKES A JOURNEY IN THE ABSENCE OF HER HUSBAND.

EILY heard Lowry Looby take his departure on the next morning with as lively a sensation of regret as if he had been a dear friend. After the unkindness of her husband, she trembled while she wept to think that it might be a long time before she could meet one more interested in her fortunes.

Happier anticipations than this might not have been so perfectly fulfilled. The first weeks of winter swept rapidly away, and Eily neither saw nor heard from Hardress. Her situation became every moment more alarming. Her host and hostess, according as she appeared to grow out of favour with their patron, became at first negligent and surly, and at last insulting. She had hitherto maintained her place on the sunny side of Poll's esteem, by supplying that virago with small sums of money from time to time, although her conscience told her that those donations were not appropriated by the receiver to any virtuous end. But now her stock was running low. Hardress —and this was from mere lack of memory—had left her almost wholly unprovided with funds.

She resolved to write to him, not with the view of obtaining mere pecuniary assistance, but in order to communicate the request which is subjoined in her own simple language:—

DANNY FULFILLING HIS MASTER'S WISHES.

"MY DEAR HARDRESS,

"Do not leave me here to spend the whole winter alone. If Eily has done anything to offend you, come and tell her so; but remember that she is now away from every friend in the whole world. Even if you are still in the same mind as when you left me, come, at all events, for once, and let me go back to my father. If you wish it, nobody besides us three, shall ever know what you were to your own

"EILY."

To this letter, which she intrusted to Danny the Lord, she received no answer, neither Hardress nor his servant being seen at the cottage for more than a week after.

Matters in the mean time grew more unpleasing between Eily and her hosts. Poll treated her with the most contemptuous rudeness, and Phil began to throw out hints which it was difficult to misconceive, respecting their poverty, and the unreasonableness of people thrusting idlers upon them, when it was as much as they could do to maintain themselves in honesty. But Poll, who possessed the national recklessness of expense, whenever her husband spoke in this niggardly humour, turned on him, not in defence of Eily, but in abuse of his "mainness," although she could herself use the very same cause of invective when an occasion offered. Thus Eily, instead of commanding like a queen, as she had been promised, was compelled to fill the pitiable situation of an insecure and friendless dependent.

The wintry year rolled on in barrenness and gloom, casting an air of iron majesty and grandeur over the savage scenery in which she dwelt, and bringing close to her threshold the first Christmas which she had ever spent away from home. The Christmas eve found her still looking anxiously forward to the return of her husband, or of his messenger. The morning had brought with it a black frost, and Eily sat down alone to a comfortless breakfast. No longer attended with that ready deference which marked the conduct of the Naughtens while she remained in favour, Eily was now obliged to procure and arrange all the materials for her repast with her own hands. There was no butter nor cream; but as this was one of the great vigils or fast days of her church, which Eily observed with a conscientious exactness, she did not miss these prohibited luxuries. There was no fast upon sugar, however, and Eily perceived, with some chagrin, that the sugar-bowl also was empty. She walked softly to the chamber-door, where she paused for a moment, with her handkerchief placed before her cheeks, in that beautiful attitude which Homer ascribes to Penelope at the entrance of the "stout-built hall." At length she raised the latch, and opened the door to a few inches only.

"Poll," she said, in a timid and gentle voice, "do you know where's the sugar?"

"It's in the *cubbert*, I suppose," was the harsh and unceremonious answer.

The fact was, Poll had begun to keep the Christmas the evening before, and treated herself to a few tumblers of hot punch, in the manufacture of which she had herself consumed the whole of Eily's sweets. And there might have been some cause of consolation, if Poll's temper had been rendered the sweeter by all the sugar she took; but this was not the case.

"There is none there, Poll," said Eily.

"Well, what hurt? Can't you put a double allowance o' crame in the tay, and dhrink it raw for once?"

"Ah, but this is a fast day," said Eily.

"Oyeh, choke it for work! Well, then, do as you plase; I can't help you. I haven't a spoonful o' groceries in the house, girl, except I went for 'em—a thing I 'd be very unfond to do on a mornin' like this."

"Well, I can do without it, Poll," said Eily, returning to the table, and sitting down to her unmetaphorically bitter draught with the meekest resignation.

"Gi' me the money by-an'-by, when I'm goin' into town for the Christmas candle, an' I 'll buy it for you, itself an' the tay."

"But I have no money, Poll."

"No money, inagh? An' isn't it upon yourself wo 're depending this way to get in the things again' to-morrow, a Christmas day?"

"Well, I have not a farthing."

"Didn't you tell me yourself, the other day, you had a half-crown keepin' for me again' Hansel Monday?"

"I gave it to Danny. I thought I'd have more for you before then."

Here Poll dashed in the door with her hand, and confronted her affrighted lodger with the look and gesture of a raging Bacchanal.

"An' is that my thanks?" she screamed aloud. "Why, then, cock you up with bread and tay this mornin'. Go look afther Danny, now, if you want your *bruk'ast*." And so saying, she seized two corners of the table-cloth, and upset the whole concern into the fireplace.

Terror and astonishment deprived Eily for some moments of the power of speech or motion; but when she saw Poll taking breath for a moment, and looking around to know what further devastation she might commit, the forlorn helplessness of her condition rushed at once upon her mind, and she fell back into her seat in a violent fit of hysterics.

This is a condition in which one woman can rarely behold another without emotion. Poll ran to her relief, uttering every sound of affectionate condolence and encouragement which arose to her lips.

"Whist, now, a'ra gal! Whist, now, missiz, a-chree! Oh, ma chree, ma'asthora, ma llanuv, you wor! Howl, now, a'ra gal! Oh! vo! vo!—howl, asthore! What ails you? Sure you know 'tis only funnin' I was .Well, see this! Tell me anything now in the wide world I 'll do it for you, a'ra gal."

"Poll," said Eily, when she had recovered a certain degree of composure, "there is one thing that you can do for me, if you like, and it will relieve me from the greatest distress."

"An' what is that, a-chree?"

"To lend me one of the ponies, and get me a boy that can show me the way to Castle Island."

"Is it goin' you're thinkin' of?"

"I will be here again," said Eily, "on to-morrow evening." Eily spoke this without any vehemence of asseition, and in the quiet manner of one who had never been accustomed to have her words doubted. So irresistible, too, is the force of simple truth, that Poll did not even entertain a suspicion of any intent to deceive.

"An' what business would carry you to Castle Island, a'ra gal?"

"I have a friend there, an uncle," Eily replied, with tears starting into her eyes at the remembrance of her old preceptor. "I am sure, Poll, that he would assist me."

"I'm in dhread 'tis goin' from uz you are now, o' count o' what I said to you. Don't mind that at all. Stop here as long as ever you like, an' no thanks. I 'll step across the road this minute, an' *borry* the sugar for you, if it 's it you want."

"No, no; I only want you to do as I have told you. I 'll engage to screen you from all blame."

"Blame! Ah! whose blame is it you think I'd be afeerd of? I 'll let you see that I 'll do what I like myself, an' get you the pony saddled an' all this minute. But you didn't ate anything hardly. Here 's more bread in the cubbert, an' strengthen yourself again' the road while I 'm away."

She left the room, and Eily, who had little hope of succeeding so easily in her request, proceeded to make her preparations for the journey with as much dispatch and animation as if she had discovered a sudden mode of release from all her anxieties. For a considerable time the prospect of meeting with her uncle filled her bosom with a sensation of unmingled pleasure. If she looked back while she tied her bonnet strings below her chin, and hurried on the plainest dress in her trunk—if she looked back to those days in which her venerable relative presided over her evening studies, and directed their application, it was only to turn her eyes again upon the future, and hope for their speedy renovation.

Having concluded her arrangements, and cautioned Poll not to say a word of her destination in case Hardress should come to the cottage, Eily now set out upon her lonely journey. The person whom Poll Naughten had procured her for a guide, was a stout-made girl, who carried an empty spirit-keg slung at her back in the tail of her gown, which she had turned up over her shoulders. She informed Eily that she was accustomed to go every Saturday to a town at the distance of fourteen miles, and to return in the evening with the keg full of spirits. "But this week," she continued, "I'm obleest to go twice, on account o' the Christmas day falling in the middle of it."

"And what does your employer want with so much whiskey?" said Eily, a little interested in the fortune of so hard-working a creature.

"Want wi' the whiskey, inagh?" exclaimed the mountain girl, turning her black eyes on her companion in surprise. "Sure isn't it she that keeps the public-house above the Gap? An' what business would she have wid a place o' the kind without a dhrop o' whiskey?"

"And what are you paid, now, for so long a journey as that?"

"Different ways I'm paid different times. If it is a cowld evening when I come home, I take a glass o' the spirits itself, in preference to anything, an' if not, the misthress pays me a penny every time!"

"One penny only!"

"One penny. Indeed, it's too little, but when I spake of it, the misthress tells me she can get it done for less. So I have nothin' to say, but do as I 'm bid."

Eily paused for some moments, while she compared the situation of this uncomplaining individual with her own. The balance of external comforts, at least, did not appear to be on the side of the poor little mountaineer.

"And have you no other way of living, now, than this?" she asked, with increasing interest.

"Illilo! Is it upon a penny a week you think I 'd live?" returned the girl, who was beginning to form no very exalted idea of her companion's intellect.

"Do you live with your mistress?"

"No, I live with my ould father. We have a spot o' ground beyant for the piatees. Sometimes I dig it; but mostly the young boys o' the place comes and digs it for us on a Sunday or a holiday mornin', an' I stick in the seed."

"And is it for the sake of the father or the daughter they take that trouble?"

"For the sake, I b'lieve, of the Almighty that made 'em both. Signs on, they have our prayers, night an' mornin'."

"Is your father quite helpless?"

"Oyeh! long from it. He's a turner; he makes little boxes, and necklaces, and things that way, of the arbutus and the black oak of the Lakes, that he sells to the English and other quollity people that comes to see them. But he finds it hard to get the timber, for none of it is allowed to be cut, and 'tis only windfalls that he can take when the stormy saison begins.

Besides, there's more in the town o' Killarney that outsells him. He makes but a poor hand of it, afther all."

"I wonder you have not got a sweetheart. You are very pretty and very good."

The girl here gave her a sidelong glance, and laughed so as to exhibit a set of teeth of the purest enamel. The look seemed to say, "Is that all you know about the matter?" but her words were different in their signification.

"Oyeh, I don't like 'em for men," she said with a half smiling, half coquettish air; "they're deceivers an' rovers, I believe, the best o' 'em."

"Well, I wouldn't think that, now, of that handsome young man in the check shirt, that nodded to you as we passed him awhile ago: he has an honest face."

The girl again laughed and blushed. "Why, then, I'll tell you," she said at length, seduced into a confidence. "If I'd b'lieve any of 'em, I think it is that boy; he is a boatman on the Lakes, and airns a sight o' money, but it goes as fast as it comes."

"How is that?"

"Oh! then, he can't help it, poor fellow. Them boatmen arn't allowed to dhrink anything while they're upon the Lakes, except at the *stations*; but then, to make up for that, they all meet at night at a hall in town, where they stay dancing and dhrinking all night, till they spend whatever the quollity gives 'em in the day. Luke Kennedy (that's this boy), would like to save if he could, but the rest wouldn't pull an oar with him if he didn't do as they do. So that's the way of it. And sometimes, after being up all night a'most, you'll see 'em out again at the first light in the mornin'. 'Tis a pity the quollity would give 'em money at all, only have it laid out for 'em in some way that it would do 'em good. Luke Kennedy is a great fencer, I'm tould. Himself an' Myles Murphy, behind, are the best about the Lakes at the stick. Sure Luke taught fencin' himself once. Did you ever hear o' the great guard he taught the boys a'bout the place?"

Fame had not informed Eily of this circumstance.

"Well, I'll tell you it. He gev it out one Sunday upon some writing, that was placed again' the chapel door, to have all the boys that wor for larnen to fence to come to him at such a place, an' he'd taich 'em a guard that would hindher 'em of ever being sthruck. Well, 'tis an admiration what a gathering he had before him. So when they wor all listenin', 'Boys,' says he, gettin' up on a table, an' lookin' round him—' boys, the guard I have to give ye, that'll save ye from all sorts o' sthrokes, is this, to keep a civil tongue in yer head at all times. Do that,' says he, 'an I'll be bail ye never'll get a sthroke.' Well, you never seen people wondher so much, nor look so foolish as they did, since the hour you wor born."

"'Twas a good advice."

"And that's a thing Luke knew how to give better than he'd take. I hardly spoke to him at all now myself."

"Why so?"

Oh! he knows himself. He wanted me a while ago to marry him, and to part my ould father."

"And you refused?" said Eily, blushing a conscious crimson.

"I hardly spoke to him after. He'd be the handsome Luke Kennedy, indeed, if he'd make me part the poor ould man that way, an' my mother dead, an' he having no one else but myself to do a ha'porth for him. What could I expect if I done that? If Luke likes me, let him come and show it by my father; if not, there's more girls in the place, an' he's welcome to pick his choice for Mary."

Every word of this speech fell like a burning coal upon the heart of Eily. She paused a moment in deep emotion, and then addressed her companion :—

"You are right, Mary—you are very right. Let nothing—let no man's love tempt you to forget your duty to your father. Oh! you dont know, much as you love him, what thoughts you would have, if you were to leave him, as you say. Let nothing tempt you to it. You would neither have luck, nor peace, nor comfort; and if your husband should be unkind to you, you could not turn to him again for consolation. But I need not be talking to you; you are a good girl, and more fit to give me advice than to listen to any I can offer you."

From this moment Eily did not open her lips to her companion until they arrived in Castle Island. The Christmas candles were already lighted in every cottage, and Eily determined to defer seeing her uncle until the following morning.

CHAPTER XXV.

HOW EILY FARED IN HER EXPEDITION.

AFTER a sharp and frosty morning, the cold sun of the Christmas noon found Father Edward O'Connor seated in his little parlour before a cheerful turf fire. A small table was laid before it, and decorated with a plain breakfast, which the fatigues of the forenoon rendered not a little acceptable. The sun shone directly in the window, dissolving slowly away the fantastic foliage of frost-work upon the window-panes, and flinging its shadow on the boarded floor. The reverend host himself sat in a meditative posture near the fire, awaiting the arrival of some fresh eggs, over the cookery of which Jim, the clerk, presided in the kitchen. His head was drooped a little; his eyes fixed upon the burning fuel, his nether lip a little protruded, his feet stretched out and crossed, and the small bulky volume in which he had been reading his daily office, half closed in his right hand, with a finger left between the leaves to mark the place. No longer a pale and secluded student, Father Edward now presented the appearance of a healthy man, with a face hardened by frequent exposure to the winds of midnight and of morn, and with a frame made firm and vigorous by unceasing exercise. His eye, moreover, had acquired a certain character of severity, which was more than qualified by a nature of the tenderest benevolence.

On the table, close to the small tray which held his simple equipage, was placed a linen bag, containing in silver the amount of his Christmas offerings. They had been paid him on the morning in crowns, half-crowns, and shillings, at the parish chapel. And Father Edward on this occasion had returned thanks to his parishioners for their liberality—the half-yearly compensation for all his toils and exertions, his sleepless nights and restless days, amounting to no less a sum than thirteen pounds fourteen shillings.

"'Tis an admiration, sir," said Jim, the clerk, as he entered, clad in a suit of Father Edward's rusty black, laid the eggs upon the tray, and moved back to a decorous distance from the table —"'tis an admiration what a sighth o' people is abroad in the kitchen, money hunting."

"Didn't I tell 'em the last time that I never would pay a bill upon a Christmas day again?"

"That's the very thing I said to 'em, sir. But 'tis the answer they made me, that they came a long distance, and 'twould cost 'em a day more if they were obliged to be coming again to-morrow."

Father Edward, with a countenance of perplexity and chagrin, removed the top of the egg, while he cast a glance alternately at the bag and at his clerk. "It is a hard case, Jim," he said at last, "that they will not allow a man even the satisfaction of retaining so much money in his possession for a single day, and amuse himself by fancying it his own. I suspect I am doomed to be no more than a mere agent to this thirteen pounds fourteen, after all—to receive and pay it away in a breath."

"Just what I was thinking myself, sir," said Jim, tossing his head.

"Well, I suppose I must not cost the poor fellows a day's work, however, Jim, if they have come such a distance. That would be a little pharisaical, I fear."

Jim did not understand this word, but he bowed, as if he would say, "Whatever your reverence says must be correct."

"Who are they, Jim?" resumed the clergyman.

"There's Luke Scanlon, the shoemaker, for your boots, sir; and Reardon, the blacksmith, for shoeing the pony; and Milesna-Coppaleen, as they call him, for the price o' the little crathur; and the printer for your reverence's subscription to the *Kerry Luminary;* an' Rawley, the carpenter, for the repairs o' the althar; an'——"

"Hut tut! he must settle that with the parishioners. But the others—let me see. Shoeing myself, fifteen shillings; shoeing my pony, thirteen, four sets. Well, the price of the 'little crathur,' as you say, seven pounds ten (and she's well worth it); and, lastly, the newspaper man, two pounds."

"But not *lastly*, intirely," said Jim, "for there's the tailor——"

"Sixteen and threepence. Jim, Jim, that will be a great reduction on the thirteen pounds fourteen."

"Just what I was thinking of myself, sir," said the clerk.

"But I suppose they must have their money. Well, bring me in their bills, and let them all write a *settled* at the bottom."

Exit Jim.

"Here they are all, sir," he said, returning with a parcel of soiled and crumpled papers in his hand; "and Myles Murphy says that the agreement about the pony was seven pound ten an' a glass o' whiskey, and that he never knew a morning he 'd sooner give your reverence a *resate* for it than a frosty one like this."

"Let him have it, Jim. That was an item in the bargain which had slipped my memory. An' as you are giving it to him, take the bottle and treat them all round. They have a cold road before them."

"It 's what I thought myself, sir," said Jim.

Father Edward emptied the bag of silver, and counted it into several sums, the amount of all the bills. When he had done so, he took in one hand the few shillings that remained, threw them into the empty bag, jingled them a little, smiled, and tossed his head. Jim, the clerk, smiled, and tossed his head in sympathy.

"It 's aisier emptied than filled, plase your reverence," said Jim, with a short sigh.

"If it were not for the honour and dignity of it," thought Father Edward after his clerk had once more left the room, "my humble curacy at St. John's were preferable to this extensive charge in so dreary a peopled wilderness. Quiet lodgings, a civil landlady, regular hours of discipline, and the society of my oldest friends—what was there in these that could be less desirable than a cold small house on a mountainside, total seclusion from the company of my equals, and a fearful increase of responsibility? Did the cause of preference lie in the distinction between the letters V. P. and P. P., and the pleasure of paying away thirteen pounds fourteen shillings at Christmas? Oh, world! world! world! You are a great stage-coach, with fools for outside passengers; a huge round lump of earth, on the surface of which men seek for peace, but find it only when they sink beneath. Would I not give the whole thirteen pounds fourteen at this moment to sit once more in my accustomed chair in that small room, with the noise of the streets just dying away as the evening fell, and my poor little Eily reading to me from the window, as of old, as innocent, as happy, and as dutiful as then? Indeed, I would, and more if I had it. Poor Mihil! Ah, Eily, Eily! You deceived me! Well, well! Old Mihil says I am too ready to preach patience to him. I must try and practise it myself."

At this moment the parlour door opened again, and Jim once more thrust in his head.

"A girl, sir, that 's abroad, an' would want to see you, if you plase."

"Who is she? What does she want? Confession, I suspect."

"Just what I was thinking of myself, sir."

"Oh! why didn't she go to the chapel yesterday, where I was sitting until ten at night?"

"It 's the very thing I said to her myself, sir, and she had no answer to make, only wanting to see you."

"Who is she? Don't you know her even by sight?"

"No, sir, in regard she keeps her head down, and her handkerchief to her mouth. I stooped to have a peep undernaith, but if I stooped low, she stooped lower, an' left me just as wise as I was in the beginning."

"Send her in," said Father Edward; "I don't like that secrecy."

Jim went out, and presently returned, ushering in, with many curious and distrustful glances, the young female of whom he had spoken. Father Edward desired her to take a chair, and then told the clerk to go out to the stable, and give the pony his afternoon feed. When the latter had left the room he indulged in a preliminary examination of the person of his visitor. She was young and well formed, and clothed in a blue cloak and bonnet, which were so disposed, as she sat, as to conceal altogether both her person and her features.

"Well, my good girl," said the clergyman, in an encouraging tone, "what is your business with me?"

The young female remained for some moments silent, and her dress moved as if it were agitated by some strong emotion of the frame. At length, rising from her seat, and tottering towards the astonished priest, she knelt down suddenly at his feet, and exclaimed, while she uncovered her face, with a burst of tears and sobbing, "Oh, uncle Edward, don't you know me?"

Her uncle started from his chair. Astonishment for some moments held him silent and almost breathless. He at last stooped down, gazed intently on her face, raised her, placed her on a chair, where she remained quite passive, resumed his own seat, and covered his face in silence with his hand. Eily, more affected by this action than she might have been by the bitterest reproaches, continued to weep aloud with increasing violence.

"Don't cry—do not afflict yourself," said Father Edward, in a quiet, yet cold tone; "there can be no use in that. The Lord forgive you, child! Don't cry! Ah, Eily O'Connor! I never thought it would be our fate to meet in this manner."

"I hope you will forgive me, uncle," sobbed the poor girl; "I did it for the best, indeed."

"Did it for the best!" said the clergyman, looking on her for the first time with some sternness. "Now, Eily, you will vex me if you say that again. I was in hopes that, lost as you are, you came to me, nevertheless, in penitence and humility, at least, which was the only consolation your friends could ever look for. But the first word I hear from you is an excuse—a justification of your crime. Did it for the best! Don't you remember, Eily, having ever read in that book that I was accustomed to explain to you in old times—don't you remember that the excuses of Saul made his repentance unaccepted? and will you imitate his example? You did it for the best, after all! I won't speak of my own sufferings since the unhappy affair; but there is your old father—I am sorry to hurt your feelings, but it is my duty to make you know the extent of your guilt—your old father has not enjoyed one moment's rest ever since you left him. He was here with me a week since, for the second time after your departure, and I never was more shocked in all my life. You cry, but you would cry more bitterly if you saw him. When I knew you together, he was a good father to you, and a happy father, too. He is now a frightful skeleton! Was that done for the best, Eily?"

"Oh, no, no, sir! I did not mean to say that I acted right, or even from a right intention. I only meant to say that it was not quite so bad as it might appear."

"To judge by your own appearance, Eily," her uncle continued in a compassionate tone, "one would say that its effects have not been productive of much happiness on either side. Turn to the light: you are very thin and pale. Poor child! poor child! Oh, why did you do this? What could have tempted you to throw away your health, your duty, to destroy your father's peace of mind, and your own honest reputation, all in a day?"

"Uncle," said Eily, "there is one point on which I fear you have made a wrong conclusion. I have been, I know, sir, very ungrateful to you, and to my father, and very guilty in the sight of Heaven, but I am not quite so abandoned a creature as you seem to believe me. Disobedience, sir," she added, with a blush of the deepest crimson, "is the very worst offence of which I can accuse myself."

"What!" exclaimed Father Edward, while his eyes lit up with sudden pleasure, "are you, then, married?"

"I was married, sir, a month before I left my father."

The good clergyman seemed to be more deeply moved by this intelligence than by anything which had yet occurred in the scene. He winked repeatedly with his eyelids, in order to clear away the moisture which began to overspread the balls, but it would not do. The fountain had been unlocked; it gushed forth in a flood too copious to be restrained, and he gave up the contest. He reached his hand to Eily, grasped hers, and shook it fervently and long, while he said, in a voice that was made hoarse and broken by emotion,—

"Well, well, Eily, that 's a great deal. 'Tis not everything, but it is a great deal. The general supposition was, that the cause of secrecy should be no other than a shameful one. I am very glad of this, Eily. This will be some comfort to your father." He again pressed her hand, and shook it kindly, while Eily wept upon his own like an infant.

"And where do you stay now, Eily—where? Who is your husband?"

Eily appeared distressed at this question, and after some embarrassment said, "My dear uncle, I am not at liberty to answer you those questions at present. My husband does not know of my having even taken this step, and I dare not think of telling what he commanded that I should keep secret."

"Secrecy still, Eily?" said the clergyman, rising from his seat, and walking up and down the room with his hands behind his back, and a severe expression returning to his eye. "I say again, I do not like this affair. Why should your husband affect this deep concealment? Is he poor? Your father will rejoice to find it no worse. Is he afraid of the resentment of your friends? Let him bring back our own Eily, and he will be received with arms as open as charity. What besides conscious guilt can make him thus desirous of concealment?"

"I cannot tell you his reasons, uncle," said Eily, timidly; "but indeed he is nothing of what you say."

"Well, and how do you live, then, Eily? With his friends, or how? If you will not tell where, you may at least tell how."

"It is not *will not* with me, indeed, uncle Edward, but *dare not*. My first act of disobedience cost me dearly enough, and I dare not attempt a second."

"Well, well," replied her uncle, a little annoyed, "you have more logic than I thought you had. I must not press you further on that head. But how do you live? Where do you hear mass on Sundays? Or do you hear it regularly at all?"

Eily's drooping head and long silence gave answer in the negative.

"Do you go to mass every Sunday at least? You used to hear it every day, and a blessing fell on you and on your house while you did so. Do you now attend it on Sunday itself?"

Eily continued silent.

"Did you hear mass a single Sunday at all since you left home?" he asked in increasing amazement.

Eily answered in a whisper between her teeth, "Not one."

The good religious lifted up his hands to heaven, and then suffered them to fall motionless by his side. "Oh, you poor child!" he exclaimed, "may the Lord forgive you your sins! It is no wonder that you should be ashamed, and afraid, and silent."

A pause of some moments now ensued, which was eventually broken by the clergyman.

"And what was your object in coming, then, if you had it not in your power to tell me anything that could enable me to be of some assistance to you?"

"I came, sir," said Eily, "in the hope that you would, in a kinder manner than anybody else, let my father know all that I have told you, and inform him, moreover, that I hope it will not be long before I am allowed to ask his pardon, with my own lips, for all the sorrow that I have caused him. I was afraid, if I had asked my husband's permission to make this journey, it might have been refused. I will now return and persuade him, if I can, to come here with me again this week."

Father Edward again paused for a considerable time, and eventually addressed his niece with a deep seriousness of voice and manner. "Eily," he said, "a strong light has broken upon me respecting your situation. I fear this man, in whom you trust so much and so generously, and to whose will you show so perfect an obedience, is not a person fit to be trusted nor obeyed. You are married, I think, to one who is not proud of his wife. Stay with me, Eily, I advise—I warn you. It appears by your own words that this man is already a tyrant; he loves you not, and from being despotic he may grow dangerous. Remain with me, and write him a letter. I do not judge the man. I speak only from general probabilities, and these would suggest the great wisdom of your acting as I say."

"I dare not, I could not, would not do so," said Eily. "You never were more mistaken in anybody's character than in his of whom you are speaking. If I did not fear, I love him far too well to treat him with so little confidence. When next we meet, uncle, you shall know the utmost of my apprehensions. At present I can say no more. And the time is passing, too," she continued, looking at the sunshine which traversed the little room with a ray more faint and more oblique. "I am pledged to return this evening. Well, my dear uncle, good-by! I hope to bring you back a better niece than you are parting now. Trust all to me for three or four days more, and Eily never will have a secret again from her uncle nor her father."

"Good-by, child—good-by, Eily!" said the clergyman, much affected. "Stay—stay!" he exclaimed, as a sudden thought entered into his head. "Come here, Eily, an instant." He took up the linen bag before mentioned, and shook out into

his hand the remaining silver of his dues. "Eily," said he, with a smile, "it is a long time since uncle Edward gave you a Christmas-box. Here is one for you. Open your hand, now, if you do not wish to offend me. Good-by—good-by, my poor darling child!" He kissed her cheeks, and then, as if reproaching himself for an excess of leniency, he added in a more stern accent, "I hope, Eily, that this may be the last time I shall have to part from my niece without being able to tell her name."

Eily had no other answer than her tears, which, in most instances, were the most persuasive arguments she could employ.

"She is an affectionate creature, after all," said Father Edward, when his niece had left the house—"a simple, affectionate little creature; but I was in the right to be severe with her," he added, giving himself credit for more than he deserved; "her conduct called for some severity, and I was in the right to exercise it as I did."

So saying, he returned to his chair by the fireside, and resumed the reading of his interrupted office.

CHAPTER XXVI.

HOW HARDRESS CONSOLED HIMSELF DURING HIS SEPARATION FROM EILY.

DANNY the Lord did not, as Eily was tempted to fear, neglect the delivery of her letter to Hardress. Night had surprised him on his way to Mr. Cregan's cottage. A bright crescent shed its light over the lofty Toomies, and flung his own stunted shadow on the limestone road as he trudged along, breathing now and then on his cold fingers, and singing,—

"Oh, did you not hear of Kate Kearney,
Who lives on de banks of Killarney?
    From de glance of her eye
    Shun danger and fly,
For fatal 's de glance of Kate Kearney."

He had turned in upon the road which led to Aghadoe, and beheld at a short distance the ruined church and the broken grave-stones which were scattered around its base. Danny, with the caution which he had learned from his infancy, suppressed his unhallowed song as he approached this mournful retreat, and stepped along with a softer pace, in order to avoid attracting the attention of any spiritual loiterers in his neighbourhood. The grave of poor Dalton, the huntsman, was amongst the many which he beheld; and Danny knew that it was generally reported amongst the peasantry that his ghost had been frequently seen in the act of exercising, after death, that vocation to which, during life, he had been so ardently attached. Danny, who had no ambition to become a subject for the view-halloo to his sporting acquaintance, kept on the shady side of the road, in the hope that by this means he might be enabled to "stale by unknownst."

Suddenly the night wind, which hurried after, bore to his ear the sound of several voices, which imitated the yelling of hounds in chase and the fox-hunter's cry. Danny started aghast with terror, a heavy and turbid sensation pressed upon his nerves, and all his limbs grew damp. He crossed himself, and drew close to the dry stone wall which bounded the road-side.

"Hoicks! Come!—come!—come away! Come away! Hoicks!" was shouted at the top of a voice that, one might easily judge, had sounded the death-knell of many a wily reynard. The cry was caught up, and echoed at various distances by three less practised voices. The ringing of horses' hoofs against the hard and frosty road was the next sound that encountered the ear of the little lord. It approached rapidly nearer, and grew too sharp and hard to suppose that it could be occasioned by any concussion of immaterial substances. It proved, indeed, to be a danger of a more positive and actual kind. Our traveller perceived, in a few minutes, that the noise proceeded from three drunken gentlemen who were returning from a neighbouring debauch, and urging their horses forward at the summit of their speed with shouts and gestures, which gave them the appearance of demoniacs.

The foremost, perceiving Danny Mann, pulled up his horse with a violent check, and the others, as they approached, imitated his example. The animals (which were worthy of kinder masters) appeared to participate in the intoxication of their riders. Their eyes flared, their mouths were hid in foam, and they snorted in impatient scorn of the delay to which they were subjected.

"Tally!" cried the first who galloped up. "Ware bailiff! Who are you?"

"A poor man, sir, dat's going de road to——"

"Hoicks! A bailiff! Come, come away! Don't I know you, you limb of mischief? Give me out your processes, or I'll beat you into jelly. Kneel down there on the road until I ride over you!"

"Dat de hands may stick to me, sir, if I have a process in de world."

"Kneel down, I say!" repeated the drunken horseman, shaking his whip loose, and applying it several times with all his worst to the shoulders of the recusant. "Lie down on the road until I ride over you, and trample your infernal brains out."

"Pink him! Sweat him! Pink the rascal!" cried another horseman, riding rapidly up, and flourishing a naked sword. "Put up your whip, Connolly; out with your sword, man, and let us pink the scoundrel."

"Do as Creagh bids you, Connolly," exclaimed a third, who was as drunk again as the other two. "Out with your blade, and pi—pink the ras—rascal."

There was nothing for it but a run, and Danny took to his heels like a fawn. This measure, however, gave a new zest to the sport. The gentlemen galloped after him with loud shouts of "Hoicks!" and "Tally!" and overtook him at a part of the road which was inclosed by hedges too close and high to admit of any escape into the fields. Knowing well the inhuman desperation with which the gentlemen of the day were accustomed to follow up freaks of this kind, Danny felt his heart sink as low as if he had been pursued by a rooted enemy. While he glanced in terror from one side to another, and saw himself cut off from all chance of safety, he received a blow on the head from the loaded handle of a whip, which stunned, staggered, and finally laid him prostrate on the earth.

"I have him," shouted his pursuer. "Here he is, as cool as charity. I'll trample the rascal's brains out."

So saying, he reined up his horse, and endeavoured, by every species of threat and entreaty, to make the chafed and fiery steed set down his iron hoof on the body of the prostrate lord; but the animal, true to that noble instinct which distinguishes the more generous individuals of his species, refused to fall in with the bloody humour of his rider. He set his feet apart, demi-vaulted to either side, and would not, by any persuasion or sleight of horsemanship, be prevailed upon to injure the fallen man.

Danny, recovering from the stunning effects of the blow, and perceiving the gentlemen hemming him round with their swords, now sought, in an appeal to their mercy, that security which he could not obtain by flight. He knelt before them, lifted up his hands, and implored compassion in accents which would have been irresistible by any but drunken gentlemen on a *pinking* frolic. But his cries were drowned in the savage shouts of his beleaguerers. Their swords gathered round him in a fearful circle, and Creagh commenced operations by a thrust in the arm, which left a gash of nearly half an inch in depth. His companions, who did not possess the same dexterity in the exercise of the weapon, and were nevertheless equally free of its use, thrust so frequently, and with so much awkwardness, that the unfortunate deformed ran a considerable risk of losing his life. He had already received several gashes in the face and limbs, and was growing faint with pain and anxiety, when the voice of a fourth horseman was heard at a little distance, and young Hardress Cregan, as little self-possessed as the rest, galloped into the group. He drew his small sword, flourished it in the moonlight with a fierce halloo, that was echoed far away among the lakes and mountains, and prepared to join in the fun. But one glance was sufficient to enable him to recognise his servant.

"Connolly, hold! Hold off, Creagh! Hold, or I'll stab you!" he cried aloud, while he struck up their swords with passion. "How dared you set upon my servant? You are both drunk! Go home, or I'll hash you!"

"Drunk!" said his father. "Pup—puppy! wha—what do you call d—d—drunk? D—d—d' you say I'm drunk? Eh?" And he endeavoured, but without much success, to assume a steady and dignified posture in his saddle.

"No, sir," said Hardress, who merited his own censure as

richly as any one present; "but n—th—these two gentlemen are."

"D'ye hear that, Creagh?" said Connolly. "Come along, and show him if we're drunk. Look here, Mister Slender-limbs! Do you see that road?"

"I—I do," said Hardress, who might have conscientiously sworn to the seeing more than one.

"And do you—look here—do you see this horse?"

"I do," said Hardress, with some gravity of deliberation.

"And do you see *me*?" shouted the querist.

> "He raised his desperate foot
> On stirrup side, and gazed about."

"Ve—very well. You see that road, and you see my horse, and you see me! Ve—very well. Now, could a drunken man do this? Yo—hoicks! Come! come! come away! hoicks!" And so saying, he drove the rowels into his horse's flanks, stooped forward on his seat, and galloped away with a speed that made the night air whistle by his ears. He was followed at an emulative rate by Hyland Creagh and the elder Cregan.

Hardress now assisted the afflicted Danny to mount behind him, and, putting spurs to his horse, rode after his companions at a pace but little inferior, in point of speed, to that which they had used.

Arrived at the cottage, he bade Danny follow him into the drawing-room, where there was a cheerful fire. The other gentlemen, in the mean time, had possessed themselves of the dining-parlour, and were singing, in astounding chorus, the melody which begins with this verse:—

> "Come, each jolly fellow
> That loves to be mellow,
> Attend unto me, and sit easy;
> One jorum in quiet,
> My boys, we will try it:
> Dull thinking will make a man crazy."

The ladies, who had spent the evening out, were not yet returned; and Hardress, much against the will of the affrighted boatman, insisted upon Danny's taking his seat before the fire in Mrs. Cregan's arm-chair.

"Sit down there!" he exclaimed, seizing him with violence by the collar, and forcing him into the seat. "Know, fellow, that if I bid you sit on a throne, you are fit to fill it! You are a king, Danny!" he added, standing unsteadily before his servant, with one hand thrust between his ample shirt-frills, and the other extended in an oratorical attitude; "you are a king in heart, though not in birth. But, tush! as Sterne says, 'are we not all relations?' Look at this hand! I admire you, Danny Mann! I respect, I venerate you: I think you a respectable person in your class—respectable in your class; and what more could be expected from a king? I admire, I love you, Danny! You are a king in heart, though not," he repeated, lowering the tone of his eulogy, while he fixed his half closed eyes upon the deplorable figure of the little lord, "though not in appearance."

Anybody who could contemplate Danny's person at this moment might have boldly joined in the assertion that he was not a "king in appearance." The poor hunchback sat forward in the chair in a crouching attitude, half terrified, and abashed by the finery with which he was surrounded. His joints were stiffened from the cold, his dress sparkling with a hoar-frost, and his face of a wretched white wherever it was not discoloured by the clotted blood. At every noise he half started from his seat, with the exclamation, "Tunder alive! it's de missez!"

"Nancy!" Hardress said, addressing the old woman who came to answer the bell; "Nancy, draw that table near to the fire, there, and slip into the dining-parlour, do you hear? and bring here the whiskey, a jug of hot water, a bowl, two glasses, and a lemon. Don't say a word to the gentlemen: I'll take a quiet glass here in comfort with Danny."

"With Danny!" exclaimed the old woman, throwing up her hands.

"Oh, dat I mightn't sin, master, if I daare do it," said Danny, springing out of the chair. "I'll be kilt by de missez."

"Stay where you are," said Hardress; "and you, woman! do as you're bid."

He was obeyed. The lord, in vain ennobled, returned to his seat; and the bewildered Nancy laid on the table the materials in demand.

"Danny," said Hardress, filling out a brimming glass to his dependent, "when the winds of autumn raved, and the noble

Shannon ruffled his grey pate against the morning sun; when the porpoise rolled his black bulk amid the spray and foam, and the shrouds sang sharp against the cutting breeze—— Do you understand me?"

"Iss, partly, sir."

"In those moments, then, of high excitement and of triumph, with that zest which danger gives to enjoyment; when every cloud that darkened on the horizon sent forth an additional blast, a fresh trumpeter amongst the Tritons to herald our destruction; when our best hope was in our own stout hands, and our dearest consolation that of the Trojan leader—

'Hæc olim meminisse juvabit.'

Do you understand that?"

"It's Latin, sir, I'm thinking."

"*Probatum est!* When the struggle grew so close between our own stout little vessel and her invisible aërial foe as to approach the climax of contention, the point of contact between things irresistible and things immovable, the 'Ημε αναειρ η εγω σε.' Do you understand?"

"More Latin, sir."

"That's Greek, you goose."

"It's all Greek to me," said Danny.

"But in those moments, my *fidus Achates*, you often joined me in a simple aquatic meal; and why not now? This is my conclusion. Why not now? *Major*—We used to eat together; *Minor*—We wish to drink together; *Conclusion*—We ought to drink together." And following up in act a conclusion so perfectly rational, the collegian (who was only pedantic in his maudlin hours) hurried swiftly out of sight the contents of his own lofty glass.

Danny timidly imitated his example, at the same time drawing from inside the lining of his hat the letter of the unhappy Eily. Intoxicated as he was, the sight of this well-known hand produced a strong effect upon her unprincipled husband. His eyelids quivered, his hand trembled, and a black expression swept across his face. He thrust the letter—opened, but still unread—into his waistcoat pocket, refilled his glass, and called on Danny for a song.

"A song, Mr. Hardress! Oh! dat I may be happy if I'd raise my voice in dis room for all Europe!"

"Sit in that chair, and sing," exclaimed Hardress, clenching his hand, and extending it towards the recusant, "or I'll pin you to that door!"

Thus enforced, the rueful Danny returned to the chair which he had once more deserted, and after clearing his throat by a fresh appeal to the glass, he sang a little melody which may yet be heard at evening in the western villages. Hardress was enchanted with the air, the words, and the style of the singer. He made Danny repeat it until he became hoarse, and assisted to bear the burden himself with more of noise than good taste or correctness. The little lord, as he dived deeper into the bowl, began to lose his self-restraint, and to forget the novelty of his situation. He rivalled his master in noise and volubility, and no longer showed the least reluctance or timidity when commanded to chant out the favourite lay for the seventh time at least:—

I.

"My mamma she bought me a camlet coat-gown,
Made in de fashion, wit de tail of it down,
A dimity petticoat whiter dan chalk,
An' a pair o' bow slippers to help me to walk,
An' it 's Oro wisha, Dan'el asthore!

II.

"I 've a nice little dog to bark at my doore,
A neat little beasom to sweep up the floore,
Everyting else dat is fit for good use,
Two ducks and a gander, besides an old goose,
An' it 's Oro wisha, Dan'el asthore."

"Well, why do you stop? What do you stare at?" Hardress asked, perceiving the vocalist suddenly lower his voice, and slinge away from the table, while his eyes were fixed on the farther end of the room. The collegian looked in the same direction, and beheld the figure of a young female, in a ball dress of unusual splendour, standing as if fixed in astonishment. Her black hair, which was decorated with one small sprig of pearls, hung loose around her head, a necklace of the same costly material rested on her bosom, and was, in part, concealed by the bright-coloured silk kerchief which was drawn around her shoulders. On one arm she held the fur-trimmed cloak

and heavy shawl which she had just removed from her person, and which were indicative of a recent exposure to the frosty air. Indeed, nothing but the uproarious mirth of the ill-assorted revellers could have prevented their hearing the wheels of the carriage as they grated along the gravel-plat before the hall door. This venerable vehicle was sent to set the ladies down by the positive desire of the hostess, and Mrs. Cregan accepted it in preference to her own open curricle, although she knew that a more crazy mode of conveyance could not be found, even among the ships marked with the very last letter on Lloyd's list.

Recognising his cousin, Hardress endeavoured to assume towards Danny Mann an air of dignified condescension and maudlin majesty, which formed a ludicrous contrast to the convivial freedom of his manner a few moments before.

"Very well, my man," he said, liquefying the consonants in every word. "Go out now, go to the kitchen, and I'll hear the remainder of your story in the morning."

Danny fell cunningly into the deception of his master, to whom he now evinced a profundity of respect, as if to banish the idea of equality, which the foregoing scene might have suggested.

"Iss, plase your honour!" he said, bowing repeatedly down to his knees, and brushing his hat back until it swept the floor. "Long life an' glory to your honour, Master Hardress; an' 'tis I dat would be lost if it wasn't for your goodness. Oh, murder, murder!" he added to himself, as he scoured out of the room, describing a wide circuit to avoid Miss Chute, "I'll be fairly flayed alive on de 'count of it."

"Well, Anne," said Hardress, rising and moving towards her with some unsteadiness of gait, "I—I am glad to see you, Anne; we're just come home; very pleasant night; pleasant fellows, very, very pleasant fellows; some cap—capital songs; I was wishing for you, Anne. Had you a pleasant night where you were? Who—who did you dance with? Come, Anne, we'll dance a minnet—min—minuet de la cour."

"Excuse me," said Anne, coldly, as she turned towards the door, "not at this hour, certainly."

"A fig for the hour, Anne. Hours were made for slaves. Anne, oh, Anne! you look beautiful—beautiful to-night! Oh, Anne! Time flies, youth fades, and age with slow and withering pace comes on before we hear his footfall!" Here he sang, in a loud but broken voice,—

"Then follow, follow,
Follow, follow,
Follow, follow pleasure!
There's no drinking in the grave."

"Oh, Anne! that's as true as if the Stagyrite had penned it. Worms, Anne, worms and silence! Come, one minuet! Lay by your cloak—

'And follow, follow,
Follow, follow,
Follow, follow pleasure!
There's no *dancing* in the grave!'"

"Let me pass, if you please," said Miss Chute, still cold and lofty, while she endeavoured to get to the door.

"Not awhile, Anne," replied Hardress, catching her hand.

"Stand back, sir!" exclaimed the offended girl, drawing up her person into the attitude of a Minerva, while her forehead glowed, and her eye flashed with indignation. "If you forget yourself, do not suppose that I am inclined to commit the same oversight." Saying this, she walked out of the room with the air of an offended princess, leaving Hardress a little struck and sobered by the sudden change in her manner.

Lifting up his eyes after a pause of some moments, he beheld his mother standing near, and looking on him with an eye in which the loftiness of maternal rebuke was mingled with an expression of sneering and satirical reproach.

"You are a wise young gentleman," she said; "you have done well. Fool that you are! you have destroyed yourself." Without bestowing another word upon him, Mrs. Cregan took one of the candles in her hand, and left the room.

Hardress had sufficient recollection to follow her example. He took the other light, and endeavoured, but with many errors, to navigate his way towards the door. "Destroyed myself!" he said as he proceeded. "Why, where's the mighty harm of taking a cheerful glass on a winter's night with a friend? A friend, Hardress? Yes, a friend; but what friend?

Danny Mann, *alias* Danny the Lord, my boatman. It won't do!" (shaking his head). "It sounds badly. I'm afraid I did something to offend Anne Chute. I am sorry for it, because I respect her. I respect you, Anne, in my very, very heart. But I am ill-used, and I ought to have satisfaction. Creagh has pinked my boatman. I'll send him a message, that's clear. I'll not be hiring boatmen for him to be pinking for his amusement. Let him pink their master if he can. That's the chat!" (snapping his fingers). "Danny Mann costs me twelve pounds a year, besides his feeding and clothing, and I'll not have him pinked by old Hyland Creagh afterwards. Pink me, if he can; let him leave my boatman alone! That's the chat! This floor goes starboard and larboard, up and down, like the poop of a ship; up and——Hallo! Who are you? Oh! it's only the door. I have broken my nose against it. And if I break my own nose without any reason, at this time o' the day, what usage can I expect from Creagh or anybody else?"

Having arrived at this wise conclusion, he sallied out of the room, rubbing with one hand the bridge of the afflicted feature, and elevating in the other the light, which he still held with a most retentive grasp. As the long and narrow hall, which lay between him and his bed-chamber, formed a direct railroad way, which it was impossible even for a drunken man to miss, he reached the little dormitory without further accident. The other gentlemen had been already borne away unresisting from the parlour, and transmitted from the arms of Mike to those of Morpheus.

CHAPTER XXVII.

HOW HARDRESS ANSWERED THE LETTER OF EILY.

"You have destroyed yourself!" Mrs. Cregan repeated on the following morning, as she sat in the breakfast parlour in angry communication with our collegian. "If you have any desire to redeem even a portion of her forfeited esteem, now is your time. She is sitting alone in the drawing-room, and I have prevailed on her to see you for a few moments. She returns in two or three days to Castle Chute, where she is to spend Christmas; and unless you are able to make your peace before her departure, I know not how long the war may last."

"Yes," said Hardress, with a look of deep anguish, "I shall go and meet her on the spot where I dared to insult her! Insult Anne Chute! Why, if my brain had turned, if lunacy instead of drunkenness had set a blind upon my reason at the time, I thought my heart at least would have directed me. Mother, don't ask me to see her there. I could tear my very flesh for anger! I never will forgive myself, and how then can I seek forgiveness from her?"

"Go, go! That speech might have done much for you, if it had been properly addressed. Go to her."

"I will," said Hardress, setting his teeth, and rising with a look of forced resolution. "I know that it is merely a courting of ruin, a hastening and confirming of my own black destiny, and yet I will go seek her. I cannot describe to you the sensation that attracts my feet at this moment in the direction of the drawing-room. There is a demon leading and a demon driving me on, and I know them well and plainly, and yet I will not choose but go! The way is torture, and the end is hell; and I know it, and I go! And there is one sweet spirit, one trembling, pitying angel, that waves me back with its pale, fair hands, and strives to frown in its kindness, and points that way to the hills! Mother! mother! the day may come when you will wish a burning brand had seared those lips athwart before they said, 'Go to her!'"

"What do you mean?" said Mrs. Cregan, with some indignant surprise.

"Well, well, am I not going? Do I not say, I go?" continued Hardress. "Is it not enough if I comply? May I not talk? May I not rant a little? My heart will burst if I do these things in silence."

"Come, Hardress, you are far too sensitive a lover——"

"A *what*?" cried Hardress, springing to his feet, and with a fierceness of tone and look that made his mother start.

"Pooh! A cousin, then—a good, kind cousin, but too sensitive."

"Yes, yes," muttered Hardress; "I am not yet damned. The sentence is above my head, but it is not spoken; the scarlet sin is willed, but not recorded. Mother, have patience with me! I will not, I cannot, I dare not, see Anne Chute this morning." And he again sank into his chair.

Mrs. Cregan, who attributed all those manifestations of reluctance and remorse which her son had evinced during their frequent interviews, to the recollection of some broken promise or boyish faith forsaken, was now surprised at their intensity.

"My dear Hardress!" she said, laying her hand affectionately on his shoulder—"my darling child! you afflict yourself too earnestly. Say what you will, there are few natures nursed in an Irish cabin that are capable of suffering so keenly the endurance of any disappointment as you do the inflicting it."

"Do you think so, mother?"

"Be assured of it. And again, why do you vex your mind about this interview? Is it not a simple matter for a gentleman to apologise politely to a lady for an unintentional affront? If you have hurt your cousin's feelings, what crime can accompany or follow a plain and gentlemanly apology?"

"That's true, that's very true," said Hardress. "There is a call upon me, and I will obey it. But politely? Politely! If I could stop at that! It is impossible. I shall first become a fool, and by-and-by a demon. But you are right, and I obey you, mother."

So saying, he walked with a kind of desperate calmness out of the room, and Mrs. Cregan heard him continue the same heavy, self-abandoned step along the hall which led to the drawing-room door.

Nothing could have been more propitiatory than the air of mournful tranquillity with which the young collegian entered the room in which his cousin was expecting him. It might resemble that of a believing Mussulman who prepared to encounter a predestined sorrow. He observed, and his pulse quickened at the sight, that his cousin's eyes were marked with a slight circle of red, as if she had been weeping. She rose as he entered, and lowered her head and her person in rather distant courtesy—a coldness which she repeated the moment her eye rested on his pale and anxious countenance.

"You see how totally all shame has left me," said Hardress, forcing a smile; "I do not even hide myself. Will any apology, Anne, be admissible after last night?"

Miss Chute hesitated, and appeared slightly confused. She did not, she said, for her own sake, look for any; but it would indeed give her pleasure to hear anything that might explain the extraordinary scene on which she had intruded.

"You are astonished," said Hardress, "to find that I could make myself so much a beast? But intoxication is not always a voluntary sin with people who sit down after dinner with such men as Creagh, and Connolly, and——" He did not add, "My father."

"But when you were aware——"

"And when I was, and *as* I was, Anne, I rose and left the table—I and young Geoghegan; but they all got up, to a man, and shut the door, and swore we should not stir. They went so far as to draw their swords. Upon my honour, I do not think we could have left the room last night sober without bloodshed. And was it so unpardonable, then? Cato himself, you know, was once found drunk."

"Yes, *once*."

"I don't think that's deserved," said Hardress, colouring slightly. "I may have often trespassed a little in that way, but I never, till last night, became as drunk as Cato. Nor even last night, for I was able to ride home at a canter, to rescue my poor hunchback out of a dilemma, and to bring him hither on my saddle; whereas Cato was unable to keep his own legs, you know."

"I heard that circumstance this morning, and I admit that it altered the posture of the transaction very considerably. But did those gentlemen who drew their swords upon you make you promise to continue drinking after your return, and to bring Danny into the drawing-room to join you?"

"And to insult my cousin?" added Hardress. "No! there my guilt begins, and unless your mercy steps in to my relief, I must bear the burden unassisted."

"To tell you the truth, Hardress," said Anne, assuming an air of greater frankness, "it is not the offence or insult, as you term it, of last night alone that perplexes and afflicts me. Your whole manner, for a long time past, is one continued enigma—one distressing series of misconceptions on my part, and of inconsistencies—I will say nothing harder—upon yours. Your

HARDRESS LEARNS THE FATE OF EILY.

whole conduct has changed since I have met you here, and changed by no means favourably. I cannot understand you. I appear to give you pain most frequently when it is farthest from my own intention, and I cannot tell you how distressed I feel upon the subject."

Hardress fixed his eyes upon her while she spoke, and remained for some moments wrapped in silent and intoxicating admiration. When she had concluded, and while a gentle anxiety still shadowed her features with an additional depth of interest, he approached her and said, "And is it possible, Anne, that the conduct of so worthless a fellow as I am should in any way affect you so deeply as you describe? Believe me, Anne, I do not mouth or rave while I declare to you that I had rather lie down and die here at your feet than give you a moment's painful thought, or seem to disregard your feelings."

"Oh, sir!" said Anne, looking more offended than usual, "I cannot sit to hear this language again repeated. You must remember how painfully those conversations have always terminated."

The intoxication of passion is not less absorbing and absolute than that which arises out of coarser sensual indulgence. Hardress was no more capable of thought or of reflection now than he was during the excesses of the foregoing night. He yielded himself slowly, but surely, to the growing delirium, and became forgetful of everything but the unspeakable happiness that seemed to thrust itself upon him.

"Anne," he said, with great anxiety of voice and manner, "let that, too, be made a subject for your forgiveness. Shall I tell you a secret? Shall I give you the key to all those perplexing inconsistencies—the solution to that long enigma of which you have complained? I can no more contain it than I could arrest a torrent. I love you! Does that explain it? If you are satisfied do not conceal your thoughts. Say it kindly—say it generously! I do not ask you to say anything that can even make you blush. If you are not displeased, say only that you forgive me, and that word will be the token of my happiness."

He paused, and Anne Chute, turning away her head, and reaching her hand, said in a low, but distinct tone, "Hardress, I am satisfied—I do forgive you."

Hardress sank at her feet, and bathed with his tears the hand which had been surrendered to him. "One moment! one moment's patience, my kindest, my sweetest Anne!" he said, as a sudden thought started into his mind. "I wish to send one line to my mother: is it your pleasure? She is in the next room, and I wish to—— Ha!"

A sudden alteration took place in his appearance. While he spoke of writing he had taken from his waistcoat pocket a pencil and an open letter, from which he tore away a portion of the back. The handwriting arrested his attention, and he looked within. The first words that met his eyes were the following:—

"If Eily has done anything to offend you, come and tell her so; but remember she is now away from every friend in the whole world. Even if you are still in the same mind as when you left me, come at all events for once, and let me go back to my father."

Whilst his eyes wandered over this letter his figure underwent an alteration that filled the heart of Anne with terror. The apparition of the murdered Banquo at the festival could not have shot a fiercer remorse into the soul of his slayer than did these simple lines into the heart of Hardress. He held the paper before him at arm's length, his cheek grew white, his forehead grew damp, and the sinews of his limbs grew faint and quivering with fear. His uneasiness was increased by his total ignorance of the manner in which the letter came into his possession.

"Hardress! what is the matter? What is it you tremble at?" said Anne in great uneasiness.

"I do not know, Anne. I think there's witchcraft here. I am doomed, I think, to live a charmed life. I never yet imagined that I was on the threshold of happiness, but some wild hurry, some darkening change, swept across the prospect, and made it all a dream. It has been always so—in my least as in my highest hopes. I think it is my doom. Even now I thought I had already entered upon its free enjoyment, and behold yourself how swiftly has it vanished!"

"Vanished!"

"Ay, vanished, and for ever! Were we not now almost one soul and being? Did we not mingle sighs? Did we not mingle tears? Was not your hand in mine, and did I not think I felt our spirits growing together in an inseparable league? And now (be witness for me against my destiny), how suddenly we have been wrenched asunder! how soon a gulf has opened at our feet, to separate our hearts and fortunes from henceforth and for ever!"

"For ever!" echoed Anne, lost in perplexity and astonishment.

"Forgive me!" Hardress continued in a dreary tone. "I did but mock you, Anne. I cannot—I must not love you! I am called away. I was mad, and dreamed a lunatic's dream; but a horrid voice has awoke me up, and warned me to be gone. I can never be the happy one I hoped—Anne Chute's accepted lover."

"Yet once again, sir!" exclaimed Miss Chute, with a burst of natural indignation; "once more must I endure those insults? Do you think I am made of marble? Do you think," she continued, panting heavily, "that you can sport with my feelings at your pleasure?"

"I can only say, forgive me!"

"I do not think you value my forgiveness. I have been always too ready to accord it, and that, I think, has subjected me to additional insult. Oh, Mrs. Cregan!" she added, as she saw that lady enter the room, and close the door carefully behind her, "why did you bring me to this house?" With these words she ran, as if for refuge, to the arms of her aunt, and fell in a fit of hysterical weeping upon her neck.

"What is the matter?" said Mrs. Cregan sternly, and standing at her full height. "What have you done?"

"I have in one breath made her a proposal, which I have broken in the next," said Hardress calmly.

"You do well to boast of it. Comfort yourself, my love; you shall have justice. Now, hear me, sir. Abandon my house this instant!"

"Mother——"

"Be silent, sir, and dare not address me by that name. My love, be comforted! I disown, I renounce you for a son of mine. If you had one drop of gentle blood in your veins it would have rebelled against such perfidy, such inhuman villany as this! Away, sir! your presence is distressing to us both! My love!

my love! my unoffending love! be comforted!" she added, gathering her niece tenderly in her arms, and pressing her head against her bosom.

"Mother," said Hardress, drawing in his breath between his teeth, "if you are wise you will not urge me farther. Your power is great upon me: if you are merciful, exercise it not at this moment."

"Do not, aunt!" said Anne in a whisper. "Let him do nothing against his own desire."

"He *shall* do it, girl!" exclaimed Mrs. Cregan. "Must the selfish boy suppose that there are no feelings to be consulted besides his own in the world? I will not speak for myself," she added; "but look there!" holding towards him the form of her niece as if in reproach. "Is there a man on earth besides yourself that——" Here the words stuck in her throat, and her eyes filled up. "Excuse me, my darling!" she said to Anne; "I must sit down. This monster will kill me!" She burst into tears as she spoke those words.

It now became Anne's turn to assume the office of comforter. She stood by her aunt's chair, with her arm round her neck, and loading her with caresses. If ever a man felt like a fiend, Hardress Cregan did so at that moment.

"I am a villain either way," he muttered below his breath. "There is no escaping it. Well whispered, fiend! I have but a choice between the two modes of evil, and there is no resisting this! I cannot hold out against this!"

"Come, Anne," said Mrs. Cregan, rising, "let us look for privacy elsewhere, since this gentleman loves so well to feast his eyes upon the misery he can occasion, that he will not afford it to us here."

"Stay, mother," said Hardress, suddenly rising and walking towards them; "I have decided between them."

"Between what?"

"I—I mean that I am ready to obey you. I am ready, if Anne will forgive me, to fulfil my pledge. I ask her pardon and yours for the distress I have occasioned. From this moment I will offend no more. Your power, mother, has prevailed—whether for good or evil, let time tell."

"But will you hold to this?"

"To death and after. Surely that may answer."

"No more discoveries?"

"None, mother, none."

"This once for all, and at every hazard?"

"Yes; and at every expense to soul or to body, here or hereafter."

"Fie, fie! Why need you use those desperate terms? Where are you running to now?"

"Merely to speak to my servant. I will return to dinner."

"Why, how you tremble! You are pale and ill."

"No, no; 'tis nothing. The air will take it away. Good-by one moment; I will return to dinner."

He hurried out of the room, leaving the ladies to speculate together on the probable cause of his vacillation. What appeared most perplexing to Anne Chute was the circumstance that she knew he loved her as deeply and as intensely as he said, and yet her admitting his addresses always seemed to occasion a feeling of terror in his mind. More than once, as his character unfolded on her view, she had been tempted to regret her hasty predilection, and had recurred, with a feeling of saddened recollection, to the quiet tenderness and cheerful affection of the rejected Kyrle Daly.

In the mean time Hardress Cregan hurried through the house in search of his boatman. Danny's wounds had become inflamed in the course of the night, and he was now lying in a feverish state in the little green-room in which Hardress had his last interview with the poor huntsman. Hither he hastened with a greater turbulence of mind than he had ever yet experienced, "They are driving me upon it!" he muttered between his teeth. "They are gathering upon me, and urging me onward in my own despite! Why, then, have at ye, devils! I am among ye. Which way must it be done? Heaven grant I may not one day weep for this; but I am scourged to it!"

He entered the room. The check blind was drawn across the little window, and he could scarcely for a moment distinguish the face of his servant, as the latter raised himself in the bed at his approach. Old Nancy was standing, with a bowl of whey in her hand, near the bedside. Hardress, as if unwilling to afford a moment's time for reflection, walked quickly to her, seized her by the shoulders, and thrust her out of the room. He then threw in the bolt of the door, and took a chair by the sick man's side. A silence of some moments ensued.

"Long life to you, Master Hardress! 'Tis kind o' you to come and see me dis mornin'," said the wounded lord.

His master made no reply, but remained for a minute with his elbows on his knees, and his face buried in his hands.

"Danny," he said at length, "do you remember a conversation which I had with you some weeks since on the Purple Mountain?"

"Oh! den, master," said Danny, putting his hands together with a beseeching look, "don't talk o' dat any more. I ax Heaven's pardon, an' I ax your pardon, for what I said; and I hope and pray your honour 'ill tink of it no more. Many is de time I was sorry for it since, and moreover now, being on my sick bed, and tinkin' of everyting."

"Pooh! you do not understand me. Do you remember your saying something about hiring a passage for Eily in an American vessel, and——"

"I do, an' I ax pardon. Let me out o' de bed, an' I'll go down on my two knees——"

"Pish! bah! be silent! When you spoke of that, I was not wise enough to judge correctly. Do you mark? If that conversation were to pass again, I would not speak, nor think, nor feel, as I did then."

Danny gaped and stared on him as if at a loss.

"Look here! You asked me for a token of my approbation. Do you remember it? You bade me draw my glove from off my hand, and give it for a warrant. Danny," he continued, plucking off the glove slowly, finger after finger, "my mind has altered. I married too young. I didn't know my own mind. Your words were wiser than I thought. I am hampered in my will. I am burning with this thraldom. Here is my glove." Danny received it, while they exchanged a look of cold and fatal intelligence.

"You shall have money," Hardress continued, throwing a purse upon the bed. "My wish is this. She must not live in Ireland. Take her to her father? No; the old man would babble, and all would come to light. Three thousand miles of a roaring ocean may be a better security for silence. She could not keep her secret at her father's. She would murmur it in her dreams. I have heard her do it. She must not stay in Ireland. And you, do you go with her—watch her—mark all her words, her wishes. I will find you money enough; and never let me see her more. Harm not, I say—oh, harm not a hair of the poor wretch's head! Never let me see her more. Do you hear? Do you agree?"

"Oh, den, I'd do more dan dat for your honour; but——"

"Enough. When?—when, then?—when?"

"Ah, den, Master Hardress, dear knows I'm so poorly after de proddin' I got from dem jettlemen dat I don't know will I be able to lay dis for a few days, I'm tinkin'."

"Well, when you go, here is your warrant."

He tore the back from Eily's letter, and wrote in answer:—

"I am still in the same mind as when I left you. I accept your proposal. Put yourself under the bearer's care, and he will restore you to your father."

He placed this black lie in the hand of his retainer, and left the room.

CHAPTER XXVIII.

HOW THE LITTLE LORD PUT HIS MASTER'S WISHES INTO ACTION.

WE lost sight of Eily after her parting with her uncle. She wasted no time on her journey homewards, but yet it was nearly dusk before the pony had turned in upon the little craggy road which led upward through the Gap. The evening was calm and frosty, and every footfall of the animal was echoed from the opposite cliffs like the stroke of a hammer. A broken covering of crystal was thrown across the stream that bubbled downwards through the wild valley; and the rocks and leafless trees in those corners of the glen which had escaped the direct influence of the sunshine were covered with drooping spars of ice. Chilled by the nipping air, and fearful of attracting the attention of any occasional straggler in the wild, Eily had drawn her blue cloak around her face, and was proceeding quietly in the direction of the cottage, when the sound of voices on the other side of a hedge by which she passed struck on her ear.

"Seven pound tin, an' a pint o' whiskey!—the same money as I had for the dead match of her from Father O'Connor, the priest, eastwards in Castle Island. Say the word now—seven pound tin, or lave it there."

"Seven pound."

"No; seven pound tin."

"I will not, I tell you."

"Well, then, being relations, as we are, I never will break your word, although she's worth that, if it was between brothers."

In her first start of surprise at hearing this well-remembered voice, Eily had dropped the mantle from her face. Before she could resume it the last speaker had sprung up on the hedge, and plainly encountered her.

At this moment—far away from home, forsaken, as it appeared, by her chosen, her own accepted love, living all alone in heart, and without even the feverish happiness of hope itself—at this mournful moment it would be difficult to convey any idea of the effect which was produced upon Eily by the sudden apparition of the first, though not the favoured love of her girlish days. Both came simultaneously to a pause, and both remained gazing each on the other's face with a feeling too sudden and too full for immediate expression. The handsome, though no longer healthy countenance of the mountaineer was expanded to a stare of pleasurable astonishment, while that of Eily was covered with an appearance of shame, sorrow, and perplexity. The pony likewise, drooping his head as she suffered the rein to slacken in her hand, seemed to participate in her confusion.

At length Myles of the Ponies, keeping his eyes still fixed on Eily, advanced towards her, step after step, with the breathless suspense of King Leontes before the feigned statue. "Eily," he said at length, laying one hand upon the shaggy neck of the little animal, and placing the other against his throat, to keep down the passion which he felt gathering within, "Oh, Eily O'Connor! is it you I see at last?"

Eily, with her eyes lowered, replied in a whisper, which was all but utterly inaudible, "'Tis, Myles."

A long pause ensued. The poor mountaineer bent down his head in a degree of emotion which it would be difficult to describe otherwise than by adverting to the causes in which it originated. He was Eily's first declared admirer, and he was the cause of her present exile from her father's fireside. He had the roughness, but at the same time the honesty, of a mountain cottager; and he possessed a nature which was capable of being deeply, if not acutely, impressed by the circumstances just mentioned. It was long, therefore, before he could renew the conversation. At last he looked up and said,—

"Why, then, when you were below at the lake, where I seen you, although I couldn't see a bit o' you but the cloak, I wondhered greatly what is it made me feel so quare in myself. Sure it's little notion I had who was in it for a cloak. Little I thought——" Here he passed his hand across his eyes. "Ah, what's the use o' talking?"

Eily was still unable to articulate a syllable.

"I saw the old man last week," continued Myles, "still at the old work on the rope-walk."

"Did you—speak to him?" whispered Eily.

"No. He gave me great anger (and justly), the next time he saw me afther you going, in regard it was on my account, he said (and justly too), that you were driven to do as you had done. Oh! then, Miss Eily, why did you do that? Why didn't you come to me unknownst to the old man, and says you, 'Myles, I make it my request o' you, you won't ax me any more, for I can't have you at all?' And sure, if my heart was to split open that minute, it's the last word you'd ever hear from Myles."

"There is only one person to blame in all this business," murmured the unhappy girl, "and that is Eily O'Connor."

"I don't say that," returned the mountaineer. "It's no admiration to me you should be heart-broken with all the persecution we gave you day after day. All I'm thinking is, I'm sorry you didn't mention it to myself in this business. Sure it would be betther for me than to be as I was afther when I heerd you were gone. Lowry Looby told me first of it, when I was eastwards. Oh, vo! such a life as I led afther! Lonesome as the mountains looked before, when I used to come home thinkin' of you, they looked ten times lonesomer afther I heerd that story. The ponies, poor crathurs—see 'em all, how they're lookin' down at us this moment—they didn't hear me spring the rattle on the mountain for a month afther. I suppose they thought it is in Garryowen I was."

Here he looked upward, and pointed to his herd, a great number of which were collected in groups on the broken cliffs above the road, some standing so far forward on the projections of rock as to appear magnified against the dusky sky. Myles sprang the large wooden rattle which he held in his hand, and in an instant all dispersed and disappeared like the clan of a Highland Chief at the sound of their leader's whistle.

"Well, Myles," said Eily at length, collecting a little strength, "I hope we'll see some happy days in Garryowen yet."

"Heaven send it! I'll pack off the boy to-night to town, or I'll go myself if you like, or I'll get you a horse and truckle, and guide it myself for you, or I'll do anything in the whole world that you'll have me. Look at this. I'd rather be doing your bidding this moment than my own mother's, and Heaven forgive me if that's a sin. Ah, Eily! they may say this and that o' you, in the place where you were born, but I'll ever hold to it, I held to it all through, an' I'll hold to it to my death, that when you darken your father's door again you will send no shame before you!"

"You are right in that, Myles."

"Didn't I know I was? And wasn't it that that broke my heart? Look! If one met me after you flitted away, an' saw me walking the road with my hands in my pocket, and my head down, an' I thinking: an' if he sthruck me on the shoulder, an' 'Myles,' says he, 'don't grieve for her, she's this an' that!' and if he proved it to me, why I'd look up that minute an' I'd smile in his face. I'd be as easy from that hour as if I never crossed your threshold at Garryowen! But knowing in my heart, and as my heart told me, that it never could be that way, that Eily was still the old girl always, an' henring what they said o' you, an' knowing that it was I that brought it all upon you—— Oh, Eily! Eily! Oh, Eily O'Connor! there is not that man upon Ireland ground that can tell what I felt. That was what kilt me! That was what drove the pain into my heart, and kept me in the doctor's hands till now."

"Were you ill, then, Myles?" Eily asked in a tone of greater tenderness and interest than she had ever shown to this faithful lover. He seemed to feel it too; for he turned away his head, and did not answer for some moments.

"Nothing to speak of," he said at length; "nothing, Eily, that couldn't be cured by a kind word or a look o' that kind. But where are you going now? The night is falling, and this is a lonesome road. The Sowlth * was seen upon the Black Lake last week, and few are fond of crossing the little bridge at dark since then."

"I am not afraid," said Eily.

"Are you going far a-past the Gap? Let me guide the pony for you."

"No, Myles; where I am going, I must go alone."

"Alone! Sure 'tisn't to part me you will, now?"

"I must, indeed, Myles."

"And what will I say to the old man when I go and tell him that I saw Eily, an' spoke to her, an' that I know no more?"

"Tell him, if you like, that Eily is sorry for the trouble she gave him, and that before many days she hopes to ask his pardon on her knees. Good night, and Heaven be with you! Myles, you are a good man."

"An' amn't I to know where you stop itself?"

"Not now. You said, Myles, that you would like to do my bidding. My bidding is now that you would neither ask, nor look after, where I'm going, nor where I stop. If you do either one or the other, you will do me a great injury."

"Say no more, a-chree!" said Myles; "the word is enough. Well, Eily, good night! your own good night back again to you, and may the angels guide you on your road! Cover up your hands in your cloak, an' hide your face from the frost. I do your bidding, but I don't like the look o' you that way, going up this lonesome glen alone, an' a winter night coming on, an' not knowing where you're steering, or who you're trusting to. Eily, be said by me, and let me go with you."

Eily again refused, and gave her hand to Myles, who retained it between his, and seemed as loath to part with it as if it were a treasure of gold. At length, however, Eily disengaged herself, and put her pony to a trot. The mountaineer remained gazing after her until her figure was lost among the shadows of the

* A gloomy spirit.

rocks. He then turned on his path, and pursued the road which led down the valley, with his eyes fixed heavily upon the ground, and his head sunk forward in an excess of deep and singular emotion. Eily, meanwhile, pursued her journey to the cottage, where, as the reader is aware, no news of her forgetful husband had as yet been heard. Some days of painful suspense and solitude elapsed, and then came Danny Mann with his young master's note.

It was the eve of Little Christmas, and Eily was seated by the fire, still listening, with the anxiety of deferred hope, to every sound that approached the cottage door. She held in her hand a small prayer book, in which she was reading, from time to time, the office of the day. The sins and negligences of the courted maiden and the happy bride came now in dread array before the memory of the forsaken wife, and she leaned forward, with her cheek supported by one finger, to contemplate the long arrear in silent penitence. They were, for the most part, such transgressions as might, in a more worldly soul, be considered indicative of innocence rather than hopeless guilt; but Eily's was a young and tender conscience, that bore the burden with reluctance and with difficulty.

Poll Naughten was arranging at a small table the three-branched candle with which the vigil of this festival is celebrated in Catholic houses. While she was so occupied a shadow fell upon the threshold, and Eily started from her chair. It was that of Danny Mann. She looked for a second figure, but it did not appear, and she returned to her chair with a look of agony and disappointment.

"Where's your masther? Isn't he coming?" asked Poll, while she applied a lighted rush to one of the branches of the candle.

"He isn't," returned Danny; "he has something else to do."

He approached Eily, who observed, as he handed her the note, that he looked more pale than usual, and that his eyes quivered with an uncertain and gloomy fire. She cast her eyes on the note, in the hope of finding there a refuge from the fears which crowded in upon her; but it came only to confirm them in all their gloomy force. She read it word after word, and then, letting her hand fall lifeless by her side, she leaned back against the wall in an attitude of utter desolation. Danny avoided contemplating her in this condition, and stooped forward with his hands expanded over the fire. The whole took place in silence, so complete that Poll was not yet aware of the transaction, and had not even looked on Eily. Again she raised the paper to her eyes, and again she read in the same well-known hand, to which her pulses had so often thrilled and quickened, the same unkind, cold, heartless, loveless words. She thought of the first time on which she had met with Hardress; she remembered the warmth, the tenderness, the respectful zeal of his young and early attachment; she recalled his favourite phrases of affection; and again she looked upon this unfeeling scrawl, and the contrast almost broke her heart. She thought that if he were determined to renounce her, he might at least have come and spoken a word at parting, even if he had used the same violence as in their last interview. His utmost harshness would be kinder than indifference like this. It was an irremediable affliction—one of those frightful visitations, from the effects of which a feeble and unelastic character, like this unhappy girl, can never be recovered.

But though the character of Eily was, as we have termed it, unelastic; though, when once bowed down by a calamitous pressure, her spirits could not recoil, but took the drooping form, and retained it even after that pressure was removed; still she possessed a heroism peculiar to herself—the noblest of which humanity is capable—the heroism of endurance. The time had now arrived for the exercise of that faculty of silent sufferance of which she had made her gentle boast [to Hardress. She saw now that complaint would be in vain, that Hardress loved her not, that she was dead in his affections, and that, although she might disturb the quiet of her husband, she never could restore her own. She determined, therefore, to obey him at once, and without a murmur. She thought that Hardress's unkindness had its origin in a dislike to her, and did not at all imagine the possibility of his proceeding to such a degree of perfidy as he, in point of fact, contemplated. Had she done so, she would not have agreed to maintain the secrecy which she had promised.

While this train of meditation was still passing in her mind,

Danny Mann advanced towards the place where she was standing, and said, without raising his eyes from her feet,—

"If you're agreeable to do what's in dat paper, Miss Eily, I have a boy below at de Gap wid a horse and car, an' you can set off to-night if you like."

Eily, as if yielding to a mechanical impulse, glided into the little room, which, during the honeymoon, had been furnished up and decorated for her own use. She restrained her eyes from wandering as much as possible, and commenced, with hurried and trembling hands, her arrangements for departure. They were few and speedily effected. Her apparel was folded into her trunk, and for once she tied on her bonnet and cloak without referring to the glass. It was all over now! It was a happy dream, but it was ended. Not a tear fell, not a sigh escaped her lips, during the course of those farewell occupations. The struggle was deep and terrible, but it was firmly mastered. A few minutes only elapsed before she again appeared at the door of the little chamber, accoutred for the journey.

"Danny," she said, in a faint, small voice, "I am ready."

"Ready!" exclaimed Poll. "Is it going you are, a-chree?"

Nothing could be more dangerous to Eily's firmness at this moment than any sound of commiseration or kindness. She felt the difficulty at once, and hurried to escape the chance of this additional trial.

"Poll," she replied, still in the same faint tone, "good-by to you. I am sorry I have only thanks to give at parting, but I will not forget you when it is in my power. I left my things within; I will send for them some other time."

"And where is it you're going? Danny, what's all this about?"

"What business is it of yours," replied her brother, in a peevish tone, "or of mine eider? It is do master's bidding, an' you can ax him why he done it when he comes, if you want to know."

"But the night will rain; it will be a bad night," said Poll. "I see the clouds gatherin' for tundher, an' I comin' down the mountain."

Eily smiled faintly and shook her head, as if to intimate that the changes of the seasons would henceforth be to her of trivial interest.

"If it be the master's bidding, it must be right, no doubt," said Poll, still looking in wonder and perplexity on Eily's dreary and dejected face; "but it is a quare story—that's what it is. Won't you ate anything?"

"Oh, not a morsel!" said Eily, with a look of sudden and intense disgust; "but perhaps Danny may."

"No, but I'll drink a drop if you have it," returned the lord, in a tone which showed that he doubted much the likelihood of any refreshment of that kind remaining long inactive in the possession of his sister. To his delight and disappointment, however, Poll handed him a bottle from the neighbouring dresser, which contained a considerable quantity of spirits. He drank off the whole at a draught, and we cannot more clearly show the strong interest which Poll Naughten felt in the situation of Eily than by mentioning that she left this circumstance unnoticed.

Without venturing to reiterate her farewell, Eily descended, with a hasty but feeble step, the broken path which led to the Gap road, and was quickly followed by the little lord. Committing herself to his guidance, she soon lost sight of the mountain cottage, which she had sought in hope and joy, and which she now abandoned in despair.

CHAPTER XXIX.

HOW HARDRESS LOST AN OLD ACQUAINTANCE.

EILY had not been many minutes absent from the cottage, when the thunder-storm predicted by Fighting Poll commenced, amid all the circumstances of adventitious grandeur by which those elemental convulsions are accompanied among the Kerry mountains. The rain came down in torrents, and the thunder clattered among the crags and precipices with a thousand short reverberations. Phil Naughten, who had entered soon after the storm began, was seated with his wife at their small supper-table, the latter complaining heavily of the assault made by Danny on her spirit flask, which she now, for the first time, discovered to be empty.

Suddenly the latch of the door was raised, and Hardress Cregan entered, with confusion and terror in his appearance. The dark frieze great-coat, in which his figure was enveloped, seemed to be drenched in rain, and his face was flushed and glistening with the beating of the weather. He closed the door with difficulty against the strong wind, and still keeping his left hand on the latch, he said,—

"I am afraid I have come too late. Is Danny here?"

"No, sir," said Phil; "he's gone these two hours."

"And Eily?"

"An' Eily along with him. He gave her papers that made her go."

Hardress heard this with an appearance of satisfaction. He leaned his back against the door, crossed his feet, and fixed his eyes upon the ground, in a silent soliloquy, which was to this effect:—

"It is done, then. I would have saved her, but it is too late. Now, my good angel, be at peace with me. I would have saved her. I obeyed your call. Amid the storm, the darkness, and the rain, I flew to execute your gentle will. But the devil had taken me at my word already, and found me a rapid minister. Would I had saved her! Ha! What whisper 's that? There can come nothing worse of it than I have ordered. Forsaken! Banished! This is the very worst that can befall her. And for the consequences, why, if she be so weak and silly a thing as to pine and die of the slight, let nature take the blame, not me. I never meant it. But if that madman should exceed my orders? And if he should," Hardress suddenly exclaimed aloud, while he started from the door, and trembled with fury; "and if he should," he repeated, extending his arms, and spreading his fingers as if in act to gripe, "wherever I meet him—in the city, or in the desert, in the lowest depth of this accursed valley, or on the summit of the mountain where he tempted me—I will tear his flesh from off his bones, and gibbet him between these fingers for a miscreant and a ruffian."

He sunk, exhausted by this frantic burst of passion, into a chair—the chair which Eily had occupied on that evening. Phil Naughten and his wife left their seats in astonishment, and gazed on him and on one another in silence. In a few minutes Hardress rose more calmly from the chair, and drew his arms out of the great-coat, which he handed to Poll, signifying, by a motion of his hand, that she should hang it near the fire. While she obeyed his wishes he resumed his seat in silence. For a considerable time he remained leaning over the back of the chair, and gazing fixedly upon the burning embers. The fatigue of his long journey on foot, and the exhaustion of his feelings, at length brought on a heavy slumber, and his head sank upon his breast in deep, though not untroubled rest. Poll and her husband resumed their meal, and afterwards proceeded to their customary evening occupations. Phil began to repair the pony's saddle, while Poll twisted the flaxen cords according as her husband required them.

"I'll tell you what, Phil," said his wife in a low whisper, "there's something going on to-night that is not right. I am sorry I let Eily go."

"Whisht, you foolish woman!" returned her husband; "what would be going on? Mind your work, an' don't wake the master. D'ye hear how he moans in his sleep?"

"I do; an' I think that moan isn't for nothing. Who is it he was talking of tearing a while ago?"

"I don't know; there's no use in thinking about it. This is a cold night with poor M'Donough in his grave—the first he ever spent there."

"And so it is. Were there many at the funeral?"

"A power. The whole coúnthry was afther the hearse. You never heard such a cry in your life as was set up in the churchyard by poor Garret O'Neil, his own *natural*, afther the grave was covered in. The whole place was in tears."

"Sure Garret wasn't with him this many a year?"

"He was not, until the very day before he died, when he seen him in his own room. You remember a long wattle that Garret used always be carrying in his hand?"

"I do, well."

"That was given to him be the masther, M'Donough himself. Garret axed him once of a Hansel Monday for his *hansel*,* and

* On the first Monday of the new year (called Hansel Monday), it is customary to bestow trifling gifts, which are denominated *hansels*.

'tis what he gave him was that wattle, as it was standing behind the parlour doore. 'Here, Garret,' says he, 'take this wattle, and when you meet with a greater fool than yourself, you may give it to him.' Garret took it without a word, and the masther never seen him afther till the other day, when he walked into his bedroom, where he was lying in his last sickness, with the wattle still in his hand. The masther knew him again the minute he looked at him. 'And didn't you part the wattle yet, Garret?' says he. 'No, sir,' says Garret; 'I can find nowhere a greater fool than I am myself.' 'You show good sense in that, any way,' says the masther. 'Ah, Garret,' says he, 'I b'lieve I'm going.' 'Going where, sir?' says Garret. 'Oh, a long journey,' says he, 'an' one that I'm but little provided for.' 'An' did you know you'd be goin' that journey?' says Garret. 'I did, Heaven forgive me,' says M'Donough. 'An' you made no preparation for it?' says Garret. 'No preparation in life,' says the masther to him again. Well, Garret moved over near the bedside, and took the masther's hand, an' put the wattle into it, just that way. 'Well,' says he, 'take your wattle again. You desired me keep it until I'd meet a greater fool than myself, an' now I found him; for if you knew you'd be taking that journey, an' made no preparation for it, you are a greater fool than ever Garret was.'"

"That was frightful!" said Poll. "Husht! Did you hear that? Well, if ever the dead woke, they ought to wake to-night! Did you ever hear such tundher?"

"'Tis great, surely. How sound Misther Hardress sleeps, an' not to be woke by that! Put the candle at this side, Poll, an' don't disturb him."

They now proceeded with their employment in silence, which was seldom broken. Any conversation that passed was carried on in low and interrupted whispers, and all possible pains were used to avoid disturbing the repose of their weary guest and patron.

But the gnawing passion haunted him even in the depth of sleep. A murmur occasionally broke from his lips, and a hurried whisper, sometimes indicative of anger and command, and sometimes of sudden fear, would escape him. He often changed his position, and it was observed by those who watched beside him that his breathing was oppressed and thick, and his brow was damp with drops of moisture.

"The Lord defend and forgive us all!" said Phil in a whisper to his wife. "I'm afeerd—I'll judge nobody, but I'm afeerd there's some bad work, as you say, going on this night."

"The Lord protect the poor girl that left us!" whispered Poll.

"Amen!" replied her husband aloud.

"Amen!" echoed the sleeper; and following the association awakened by the response, he ran over, in a rapid voice, a number of prayers, such as are used in the service of his Church.

"He's saying his litanies," said Poll. "Phil, come into the next room, or wake him up, either one or the other; I don't like to be listenin' to him. 'Tisn't right of us to be taking advantage of anybody in their dhrames. Many is the poor boy that hung himself that way in his sleep."

"'Tis a bad business," said Phil. "I don't like the look of it at all, I tell you."

"My glove!—my glove!" said the dreaming Hardress; "you used it against my meaning. I meant but banishment. We shall both be hanged—we shall be hanged for this——"

"Come, Phil! Come—come!" cried Poll Naughten with impatience.

"Stop, eroo!—stop!" cried her husband. "He's choking, I b'lieve! Poll! Poll!—the light! the light! Get a cup o' wather."

"Here it is! Shake him, Phil! Masther Hardress!—wake, a'ra gal!"

"Wake, Masther Hardress. Wake, sir, if you plase!"

The instant he was touched Hardress started from his chair, as if the spring that bound him to it had been suddenly struck, and remained standing before the fire in an attitude of extreme terror. He did not speak—at least, the sounds to which he gave utterance could not be traced into any intelligible form; but his look and gesture were those of a man oppressed with a horrid apprehension. According, however, as his nerves recovered their waking vigour, and the real objects surrounding him became known to his senses, a gradual relief appeared to steal upon his spirits, his eyelids dropped, his muscles were re-

laxed, and a smile of intense joy was visible upon his features. He let his arms fall slowly by his side, and sank down once more, with a murmur of painful satisfaction, into the chair which he had left.

But the vision with which he had been terrified was too deeply impressed on his imagination to be at once removed. His dream had merely represented in act a horrid deed, the apprehension of which had shaken his soul with agony when awake, and had brought him amid those obstacles of storm and darkness to the cottage of his neglected wife. His fears were still unquieted. The frightful image that bestrode his slumbers yet haunted him awake, and opposed itself with a ghastly vigour to his eyes, in whatever direction they were turned. Unable to endure the constant recurrence of this unvarying suggestion, he at length hurried out of the cottage. He paid no attention to the voice of Poll Naughten, who followed him to the door, with his great-coat in her hand, but ran down the crags, and in the direction of his home, with the speed of one distracted.

The light which burned in the drawing-room window showed that all the family had not yet retired. His mother, as he learned from old Nancy, was still expecting his return. She was almost alone in the house, for Cregan had left the cottage about a fortnight before in order to escort Miss Chute to her own home. She was seated at a table, and reading some work appropriate to the coming festival, when Hardress made his appearance at the door, still drenched in rain, and pale with agitation and fatigue. He remained on the threshold, leaning with one arm against the jamb, and gazing on the lady.

"What! up yet, mother?" he said at length. "Where's Anne?"

"Ha! Hardress! Oh! my dear child, I have been anxiously expecting you. Anne! Do you forget that you took leave of her a fortnight since?"

"I had forgotten it. I now remember. But not for ever?"

"Why should you say so? What do you mean?" said Mrs. Cregan. "Is not your bridal fixed for the 2nd of February? But I have mournful news to tell you, Hardress."

"Let me hear none of it!" exclaimed the unhappy youth with great vehemence. "It will drive me mad at last. Nothing but mournful news! I'm sick of it. Wherever I turn my eyes, they encounter nothing now but mourning. Coffins and corpses, graves and darkness, all around me! Mother, your son will end his days in Bedlam. Start as you will, I say but what I feel and fear. I find my reason going fast to wreck. Oh! mother, I shall die an idiot yet!"

"My child!"

"Your child!" Hardress reiterated with petulant emphasis. "And if I am your child, could you not care more kindly for my happiness? It was you that urged me on to this. Mind, I comply; but it was you that urged me. You brought me into the danger; and when I would have withdrawn, you held me there. I told you that I was engaged; that Heaven had heard, and earth recorded, my pledge, and that I could not break it. Oh! mother, if you were a mother, and if you saw your son caught by a treacherous passion—if you saw that he was weak, and yielding, and likely to be overcome, you should have strengthened him. It would have been a mother's part to warn him off—to take the side of honesty against his weakness, and make him virtuous in his own despite. But this you did not. I was struggling for my failing honesty, and you strove against me. I rose again and again, almost discomfited, yet still unwilling to yield up all claim to truth, and again and again you struck me down. Behold me now! You have succeeded fully. I am free now to execute your will—to marry or hang, whichever you please."

"Hardress!" exclaimed his mother in an agony, I——"

"Oh! no more remonstrance, mother. Your remonstrances have been my curse and bane: they have destroyed me for this world and for the next."

"You shock me to the soul!"

"Well, I am sorry for it. Go on. Tell me this mournful news. It cannot be but another drop in the ocean. I told you that my reason was affected, and so it is. I know it by the false colouring that has grown upon my senses. My imagination is filled continually with the dreariest images, and there is some spirit within me that tinges, with the same hue of death, the real objects I behold. At morning, if I look upon the east, I think it has the colour of blood; and at night, when I gaze on the advancing shadows, I think of palls, and hearse-plumes, and habits of mourning. Mother, I fear I have not long to live."

"Fie, Hardress!—fie! Are you growing superstitious? For shame! I will not talk with you to-night upon that subject, nor will I tax you with the manifest unkindness of your charges on myself, so often refuted, yet now again repeated. I have a matter of weightier interest to communicate. You know Mrs. Daly, the mother of your young friend, Kyrle?"

"There again!" exclaimed Hardress, starting from his seat, and speaking with passionate loudness. "There again, mother! Another horrid treason! Why, the whole world is joining in one cry of reprobation on my head. Another black and horrid perfidy! Oh! Kyrle, my friend, my calm, high-minded, virtuous, and serene companion! He trusted me with every-thing, told me his secrets, showed me his fears, and commended his hopes to my patronage. And what have I done? I pledged myself to be his friend. I lied! I have supplanted him! How shall I meet him now for evermore? I feel as if the world were met to spit upon my face. This should be my desert. Oh, fool! blind fool! Anne Chute! What was Anne Chute to me, or I to her, that I should destroy my own repute, betray my friend, resist my Maker, and forsake my——?" Suddenly arresting his speech at this conjuncture, he sank back into his chair, and added in a low murmur, "Well, mother, tell this mournful news at once."

"It is soon told," said Mrs. Cregan, who had now become too well accustomed to those bursts of transient passion in her son to afford them any angry consideration. "Poor Mrs. Daly is dead."

"Dead!"

"But this evening I heard it. The circumstance is one of peculiar melancholy. She died quite unexpectedly in her ac-couchment."

"And if the virtuous are thus visited," said Hardress, after a pause, lifting up his hands and eyes, "what should not I ex-pect? I wish I were fit to pray, that I might pray for that kind woman."

"There is one act of mercy in your power," said his mother; "you will be expected at the wake and funeral."

"And there I shall meet with Kyrle!"

"What then?"

"Oh, nothing, nothing!" He paused for several minutes, during which he leaned on the table in a meditative posture. His countenance at length assumed an appearance of more peaceful grief, and it became evident, from the expression of his eye, that a more quiet train of feeling was passing through his mind. "Poor Mrs. Daly!" he said at last. "If one would be wise at all times, how little he would sacrifice to the gratifi-cation of simple passion in such a world as this! Imprimis," he continued, counting on his finger-ends. "Imprimis, a cradle; item, clothing; item, a house; item, fire; item, food; item, a coffin. The best require no more than these; and for the worst, you need only add—item, a gallows, and you have said enough."

Mrs. Cregan heard this speech without the keen anxiety which she would have felt if Hardress had been less passionate in his manner and less extravagant in his mode of speech. But knowing this, she heeded little in him what would have filled her with terror in another.

"Well, will you go to the wake, Hardress?" she said. "You must set out to-morrow morning early."

"I will," said Hardress. "It's a long distance; but I can be there, at all events, by nightfall. When does the funeral take place?"

"I suppose after to-morrow. I will have the curricle at the door by daybreak, for you must set me down at Castle Chute. Go now and change your dress at once, or you will suffer for it. Nancy shall take you a warm footbath and a hot drink when you are in your room."

Hardress retired without farther question. The idea of meeting with Kyrle Daly, after the unmanly neglect, and even betrayal of his interests, was now the one which occupied his sole attention. Half love is vanity; at least, a fair moiety of Hardress Cregan's later passion might be placed to the account of that effeminate failing. It could not, therefore, continue to maintain its hold upon his heart against a passion so new and terrible as that of remorse. His love for Ann Chute was now

entirely dormant in his mind, and his reason was at full liberty to estimate the greatness of his guilt, without even the sugges-tion of a palliative. When we add to this his cruel uncertainty with respect to the fate of Eily O'Connor, it is probable that few who hear the story will envy the repose of Hardress Cregan.

For one instant only, during his conversation with Danny Mann, the idea of Eily's death had flashed upon his mind, and for that instant it had been accompanied with a sensation of wilful pleasure. The remembrance of this guilty thought now haunted him with a deep feeling of remorse, as if that mo-mentary assent had been a positive act. Whenever his eyelids dropped, a horrid chain of faces passed before his imagination, each presenting some characteristic of death or pain—some appearing to threaten, and others to deride him. In this manner the long and lonely night crept by, and the dreary winter dawn found him still unrefreshed and feverish.

CHAPTER XXX.

HOW HARDRESS GOT HIS HAIR DRESSED IN LISTOWEL, AND HEARD A LITTLE NEWS.

HE rose, and found that his mother was already equipped for the journey. They took a hurried breakfast by candlelight, while Mike was employed in putting the horse to the curricle. The lakes were covered by a low mist, that concealed the islands and the distant shores, and magnified the height of the gigantic mountains by which the waters are walled in. Far above this slumbering cloud of vapour, the close and wide-spread forests were seen along the sides of the stupendous ridge, the trees so much diminished by the distance, and by the illusion produced by the novelty of the point of vision, as to resemble a garden of mangold-wurtzel.

Hardress had just taken his seat in the vehicle beside his mother, when a servant in livery rode up to the door, and, touching his hat, put a letter into his hand. It contained an invitation from Hepton Connolly to a hunting dinner, which he was about to give in the course of the month. Hardress remained for a moment in meditation.

"Well, how long am I to stop here waiting for my answer?" asked the messenger—the insolent groom alluded to in an early portion of the narrative. Hardress stared on him in silence for some moments.

"You had better go in and breakfast, I think," he said; "you don't intend to return without alighting?"

"Is it for Hepton Connolly? Why, then, you may take your vido I don't, nor for any other masther under the sun. I was going to breakfast over at the inn, but as you make the offer, I'll not pass your doore."

"You do me a great deal of honour. When does the hunt take place?"

"In three weeks' time, I believe, or something thereabouts."

"Not sooner?"

"No. I wanted him to have it at once, for he couldn't have finer weather, an' the mare is in fine condition for it. But when Connolly takes a thing into his head, you might as well be talking to an ass."

"Well," said Hardress, "tell your master that you found me just driving from home, and that I will come."

Saying this he drove away, while his mother remained still wrapped in silent astonishment at the fellow's impudence.

"Such," said Hardress, "is the privilege of a clever groom. That rogue was once a simple, humble cottager, but fortune favoured him. He assisted Connolly to win a sweepstakes, which gained him a reputation on the turf; and fame has since destroyed him. You would not know whether to choose between indignation or laughter, if you were present at the conversations that sometimes take place between him and his master."

"If, instead of winning me the king's plate, he could win me the king's crown, I could not endure him," said the proud mother.

"Nor I," returned her prouder son; "nor I, indeed."

About noon they stopped to bait and hear mass at the town of Listowel. Mrs. Cregan and her son were shown into a little parlour at the inn, the window of which looked out upon the square. The bell of the chapel on the other side was ringing for last mass, and numbers of people, in their holiday attire, were seen in the wide area, some hurrying towards the chapelgate, some loitering in groups about the square, and some sitting on the low window-sill stones.

The travellers joined the first-mentioned portion of the crowd, and performed their devotions; at least, they gave the sanction of their presence to the ceremonial of the day. When they had returned to the inn, and taken their places in the little parlour, Mrs. Cregan, after fixing her eyes for a moment on her son, exclaimed,—

"Why, Hardress, you are a perfect fright! Did you dress to-day?"

"Not particularly."

"Do you intend to call in at Castle Chute?"

"Just to visit in passing."

"Then I would advise you, by all means, to do something to your toilet before you leave this."

Hardress took up a miror which lay on the wooden chimney-piece, and satisfied himself, by a single glance, of the wisdom of his mother's suggestion. His eyes were bloodshot, his beard grown and grisly, and his hair hanging about his temples in most ungraceful profusion. He rang the little bell which lay on the table, and summoned the landlady to his presence. It would be difficult, she told him, to procure a hair-cutter to-day, being a holiday, but there was one from Garryowen below, that would do the business as well as any one in the world, if he had only got his scissors with him.

Hardress started at the name of Garryowen; but as he did not remember the hair-cutter, and felt an anxiety to hear news from that quarter, he desired the stranger to be shown into another room, where he proposed effecting the necessary changes in his attire.

He had scarcely taken his seat before the toilet, when a soft tap at the door, and the sound of a small, squeaking voice, announced the arrival of a tailor. On looking round him, Hardress beheld a small, thin-faced, red-haired little man, with a tailor's shears dangling from his finger, bowing and smiling with a timid and conciliating air. In an evil hour for his patience, Hardress consented that he should commence operations.

"The piatez were very airly this year, sir," he modestly began, after he had wrapped a check apron about the neck of Hardress, and made the other necessary arrangements.

"Very early indeed. You needn't cut so fast."

"Very airly, sir—the white-eyes especially. Them white-eyes are fine piatez. For the first four months I wouldn't ax a better piatie than a white-eye, with a bit o' bacon, if one had it; but afther that the meal goes out of 'em, and they gets wet and bad. The cups arn't so good in the beginnin' o' the saison, but they hould better. Turn your head more to the light, sir, if you plase. The cups, indeed, are a fine, substantial, lasting piatie. There's great nutriment in 'em for poor people, that would have nothin' else with them but themselves or a grain o' salt. There's no piatie that eats better, when you have nothin' but a bit o' the little one (as they say) to eat with a bit o' the big. No piatie that eats so sweet with point."

"With point?" Hardress repeated, a little amused by this fluent discussion of the poor hair-cutter upon the varieties of a dish which, from his childhood, had formed almost his only article of nutriment, and on which he expatiated with as much cognoscence and satisfaction as a fashionable gourmand might do on the culinary productions of Eustache Ude. "What is point?"

"Don't you know what that is, sir? I'll tell you in a minute. A joke that them that has nothin' to do, an' plenty to eat, make upon the poor people that has nothin' to eat, and plenty to do. That is, when there's dry piatez on the table, and enough of hungry people about it, and the family would have, maybe, only one bit o' bacon hanging up above their heads, they'd peel a piatie first, and then they'd point it up at the bacon, and they'd have the taste o' the mait when they'd be aitin' it after. That's what they call point, sir. A cheap sort o' diet it is (Lord help us!) that's plenty enough among the poor people in this country. A great plan for making a small bit o' pork go a long way in a large family."

"Indeed, it is but a slender sort of food. Those scissors you have are dreadful ones."

"Terrible, sir. I sent my own over to the forge before I left home, to have any eye put in it; only for that I'd be smarter a deal. Slender food it is, indeed. There's a deal o' poor people here in Ireland, sir, that are run so hard at times, that the wind of a bit o' mait is as good to 'em as the mait itself to them that would be used to it. The piatez are everythin'—the *kitchen* little or nothin'. But there's a sort of piatez (I don't know did your honour ever taste 'em) that's gettin' greatly in vogue now among 'em, an' is killin' half the country—the white piatez—a piatie that has great produce, an' requires but little manure, an' will grow in very poor land, but has no more strength nor nourishment in it than if you had boiled a handful o' sawdust and made gruel of it, or put a bit of deal boord between your teeth and thought to make a breakfast of it. The black bulls themselves are better. Indeed, the black bulls are a deal a better piatie than they're thought. When you'd peel 'em, they'd look as black as indigo, an' you'd have no mind to 'em at all; but I declare they're very sweet in the mouth, an' very strengthenin'. The English reds are a nate piatio too; and the apple piatie (I don't know what made 'em be given up), an' the kidney (though delicate of rearing); but give me the cups for all, that will hould the meal in 'em to the last, and won't require any inthricket tillage. Let a man have a middling-sized pit o' cups again' the winter, a small *caish* † to pay his rent, an' a handful o' turf behind the doore, an' he can defy the world."

"You know as much, I think," said Hardress, "of farming as of hair-cutting."

"Oyeh, if I had nothing to depend upon but what heads comes across me this way, sir, I'd be in a poor way enough. But I have a little spot o' ground besides."

"And a good taste for the produce."

"'Twas kind father for me to have that same. Did you ever hear tell, sir, of what they call limestone broth?"

"Never."

"'Twas my father first made it. I'll tell you the story, sir, if you'll turn your head this way a minute."

Hardress had no choice but to listen.

"My father went once upon a time about the country, in the idle season, seeing would he make a penny at all by cutting hair, or setting razhurs and penknives, or any other job that would fall in his way. Well an' good—he was one day walking alone in the mountains of Kerry, without a hai'p'ny in his pocket (for though he travelled afoot, it cost him more than he earned), an' knowing there was but little love for a county Limerick man in the place where he was, on being half perished with the hunger, an' evening drawing nigh, he didn't know well what to do with himself till morning. Very good—he went along the wild road, an' if he did, he soon see a farm-house at a little distance, o' one side—a snug-looking place, with the smoke curling up out of the chimney, an' all tokens of good living inside. Well, some people would live where a fox would starve. What do you think did my father do? He wouldn't beg (a thing one of our people never done yet, thank Heaven!), an' he hadn't the money to buy a thing; so what does he do? He takes up a couple o' the big limestones that were lying on the road in his two hands, an' away with him to the house. 'Lord save all here!' says he, walkin' in the door. 'And you kindly,' says they. 'I'm come to your,' says he, this way, looking at the two limestones, 'to know would you let me make a little limestone broth over your fire, until I'll make my dinner?' 'Limestone broth!' says they to him again; 'what's that, eroo?' 'Broth made o' limestone,' says he; 'what else?' 'We never heard of such a thing,' says they. 'Why, then, you may hear it now,' says he, 'an see it also, if you'll gi' me a pot an' a couple o' quarts o' soft water.' 'You can have it an' welcome,' says they. So they put down the pot an' the water, an' my father went over an' tuk a chair hard by the pleasant fire for himself, an' put down his two limestones to boil, and kept stirrin' them round like stirabout. Very good—well, by an' by, when the wather began to boil—'Tis thickening fine,' says my father; 'now, if it had a grain o' salt at all, 'twould be a great improvement to it.' 'Raich down the salt-box, Nell,' says the man o' the house to his wife. So she did. 'Oh! that's the very thing just,' says my father, shaking some of it into the pot. So he stirred it again a while, looking as sober as a minister. By an' by, he takes the spoon he had stirring it, an' tastes it. 'It is very good now,' says he, 'although it wants something yet.' 'What is it?' says they. 'Oyeh, wisha, nothing,' says he; 'maybe 'tis only fancy o'me. 'If it's anything we can give you,'

* Anything eaten with potatoes.   † A pig.

72

FIGHTING POLL'S ENTRY INTO COURT.

ays they, 'you're welcome to it.' 'Tis very good as it is,' says
he; 'but when I'm at home, I find it gives it a fine flavour just
to boil a little knuckle o' bacon, or mutton trotters, or anything
that way, along with it.' 'Raich hether that bone o' sheep's
head we had at dinner yesterday, Nell,' says the man o' the
house. 'Oyeh, don't mind it,' says father; 'let be as it is.'
Sure if it improves it, you may as well,' says they. '*Baither-*
*hin !'** says my father, putting it down. So after boiling it a
good piece longer, ''Tis as fine limestone broth,' says he, 'as
ever was tasted; an' if a man had a few piatez,' says he, looking
at a pot of 'em that was smokin' in the chimney corner, 'he
couldn't desire a better dinner.' They gave him the piatez, and
he made good dinner of themselves an' the broth, not forgetting
the bone, which he polished equal to chaney before he let it go.
'he people themselves tasted it, an' thought it as good as any
mutton broth in the world."

"Your father, I believe, knew how to amuse his friends after
short journey as well as any other traveller."

* Be it so.

The fellow leered at Hardress, thrust out his lips, and winked
with both eyes, in a manner which cannot be expressed. "He
was indeed a mighty droll funny man. Not interruptin' you,
sir, I'll tell you a thing that happened him in the hair-cuttin'
line, that flogs all Munster I think for 'cuteness."

"I am afraid I cannot wait to hear it. I have a great way to
go to-day, and a great deal to do before I set off."

"That's just biddin' me go on with my story, sir; for the
more I talk, the faster I work, for ever. Just turn your head
this way, sir, if you plase. My father—a little more to the
light, sir—my father was sittin' one fine mornin' in his little
shop, curlin' a front curl belongin' to a lady (we won't mention
who) in the neighbourhood, with the sun shinin' in the door,
and he singin' a little song for himself, an' meself, a craithur,
sittin' by the fire, lookin' about me, an' sayin' nothin'. Very
well; all of a sudden a gentleman, tall and well mounted, rode
up to the doore, an', 'Hello!' says he, callin' out,' 'can I get
myself shaved here?' says he. 'Why not, plase your honour?'
says my father, startin' up, and layin' by the front out of his

hand. So he 'lit off his horse, an' come in. He was a mighty bould, fierce-looking gentleman, with a tundherin' long sword be his side, down, an' a pair o' whiskers as big an' as red as a fox's brush, an' eyes as round as them two bull's eyes in the window-panes, an' they having a strange twisht in 'em, so that when he'd be lookin' you straight in the face, you'd think it's out at the door he'd be lookin'. Besides that, when he'd spake, he used to give himself a loud roisterin' way, as if you were a mile off, an' not willin' to come near or to be said by him. 'Do you mind, now,' says he, an' he takin' a chair oppozzit the windee, while my father smartened himself, an' bate up a lather—'ever and always, since I was the height of a bee's knee,' says he, 'I had a mortal ennity to seein' a drop o' my own blood, an' I'll tell you what it is,' says he. 'What is it, sir?' says my father. 'I'll make a clear bargin with you now,' says the gentleman. So he took out a half crown, an' laid it upon the table, au' after that he drew his swoord, and laid it hard by the half-crown. 'Do you see them two now?' says he. 'I do, surely,' says my father. 'The half-crown will be yours,' says the gentleman, 'if you'll shave me without drawin' my blood; but if I see as much as would make a breakfast for—(he named an animal that I won't mention after him now)—if I see as much after you,' says he, 'I'll run this swoord through your body, as sure as there's mait in mutton. So look before you lep; if you won't take the bargain, say it, and let me ride away,' says he. This was in times when a gentleman that way would think as little a'most of doin' a thing o' the kind to a poor Catholic as he would now of sayin' it; so well became my father to look to himself. "You'll never have it to say o' me,' says my father, 'that I wouldn't trust my hand so far at any rate in the business I was bred to.' So to it they fell, an' as Providence ordered it, my father shaved him without one gash, an' put the half-crown in his pocket. 'Well, now 'tis done,' says the gentleman, 'but you're a foolish man.' 'How so, sir?' says my father. 'Because, so sure as I saw the blood,' says the other, 'I'd make my word good.' 'But you never would see the blood, sir,' says my father, quite easy, 'because I'd see it before you, an' I'd cut your throat with the razhur.' Well, 'twas as good as a play to see the look the gentleman gave him when he said that. He didn't answer him a word, but mounted his horse, and rode away.'

"He found his match in the hair-cutter," said Hardress, rejoiced as the story ended.

"I'll be bound, sir, he was in no hurry to make bargains o' that kind any more. 'Twas a mighty good answer, sir, wasn't it?"

"A desperate one at all events."

"Ah, desperate, you may say that; but my father was sure of his hand. I'll tell you another droll thing that happened my father once, when——"

But the patience of his listener was here completely stranded. The hair-cutter had got such a miserable pair of shears, that he was obliged to use as much exertion in clipping the hair as a tinker or a plumber might do in cutting sheet lead. Besides, being accustomed to that professional flippancy of movement which, with proper instruments, might have expedited the operation, he made no allowance for the badness of his scissors, but clipped and plucked away as fast as usual, thus contriving to tear up half as much by the roots as he removed in the usual course of business. This and other circumstances induced Hardress to place a decided negative in the way of his anecdotes until he had concluded his task.

This being accomplished, Hardress raised his hand to his head, and experienced a sensation on the palm somewhat similar to that which would be produced by placing it on an inverted hair-brush. On looking in the glass, he discovered that his hair had been cut into a fashion which enjoys a lasting popularity at fairs and cottage merry-makings; but, however consistent with the interests of persons who only employed a barber once in a quarter, and then supposed that the closer he cut the better value he gave for the money, it was by no means in accordance with the established notions of good taste. There were, indeed, no gaps, as he boasted, for he had cut it almost as bare as a wig-block, leaving only a narrow fringe in front, from ear to ear, like the ends of a piece of silk. There was no help, however, for such mischief once effected, so that Hardress paid him without remark, and paid him liberally.

The little hair-cutter took it for granted, by the handsome manner in which his customer had compensated for his services, that he was highly gratified with the manner in which they had been performed.

"If your honour," he said, bowing very low, "would be passing through Garryowen, an' would be inclined to lave any o' your hair behind you, maybe you'd think of Dunat O'Leary's shop, on the right-hand side o' the sthreet, three doores down from Mihil O'Connor's, the rope-maker's."

"I will, I will," said Hardress, turning suddenly away.

Mr. O'Leary walked slowly to the door, and again returned.

"There's a great set o' lads about the place, sir," he said, in his usual shrill voice, while a slight degree of embarrassment appeared in his manner, "an' they're for ever christenin' people out o' their names, till a man is better known by a nickname than by his own. 'Tis ten to one, plase your honour, that you'll be the surer of finding me by asking for Foxy Dunat than for my own lawful name; they're such a set o' lads."

"Very well; good morning, Foxy Dunat."

"Yes, sir, Foxy, in regard of the red hair that's on me. Ah, there's no standing them lads."

"Very well; good morning, Foxy Dunat. I'll remember."

"Good morning to your honour. Stay!" he once more returned from the door. "See what I was doing—carrying your honour's hair away with me!"

"Well, and what business do you suppose I have of it now? I am not a wig-maker."

"I don't know, sir, but people mostly likes to put it up in some safe place again' the day of judgment, as they say."

"The day of judgment!"

"Yes, plase your honour. We must have everything about us then that ever belonged to us, an' a man would look droll that time without his hair."

Hardress was not in a humour for jesting, but he could not avoid smiling in secret at this conceit.

"Very well," said he, tapping the hair-cutter upon the shoulder, and looking gravely in his face. "As I am going a long journey at present I will feel obliged by your keeping it for me until then, and I will call on you if I want it."

"As your honour feels agreeable," said Dunat, again bowing low, and moving towards the door. Nevertheless, he did not leave the room until he had made the young gentleman acquainted with all the circumstances that occasioned his absence from home at this moment. In doing so he unwarily touched Hardress to the quick. He had come, he said, in consequence of a letter he had received from a neighbour's daughter that had run away from her father, and was hid somewhere among the Kerry mountains.

"A letter you received!" exclaimed Hardress in strong surprise.

"Yes, sir, telling me she was alive, and bidding me let the old man know of it, the old rope-maker I mentioned a while ago. Since I came it reported at Castle Island this morning that she was drownded somewhere in the Flesk."

"Drowned! Eily drowned!" Hardress suddenly exclaimed, starting from a reverie, as the single word struck upon his hearing.

"Eily was her name, sure enough," replied O'Leary, staring on him, "howsomdever you come to know it."

"I—I—you mentioned that name, I think—did you not?"

"Maybe it slipped from me, sir. Well, as I was saying, they thought she was drownded there, an' they wor for havin' a sheaf o' reeds, with her name tied upon it, put out upon the sthrame; for they say, when a person dies by water, the sheaf o' reeds will float against the sthrame, or with the sthrame, until it stops over the place where the body lies, if it had to go up O'Sullivan's cascade itself. But Father Edward O'Connor desired 'em to go home about their business, that the sheaf would go with the current, an' no way else, if they were at it from this till doomsday. To be sure he knew best."

At this moment the landlady knocked at the door to inform our collegian that Mrs. Cregan was expecting him without. Having concluded his toilet, he hurried out of the room, not displeased at his release from the observation of this stranger, at a moment when he felt his agitation increasing to an extent that was almost ungovernable.

CHAPTER XXXI.

HOW KYRLE DALY HEARS OF THE HANDSOME CONDUCT OF HIS FRIEND HARDRESS.

PREVIOUS to Anne Chute's departure from the cottage of her aunt all the arrangements necessary for her marriage with Hardress had been verbally agreed upon. A feeling of decorum only prevented the legal preliminaries from being put in form before her return to her mother's castle. The singularly unequal and unaccountable behaviour of her intended husband, during the whole course of wooing, had left her mind in a condition of distressing annoyance and perplexity. Though she still loved Hardress well, it was with an anxious and uneasy affection, such as she should entertain for a mysterious being whose talents had fascinated her will, but of whose real nature she yet remained in troubled ignorance. Fame, who never moves her wings so swiftly as when she has got a tale to tell of death or marriage, soon spread the information far and wide. The manner in which it reached the ears of Kyrle Daly was sudden as it was unwelcome.

He had gone down to the dairy-farm for the purpose of shore-shooting, and was returning in order to spend the Little Christmas at home. It was about noon when he rode by the gate at Castle Chute. The door of the dwelling-house stood open, and several figures appeared on the broad stone steps. They were too distant to be recognised; but Kyrle glanced with a beating pulse towards that part of the building which contained the sleeping-chamber of his mistress. The window-shutters were unclosed, and it was evident that Anne Chute had once more become a resident in the castle.

In order to be assured of the reality of this belief, young Daly spurred on his horse as far as the caravansary of Mr. Normile, already celebrated in an early part of our history. That individual, whom he found in the act of liberating an unruly pig, after payment of pound fees, informed him of the arrival at Castle Chute, a fortnight previously, of its young heiress and her uncle.

He rode on, unwilling to trust himself with any lengthened conversation on this subject while under the shrewd eye of an Irish peasant. All his former passion returned in an instant, and with an intensity which surprised himself. It had been the labour of his life, since his last interview with the young lady above named, to remove her quietly from his recollection, and he flattered himself that he had, in a great degree, succeeded. He was no believer in the romantic and mischievous supposition that true love never changes nor decays, even when hope has left it. He knew that there were many effeminate and sensitive characters, who, having once permitted their imaginations to become deeply impressed, are afterwards weak enough to foster that impression, even while it is making inroads upon their health and peace; but such beings were the objects of his pity, not of his esteem. He was neither a fanatic nor a voluptuary in the passion. If, therefore, he had discovered that any one of those rational considerations on which his love was founded, had been erroneously taken up—if he had discovered that the lady was, in reality, unworthy of the place to which he had raised her, we do not say he would at once have ceased to love, but he would certainly have experienced much less difficulty in subduing the frequent agitations of the passion. But he had not the assistance of such a conviction; and it was only after a long and vigilant exercise of his habitual firmness that he had reduced his mind to a state of dormant tranquillity.

Opportunity, therefore, was only needed to rouse it up once more in all its former strength. That opportunity had now arrived, and Kyrle Daly found that the trial was a more searching one than he had been led to think. He yielded for a moment to the reflections which pressed upon him, and slackened the pace of his steed. He looked upon the castle and its quiet bay, the point, the wood, the waves, and the distant hills of Clare. He passed the little sandy slope on which he had witnessed the festivities of the saddle-race, and which now looked wintry, lone, and bleak in the December blast. The face of the river was dark and troubled—the long waves of the half-flood tide rolled in, and broke upon the sands, leaving a track of foam upon the water's verge, while a long black line of seaweed marked the height to which it had arisen on the shore. He glanced at the pathway from the road, on which his hopes had experienced their last decisive and severe repression. His feelings, at this moment, approached the limits of pain too nearly, and he spurred on his horse to hurry away from them, and from the scene on which they had been first called into action.

He had not ridden far when he heard loud bursts of laughter, and the tramp of many horses on the road behind him. The voices were raised high in the competition to obtain a hearing, and he thought the accents were not those of strangers. The proud politeness of an Irish gentleman, which was rather conventional than natural with Kyrle Daly, prevented his looking round to satisfy his curiosity until the party had ridden up, and he heard his own name coupled with a familiar greeting by many voices. Turning on his saddle, he beheld Mr. Connolly, Mr. Hyland Creagh, Dr. Leake, and Captain Gibson, riding abreast, and laughing immoderately.

"Connolly, how are you? How are you, doctor? Mr. Creagh—captain," touching his hat slightly to the latter, "what's all the fun about?"

"I'll tell Daly," said Connolly; "he's a lawyer."

"Pish!" replied Dr. Leake, "'tis too foolish a thing; you will make him laugh at you."

"Foolish! It is the best story I ever heard in my life. Eh, captain?"

Captain Gibson replied by an excessive roar of laughter, and Hyland Creagh protested it was worthy of the days of the Hell-fire Club. Connolly looked down in scornful triumph upon the doctor, who tossed his head, and sneered in silence.

"I'll tell you how it was," said Connolly. "I believe 'tis no secret to you, Daly, or any other acquaintance of mine, that I owe more money to different friends than I am always willing to pay,—

> 'Owen Moore ran away,
> Owing more than he could pay;'

so, if I should come to borrow money of you, you had better keep it in your pocket, I advise you. But it so happened that we spent the other evening at a friend's in the neighbourhood, who could not afford me a bed, so I went to hammock at Normile's inn. In the morning I stepped out to the stable to see how my horse had been made up in the night, when I felt a tap on the shoulder—just like that—do you feel it at all electrical?"—(he touched Kyrle's shoulder)—"*I* do always. I turned, and saw a fellow in a brown coat, with a piece of paper in his hand. I was compelled to accept his invitation, so I requested that he would step into the inn while I was taking a little breakfast. While I was doing so, and while he was sitting at the other side of the fire, in walked Pat Falvey, Mrs. Chute's footman, with his mistress's compliments, to thank me for a present of baking apples I had sent her. I winked at Pat, and looked at the bailiff. 'Pat,' says I, 'tell your mistress not to mention it; and Pat,' says I, dropping to a whisper, 'I am a prisoner.' 'Very well, sir,' says Pat aloud, and bowing as if I had given him some message. He left the room, and in ten minutes I had the whole parish about the windows. They came in, they called for the bailiff, they seized him, and beat him until they didn't leave him worth looking at. Dooly, the nailer, caught his arm, and O'Reilly, the blacksmith, took him by the leg, and another by the hair, and another by the throat; and such a show as they made of him before five minutes, I never contemplated. But here was the beauty of it. I knew the law, so I opposed the whole proceeding. 'No rescue,' says I; 'I am his prisoner, gentlemen, and I will not be rescued; so don't beat the man!—don't toss him in a blanket!—don't drag him in the puddle!—don't plunge him into the horse-pond, I entreat you!' By some fatality my intentions were wholly misconceived, and they performed exactly the things that I warned them to avoid. They did beat him—they did toss him in a blanket—they did drag him through the puddle—and they did plunge him into the horse-pond! Only imagine what were my chagrin and disappointment. Dr. Leake maintains that it is a misprision of battery—a law term I never heard in my life. As if, by desiring them not to drag him through the horse-pond, I *imagined* their doing it. Then it was an overt act of dragging him through the horse-pond. *Compassing* the dragging him through would have been an actual act of battery, but the imagining of it is only an overt act; as among the English regicides, by cutting off the head of Charles, they were said to *imagine* his death, which was an *overt act* of treason, whereas compassing his death was the actual treason itself. But in this case I deny both the *compassing* and the imagination. What do you think of it, Mr. Daly?"

"I think," said Kyrle with a smile, "that you ought to come and take my opinion on it some day or other."

"Ah, ah!" replied Connolly, shaking his head. "I understand you, young lawyer! Well, when I have a fee to spare, you shall have it. But here is the turn up to my house. *Est ubi locus*—how I forget my Latin! Daly, will you come up and dine with me?"

"I cannot, thank you."

"Well, I'm sorry for it. Creagh, you're not going?"

"I must."

"Stop and dine."

"No. I'll see you to-morrow. I have business in town."

The party separated, Kyrle Daly and Creagh continuing to ride in the same direction, while the rest wheeled off by a narrow by-road.

"You will be at the wedding, I suppose, Mr. Daly?" said the latter gentleman, after a silence of some minutes.

"What wedding?" asked Kyrle in some surprise.

"Why, have you not heard of it? Miss Chute's wedding."

"Miss Chute!" Kyrle repeated faintly.

"Yes. Everything, I understand, has been arranged for the ceremony, and Cregan tells me it is to take place next month. She would be a magnificent wife for any man!"

It was some moments before Kyrle could recover breath to ask another question.

"And—a—of course you heard who is to be the bridegroom?" he said with much hesitation.

"O yes! I thought he was a friend of yours. Mr. Hardress Cregan."

"Cregan!" exclaimed Kyrle aloud, and starting as if he had received a galvanic shock; "it is impossible!"

"Sir!" said Creagh sternly.

"I think," said Kyrle, governing himself by a violent exertion, "you must have been misinformed. Hardress Cregan is, as you say, my friend, and he cannot be the man."

"I seldom, sir," said Creagh, with a haughty curl on his lip, "converse with any person who is capable of making false assertions; and, in the present instance, I should think the gentleman's father no indifferent authority."

Again Kyrle Daly paused for some minutes in an emotion of deep apprehension. "Has Mr. Cregan, then, told you," he said, "that his son was to be the bridegroom?"

"I have said he has."

Daly closed his lips hard, and straightened his person, as if to relieve an internal pain. This circumstance accounted for the enigmatical silence of his friend. But what a horrible solution!

"It is very strange," he said, "notwithstanding. There are many impediments to such a marriage. He is her cousin."

"Pooh, pooh! that's a name of courtesy. It is only a connection by affinity. Cousin! Hang them all, cousins on a string, say I! They are the most dangerous rivals a man can have. Any other man you can call out and shoot through the head, if he attempts to interfere with your prospects, but cousins must have a privilege. The lady may walk with her cousin (hang him!), and she may dance with her cousin, and write to her cousin, and it is only when she has run away with her cousin that you find that you have been cozened with a vengeance."

While Creagh made this speech Kyrle Daly was running over in his mind the entire circumstances of young Cregan's conduct, and the conclusion to which his reflections brought him was, that a more black and shameful treason had never been practised between man and man. For the first time in his life Kyrle Daly wholly lost his self-government. Principle, religion, duty, justice, all vanished for the instant from his mind, and nothing but the deadly injury remained to stare him in the face.

"I will horsewhip him!" he said within his mind; "I will horsewhip him at the wedding feast. The cool, dark hypocrite! I suppose, sir," he said aloud, turning to Creagh with a smile of calm and dignified courtesy, "I suppose I may name you as my authority for this?"

"Certainly, certainly," returned the old duellist with a short

bow, while his eyes lit up with pleasure at the idea of an affair of honour. "Stay a moment, Mr. Daly," he added, as the young gentleman was about to quicken his pace, "I perceive, sir, that you are going to adopt, in this business, the course that is usual among men of honour. Now, I have had a little experience in these affairs, and I am willing to be your friend——"

"Pardon me, Mr. Creagh, I——"

"Nay, pardon *me*, Mr. Daly, if you please. I do not mean your friend in the usual acceptation of the term; I do not mean your second; you may have a desire to choose for yourself in that respect; I merely wished to say that I could afford you some useful hints as to your conduct on the ground. In the first instance, look to your powder. Dry it yourself overnight on a plate, which you may keep hot over a vessel of warm water. Insert your charge at the breech of the pistol, and let your ball be covered with kid leather, softened with the finest salad oil. See that your barrel is polished and free from dust. I have known many a fine fellow lose his life by purchasing his ammunition at a grocer's on the morning of the duel. They bring it him out of some cask in a damp cellar, and of course it hangs fire. Do you avoid that fault. Then, when you come to the ground—level ground of course—fix your eye on some object beyond your foe, and bring him in a line with that; then let your pistol hang by your side, and draw an imaginary line from the mouth of the barrel to the third button of your opponent's coat. When the word is given, raise your weapon rapidly along that line, and fire at the button. He will never hear the shot."

"Tell me, Mr. Creagh," said Kyrle in a grave tone, after he heard these murderous directions to the end, "are not you a friend of Mr. Cregan?"

"Yes. Very old friends."

"Do you not dine at his table, and sleep under his roof from day to day?"

"Pray what is the object of these curious questions?"

"It is this," said Kyrle, fixing his eyes upon the man: "I find it impossible to express the disgust I feel at hearing you, the professed and bounden friend of that family, thus practise upon the life of one of its chief members—the son of your benefactor. Away, sir, with your bloody science to those who will become your pupils! I hope the time will come in Ireland when you and your mean and murderous class shall be despised and trampled on as you deserve."

"How am I to take this, Mr. Daly?"

"As you will!" exclaimed Kyrle, driven wholly beyond the bounds of self-possession, and tossing a desperate hand towards the duellist. "I have done with you."

"Not yet, please the fates," Creagh said, in his usual restrained tone, while Kyrle Daly galloped away in the direction of his father's house. "To-morrow morning, perhaps, you may be enabled to say that with greater certainty. He is a fine young fellow. I didn't think it was in him. Now, whom shall I have? Connolly? Cregan? I owe it to Connolly, as I performed the same office for him a short time since; and yet I'd like to pay old Cregan the compliment. Well, I can think about it as I ride along."

CHAPTER XXXII.

HOW KYRLE DALY'S WARLIKE ARDOUR WAS CHECKED BY AN UNTOWARD INCIDENT.

A JOYOUS piece of news awaited Kyrle Daly at the door of his own home. Lowry Looby met him on the avenue, his little arms outstretched, and his huge mouth expanded with an expression of delighted astonishment.

"Oh, Master Kyrle!" he said, "you're just come in time. I was goin' off for you. Hurry in—hurry in, sir! There's a new little sister within waiting for you this way."

"And your mistress, Lowry?" said Kyrle, springing from his horse, and tossing the reins to the servant.

"Finely, finely, sir, thank Heaven!"

"Thank Heaven indeed!" echoed Daly, hurrying on with a flushed and gladdened face towards the hall-door. Everything of self, his disappointment, the treachery of his friend, the loss of his mistress, and his dilemma with the duellist, were all forgotten in his joy at the safety of his mother.

The door stood open, and the hall was crowded with servants, children, and tenants. In the midst of a hundred exclamations of wonder, delight, and affection, which broke from the lips of the group, the faint cry of a baby was heard, no louder than the wail of a young kitten. He saw his father holding the little stranger in his arms, and looking in its face with a smile, which he was in vain endeavouring to suppress. The old kitchen-maid stood on his right, with her apron to her eyes, crying for joy. One or two younger females, the wives of tenants, were on the other side, gazing on the red and peevish little face of the innocent with a smile of maternal sympathy and compassion. A fair-haired girl clung to her father's skirt, and petitioned loudly to be allowed to nurse it for a moment. Another looked rebukingly upon her, and told her to be silent. North-east and Charles had clambered upon a chair to over-look the throng which they could not penetrate. Patcy stood near the parlour door, jumping with all his might, and clapping his hands like one possessed. There appeared only one dis-contented figure on the scene. It was that of little Sally, hitherto the pet and plaything of the family, who stood in a distant corner, with her face turned to the wall, her lip pouting, and her blue eye filling up with jealous tears.

The moment Kyrle made his appearance at the door the uproar was redoubled. "Kyrle! Kyrle! Here's Kyrle! Kyrle, look at your sister! look at your sister!" exclaimed a dozen voices, while the group at the same moment opened, and admitted him into the centre.

"Poor little darling!" said Kyrle, patting it on the cheek. "Is it not better to take it in out of the cold, sir?"

"I think so, Kyrle. Nurse! Where's the nurse?"

The door of Mrs. Daly's sleeping-chamber opened, and a woman appeared on the threshold, looking rather anxious. She ran hastily through the hall, got a bowl of water in the kitchen, and hurried back again into the bedroom.

"Why doesn't she come?" said Mr. Daly. "The little thing cries so, I am afraid it is pinched by the air."

"I suppose she is busy with my aunt O'Connell and her patient yet," said Kyrle.

A hurried tramping of feet was now heard in the bedroom, and the sound of rapid voices in anxiety and confusion. A dead silence sank upon the hall. Mr. Daly and his son ex-changed a glance of thrilling import. A low moan was the next sound that proceeded from the room. The husband placed the child in the arms of the old woman, and hurried to the chamber door. He was met at the threshold by his sister, Mrs. O'Connell (a grave-looking lady in black), who placed her hands against his breast, and said, with great agitation of manner,—

"Charles, you must not come in yet."

"Why so, Mary? How is she?"

"Winny," said Mrs. O'Connell, addressing the old woman who held the infant, "take the child into the kitchen until the nurse can come to you."

"How is Sally?" repeated the anxious husband.

"You had better go into the parlour, Charles. Recollect yourself now, my dear Charles; remember your children——"

The old man began to tremble. "Mary," he said, "why will you not answer me? How is she?"

"She is not better, Charles."

"Not better!"

"No, far otherwise."

"Far otherwise! Come, woman, let me pass into the room!"

"You must not, indeed you must not, Charles!" exclaimed his sister, flinging her arms round his neck, and bursting into tears. "Kyrle, Kyrle! speak to him!"

Young Daly caught his father's arm. "Well, well," said the latter, looking round him with a calm, yet ghastly smile, "if you are all against me, I must of course submit."

"Come with me to the parlour," said Mrs. O'Connell, "and I will explain to you."

She took him by the arm, and led him, with a vacant countenance and passive demeanour, through the silent and astonished group. They entered the parlour, and the door was closed by Mrs. O'Connell. Kyrle Daly remained fixed like a statue in the same attitude in which his aunt had left him, and a moment of intense and deep anxiety ensued. The rare and horrid sound, the scream of an old man in suffering, was the first that broke on that portentous stillness. It acted like a spell upon the group in the hall. They were dispersed in an instant. The women ran shrieking in various directions. The

men looked dismayed, and uttered hurried sentences of wonder and affright. The children, terrified by the confusion, added their shrill and helpless wailings to the rest. The death-cry re-echoed in the bedroom, in the parlour, and in the kitchen. From every portion of the dwelling the funeral shriek ascended to the heavens; and Death and Sorrow, like armed conquerors, seemed to have possessed themselves by sudden storm of this little hold, where peace and happiness had reigned so long and calmly.

Kyrle's first impulse, on hearing his father's voice, made him rush to the bedroom of his mother. There was no longer any opposition at the door, and he entered with a throbbing heart. The nurse was crying aloud, and wringing her hands at the fireplace. Mrs. Leahy, the midwife, was standing near the bedside with a troubled and uneasy countenance, evidently as much concerned for the probable injury to her own reputation as for the affliction of the family. Kyrle passed them both, and drew back the curtain of the bed. His mother was lying back quite dead, and with an expression of languid pain upon her features.

"I never saw a case o' the kind in my life," muttered Mrs. Leahy. "I have attended hundreds in my time, an' I never saw the like. She was sitting up in her bed, sir, as well as I'd wish to see her, an' I just stepped to the fire to warm a little gruel, when I heard Mrs. O'Connell calling me. I ran to the bed, an' sure there I found her dying! She just gave one moan, and 'twas all over. I never heard of such a case. All the skill in the world wouldn't be any good in such a business."

Kyrle Daly felt no inclination to dispute the point with her. A heavy, dizzy sensation was in his brain, which made his actions and his manners resemble those of a person who walks in his sleep. He knelt down to pray, but a feeling like lethargy disqualified him for any exercise of devotion. He rose again, and walked listlessly into the hall.

Almost at the same moment Mr. Daly appeared at the parlour door, followed by his aged sister, who was still in tears. The old man glanced at his children, and waved his hands before him. "Take them from my sight," he said in a low voice; "let the orphans be removed; go now, my children, we never shall be happy here again."

"Charles, my dear Charles!" said his sister, in a tone of gentle remonstrance, while she laid her hand upon his shoulder.

"Well, Mary, I will do whatever you like. Heaven knows I am not fit to direct myself now. Ha! Kyrle, are you returned? I remember I wrote you word to come home to conclude the Christmas with us. I did not think you would have so mourn-ful a home to come to. When did you come?"

"You forget, Charles, that you saw Kyrle a while ago," said Mrs. O'Connell.

"Did I? I had forgotten it," returned Mr. Daly, tossing his head. He extended his hand to Kyrle, and burst into tears. Kyrle could not do so. He passed his father and aunt, and entered the parlour which was now deserted. He sat down at a small table before the window, and, leaning on his elbow, looked out upon the face of the river. The wintry tide was flowing against a sharp and darkening gale, and a number of boats, with close-reefed sails and black hulls, heeling to the blast, were beating through the yellow waves; the sky was low and dingy; the hills of Cratloe rose on the other side in all their bleak and barren wildness of attire. A harsh wind stirred the dry and leafless woodbines that covered the front of the cottage, and every object in the landscape seemed to wear a character of dreariness and discomfort.

Here he remained for several hours in the same dry and stolid mood of reflection. Not a single tear, not a single sound of sorrow, was added by him to the general clamour of the household. He never before had been tried by an occasion of this nature, and his present apathy filled him with alarm and astonishment. He listened to the wailings of the women and children, and he looked on the moistened faces of those who hurried past his chair from time to time, until he began to accuse himself of want of feeling and affection.

While he sat thus silent the door was opened, and Lowry Looby thrust in his head to inform him that the family were assembled to say a litany in the other room. Kyrle rose, and proceeded thither without reply or question; while Lowry, oppressed with grief, made his retreat into the kitchen. Here he was met by the nurse, who asked him for some halfpence, that she might lay them, according to custom, on the lips and eyes of the corpse.

"I didn't like," she said, "to be tazing any o' the family about it, an' they in throuble."

"Surely, surely," said Lowry, while he searched his pockets for the coin. "Ah, nurse! so that's the way ye let her go between ye! Oh, asthora, Mrs. Daly! an' 'tis I that lost the good misthress in you this day! Soft and pleasant be your bed in heaven this night! An' so it will. You never refused to feed the hungry here, an' God won't refuse to feed you where you are gone. You never turned the poor out o' your house in this world, and God won't turn you out of his house in the other. Soft and pleasant be your bed in heaven this night, Mrs. Daly! Winny, eroo, wasn't it you was telling me that the misthress's three first childher died at nurse?"

Old Winny was sitting by the fireside dandling the now forgotten little infant in her arms, and lulling it with an ancient ditty, of which the following beautiful fragment formed the burden:—

> "Gilli beg le m' onum thu!
> Gilli beg le m' chree!
> Coth yani me von gilli beg,
> 'N heur re thu more a creena." *

"They did," she said, in answer to Lowry's question; "all before Master North-aist went off so fast as they wor wained."

"See that!" said Lowry. "She cried—I wasn't in the family then—but still I know she cried a pottle for every one o' them. An' see how it is now—she has them three little angels waitin' to resaive her at the gate of heaven this day. Here is the money, nurse, an' I wish every coin of it was goold for the use you're going to make of it."

The nurse left the kitchen, and Lowry took his seat upon the settle-bed, where he remained for some time looking downwards, and striking the end of his walking-stick against the floor, gently and at regular intervals. The crying of the child disturbed his meditations, and he frequently lifted his head and stared with a look of stern remonstrance at the unconscious innocent.

"The Lord forgive you, you little disciple!" said Lowry. "'Tis little you know what harm you done this day! Do all you can —grow up as fine as a queen, an' talk like an angel—'twill set you to fill up the place o' the woman you took away from us this day. Howl your tongue, again I tell you; 'tis we that have raison to cry, an' not you."

The news of this unexpected visitation became diffused throughout the country with a speed resembling that of sound itself. Friend after friend dropped in as evening fell, and the little parlour was crowded before midnight. It was a dreadful night without, the same (it will be remembered) on which Eily O'Connor left the cottage in the Gap. The thunder clattered close overhead, the rain fell down in torrents, and the reflection of the frequent lightning-flashes danced upon the glasses and bowl, around which the company were seated in the parlour. It was yet too soon for the report to have reached the ears of the real friends of the family, whose condolence might have been more efficacious than that of the humbler crowd of distant relatives and dependents who were now assembled in the house of mourning. Kyrle considered this, and yet he could not avoid a certain dreary and desolate feeling as he looked round upon the throng of persons by whom their hearth was girded. But though he could not receive from them the delicate condolence which his equals might have afforded, their sympathy was not less cordial and sincere.

The night passed away in silence and watching. A few conversed in low whispers, and some pressed each other by signs to drink, but this courtesy was for the most part declined by a gathering of the brows and a shake of the head. The grey and wintry morning found the dwelling thronged with pale, unwashed, and lengthened faces. Some strayed out on the little lawn to breathe the river air. Others thronged the room of death, where an early mass was celebrated for the soul of the departed. At intervals a solitary cry of pain and grief was heard to break from some individual of the crowd, but it was at once repressed by the guests, with low sounds of anger and surprise.

---

* "My soul's little darling you are!
My heart's little darling!
What will I do without my little darling
When you're grown up and old?"

The family were silent in their woe, and it was thought daring in a stranger to usurp their prerogative of sorrow.

The arrivals were more frequent in the course of the second evening, and a number of gigs, curricles, and outside jaunting-cars were laid by in the yard. No circumstance could more fully demonstrate the estimation in which this family was held than the demeanour of the guests as they entered the house. Instead of the accustomed ceremonials which friends use at meeting, they recognised each other in silence and with reserve, as in a house of worship. Sometimes a lifting of the eyelid, and a slight elevation of the hand, expressed their dismay and their astonishment; and if they did exchange a whisper, it was only to give expression to the same feeling—"It was a dreadful loss! Poor man! What will become of the children?"

About nightfall on the second evening Kyrle was standing at the window of the room in which the corpse was laid out. The old nurse was lighting the candles that were to burn on either side of the deathbed. The white curtains were festooned with artificial roses, and a few were scattered upon the counterpane. Kyrle was leaning with his arm against the window-sash, and looking out upon the river, when Mrs. O'Connell laid her hand upon his shoulder.

"Kyrle," said she, "I wish you would speak to your father, and make him go to bed to-night. It would be a great deal too much for him to go without rest the two nights successively."

"I have already spoken to him, aunt, and he has promised me that he will retire early to his room. We ought to be all obliged to you, aunt, for your attention; it is in conjunctures like this that we discover our real friends. I am only afraid that you will suffer from your exertions. Could you not find somebody to attend to the company to-night, while you are taking a little rest?"

"Oh! I am an old nurse-tender," said Mrs. O'Connell. "I am accustomed to sit up. Do not think of me, Kyrle."

She left the room, and Kyrle resumed his meditative posture. Up to this moment he had not shed a single tear, and the nurse was watching him, from time to time, with an anxious and uneasy eye. As he remained looking out, an old man, dressed in dark frieze, and with a stooping gait, appeared upon the little avenue. The eye of Kyrle rested on his figure as he walked slowly forward, assisting his aged limbs with a seasoned blackthorn stick. He figured involuntarily, to his own mind, the picture of this poor old fellow in his cottage, taking his hat and stick, and telling his family that he would "step over to Mrs. Daly's wake." To Mrs. Daly's wake! His mother, with whom he had dined on the Christmas day just past, in perfect health and security! The incident was slight, but it struck the spring of nature in his heart. He turned from the window, threw himself into a chair, extended his arms, let his head hang back, and burst at once into a loud and hysterical passion of grief.

Instantly the room was thronged with anxious figures. All gathered around his chair with expressions of compassion and condolence.

"Come out—come out into the air, Masther Kyrle," said the nurse, while she added her tears to his. "Don't, a'ra gal! Don't now, asthora ma chree! Oh, then, 'tis little wondher you should feel your loss!"

"Kyrle," said Mrs. O'Connell, in a voice nearly as convulsive as his whom she sought to comfort, "remember your father, Kyrle; don't disturb him."

"Let me alone—oh, let me alone, aunt Mary!" returned the young man, waving his hands, and turning away his head, in deep suffering. "I tell you I shall die if you prevent me." And he abandoned himself once more to a convulsive fit of weeping.

"Let him alone, as he says," whimpered old Winny. "I'm sure I thought it wasn't natural he should keep it on his heart so long. It will do him good. Oh, vo, vo! it is a frightful thing to hear a man crying."

Suddenly Mr. Daly appeared amid the group. He walked up to Kyrle's chair, and took him by the arm. The latter checked his feelings on the instant, and arose with a calm and ready obedience. As they passed the foot of the bed, the father and son paused, as if by a consent of intelligence. They exchanged one silent glance, and then flinging themselves each on the other's neck, they wept long, loudly, and convulsively together. There was no one now to interfere. No one dared at this moment to assume the office of comforter, and every individual acted the part of a principal in the affliction. The geneal wail of sorrow which issued from the room was once more echoed in the other parts of the dwelling, and the winds bore it to the ear of Hardress Cregan as he approached the avenue.

CHAPTER XXXIII.

HOW HARDRESS MET A FRIEND OF EILY'S AT THE WAKE.

He entered the house with that species of vulgar resolution which a person feels who is conscious of deserving a repulse, and determined to outface it; but his bravery was wholly needless. Poor Kyrle was busy now with other thoughts than those of Cregan's treachery.

He was shown into the parlour, in which the gentlemen were seated round the fire, and listening to the mournful clamour which yet had hardly subsided in the distant room. The table was covered with decanters of wine, bowls of whiskey-punch, and long glasses. A large turf fire blazed in the grate, and Lowry Looby was just occupied in placing on the table a pair of plated candlesticks almost as long as himself. Mr. Barnaby Cregan, Mr. Connolly, Dr. Leake, and several other gentlemen were seated at one side of the fire. On the other stood a vacant chair, from which Mr. Daly had been summoned a few minutes before by the voice of his son in suffering. A little farther back, on a row of chairs which were placed along the wall, the children were seated—some of them with countenances touchingly dejected, and a few of the very youngest appearing still more touchingly unconscious of their misfortune. The remainder of the circle (which, though widened to the utmost limit, completely filled the room) consisted of the more fortuneless connections of the family, their tradesmen, and some of the more comfortable class of tenants. One or two persons took upon themselves the office of attending to the company, supplying them with liquor, and manufacturing punch, according as the fountain was exhausted.

When Hardress appeared at the door his eye met that of Connolly, who beckoned to him in silence, and made room for him upon his own chair. He took his place, and looked round him for some members of the family. It was, perhaps, rather to his relief than disappointment that he could not discern Kyrle Daly or his father among the company.

Shortly afterwards two or three clergymen made their appearance, and were with difficulty accommodated with places. While Hardress was occupied in perusing the countenances of these last, he felt his arm grasped, and turning round, received a nod of recognition and a hand-shake (such as was then in fashion) from Dr. Leake.

"A dreadful occasion this, doctor," whispered Hardress.

The doctor shut his eyes, knit his brows, thrust out his lips, and shook his head with an air of deep reproof. Laying his hand familiarly on Hardress's knee, and looking fixedly in his face, he said,—

"My dear Cregan, 'tis a warning—'tis a warning to the whole country. This is what comes of employing unscientific persons."

Some whispering conversation now proceeded amongst the guests, which, however, was suddenly interrupted by the appearance of Kyrle Daly at the parlour door. He walked across the room with that port of mournful ease and dignity which men are apt to exhibit under any deep emotion, and took possession of the vacant chair before alluded to. Not forgetful in his affliction of the courtesy of a host, he looked around to see what new faces had entered during his absence. He recognised the clergymen, and addressed them with a calm, yet cordial politeness.

"I hope," he said, smiling courteously, yet sadly, as he looked upon the circle, " I hope the gentlemen will excuse my father for his absence. He was anxious to return, but I prevented him. I thought a second night's watching would have been too severe a trial of his strength."

A general murmur of assent followed this appeal, and the speaker, resting his forehead on his hand, was silent for an instant.

"I wish you would follow his example, Kyrle," said Mr. Cregan. " I am sure we can all take care of ourselves, and you must want rest."

"It is madness," said Connolly, "for the living to injure their health, when it can be of no possible use."

"Pray do not speak of it," said Kyrle; "if I felt in the least degree fatigued, I should not hesitate. Lowry," he added, calling to his servant, who started and turned round on his heel with a serious eagerness that would at any other time have been comic in its effect—" Lowry, will you tell Mrs. O'Connell to send in some tea? Some of the gentlemen may wish to take it."

Lowry disappeared, and Kyrle relapsed into his attitude of motionless dejection. A long silence ensued, the guests conversing only by secret whispers, signs, and gestures, and significant contortions of the face. It was once more broken by Kyrle, who, looking at Mr. Cregan, said, in a restrained and steady voice, "Has Hardress returned from Killarney yet, Mr. Cregan?"

Hardress felt his blood rush through his veins, like that of a convict when he hears from the bench those fearful words, "Bring him up for judgment!" He made a slight motion in his chair, while his father answered the question of Kyrle.

"Hardress is here," said Mr. Cregan; "he came while you were out."

"Here! is he? I ought to be ashamed of myself," said Kyrle, rising slowly from his chair, and meeting his old friend half way with an extended hand. They looked, to the eye of the guests, pale, cold, and passionless, like two animated corpses. "But Hardress," continued Kyrle, with a ghastly lip, "will excuse me, I hope. Did you leave Mrs. Cregan well?"

"Quite well," muttered Hardress, with a confused bow.

"I am glad of it," returned Kyrle in the same tone of calm, dignified, and yet mournful politeness. "You are fortunate, Hardress, in that. If I had met you yesterday, I would have answered a similar question with the same confidence. And see how short——"

A sudden passion choked his utterance, he turned aside, and both the young men resumed their seats in silence.

There was something to Hardress infinitely humiliating in this brief interview. The manner of Kyrle Daly, as it regarded him, was merely indifferent. It was not cordial, for then it must necessarily have been hypocritical, but neither could he discern the slightest indication of a resentful feeling. He saw that Kyrle Daly was perfectly aware of his treason; he saw that his esteem and friendship were utterly extinct; and he saw, likewise, that he had formed the resolution of never exchanging with him a word of explanation or reproach, and of treating him in future as an indifferent acquaintance, who could not be esteemed, and ought to be avoided. This calm avoidance was the stroke that cut him to the quick.

Lowry now entered with tea, and a slight movement took place amongst the guests. Many left their places, and order being restored, Hardress found himself placed between two strangers, of a rank more humble than his own. He continued to sip his tea for some time in silence, when a slight touch on his arm made him turn round. He beheld on his right an old man dressed in dark frieze, with both hands crossed on the head of his walking-stick, his chin resting upon them, and his eye fixed upon Hardress with an air of settled melancholy. It was the same old man whose appearance in the avenue had produced so deep an effect on Kyrle Daly—Mihil O'Connor, the rope-maker.

"I beg your pardon, sir," he said gently; "but I think I have seen your face somewhere before now. Did you ever spend an evening at Garryowen?"

If, as he turned on his chair, the eye of Hardress had encountered that of the corpse which now lay shrouded and coffined in the other room, he could not have experienced a more sudden revulsion of affright. He did not answer the question of the old man (his father-in-law! the plundered parent!), but remained staring and gaping on him in silence. Old Mihil imagined that he was at a loss, and labouring to bestir his memory. "Don't you remember, sir," he added, " on a Patrick's eve, saving an old man and a girl from a parcel o' the boys in Mungret Street?"

"I do," answered Hardress in a low and hoarse voice.

"I thought I remembered the face and the make," returned Mihil. "Well, sir, I 'm that same old man, and many's the time, since that night, that I wished (if it was Heaven's will) that both she and I had died that night upon the spot together! I wished that when you seen us that time you passed us by and never ris a hand to save us—always if it was Heaven's will, for

I'm submissive. The will of Heaven be done, for I'm a great sinner, and I deserved great punishment, and great punishment I got—great punishment that's laid on my old heart this night!"

"I pity you," muttered Hardress involuntarily. "I pity you, although you may not think it."

"For what?" exclaimed the old man, still in a whisper, elevating his person, and planting his stick upright upon the floor. "For what would you pity me? You know nothing about me, man, that you'd pity me for. If I was to tell you my story, you'd pity me, I know; for there isn't that man living, with a heart in his breast, that wouldn't feel it. But I won't tell it to you, sir. I'm tired of telling it, that's what I am. I'm tired of talking of it, an' thinking of it, an' dreaming of it, an' I wisht I was in my grave, to be done with it for ever for a story—always, always," he added, lifting his eyes in devout fear—"always if it was Heaven's will. Heaven forgi' me! I say what I oughtn't to say sometimes, thinkin' of it."

"I understand," muttered Hardress incoherently. The old man did not hear him.

"An' still, for all," Mihil added after a pause, "as I spoke of it at all, I'll tell you something of it. That girl you saw that night with me—she was a beautiful little girl, sir, wasn't she?"

"Do you think so?" Hardress murmured, still without knowing what he said.

"Do I think so?" echoed the father with a grim smile. "It's little matter what her father thought. The world knew her for a beauty, but what was the good of it? She left me there, afther that night, an' went off with a stranger."

Hardress again said something, but it resembled only the delirious murmurs of a person on the rack.

"Oh, yo, Eily! that night, that woeful night!" continued the old man. "I'm ashamed o' myself to be always this way, like an ould woman, moaning and ochoning among the neighbours, like an ould goose that would be cackling afther the flock, or a fool of a little bird whistling upon a bough of a summer evening afther the nest is robbed."

"How close this room is!" said Hardress; "the heat is suffocating."

"I thought at first," continued Mihil, "that it is dead she was, but a letther come to a neighbour o' mine to let me know that she was alive and hearty. I know how it was. Some villyan that enticed her off. I sent the neighbour westwards to look afther her, an' I thought he'd be back to-day, but he isn't. I tould him to call at my brother's, the priest's, in Castle Island. Sure, he writes me word, he seen her himself of a Christmas day last, an' that she tould him she was married, and coming home shortly. Ayeh, I'm afraid the villyan desaived her, an' that she is not rightly married; for I made it my business to inquire of every priest in town and country, an' none of 'em could tell me a word about it. She desaived me, an' I'm afeerd he's desaivin' her. There let him! there let him! But there's a throne in heaven, and there's One upon it, an' that man, an' my daughter, an' I will stand together before that throne one day!"

"Let me go!" cried Hardress aloud, and breaking from the circle with violence. "Let me go! let me go! Can any one bear this?"

Such an incident, amid the general silence, and on this solemn occasion, could not fail to produce a degree of consternation amongst the company. Kyrle looked up with an expression of strong feeling. "What's the matter?" "What has happened?" was asked by several voices. "It is highly indecorous." "It is very unfeeling," was added by many more.

Hardress stayed not to hear their observations, but struggled through the astonished crowd, and reached the door. Kyrle, after looking in vain for an explanation, once more leaned down with his forehead on his hand, and remained silent.

"He's a good young gentleman," said Mihil O'Connor, looking after Hardress and addressing those who sat around him. "I was telling him the story of my daughter. He's a good young gentleman—he has great nature."

The unfortunate Hardress in the mean time strayed onward through the hall of the cottage, with the feeling of a man who has just escaped from the hands of justice. He entered another room appropriated to the female guests, where Mrs. O'Connell presided at the tea-table. The gradation of ranks in this apartment was similar to that in the other, but the company were not quite so scrupulous in the maintenance of silence. A general and very audible whispering conversation was carried on, in which a few young gentlemen, who were sprinkled among the ladies, took no inactive part. A hush, of some moments' duration, took place on the entrance of Hardress, and a hundred curious eyes were turned on his figure. His extreme paleness, the wildness of his eyes, and the ghastly attempt at courtesy which he made as he entered, occasioned a degree of general surprise. He passed on, and took his seat by the side of Mrs. O'Connell, who, like Mihil, placed his agitation to the account of sympathy, and entered him at once upon her list of favourites.

A number of young ladies were seated on the right of this good lady, and at a distance from the long table, round which were placed a number of females of a humbler rank, dressed out in all their finery, and doing honour to Mrs. O'Connell's tea and coffee. One or two young gentlemen were waiting on the small circle of ladies, who sat apart near the fire, with tea, cakes, toast, &c. The younger of the two, a handsome lad, of a cultivated figure, seemed wholly occupied in showing off his grace and gallantry. The other, a grave wag, strove to amuse the ladies by paying a mock ceremonious attention to the tradesmen's wives and daughters at the other side of the fire, and to amuse himself by provoking the ladies to laugh.

Revolutions in private, as in public life, are occasions which call into action the noblest and meanest principles of our nature—the extremes of generosity and of selfishness. As Lowry Looby took away the tea-service, he encountered, in the hall and kitchen, a few sullen and discontented faces. Some complained that they had not experienced the slightest attention since their arrival, and others declared they had not got "as much as one cup o' tay."

"Why, then, mend ye!" said Lowry. "Why didn't ye call for it? Do you think people that's in trouble that way has nothing else to do but to be thinkin' o' ye, an' o' yer aitin' an' drinkin'? What talk it is! There's people in this world, I b'lieve, that thinks more o' their own little finger than o' the lives an' fortunes o' all the rest."

So saying, he took a chair before the large kitchen fire, which, like those in the two other apartments, was surrounded by a class of watchers. On a wooden form at one side were seated the female servants of the house, and opposite to them the hearse-driver, the mutes, the drivers of two or three hack carriages, and one or two of the gentlemen's servants. The table was covered with bread, jugs of punch, and Cork porter. A few, exhausted by the preceding night's watching, and overpowered by the heat of the fire, were lying asleep in various postures on the settle-bed at the further end.

"'Twill be a good funeral," said the hearse-driver, laying aside the mug of porter, from which he had just taken a refreshing draught.

"If it isn't it ought," said Lowry; "they're people, sir, that are well known in the country."

"Surely, surely," said one of the hack-coachmen, taking a pipe from the corner of his mouth, "an' well liked, too, by all accounts."

A moan from the females gave a mournful assent to this proposition.

"Ah, she was a queen of a little woman!" said Lowry. "She was too good for this world. Oh, vo! where's the use o' talking at all? Sure 'twas only a few days since I was saltin' the bacon at the table over, an' she standin' a near me knitting. 'I'm afraid, Lowry,' says she, 'we won't find that bacon enough. I'm sorry I didn't get another o' them pigs killed.' Little she thought that time that they'd outlast herself. She never lived to see 'em in pickle."

A pause of deep affliction followed this speech, which was once more broken by the hearse-driver.

"The grandest funeral," said he, "that ever I see in my life was that of the Marquis of Watherford, father to the present man. It was a sighth for a king. There was six men marching out before the hearse, with goold sticks in their hands, an' as much black silk about 'em as a lady. The coffin was covered all over with black velvet an' goold, an' there was his name above upon the top of it, on a great goold plate intirely, that was shining like the sun. I never seen such a sighth before, nor since. There was forty-six carriages after the hearse, an' every one of 'em belonging to a lord, or an estated man at the

A PEASANT GREETING.

laste. It flogged all the shows I ever see since I was able to walk the ground."

The eyes of the whole party were fixed in admiration upon the speaker while he made the above oration with much importance of look and gesture. Lowry, who felt that poor Mrs. Daly's funeral must necessarily shrink into insignificance in comparison with this magnificent description, endeavoured to diminish its effect upon the imaginations of the company by a few philosophical remarks.

"'Twas a great funeral, surely," he began.

"Great!" exclaimed the hearse-driver; "it was worth walking to Watherford to see it."

"Them that has money," added Lowry, "can easily find means to sport it. An' still, for all, now, sir, if a man was to look into the rights o' the thing, what was the good o' all that? What was the good of it for him that was in the hearse, or for them that wor afther it? The Lord save us, it isn't what goold an' silver they had upon their hearses, they'll be axed where they are going; only what use they made of the goold an' silver that was given them in this world. 'Tisn't how many carriages was afther 'em, but how many good actions went before 'em; nor how they were buried, they'll be axed, but how they lived. Them are the questions, the Lord save us, that'll be put to us all one day; an' them are the questions that Mrs. Daly could answer this night as well as the Marquis of Watherford, or any other lord or marquis in the land."

The appeal was perfectly successful. The procession of the marquis, the gold sticks, the silks, the velvet, and the forty-six carriages were forgotten. The hearse-driver resumed his mug of porter, and the remainder of the company returned to their attitudes of silence and dejection.

CHAPTER XXXIV.

HOW THE WAKE CONCLUDED.

It was intended that the funeral should proceed at daybreak. Towards the close of a hurried breakfast, which the guests took by candlelight, the tinkling of a small silver bell summoned them to an early mass, which was being celebrated in the room of the dead. As Hardress obeyed its call, he found the apartment already crowded, and a number of the domestics and other dependents of the family kneeling at the door and in the hall. The low murmur of the clergyman's voice was only interrupted occasionally by a faint moan, or a short, thick sob, heard amid the crowd. The density of the press around the door prevented Hardress from ascertaining the individuals from whom those sounds of affliction proceeded.

When the ceremony had concluded, and when the room became less thronged, he entered and took his place near the window. There was some whispering between Mrs. O'Connell, his father, Hepton Connolly, and one or two other friends of the family. They were endeavouring to contrive some means for withdrawing Kyrle and his father from the apartment while the most mournful crisis of this domestic calamity was carried on—the removal of the coffin from the dwelling of its perished inmate. Mr. Daly seemed to have some suspicion of an attempt of this kind, for he had taken his seat close by the bed's head, and sat erect in his chair, with a look of fixed and even gloomy resolution. Kyrle was standing at the head of the coffin, his arms crossed upon the bed, his face buried between them, and his whole frame as motionless as that of one in a deep slumber. The priest was unvesting himself at a table near the window, which had been elevated a little, so as to serve for an altar. The clerk was at his side, placing the chalice, altar-cloths, and vestments in a large ticken-bag, according as they were folded. A few old women still remained kneeling at the foot of the bed, rocking their persons from side to side, and often striking their bosoms with the cross of the long rosary. The candles were now almost burnt down and smouldering in their sockets, and the winter dawn, which broke through the open window, was gradually overmastering their yellow and imperfect light.

"Kyrle," said Hepton Connolly in a whisper, touching the arm of the afflicted son, "come with me into the parlour for an instant; I want to speak to you."

Kyrle raised his head, and stared on the speaker like one who suddenly wakes from a long sleep. Connolly took him by the sleeve, with an urgent look, and led him passively out of the apartment.

Mr. Daly saw the manœuvre, but he did not appear to notice it. He kept the same rigid, set position, and looked straight forwards with the same determined and unwinking glance, as if he feared the slightest movement might unhinge his resolution.

"Daly," said Mr. Cregan, advancing to his side, "Mr. Neville, the clergyman, wishes to speak with you in the middle room."

"I will not leave this!" said the widower in a low, short, and muttering voice, while his eyes filled up with a gloomy fire, and his manner resembled that of a tigress which suspects some invasion of her young, but endeavours to conceal that suspicion until the first stroke is made. "I will not stir from this, sir, if you please."

Mr. Cregan turned away at once, and cast a desponding look at Mrs. O'Connell. That lady lowered her eyelids significantly, and glanced at the door. Mr. Cregan at once retired, beckoning to his son that he might follow him.

Mrs. O'Connell now took upon herself the task which had proved so complete a failure in the hands of Mr. Cregan. She leaned over her brother's chair, laid her hand on his, and said in an earnest voice,—

"Charles, will you come with me to the parlour for one moment?"

"I will not," replied Mr. Daly in the same hoarse tone; "I will not go, ma'am, if you please."

Mrs. O'Connell pressed his hand, and stooped over his shoulder. "Charles," she continued, with increasing earnestness, "will you refuse me this request?"

"If you please," said the bereaved husband, "I will not go—indeed, ma'am, I won't stir!"

"Now is the time, Charles, to show that you can be resigned. I feel for you—indeed I do—but you must deny yourself. Remember your duty to Heaven, and to your children, and to yourself. Come with me, my dear Charles."

The old man trembled violently, turned round on his chair, and fixed his eyes upon his sister.

"Mary," said he with a broken voice, "this is the last half hour that I shall ever spend with Sally in this world, and do not take me from her."

"I would not," said the good lady, unable to restrain her tears; "I would not, my dear Charles; but you know her well. You know how she would act if she were in your place. Act that way, Charles, and that is the greatest kindness you can show to Sally now."

"Take me where you please," cried the old man, stretching out his arms, and bursting into a fit of convulsive weeping. "Oh, Sally!" he exclaimed, turning round, and stretching his arms towards the coffin as he reached the door—oh, Sally! is this the way that we are parted, after all? This day I thought your friends would have been visiting you and your babe in health and happiness. They *are* come to visit you, my darling, but it is in your coffin, not in your bed, they find you! They are come, not to your babe's christening, but to your own funeral. For the last time now, good-by, my darling Sally. It is not now to say good-by for an hour, or good-by for a day, or for a week, but for ever and for ever. God be with you, Sally! For ever and for ever! They are little words, Mary," he added, turning to his weeping sister, "but there's a deal of grief in them. Well, now, Sally, my days are done for this world. It is time for me now to think of a better life. I am satisfied. Far be it from me to murmur. My life was too happy, Mary, and I was becoming too fond of it. This will teach me to despise a great many things that I valued highly until yesterday, and to warn my children to despise them likewise. I believe, Mary, if everything in this world went on as we could wish, it might tempt us to forget that there was another before us. This is my comfort, and it must be my comfort now for evermore. Take me where you please now, Mary, and let them take *her*, too, wherever they desire. Oh! Sally, my poor love, it is not to-day, nor to-morrow, nor the day after, that I shall feel your loss; but when weeks and months are gone by, and when I am sitting all alone by the fireside, or when I am talking of you to my orphan children. It is then, Sally, that I shall feel what happened yesterday! That is the time when I shall think of you, and of all our happy days, until my heart is breaking in my bosom!" These last sentences the old man spoke standing erect, with his hands clenched and trembling above his head, his eyes filled up and fixed on the coffin, and every feature swollen and quivering with strong emotion. As he concluded, he sank, exhausted by the passionate lament, upon the shoulder of his sister.

Almost at the same instant little Sally came peeping in at the door with a face of innocent wonder and timidity. Mrs. O'Connell, with the quick feeling of a woman, took advantage of the incident to create a diversion in the mind of her brother.

"My dear Charles," she said, "do try and conquer this dejection. You will not be so lonely as you think. Look there, Charles—you have got a Sally still to care for you."

The aged father glanced a quick eye around him, and met the sweet and simple gaze of the little innocent upturned to seek his own. He shook his sister's hand forcibly, and said with vehemence,—

"Mary, Mary! I thank you! From my heart I am obliged to you for this!"

He caught the little child to his breast, devoured it with kisses and murmurs of passionate fondness, and hurried with it, as with a treasure, to a distant part of the dwelling.

Mr. Cregan, in the mean while, had been engaged, at the request of Mrs. O'Connell, in giving out the gloves, scarfs, and cypresses, in the room which, on the preceding night, had been allotted to the female guests. In this matter, too, the selfishness of some unworthy individuals was made to appear in their struggles for precedence, and in their dissatisfaction at being neglected in the allotment of the funeral favours. In justice, however, it should be stated that the number of those unfeeling individuals was inconsiderable.

The last and keenest trial was now begun. The coffin was borne on the shoulders of men to the hearse, which was drawn up at the hall door. The hearse-driver had taken his seat, the mourners were already in the carriages, and a great crowd of horsemen and people on foot was assembled around the front of the house, along the avenue, and on the road. The female servants of the family were dressed in scarfs and huge head-dresses of white linen. The housemaid and Winny sat on the coffin, and three or four followed on an outside jaunting-car. In this order the procession began to move, and the remains of this kind mistress and affectionate wife and parent were borne away for ever from the mansion which she had blessed so many years by her gentle government.

The scene of desolation which prevailed from the time at which the coffin was first taken from the room, until the whole procession had passed out of sight, it would be a vain effort to describe. The shrieks of the women and children pierced the ears and the hearts of the multitude. Every room presented a picture of affliction: female figures flying to and fro, with ex-panded arms and cries of heart-broken sorrow; children weep-ing and sobbing aloud in each other's arms; men clenching their hands close, and stifling the strong sympathy that was making battle for loud utterance in their breasts; and the low groans of exhausted agony which proceeded from the mourning coaches that held the father, Kyrle Daly, and the two nearest sons. In the midst of these affecting sounds the hearse began to move, and was followed to a long distance on its way by the wild lament that broke from the open doors and windows of the now forsaken dwelling.

" Oh, mistress!" exclaimed Lowry Looby, as he stood at the avenue gate, clapping his hands and weeping, while he gazed, not without a sentiment of melancholy pride, on the long array which lined the uneven road, and saw the black hearse-plumes becoming indistinct in the distance, while the rear of the funeral train was yet passing him by—" oh, mistress! mistress! 'tis now I see that you are gone in airnest. I never would believe that you wor lost until I saw your coffin goin' out o' the doores!"

From the date of this calamity a change was observed to have taken place in the characters and manners of this amiable family. The war of instant affliction passed away, but it left deep and perceptible traces in the household. The Dalys became more grave and more religious, their tone of conversation of a deeper turn, and the manner even of the younger children more staid and thoughtful. Their natural mirth (the child of good-nature and conscious innocence of heart) was not extinguished; the flame lit up again as time rolled on, but it burned with a calmer, fainter, and perhaps a purer radiance. Their merri-ment was frequent and cordial, but it never again was boisterous. With the unhappy father, however, the case was different. He never rallied; the harmony of his existence was destroyed, and he seemed to have lost all interest in those occupations of rural industry which had filled up a great proportion of his time from boyhood. Still, from a feeling of duty, he was exact and dili-gent in the performance of those obligations; but he executed them as a task, not as a pleasure. He might still be found at morning, superintending his workmen at their agricultural em-ployments, but he did not join so heartily as of old in the merry jests and tales which made their labour light. It seemed as if he had, on that morning, touched the perihelion of his exist-ence, and from that hour the warmth and sunshine of his course were destined to decline from day to day.

CHAPTER XXXV.

HOW HARDRESS AT LENGTH RECEIVED SOME NEWS OF EILY.

THE marriage of Hardress Cregan and Anne Chute was post-poned for some time in consequence of the affliction of their old friends. Nothing, in the mean time, was heard of Eily or her escort; and the remorse and the suspense endured by Hardress began to affect his mind and health in a degree that excited great alarm in both families. His manner to Anne still con-tinued the same as before they were contracted; now tender, passionate, and full of an intense affection, and now sullen, short, intemperate, and gloomy. Her feeling, too, towards him continued still unchanged. His frequent unkindness pained her to the soul, but she attributed all to a natural or acquired weakness of temper, and trusted to time and to her own assidu-ous gentleness to cure it. He had yet done nothing to show himself unworthy of her esteem, and while this continued to be the case, her love could not be shaken by mere infirmities of

manner, the result, probably, of his uncertain health, for which he had her pity, rather than resentment.

But on Mrs. Cregan it produced a more serious impression. In her frequent conversations with her son, he had, in the agony of his heart, betrayed the workings of a deeper passion and a darker recollection than she had ever imagined possible. It became evident to her, from many hints let fall in his paroxysms of anxiety, that Hardress had done something to put himself within the power of outraged justice, as well as that of an aveng-ing conscience. From the moment on which she arrived at this discovery she avoided as much as possible all farther con-versation on those topics with her son, and it was observed that she, too, had become subject to fits of abstraction and of serious-ness in her general manner.

While the fortunes of the family remained thus stationary, the day arrived on which Hepton Connolly was to give his hunting-dinner. Hardress looked forward to this occasion with some satisfaction, in the hope that it would afford a certain degree of relief to his mind under its present state of depression; and when the morning came he was one of the earliest men upon the ground.

The fox was said to have kenneled in the side of a hill near the river side, which on one side was grey with limestone crag, and on the other covered with a quantity of close furze. To-wards the water, a miry and winding path among the under-wood led downward to an extensive marsh or corcass, which lay close to the shore. It was overgrown with a dwarfish rush, and intersected with numberless little creeks and channels, which were never filled, except when the spring-tide was at the full. On a green and undulating champaign above the hill were a considerable number of gentlemen mounted, conversing in groups, or cantering their horses around the plain, while the huntsman, whippers in, and dogs were busy among the furze, endeavouring to make the fox break cover. A crowd of peasants, boys, and other idlers, were scattered over the green, awaiting the commencement of the sport, and amusing themselves by criticising, with much sharpness of sarcasm, the appearance of the horses, and the action and manners of their riders.

The search after the fox continued for a long time without avail. The gentlemen became impatient, began to look at their watches, and to cast from time to time an apprehensive glance at the heavens. This last movement was not without a cause; the morning, which had promised fairly, began to change and darken. It was one of those sluggish days which frequently usher in the spring season in Ireland. On the water, on land, in air, on earth, everything was motionless and calm. The boats slept on the bosom of the river. A low and dingy mist concealed the distant shores and hills of Clare. Above, the eye could discern neither cloud nor sky. A heavy haze covered the face of the heavens from one horizon to the other. The sun was wholly veiled in mist, his place in the heavens being indi-cated only by the radiance of the misty shroud in that direction. A thin, drizzling shower, no heavier than a summer dew, de-scended on the party, and left a hoary and glistening moisture on their dresses, on the manes and forelocks of the horses, and on the face of the surrounding landscape.

" No fox to-day, I fear," said Mr. Cregan, riding up to one of the groups before mentioned, which comprised his son Har-dress and Mr. Connolly. " At what time," he added, addressing the latter, " did you order dinner? I think there is little fear of our being late for it."

" You all deserve this," said a healthy-looking old gentleman, who was one of the group; " feather-bed sportsmen every one of you. I rode out to-day from Limerick myself, was at home before seven, went out to see the wheat shaken in, and on arriving on the ground at ten, found no one there but this young gentleman, whose thoughts seem to be hunting on other ground at this moment. When I was a young man daybreak never found me napping that way."

" Good people are scarce," said Connolly; " it is right we should take care of ourselves. Hardress, will you canter this way?"

" He is cantering elsewhere," said the same old gentleman, looking on the absent boy. " Mind that sigh. Ah! she had the heart of a stone."

" I suspect he is thinking of his dinner rather," said his father.

" If Miss Chute had asked him to make a circuit with her,"

said Connolly, "she would not have found it so hard to get an answer."

"Courage, sir," exclaimed the old gentleman; "she is neither wed nor dead."

"Dead, did you say?" cried Hardress, starting from his reverie. "Who says it? Ah! I see."

A burst of laughter from the gentlemen brought the young man to his recollection, and his head sank in silence and confusion.

"Come, Hardress," continued Connolly, "although you are not in love with me, yet we may try a canter together. Hark! What is that? What are the dogs doing now?"

"They have left the cover on the hill," cried a gentleman who was galloping past, "and are trying the corcass."

"Poor Dalton," said Mr. Cregan; "that was the man that would have had old reynard out of cover before now."

"Poor, Dalton!" exclaimed Hardress, catching up the word with passionate emphasis, "poor—poor Dalton! Oh, days of my youth!" he added, turning aside on his saddle, that he might not be observed, and looking out upon the quiet river. "Oh, days—past happy days! my merry boyhood, and my merry youth! my boat! the broad river, the rough west wind, the broken waves, and the heart at rest! Oh, miserable wretch! what have you now to hope for? My heart will burst before I leave this field!"

"The dogs are chopping," said Connolly; "they have found him. Come! come away!"

"'Tis a false scent," said the old gentleman. "'Ware hare!"

"'Ware hare!" was echoed by many voices. A singular hurry was observed amongst the crowd upon the brow of the hill which overlooked the corcass, and presently all descended to the marsh.

"There is something extraordinary going forward," said Cregan. "What makes all the crowd collect upon the marsh?"

A pause ensued, during which Hardress experienced a degree of nervous anxiety for which he could not account. The hounds continued to chop in concert, as if they had found a strong scent, and yet no fox appeared.

At length a horseman was observed riding up the miry pass before mentioned, and galloping towards them. When he approached they could observe that his manner was flurried and agitated, and his countenance wore an expression of terror and compassion. He tightened the rein suddenly as he came upon the group.

"Mr. Warner," he said, addressing the old gentleman already alluded to, "I believe you are a magistrate?"

Mr. Warner bowed.

"Then come this way, sir, if you please. A terrible occasion makes your presence necessary on the other side of the hill."

"No harm, sir, to any of our friends, I hope?" said Mr. Warner, putting spurs to his horse, and galloping away. The answer of the stranger was lost in the tramp of the hoofs as they rode away.

Immediately after, two other horsemen came galloping by. One of them held in his hand a straw bonnet, beaten out of shape, and draggled in the mud of the corcass. Hardress just caught the word "horrible" as they rode swiftly by.

"What's horrible?" shouted Hardress, rising on his stirrup.

The two gentlemen were already out of hearing. He sank down again on his seat, and glanced aside at his father and Connolly. "What does he call horrible?" he repeated.

"I did not hear him," said Connolly. "Come down upon the corcass, and we shall learn."

They galloped in that direction. The morning was changing fast, and the rain was now descending in much greater abundance. Still there was not a breath of wind to alter its direction, or to give the slightest animation to the general lethargic look of nature. As they arrived on the brow of the hill, they perceived the crowd of horsemen and peasants collected into a dense mass around one of the little channels before described. Several of those in the centre were stooping low, as if to assist a fallen person. The next rank, with their heads turned aside over their shoulders, were employed in answering the questions of those behind them. The individuals who stood outside were raised on tiptoe, and endeavoured, by stretching their heads over the shoulders of their neighbours, to peep into the centre. The whipper-in, meanwhile, was flogging the hounds away from the crowd, while the dogs reluctantly obeyed. Mingled with the press were the horsemen, bending over their saddle-bows, and gazing downward on the centre.

"Bad manners to ye!" Hardress heard the whipper-in exclaim as he passed, "what a fox ye found us this morning. How bad ye are, now, for a taste o' Christian's flesh!"

As he approached nearer to the crowd he was enabled to gather farther indications of the nature of the transaction from the countenance and gestures of the people. Some had their hands elevated in strong fear, many brows were knitted in eager curiosity, some raised in wonder, and some expanded in affright. Urged by an unaccountable impulse, and supported by an energy he knew not whence derived, Hardress alighted from his horse, threw the reins to a countryman, and penetrated the group with considerable violence. He dragged some by the collars from their places, pushed others aside with his shoulder, struck those who proved refractory with his whip-handle, and in a few moments attained the centre of the ring.

Here he paused, and gazed in motionless horror upon the picture which the crowd had previously concealed.

A small space was kept clear in the centre. Opposite to Hardress stood Mr. Warner, the magistrate and coroner of the county, with a small note-book in his hand, in which he made some entries with a pencil. On his right stood the person who had summoned him to the spot. At the feet of Hardress was a small pool, in which the waters now appeared disturbed and thick with mud, while the rain, descending straight, gave to its surface the semblance of ebullition. On the bank at the other side, which was covered with sea-pink and a species of short moss peculiar to the soil, an object lay on which the eyes of all were bent with a fearful and gloomy expression. It was for the most part concealed beneath a large blue mantle, which was drenched in wet and mire, and lay so heavy on the thing beneath as to reveal the lineaments of a human form. A pair of small feet, in Spanish-leather shoes, appearing from below the end of the garment, showed that the body was that of a female; and a mass of long, fair hair, which escaped from beneath the capacious hood, demonstrated that this death, whether the effect of accident or malice, had found the victim untimely in her youth.

The cloak, the feet, the hair, all were familiar objects to the eye of Hardress. On very slight occasions he had often found it absolutely impossible to maintain his self-possession in the presence of others. Now, when the full solution of all his anxieties was exposed before him; now, when it became evident that the guilt of blood was upon his head; now, when he looked upon the shattered corpse of Eily, of his chosen and once beloved wife, murdered in her youth, almost in her girlhood, by his connivance; it astonished him to find that all emotion came upon the instant to a dead pause within his breast. Others might have told him that his face was rigid, sallow, and bloodless as that of the corpse on which he gazed. But he himself felt nothing of this. Not a sentence that was spoken was lost upon his ear. He did not even tremble, and a slight anxiety for his personal safety was the only sentiment of which he was perceptibly conscious. It seemed as if the great passion, like an engine embarrassed in its action, had been suddenly struck motionless, even while the impelling principle remained in active force.

"Has the horse and car arrived?" asked Mr. Warner, while he closed his note-book. "Can any one see it coming? We shall all be drenched to the skin before we get away."

"Can we not go to the nearest inn, and proceed with the inquest," said a gentleman in the crowd, "while some one stays behind to see the body brought after?"

"No, sir," said Mr. Warner with some emphasis, "the inquest must be held *super visum corporis*, or it is worth nothing."

"Warner," whispered Connolly to Cregan with a smile, "is afraid of losing his four-guinea fee. He will not let the body out of his sight."

"You know the proverb," returned Cregan, 'a bird in the hand,' etc. What a fine fat fox *he* has caught this morning!"

At this moment the hounds once more opened in a chopping concert; and Hardress, starting from his posture of rigid calmness, extended his arms, and burst at once into a passion of wild fear.

"The hounds! the hounds!" he exclaimed. "Mr. Warner, do you hear them? Keep off the dogs! They will tear her if ye let them pass! Good sir, will you suffer the dogs to tear her? I had rather be torn myself than look upon such a sight. Ye may stare as ye will, but I tell you all a truth, gentlemen. A truth, I say—upon my life, a truth!"

"There is no fear," said Warner, fixing a keen eye upon him.

"Ay, but there is, sir, by your leave," cried Hardress. "Do you hear them now? Do you hear that yell for blood? I tell you I hate that horrid cry. It is enough to make the heart of a Christian burst. Who put the hounds upon that horrid scent —that false scent? I am going mad, I think. I say, sir, do you hear that yelling now? Will you tell me now there is no fear? Stand close! Stand close, and hide me—her, I mean. Stand close!"

"I think there is none whatever," said the coroner, probing him.

"And I tell you," cried Hardress, grasping his whip, and abandoning himself to an almost delirious excess of rage, "I tell you there is. If this ground should open before me, and I should hear the hounds of Satan yelling upward from the deep, it could not freeze me with a greater fear! But, sir, you can pursue what course you please," continued Hardress, bowing and forcing a smile; "you are here in office, sir. You are at liberty to contradict you as you please, sir; but I have my remedy. You know me, sir, and I know you. I am a gentleman. Expect to hear farther from me on this subject."

So saying, and forcing his way through the crowd with as much violence as he used in entering, he vaulted with the agility of a Mercury into his saddle, and galloped, as if he were on a steeple-chase, in the direction of Castle Chute.

"If you are a gentleman," said Mr. Warner, "you are as ill-tempered a gentleman as ever I met, or something a great deal worse."

"Take care what you say, sir," said Mr. Cregan, riding rapidly up, after a vain effort to arrest his son's flight, and after picking up from a straggler, not three yards from the scene of action, the exaggerated report that Hardress and the coroner had given each other the lie. "Take care what you say, sir," he said. "Remember, if you please, that the gentleman, ill-tempered or otherwise, is my son."

"Mr. Cregan," exclaimed the magistrate, at length growing somewhat warm, "if he were the son of the lord lieutenant, I will not be interrupted in my duty. There are many gentlemen here present; they have witnessed the whole occurrence, and if they will tell you that I have done or said anything unbecoming a gentleman, I am ready to give you, or your son either, the satisfaction of a gentleman."

With this pacificatory and Christian-like speech, the exemplary Irish peace-preserver turned upon his heel, and went to meet the carman, who was now within a few paces of the crowd.

While the pitying and astonished multitude were conveying the shattered remains of Eily O'Connor to the nearest inn, her miserable husband was flying with the speed of fear in the direction of Castle Chute. He alighted at the Norman archway by which Kyrle Daly had entered on the day of his rejection, and, throwing the reins to Falvey, rushed without speaking up the stone staircase. That talkative domestic still retained a lingering preference for the discarded lover, and saw him with grief supplanted by this wild and passionate young gentleman. He remained for a moment holding the rein in his hand, and looking back with a gaze of calm astonishment at the flying figure of the rider. He then compressed his lips—moved to a little distance from the horse—and began to contemplate the wet and reeking flanks and trembling limbs of the beautiful animal. The creature presented a spectacle calculated to excite the compassion of a practised attendant upon horses. His eyes were wide and full of fire—his nostrils expanded, and red as blood. His shining coat was wet from ear to flank, and corded by numberless veins that were now swollen to the utmost by the accelerated circulation. As he panted and snorted in his excitement, he scattered the flecks of foam over the dress of the attendant.

"Oh! murther, murther!" exclaimed the latter, after uttering that peculiar sound of pity which is used by the vulgar in Ireland, and in some continental nations. "Well, there 's a man that knows how to use a horse! Look at that crather! Well, he ought to be ashamed of himself, so he ought—any gentleman to use a poor dumb crather that way. As if the hunt wasn't hard enough upon her, without bringin' her up in a gallop to the very doore!"

"An' as if my throuble wasn't enough besides," grumbled the groom, as he took the rein out of Falvey's hand. "He ought to stick to his boating, that 's what he ought, an' to lave horses for those that knows how to use 'em."

"Who rode that horse?" asked old Dan Dawley, the steward, as he came along sulky and bent by age to the hall door.

"The young masther we 're gettin'," returned Falvey.

"Umph!" muttered Dawley, as he passed into the house, "that's the image of the thratement he 'll give all that he gets into his power."

"It's thrue for you," said Falvey.

Dawley paused, and looked back over his shoulder. "It 's thrue for me!" he repeated gruffly. "It 's you that say that, an' you were the first to praise him when he came into the family."

"It stood to raison I should," said Falvey. "I liked him betther than Masther Kyrle himself, for bein' an offhand gentleman and aisily spoken to. But sure a Turk itself couldn't stand the way he 's goin' on of late days!"

Dawley turned away with a harsh grunt; the groom led out the heated steed upon the lawn, and Falvey returned to make the cutlery refulgent in the kitchen.

CHAPTER XXXVI.

HOW HARDRESS MADE A CONFIDANT.

HARDRESS CREGAN, in the mean time, had proceeded to the antique chamber, mentioned in a former chapter, which led to the drawing-room in the more modern part of the mansion. He flung himself into a chair which stood near the centre of the apartment, and remained motionless for some moments, with hands clasped, and eyes fixed upon the floor. There were voices and laughter in the drawing-room, and he could hear the accents of Anne Chute resisting the entreaties of Mrs. Cregan and her mother, while they endeavoured to prevail on her to sing some favourite melody.

"Anne," said Mrs. Chute, "don't let your aunt suppose that you can be disobliging. What objection is there to your singing that song?"

"One, I am sure, which aunt Cregan won't blame me for, mamma. Hardress cannot endure to hear it."

"But Hardress is not here now, my dear."

"Ah! ah! aunt, is that your principle? Would you teach me to take advantage of his absence, then, to foster a little will of my own?"

"Go, go, you giddy girl," said Mrs. Chute. "Have you the impudence to make your aunt blush?"

"My dear Anne," said Mrs. Cregan, "if you never make a more disobedient use of your husband's absence than that of singing a little song which you love, and which you can't sing in his presence, you will be the best wife in Ireland."

"Very well, aunt, very well. You ought to know the standard of a good wife. You have had some experience, or my uncle (I should say) has had some experience of what a good wife ought to be. Whether his knowledge in that way has been negatively or positively acquired, is more than I 'll venture to say."

Hardress heard her run a tender prelude along the keys of her instrument before she sung the following words:—

> " My Mary of the curling hair,
>   The laughing teeth and bashful air,
>   Our bridal morn is dawning fair,
>   With blushes in the skies.
> Shule! Shule! Shule, agra!
> Shule aucur, agus shule, aroon.*
>   My love! my pearl!
>   My own dear girl!
>   My mountain maid, arise!
>
> " Wake, linnet of the osier grove!
>   Wake, trembling, stainless, virgin dove!
>   Wake, nestling of a parent's love.
>   Let Moran see thine eyes.
> Shule! Shule! etc.
>
> " I am no stranger, proud and gay,
>   To win thee from thy home away,
>   And find thee, for a distant day,
>   A theme for wasting sighs.
> Shule! Shule! etc.
>
> * Come! come! Come, my darling!
>   Come softly, and come, my love!

"But we were known from infancy;
Thy father's hearth was home to me;
No selfish love was mine for thee,
Unholy and unwise.
Shule! Shule! etc.

"And yet (to see what love can do!)
Though calm my hope has burned, and true,
My cheek is pale and worn for you,
And sunken are mine eyes!
Shule! Shule! etc.

"But soon my love shall be my bride,
And happy by our own fireside,
My veins shall feel the rosy tide,
That lingering Hope denies.
Shule! Shule! etc.

"My Mary of the curling hair,
The laughing teeth and bashful air,
Our bridal morn is dawning fair,
With blushes in the skies.
*Shule! Shule! Shule, agra!
Shule asucur, agus shule, aroon!
My love! my pearl!
My own dear girl!
My mountain maid, arise!*"

After the song was ended Hardress heard the drawing-room door open and shut, and the stately and measured pace of his mother along the little lobby, and on the short flight of stairs which led to the apartment in which he sat. She appeared at the narrow stone doorway, and used a gesture of surprise when she beheld him.

"What, Hardress!" she exclaimed, "already returned! Have you had good sport to-day?"

"Sport!" echoed Hardress, with a burst of low, involuntary laughter, and without unclasping his wreathed hands, or raising his eyes from the earth. "Yes, mother, very good sport—sport, I think, that may bring my neck in danger one day."

"Have you been hurt, then, child?" said Mrs. Cregan, compassionately bending over her son.

Hardress raised himself in his seat, and fixed his eye upon hers for a few moments in gloomy silence.

"I have," he said. "The hurt that I feared so long I have got at length. I am glad you have come. I wished to speak with you."

"Stay a moment, Hardress. Let me close those doors. Servants are so inquisitive and apt to pry."

"Ay, now," said Hardress, "now, and from this time forth, we must avoid those watchful eyes and ears. What shall I do, mother? Advise me, comfort me! Oh! I am utterly abandoned now; I have no friend, no comforter but you! That terrible hope, that looked more like a fear, that kept my senses on the rack from morn to morn, is fled, at last, for ever. I am all forsaken now."

"My dear Hardress," said his mother, much distressed, "when will you cease to afflict yourself and me with those fancies? Forsaken, do you say? Do your friends deserve this from you? You ask me to advise you, and my advice is this. Lay aside those thoughts, and value, as you ought to do, the happiness of your condition. Who, with a love like Anne, with a friend like your amiable college companion, Daly, and with a mother at least devoted in intention, would deliver himself up, as you do, to fantastic dreams of desolation and despair? If, as you seem to hint, you have a cause for suffering in your memory, remember, Hardress, that you are not left on earth for nothing. All men have something to be pardoned, and all time here is capable of being improved in the pursuit of mercy."

"Go on," said Hardress, setting his teeth, and fixing a wild stare upon his parent; "you but remind me of my curses. With a love like Anne! One whisper in your ear. I love her not. While I was mad I did; and in my senses, now, I am dearly suffering for that frantic treason. She was the cause of all my sin and sorrow, my first and heaviest curse. With such a friend! Why, how you laugh at me! You know how black and weak a part I have played to him, and yet you will remind me that he was my friend, That's kindly done, mother. Listen!" he continued, laying a firm grasp upon his mother's arm. "Before my eyes, wherever I turn me, and whether it be dark or light, I see One painting the hideous portrait of a fiend. Day after day he comes, and adds a deeper and a blacker tint to the resemblance. Mean fear, and selfish pride, the coarser half of love, worthless inconstancy, black falsehood,

and red-handed murder, those are the colours that he blends and stamps upon my soul. I am stained in every part. The proud coward that loved and was silent when already committed by his conduct, and master of the conquest that he feared to claim. The hypocrite that volunteered a friendship, to which he proved false almost without a trial. The night-brawler, the drunkard, the faithless lover, and the perjured husband! Where—who has ever run a course so swift and full of sin as mine? You speak of heaven and mercy! Do you think I could so long have endured my agonies without remembering that? No; but a cry was at its gates before me, and I never felt that my prayer was heard. What that cry was, I have this morning learned. Mother," he added, turning around with great rapidity of voice and action, "I am a murderer!"

Mrs. Cregan never heard the words. The look and gesture, coupled with the foregoing speech, had pre-informed her, and she fell back, in a death-like faint, into the chair.

When she recovered she found Hardress kneeling by her side, pale, anxious, and terrified, no longer supported by that horrid energy which he had shown before the revealment of his secret, but motionless and helpless—desolate as an exploded mine. For the first time the mother looked upon her child with a shudder in which remorse was mingled deeply with abhorrence. She waved her hand two or three times, as if to signify that he should retire from her sight. It was so that Hardress understood and obeyed the gesture. He took his place behind the chair of his parent, awaiting with gaping lip and absent eye the renewal of her speech. The unhappy mother, meanwhile, leaned forward in her seat, covering her face with her hands, and maintained for several minutes that silent communion with herself which was usual with her when she had received any sudden shock. A long pause succeeded.

"Are you still in the room?" she said at length, as a slight movement of the guilty youth struck upon her hearing.

Hardress started, as a schoolboy might at the voice of his preceptor, and was about to come forward, but the extended arm of his parent arrested his steps.

"Remain where you are," she said; "it will be a long time now before I shall desire to look upon my son."

Hardress fell back, stepping noiselessly on tiptoe, and letting his head hang dejectedly upon his breast.

"If those things are not dreams," Mrs. Cregan again said in that calm, restrained tone which she always used when her mind was undergoing the severest struggles; "if you have not been feeding a delirious fancy, and can restrain yourself to plain terms for one quarter of an hour, let me hear you repeat this unhappy accident. Nay, come not forward; stay where you are, and say your story there. Unfortunate boy! We are a miserable pair!"

She again leaned forward with her face buried in her expanded hands, while Hardress, with a low, chidden, and timid voice and attitude, gave her in a few words the mournful history which she desired. So utterly abandoned was he by that hectoring energy which he displayed during his former conversations with his parent, that more than half the tale was drawn from him by questions, as from a culprit fearful of adding to the measure of his punishment.

When he had concluded, Mrs. Cregan raised her head with a look of great and evident relief.

"Why, Hardress," she said, "I have been misled in this. I overleaped the mark in my surmise. You are not, then, the actual actor of this horrid work?"

"I was not the executioner," said Hardress. "I had a deputy," he added with a ghastly smile.

"Nor did you, by word or act, give warrant for the atrocity of which you speak?"

"Oh! mother, if you esteem it worth your while to waste any kindness on me, forbear to torture my conscience with that wretched subterfuge. I *am* the murderer of Eily! It matters not that my finger has not gripped her throat, nor my hand been reddened with her blood. My heart, my will, have murdered her. My soul was even beforehand with the butcher who has sealed our common ruin by his bloody disobedience, I am the murderer of Eily! No, not in act, as you have said. nor even in word! I breathed my bloody thoughts into no living ear. The dark and hell-born flame was smouldered where it rose, within my own lonely breast. Not through a single chink or cleft in all my conduct could be unnatural rage be evident. When he tempted me aloud, aloud I answered, scorned, and defied him; and when, at our last fatal interview, I gave him that charge which he has stretched to bloodshed, my speech was urgent for her safety."

"Ay?"

"Ay, mother, it is truth. I answer *you* as I shall answer at that dreadful bar before that throne the old man told me of, when he and she shall stand to blast me there."

He stood erect, and held up his hand, as if already pleading to the charge. Mrs. Cregan at the same moment rose, and was about to address him with equal energy and decision of manner.

"But still," he added, preventing her, "still I am Eily's murderer. If I had an enemy who wished to find me a theme for lasting misery, he could not choose a way more certain than that of starting a doubt upon that subtle and worthless distinction. I am Eily's murderer! That thought will ring upon my brain, awake or asleep, for evermore. Are these things dreams? Oh, I would give all the world of realities to find that I had dreamed a horrid dream, and awake and die!"

"You overrate the measure of your guilt," said Mrs. Cregan, and was about to proceed, when Hardress interrupted her.

"Fool that I was!" he exclaimed with a burst of grief and self-reproach. "Fool! mad fool and idiot that I was! How blind to my own happiness! for ever longing for that which was beyond my reach, and never able to appreciate that which I possessed! In years gone by the present seemed always stale, and flat, and dreary; the future and the past alone looked beautiful. Now I must see them all with altered eyes. The present is my refuge; for the past is red with blood, and the future burning hot with shame and fire."

"Sit down and hear me, Hardress, for one moment."

"Oh, Eily!" the wretched youth continued, stretching out his arms to their full extent, and seeming to apostrophise some listening spirit. "Oh, Eily! my lost, deceived, and murdered love! Oh, let it not be thus without recall! Tell me not that the things done in those hideous months are wholly without remedy! Come back! come back, my own abused and gentle love! If tears, and groans, and years of self-inflicted penitence can wash away that one accursed thought, you shall be satisfied. Look there!" he suddenly exclaimed, grasping his mother's arm with one hand, and pointing with the other to a distant corner of the room. "That vision comes to answer me!" He followed a certain line with his finger through the air, as if tracing the course of some hallucination. "As vivid, and as ghastly real, as when I saw it lying, an hour hence, on the wet, cold bank—the yellow hair uncurled, the feet exposed, the feet that I first taught to stray from duty!—the dank, blue mantle, covering and clinging round the horrid form of death that lay beneath. Four times I have seen it since I left the spot, and every time it grows more deadly vivid. From this time forth my fancies shall be changed; for gloomy visions, gloomier realities; for ghastly fears, a ghastlier certainty."

Here he sank down into the chair which his mother had drawn near her own, and remained for some moments buried in deep silence. Mrs. Cregan took this opportunity of gently bringing him into a more temperate vein of feeling; but her feelings carried her beyond the limit which she contemplated.

"Mistake me not," she said, "unhappy boy! I would not have you slight your guilt. It is black and deadly, and such as Heaven will certainly avenge. But neither must you fly to the other and worse extreme, where you can only cure presumption by despair. You are *not* so guilty as you deem. That you willed her death was a dark and deadly sin; but nothing so hideous as the atrocious act itself. One thing, indeed, is certain, that, however this affair may terminate, we are an accursed and miserable pair for this world—I in you, and you in me. Most weak and wicked boy! It was the study of my life to win your love and confidence, and my reward has been distrust, concealment, and——"

"Do you reproach me, then?" cried Hardress, springing madly to his feet, clenching his hand, and darting an audacious scowl upon his parent. "Beware, I warn you! I am a fiend, I grant you; but it was by your temptation that I changed my nature. You, my mother! you have been my fellest foe! I drank in pride with your milk, and passion under your indulgence. You sport with one possessed and desperate. This

whole love-scheme, that has begun in trick and cunning, and ended in blood, was all your work! And do you now——"

"Hold!" cried his mother, observing the fury of his eye, and his hand raised and trembling, though not with the impious purpose she affected to think. "Monster! would you dare to strike your parent?"

As if he had received a sudden blow, Hardress sank down at her feet, which he pressed between his hands, while he lowered his forehead to the very dust. "Mother!" he said in a changing and humble voice, "my first, my constant and forbearing friend, you are right. I am not quite a demon yet. My brain may fashion wild and impious words, but it is your son's heart that still beats within my bosom. I did not dream of such a horrid purpose."

After a silence of some minutes the wretched young man arose, with tears in his eyes, and took his seat in the chair. Here he remained fixed in the same absent posture, and listening, but with a barren attention, to the many soothing speeches which were addressed to him by his mother. At length, rising hastily from his seat, with a look of greater calmness than he had hitherto shown, he said,—

"Mother, there is one way left for reparation. I will give myself up."

"Hold, madman!"

"Nay, hold, mother. I will do it. I will not bear this fire upon my brain. I will not still add crime to crime for ever. If I have outraged justice, it is enough. I will not cheat her. Why do you hang upon me? I am weak and exhausted; a child could stay me now—a flaxen thread could fetter me. Release me, mother! There is peace, and hope, and comfort, in this thought. Elsewhere I can find naught but fire and scourges. Oh! let me make this offering of a wretched life to buy some chance of quiet. I never shall close an eye in sleep again until I lie on a dungeon floor. I never more shall smile until I stand upon the scaffold. Well, well, you will prevail—you will prevail," he added, as his mother forced him back into the chair which he had left; "but I may find a time. My life, I know, is forfeited."

"It is *not* forfeited."

"Not forfeited! Hear you, just Heaven and judge! The ragged wretch that pilfers for his food must die—the starving father who counterfeits a wealthy name to save his children from a horrid death must die—the goaded slave who, driven from a holding of his fathers, avenges his wrong upon the usurper's property, must die—and I, who have pilfered for my passion—I, the hypocrite, the false friend, the fickle husband, the coward, traitor, and murderer (I am disgusted while I speak)—*my* life has not been forfeited! I alone stand harmless beneath these bloody laws! I said I should not smile again, but this will force a laugh in spite of me."

Mrs. Cregan prudently refrained from urging the subject farther for the present, and contented herself with appealing to his affectionate consideration of her own feelings, rather than reminding him of his interest in the transaction. This seemed more effectually to work upon his mind. He listened calmly and with less reluctance, and was about to express his acquiescence, when a loud and sudden knocking at the outer door of the chamber made him start from his chair, turn pale, and shake in every limb like one convulsed. Mrs. Cregan, who had herself been startled, was advancing towards the door, when the knocking was heard again, though not so loud, but that which led to the drawing-room. Imagining that her ear, in the first instance, had deceived her, she turned on her steps, and was proceeding toward the latter entrance, when the sound was heard at both doors together, and with increased loudness. Slight as this accident appeared, it produced so violent an effect upon the nerves of Hardress, that it was with difficulty he was able to reach the chair which he had left without falling to the ground. The doors were opened—the one to Anne Chute, and the other to Mr. Cregan.

"Dinner is on the table, aunt," said the former.

"And I am come on the very point of time to claim a neighbour's share of it," said Mr. Cregan.

"We are more fortunate than we expected," said Anne. "We thought you would have dined with Mr. Connolly."

"Thank you for that hint, my good niece."

"Oh! sir, don't be alarmed; you will not find us unprovided, notwithstanding. Mr. Hardress Cregan," she continued, moving towards his chair with a lofty and yet playful carriage, "will you allow me to lead you to the dining-room?"

"He is ill, Anne—a little ill," said Mrs. Cregan in a low voice.

"Dear Hardress, you have been thrown!" exclaimed Anne, suddenly stooping over him with a look of tender interest and alarm.

"No, Anne," said Hardress, shaking her hand in grateful kindness; "I am not so indifferent a horseman. I shall be better presently."

"Go in—go in, ladies," said Mr. Cregan. "I have a word on business to say to Hardress. We will follow you in three minutes."

The ladies left the room, and Mr. Cregan, drawing his son into the light, looked on his face for some moments with silent scrutiny.

"I don't know what to make of it," he said at length, tossing his head. "You're not flagging, Hardress, are you?"

"Flagging, sir?"

"Yes. You do not feel a little queer about the heart now in consequence of this affair?"

Hardress started and shrank back.

"Whew!" the old sportsman gave utterance to a prolonged sound that bore some resemblance to a whistle. "'Tis all up! That start spoke volumes. You've dished yourself for ever. Let nobody see you. Go—go along into some corner, and hide yourself: go to the ladies; that's the place for you. What a fool I was to leave a pleasant dinner party, and come here to look after a—— Well, I have seen you stand fire stoutly once. So it is with all cowards. The worm will turn when trod upon; and you were primed with strong drink, moreover. But how dared you—this is my chief point—this—how dared you stand up, and give any gentleman the lie, when you have not the heart to hold to your words? What do you stare at? Answer me."

"Give any gentleman the lie!" echoed Hardress.

"Yes, to be sure. Didn't you give Warner the lie a while ago upon the corcass?"

"Not I, I am sure."

"No! What was your quarrel, then?"

"We had no quarrel. You are under some mistake."

"That's very strange. That's another affair. It passes all that I have ever heard. The report all over the ground was that you had exchanged the lie, and some even went so far as to say that you had horsewhipped him. It leaves me at my wits' end."

At this moment Falvey put in his head at the door, and said,—

"Dinner, if ye plase, gentlemen; the ladies is waitin' for ye."

This summons ended the conversation for the present, and Hardress followed his father into the dining-room.

CHAPTER XXXVII.

HARDRESS FINDS THAT CONSCIENCE IS THE SWORN FOE OF VALOUR.

HE who, when smitten by a heavy fever, endeavours, with bursting head and aching bones, to maintain a cheerful seeming among a circle of friends, may imagine something of Hardress Cregan's situation on this evening. His mother contrived to sit near him during the whole time, influencing his conduct by word and gesture, as one would regulate the movements of an automaton.

The company consisted only of that lady, her son, her husband, and the two ladies of the mansion. The fire burned cheerfully in the grate, the candles were lighted, Anne's harpsichord was thrown open, and, had the apartment at that moment been unroofed by *Le Diable Boiteux* in the sight of his companion, Don Cleofas would have pronounced it a scene of domestic happiness and comfort.

It appeared, from the conversation which took place in the course of the evening, that the coroner had not even found any one to recognise the body, and the jury, after giving the case a long consideration, had come to the only conclusion for which there appeared to be satisfactory evidence. They had returned a verdict of "Found drowned."

"He would be a sharp lawyer," continued Mr. Cregan, "that could take them up on that verdict. I thought there were some symptoms of murder in the case, and wished them to adjourn the inquest, but I was overruled. After all, I'll venture to say it was some love business. She had a wedding ring on."

"Be calm," whispered Mrs. Cregan, laying her hand on her son's arm. "Some young husband, perhaps, who found he had

made a bad bargain. Take care of yourself, Anne; Hardress may learn the knack of it."

Hardress acknowledged the goodness of this jest by a hideous laugh.

"It was a shocking business!" said Mrs. Chute. "I wonder, Hardress, how you can laugh at it. Depend upon it, it will not terminate in that way. Murder is like fire—it will out at some cleft or another."

"That is most likely to be the case in the present instance," said Mr. Cregan, "for the clothes, in all likelihood, will be identified, and Warner has sent an advertisement to all the newspapers and to the parish chapels, giving an account of the whole transaction. It is, indeed, quite certain that the case will be cleared up, and the foul play, if there be any, discovered. Whether the perpetrators will be detected or not is a different question."

Mrs. Cregan, who was in an agony during this conversation, felt a sudden relief when it was ended by Anne Chute's calling on her uncle for a song.

Mr. Cregan, who was always very funny among young people, replied that he would with all his heart; and accordingly, with a prefatory hem, he threw back his head, raised his eyes to the cornice, dropped his right leg over the left knee, and treated the company to the following effusion, humouring the tune with his head by slightly jerking it from side to side:—

"*Gilli ma chree,*
Sit down by me;
We now are joined, and ne'er shall sever;
This hearth's our own,
Our hearts are one,
And peace is ours for ever!
When I was poor,
Your father's door
Was closed against your constant lover.
With care and pain
I tried in vain
My fortunes to recover.
I said, 'To other lands I'll roam,
Where fate may smile on me, love!'
I said, 'Farewell, my own old home!'
And I said, 'Farewell to thee, love!'
Sing *Gilli ma chree,* etc.

"I might have said,
'My mountain maid,
Come live with me, your own true lover;
I know a spot,
A silent cot,
Your friends can ne'er discover,
Where gently flows the waveless tide
By one small garden only,
Where the heron waves his wings so wide,
And the linnet sings so lonely.'
Sing *Gilli ma chree,* etc.

"I might have said,
'My mountain maid,
A father's right was never given
True hearts to curse
With tyrant force,
That have been blessed in heaven.'
But then I said, 'In after years,
When thoughts of home shall find her,
My love may mourn, with secret tears,
Her friends thus left behind her.'
Sing *Gilli ma chree,* etc.

"'O no!' I said,
'My own dear maid,
For me, though all forlorn for ever,
That heart of thine
Shall ne'er repine
O'er slighted duty—never.
From home and thee, though wandering far,
A dreary fate be mine, love,
I'd rather live in endless war
Than buy my peace with thine, love.'
Sing *Gilli ma chree,* etc.

"Far, far away,
By night and day,
I toiled to win a golden treasure;
And golden gains
Repaid my pains
In fair and shining measure.
I sought again my native land;
Thy father welcomed me, love;
I poured my gold into his hand,
And my guerdon found in thee, love!
Sing *Gilli ma chree,*
Sit down by me;
We now are joined, and ne'er shall sever;
This hearth's our own,
Our hearts are one,
And peace is ours for ever.'"

MRS. CREGAN'S DESPAIR.

It was not until he courted rest and forgetfulness in the solitude of his chamber that the hell of guilt and memory began to burn within the breast of Hardress. Fears which, until this moment, he had despised as weak and childish, now oppressed his imagination with all the force of a real and imminent danger. The darkness of his chamber was crossed by horrid shapes, and the pillow seemed to burn beneath his cheek, as if he lay on fire. If he dozed, he seemed to be rocked on his bed, as if borne upward on the back of a flying steed, and the cry of hounds came yelling on his ear with a discord even more terrible than that which rang upon the ear of the hunted Acteon in the exquisite fiction of the ancients. That power of imagination in which he had been often accustomed to take pride, as in a high intellectual endowment, became now his most fearful curse; and, as it had been a chief instrument in his seduction, was also made a principal engine of retribution..

Several circumstances, trifling in themselves, but powerful in their operation upon the mind of the guilty youth, occurred in the course of the ensuing week to give new fuel to the passion which preyed upon his nerves. A few of these we will relate, if only for the purpose of showing how slight a breath may shake the peace of him who has suffered it to be sapped in the foundation.

When the first agony of his remorse went by, the love of life —triumphant even over that appalling passion—made him join his mother in her fears of a discovery, and her precautions for its prevention. He sought, therefore, many opportunities of misleading the observation of his acquaintances, and affected to mingle in their amusements with a greater carelessness than he had ever assumed during the period of his uncertainty respecting Eily's fate.

A small party had been formed one morning for the purpose of snipe-shooting, and Hardress was one of the number. In a rushy swamp, adjoining the little bay which had been selected as the scene of the saddle-race so many months before, the game were said to exist in great quantities, and thither, accordingly, the sportsmen first repaired. A beautiful, but only half-educated pointer which Hardress procured in Kerry, in his eagerness for sport, had repeatedly broken out of bound, in disregard of all the menaces and entreaties of his owner, and by these means on many occasions narrowly escaped destruction. At length, while he was indulging in one of those wild gambols, a bird rose, with a sudden shriek, from the very feet of Hardress, and flew forward, darting and wheeling in a thousand eccentric circles. Hardress levelled and fired. The snipe escaped; but a mournful howl of pain from the animal before alluded to seemed to announce that the missile had not sped upon a fruitless errand. In a few seconds the poor pointer was seen crawling out of the rushes, and turning at every step to whine and lick its side, which was covered with blood. The slayer ran, with an aching heart, towards the unfortunate creature, and stooped to assist and caress it. But the wound was past all remedy. The poor quadruped whimpered and fawned upon his feet, as if to disarm the suspicion of resentment, and died in the action.

"Oh, murther, murther!" said Pat Falvey, who accompanied the party, "the poor thing was all *holed* with the shot! Oh, look at the limbs stiffening, and the light that's gatherin' in the eyes! There's death, now, Masther Hardress, the Lord save us!—there's death!"

"Where?" said Hardress, looking round with some wildness of eye, and a voice which was indicative at the same time of anger and of bodily weakness.

"There, before your eye, sir," said Falvey. "There's what we'll all have to go through one time or another, the Christian as well as the baste! 'Twould be well for some of us if we had as little to answer for as that poor pointher, afther our doin's in this world."

The other gentlemen had now collected around, with many expressions of condolence on the fate of the poor servant of the chase. Hardress appeared to be affected in a peculiar manner by the transaction which he had witnessed. His glances were vague and unsettled, his cheek was deadly pale, and his limbs trembled exceedingly. This was the first shot he had fired in the course of the day; and the nature of the sport in which he was engaged had not once occurred to him until he saw the blood flowing at his feet. To a mind like his, always sensitive and reflective, and rendered doubly so by the terrific associations of the last few months, the picture of death in this poor quadruped was scarcely less appalling than it might have been in the person of a fellow-mortal. He felt his head grow dizzy as he turned away from the spot; and, after a few feeble paces, he fell senseless among the rushes.

The gentlemen hastened to his relief with looks of astonishment rather than of pity. Some there were imperfectly acquainted with his character, or perplexed by the extraordinary change which it had lately undergone, who winked and sneered apart when he was lifted from the earth; and though no one ventured openly to impute any effeminacy of character to the young gentleman, yet, whenever they spoke of the occurrence in the course of the day, it was not without exchanging a conscious smile. On another occasion a boating party was formed, when Hardress, as usual, took the rudder in hand. His father, on entering the little vessel, was somewhat surprised at seeing a new boatman seated on the forecastle.

"Hello!" he said, "what's your name, my honest fellow?"

"Larry Kett, sir, plase your honour," returned the man, a sturdy old person, with a face as black as a storm.

"Why, Hardress, had you a quarrel with your little hunchback?"

Hardress stooped suddenly down, as if for the purpose of arranging a block, and after a little silence replied,—

"No quarrel, sir; but he chose to seek another service, and I do not think I have made a bad exchange."

The conversation changed, and the party (among whom was Anne Chute) proceeded on their excursion. The wind freshened considerably in the course of the forenoon, and before they had reached that part of the river which flowed by the dairy-cottage of Mr. Daly, it blew a desperate gale. The boatman, more anxious for the comfort of the ladies than really apprehensive for the boat, suggested the expediency of putting about on the homeward course before the tide should turn."

"If you hold on," said the man with a significant look, "until the wind an' tide come contrary, there 'ill be a swell in the

channel that it is as much as you can do to come through it with the two reefs."

Hardress assented, but it was already too late. They were now a considerable distance below the cottage, with a strong westerly wind, and a tide within twenty minutes of the flood.

"What are you doing, Masther Hardress?" said the boatman. "Won't you haul home the mainsheet and jib?"

Hardress, whose eyes had been fixed on the rocky point before the cottage, started suddenly, and proceeded to execute the nautical manœuvre in question. The little vessel, as docile to her helm as a well-mounted hunter to his rider, threw her bow away from the wind, and rushed roaring through the surges with a fuller and a fiercer energy. After suffering her to run for a few minutes before the wind, Hardress commenced, with due caution, the dangerous process of jibbing or shifting the mainsail from one side of the vessel to the other.

"Down with yer heads, ladies, if ye plase! Take care of the boom."

All the heads were lowered, and the boom swung rapidly across, and the vessel heeled with the sudden impulse, until her leeward gunwale sipped the brine.

"Give her a free sheet now, Masther Hardress," said Kett, "and we'll be up in two hours."

All boatmen know that it requires a much steadier hand and more watchful eye to govern a vessel when the wind is fair than when it is adverse. A still greater nicety of attention was requisite in the present instance, as the wind was high; and the now returning tide occasioned, as the boatman predicted, a heavy sea in the channel. It was, therefore, with considerable chagrin that Larry Kett perceived his master's mind wandering, and his attention frequently altogether withdrawn from the occupation which he had in hand. That nervous disease, to which he had become a slave for many weeks, approached a species of paroxysm when Hardress found himself once more upon the very scene where he had first encountered danger with the unfortunate Eily, and before that dwelling beneath whose roof he had plighted, to his forgotten friend, the faith which he had since betrayed. It was impossible his reason could preserve its calmness amid those terrible remembrances. As the shades of evening fell, assisted by the gloomy clouds that scowled upon the brow of heaven, he became subject to the imaginative weakness of a child. The faces of his companions darkened and grew strange in his eye. The roar of the waters was redoubled, and the howling of the wind along the barren shores brought to his mind the horrid cry of the hounds, by which his guilt and his misery had been so fearfully revealed. The shapes of those whom he had wronged seemed to menace him from the gloomy chasms that gaped around between the enormous billows; and the blast came after with a voice of reproach, as if to hurry him onward to a place of dreadful retribution. Sometimes the corpse of Eily, wrapped in the blue mantle which she generally wore, seemed to be rolled downward from the ridge of a foaming breaker; sometimes the arms seemed stretched to him for aid; and sometimes the pale and shrouded figure of Mrs. Daly seemed, from the gloom, to bend a look on him of quiet sadness and upbraiding. While wholly absorbed in the contemplation of these phantoms, a rough grasp was suddenly laid upon his arm, and a rough voice shouted in his ear,—

"Are you deaf or dreaming? Mind your hand, or you'll put us down!"

Hardress looked around like one who suddenly awakes from slumber, and saw his father looking on him with an inflamed and angry countenance. In his reverie a change had taken place, of which he was totally unconscious. A heavy shower drove full upon the party, the sky had grown still darker, and the wind had risen still higher. The time had long gone by when the spirits of Hardress caught fire from the sight of danger, and when his energies were concentrated by difficulty, as the firmness of an arch is augmented by the weight which it is made to sustain. The suddenness of his father's action startled him to the very heart; the strange, and as it appeared to him sudden, change in the weather, confirmed the disorder of his senses; and springing forward, as a culprit might do from the sudden arrest of an officer of justice, he abandoned the rudder, and fled with murmurs of affright into the centre of the boat, where he sank exhausted upon the ballast.

The scene of confusion which ensued it is not needful that

we should describe. Larry Kett, utterly unable to comprehend what he beheld, took charge of the helm, while the remainder of the party busied themselves in restoring Hardress to some degree of composure. There was no remark made at the time, but, when the party were separating, some touched their foreheads and compressed their lips in a serious manner; while others, in secret whispers, ventured, for the first time, to couple the name of Hardress Cregan with that epithet which is so deeply dreaded by young men, that they will burst the ties of moral justice, of religion, of humanity, and even incur the guilt of murder, to avoid its imputation—the epithet of coward.

Never was there a being more constitutionally formed for deeds of courage and of enterprise than Hardress, and yet (such is the power of conscience) never was a stigma affixed with greater justice. He hurried early to his room, where he passed a night of feverish restlessness, secured, indeed, from the observation of others, but still subjected to the unwinking gaze of memory, whose glance, like the diamond eyes of the famous idol, seemed to follow him whithersoever he turned with the same deadly and avenging expression.

CHAPTER XXXVIII.

HOW THE SITUATION OF HARDRESS BECAME MORE CRITICAL.

ANOTHER occurrence, mingled with somewhat more of the ridiculous, but not less powerful in its effect upon the mind of Hardress, took place in a few days afterwards.

In the lack of some equally exciting exercise, and in order to form a pretext for his frequent absence from the castle, Hardress was once more tempted to take up his gun, and look for shore-fowl in the neighbourhood. One morning, when he was occupied in drawing a charge in the hall, Falvey came running in to let him know that a flock of May-birds had pitched in one of the gullies in the creek, which was now almost deserted by the fallen tide.

"Are there many?" said Hardress, a little interested.

"Oceans, oceans of 'em, sir," was the reply of the figurative valet.

"Very well; do you take this bag, and follow me to the shore. I think we shall get at them conveniently from behind the lime-kiln."

This was a commission which Falvey executed with the worst grace in the world. This talkative person was, in fact, a perfect and even absurd coward, nor did he consider the absence of any hostile intention as a security, when the power of injury was in his neighbourhood. His dread of fire-arms, like that of Friday, approached to a degree of superstition, and it would appear from his conduct that he had anything but a steady faith in the common opinion that a gun must throw its contents in the direction of the bore. Accordingly, it was always with considerable reluctance and apprehension that he accompanied his young master on his shooting excursions. He followed him now with a dejected face, and a sharp and prudent eye, directed ever and anon at the loaded weapon which Hardress balanced in his hand.

They approached the game under cover of a low, ruined building, which had been once used as a lime-kiln, and now served as a blind to those who made it an amusement to scatter destruction among the feathered visitants of the little creek. Arrived at this spot, Hardress perceived that he could take the quarry at a better advantage from a sand-bank at some distance on the right. He moved, accordingly, in that direction, and Falvey, after conjecturing how he might best get out of harm's way, crept into the ruined kiln, and took his seat on the loose stones at the bottom. The walls, though broken down on every side, were yet of a sufficient height to conceal his person, when in a sitting posture, from all observation of man or fowl. Rubbing his hands in glee, and smiling to find himself thus snugly ensconced from danger, he awaited with an anxiety, not quelled, indeed, but yet somewhat diminished, the explosion of the distant engine of death.

But his evil genius, envious of his satisfaction, found means of putting his tranquillity to naught. Hardress altered his judgment of the two stations, and accordingly crept back to the lime-kiln with as little noise as he had used in leaving it. He marvelled what had become of Falvey; but reserving the search for him until he had done his part upon the curlews, he went on his knee, and rested the barrel of his piece on the grass.

covered wall of the ruin, in such a manner that the muzzle was two inches above the head of the unseen, and smiling, and unconscious Falvey. Having levelled on the centre of the flock, he fired, and an uproar ensued which it is almost hopeless to describe. Half a dozen of the birds fell without hearing the shot; several fluttered a few paces, and then sank gasping on the slob. The great mass of the flock rose screaming into the calm air, and were chorused by the whistling of myriads of sea-larks, redshanks, and other diminutive water-fowl. But the most alarming strain in the concert was played by poor Falvey, who gave himself up for dead on hearing the shot fired close to his ear in so unexpected a manner. He sprang at one bound clear out of the lime-kiln, and fell flat on his face and hands upon the short grass, roaring and kicking his heels in the air like one in the agonies of the *colica pictorum*. Terrified to the soul by this startling incident, Hardress threw down his gun, and fled as from the face of a fiend.

In the mean time the cries of the prostrate Falvey attracted to his relief a stranger, who had hitherto lain concealed under a projection of the bank. He jumped upon the wall of the kiln, and remained gazing for some moments on the fallen man with an expression which partook more of curiosity than of compassion. Seeing the gun, he imagined that Falvey had fired the shot himself, and experienced some injury from the recoil. It was with a kind of sneer, therefore, that he took up the weapon, and proceeded to question the sufferer.

"What's de matter wid you, man alive? What makes you be roarin' dat way?"

"I'm *hot!*"* returned Falvey, with a groan. "I'm hot. The masther holed me with the shot. Will I get the priest? Will I get the priest itself?"

"Where did he hole you?"

"There, in the lime-kiln, this minute. Will I get the priest?"

"I mane, where are you hot? In what part o' your body?"

"Oyeh, it is all one," said Falvey, a little perplexed by the question. "I felt it in the very middle o' my heart. Sure I know I'm a gone man!"

"How do you know it, ayeh? Straighten yourself, an' sit up a bit. I don't see any signs of a hole."

Falvey sat up, and began to feel his person in various places, moaning the whole time in the most piteous tone, and looking occasionally on his hands, as if expecting to find them covered with blood. After a minute examination, however, no such symptom could be discovered.

"Ah, dere's nottin' de matter wid you, man," said the stranger. "Stand up, man; you're as well as ever you wor."

"Faiks, maybe so," returned Falvey, rising and looking about him with some briskness of eye. "But sure I know," he added, suddenly drooping, "'tis the way always with people when they are holed by a gun; they never feel it until the moment they dhrop."

"Well, an' isn't it time for you to tink of it when you begin to feel it?" returned the stranger.

"Faiks, maybe so," returned Falvey, with increasing confidence. "That I may be blest," he added, swinging his arms, and moving a few paces with greater freedom, "that I may be blest if I feel any pain! Faiks, I thought I was *hot*. But there's one thing, any way: as long as ever I live, I never again will go shooting with any man, gentle or simple, during duration."

"Stay a minute," said the stranger. "Won't you go out for the curlews?"

"Go out for 'em yourself, an' have 'em if you like," returned Falvey; "it's bother enough I got with them for birds."

He took up the gun and pouch, and walked slowly away, while the stranger, after slipping off his shoes and stockings, and turning up the knees of his under-garment, walked out for the game. He had picked up one or two of the birds, and was proceeding farther along the brink of the gully, when a sudden shout was heard upon the rocky shore on the other side of the creek. The stranger started, and looked like a frighted deer in that direction, where Falvey beheld a party of soldiers running down the rocks, as if with the purpose of intercepting his passage round a distant point by which the high road turned. The stranger, possibly aware of their intention, left his shoes, the game, and all behind him, and fled

* An Irish preterite for the word *hit*.

rapidly across the slob, in the direction of the point. It was clear the soldiers could not overtake him. They halted, therefore, on the shore, and, levelling their pieces with deliberation, fired several shots at the fugitive, as after a runaway prisoner. With lips a gape with horror, Falvey beheld the shining face of the mud torn up by the bullets within a few feet of the latter. He still, however, continued his course unhurt, and was not many yards distant from the opposite shore, when (either caught by a trip, or brought down by some bullet better aimed) he staggered and fell in the marl. He rose again, and again sank down upon his elbow, panting for breath, and overpowered by fatigue and fear. Falvey delayed to see no more, being uncertain at whom their muskets would be next directed. Lowering his person as far as might be consistent with a suitable speed, he ran along the hedgeways in the direction of the castle.

In the mean time Hardress, full of horror at the supposed catastrophe, had hurried to his sleeping-room, where he flung himself upon the bed, and sought, but found not, relief in exclamations of terror and of agony. "What!" he muttered through his clenched teeth, "shall my hands be always bloody? Can I not move but death must dog my steps? Must I only breathe to suffer and destroy?"

A low and broken moan, uttered near his bedside, made him start with a superstitious apprehension. He looked round, and beheld his mother kneeling at a chair, her face pale, excepting the eyes, which were inflamed with tears. Her hands were wreathed together, as if with a straining exertion, and sobs came thick and fast upon her breath, in spite of all her efforts to restrain them. In a few minutes, while he remained gazing on her in some perplexity, she arose, and, standing by his bedside, laid her hand quietly upon his head.

"I have been trying to pray," she said, "but I fear in vain. It was a selfish prayer—it was offered up for you. If you fear death and shame, you will soon have cause to tremble. For a mother who loves her son, guilty as he is, and for a son who would not see his parents brought to infamy, there have been fearful tidings here since morning."

Hardress could only look the intense anxiety which he felt to learn what those tidings were.

"In a few words," said Mrs. Cregan, "the dress of that unhappy girl has been recognised, and by a train of circumstances (command yourself awhile!)—circumstances which this sick head of mine will hardly allow me to detail, suspicion has fallen upon your former boatman and his family. Do you know where he is?"

"I have not seen him since the—the—I know not. My orders were that he should leave the country, and I gave him money for the purpose."

"Thank Heaven for that!" Mrs. Cregan exclaimed, with her usual steady energy, while she clasped her hands together, and looked upward with a rapt fervour of expression. The action, however, was quickly altered to a chilly shudder. She looked suddenly to the earth, veiling her eyes with her hand, as if a rapid light had dazzled her. "Thank Heaven!" she repeated in a tone of terrified surprise. "Oh! mighty Being, Origin of justice, and Judge of the guilty, forgive me for that impious gratitude! Oh! Dora Cregan, if any one had told you in your youth that you should one day thank Heaven to find a murderer safe from justice! I do not mean you, my child," she said, turning to Hardress; "you are no murderer."

Hardress made no reply, and Mrs. Cregan remained silent for a few minutes, as if deliberating on the course which it would be necessary for her to adopt. The deception practised on Anne Chute was not among the least of those circumstances which made her situation one of agonising perplexity. But her fate had been already decided, and it would be only to make the ruin of her son assured, if she attempted now to separate the destiny of Anne from theirs.

"We must hasten this marriage," Mrs. Cregan continued, after a silence of some minutes, "and, in the mean time, endeavour to get those people, the Naughtens, out of the way. They will be sought for without delay. Mr. Warner has been inquiring for you, that he might obtain information of your boatman. I told him that you had parted with the man long since, and you did not know whither he had gone. Do you think you could sustain an interview with him?"

Hardress, who was now sitting upon the bedside, pale, and with features distorted by terror, replied to this question by a chilly shudder and a vacant stare.

"We must keep him out, then," said his mother; "or, if he must see you, it shall be in your chamber. There is still one way by which you might be saved—the way which you proposed yourself, though I was not then sufficiently at ease to perceive its advantages. Go boldly forward and denounce this wretch, lay all the information in your power before the magistrates, and aid the officers of justice in bringing him to punishment."

Hardress turned his dull and bloodshot eyes upon his mother, as if to examine whether she was serious in this proposition. If a corpse, rigid in death, could be stimulated to a galvanic laugh, one might expect to find it such a hideous convulsion as Hardress used on discovering that she did not mock.

"No, mother," he said, curbing the sardonic impulse, "I am not innocent enough for that."

"Why will you so perversely wrong yourself?" said Mrs. Cregan. "Neither in your innocence nor in your culpability do you seem to form a true estimate of your conduct. You are not so guilty as——"

"Very true, mother," said Hardress, impatient of the subject, and cutting it short with a burst of fierceness scarcely less shocking than his laughter. "If the plea of conscious guilt will not suffice, you may take my refusal upon your own ground. I am too innocent for that. I am not fiend enough for such a treachery. Pray let me hear no more of it, or I shall sicken. There's some one has knocked three times at the room door. I am quite weary of playing the traitor, and if I had nothing but pure heart-sickness to restrain me, I should yet long for a reform. My brain will bear no more; a single crime would crush it now. Again! There's some one at the door."

"Well, Hardress, I will speak with you of this at night."

"With all my heart. You say things sometimes that go near to drive me mad; but yet you always talk to me as a friend, for my own sake, and kindly. Mother!" he added, suddenly laying his hand on her arm as she passed him, and as the light fell brighter on her thin and gloomy features; "mother, how changed you are since this unhappy act! You are worn out with fears and sorrows. It has been my fate or fault (I will not contend for the distinction) to scatter poison in the way of all who knew me. A lost love for one; for another, falsehood, desertion, death; for a third, duplicity and ingratitude; and even for you, my mother, ill health, a sinking heart, and a pining frame. I can promise nothing now. My mind is so distracted with a thousand images and recollections (each one of which, a year since, I would have thought sufficient to unsettle my reason), that I know not how to offer you a word of comfort. But if these gloomy days should be destined to pass away, and (whether by penitence or some sudden mercy) my heart should once again be visited with a quieter grief, I will then remember your affection."

There was a time when this speech would have been moonlight music to the ear of Mrs. Cregan. Now, her esteem for Hardress being fled, and a good deal of self-reproach brought in to sour the feeling with which she regarded his conduct, it was only in his moments of danger, of anger, or distress, that her natural affections were forcibly aroused in his behalf. Still, however, it did not fail to strike upon her heart. She sank weeping upon his neck, and loaded him with blessings and caresses.

"I do not look for thanks, Hardress," she said at length, disengaging herself, as if in reproof of her weakness, "because I do the part of a mother. All that you have said, my child, in my regard, is very vain and idle. A quiet, at least a happy, fireside is a blessing that I never more can enjoy, nor do I even hope for it. It is not because I think your guilt not worthy of the extreme punishment of the laws, that therefore I should deem it possible we can either of us forget our share in the horrid deed that has been done. Let us not disguise the truth from our own hearts. We are a wretched and a guilty pair, with enough of sin upon our hands to make our future life a load of fear and penitence."

"I did but speak it," said the son with some peevishness of tone, "in consideration of your suffering."

"I wish, Hardress, that you had considered me a little more early."

"You did not encourage me to a confidence," said Hardress. "You repressed it."

"You should not," retorted the mother, "have needed encouragement under circumstances so decisive. Married! If you had breathed a word of it to me, I would have sooner died than urge you as I did."

"I told you I was pledged."

"You did: ay, there, indeed, my son, your reproach strikes home. I thought that you would only break a verbal truth, and most unjustly did I wish that you should break it. How fearfully has Heaven repaid me for that selfish and unfeeling act! But you were all too close and secret for me. Go, go, unhappy boy! you taunt me with the seduction which was only the work of your own shameful passion."

This painful dialogue, which, perhaps, would have risen to a still more bitter tone of recrimination, was broken off by a renewal of the summons at the door. It appeared as if the applicant for admission had gone away in despair, and again returned after a fruitless search elsewhere. On opening the door, Mrs. Cregan encountered the surly visage of Dan Dawley, who informed her that her presence was required in the ball-room: such was the name given to that apartment in which Hardress had made to her a confession of his guilt. When she had left the chamber, Hardress, who grew momentarily more weak and ill, prepared himself for bed, and bade the old steward send him one of the servants. This commission the surly functionary discharged on returning to the servants' hall, by intimating his master's desire to Pat Falvey, who had entered some time before.

Mrs. Cregan, in the mean time, proceeded to the chamber above mentioned, which she could only reach by passing through the narrow hall and winding staircase near the entrance. The former presented a scene calculated to alarm and perplex her. A number of soldiers, with their soaped and powdered queues, and musket-barrels shining like silver, were stuck up close to the wall on either side, like the wax figures in the shop of a London tailor. On the gravel before the door she could see a number of country people, who had collected about the door, wondering what could have brought "the army" to Castle Chute. From the door of the kitchen and servants' hall a number of heads were thrust out, with faces indicative of a similar degree of astonishment and curiosity.

Passing through this formidable array, Mrs. Cregan ascended the stairs, and was admitted at the door of the ball-room by a figure as solemn and formidable as those below. The interior of the room presented a scene of still more startling interest. A table was spread in the centre, around which were standing Mr. Warner, the magistrate, Mr. Barnaby Cregan, Captain Gibson, and a clerk. At the farther end of the table, his arm suspended in a cotton handkerchief, stood a low, squalid, and ill-shaped figure, his dress covered with mud, and his face, which was soiled with blood and marl, rather expressive of surprise and empty wonder than of apprehension or of suffering.

Mrs. Cregan, who recognised the figure, paused for a moment in a revulsion of the most intense anxiety, and then walked calmly forward with that air of easy dignity which she could assume even when her whole nature was at war within her. This power of veiling her inward struggles, even to the extremity of endurance, made her resemble a fair tower sapped in the foundation, which shows no symptom of a weakness up to the very instant of destruction, and is a ruin even before the sentiment of admiration has faded on the beholder's mind.

CHAPTER XXXIX.

HOW THE DANGER TO THE SECRET OF HARDRESS WAS AVERTED BY THE INGENUITY OF IRISH WITNESSES.

MR. WARNER informed her that it was no longer necessary that her son's assistance should be afforded them, as they had had the good fortune to apprehend the object of their suspicions. They should, however, he said, be compelled to await the arrival of their witnesses, for nothing had been gained by putting the fellow on his examination. His answers were all given in the true style of an Irish witness, seeming to evince the utmost frankness, yet invariably leaving the querist in still greater perplexity than before he put the question. Every hour, he said, they expected the arrival of this man's brother and sister from Killarney, and they should then have an opportunity of confronting them with him and with the previous witnesses.

"I have already sent off a messenger," continued Mr. Warner, "to my own little place, to see if they have yet arrived, in order that they may be brought hither and examined on the spot. The inconvenience to Mrs. Chute I hope she will excuse, and my principal reason for wishing to see you, Mrs. Cregan, was that you might bear our explanation to that lady. On occasions of this kind all good subjects are liable to be trespassed on, perhaps more than courtesy might warrant."

"I will answer for my sister," said Mrs. Cregan coldly; "she will not, of course, withhold any accommodation in her power. But this man—has he been questioned, sir?"

"He has."

"Might I be allowed to see the examination?"

"By all means, Mrs. Cregan. Mr. Houlahan, will you hand that book to the lady?"

Mr. Houlahan, after sticking his pen behind his ear, rose and delivered the volume accordingly, with a smirk and bow, which he meant for a wonder of politeness. The lady, whose thoughts were busy with other matters than with Mr. Houlahan's gallantry, received it, nevertheless, with a calm dignity, and opening her reading-glass, stooped to the page which that gentleman had pointed out. She glanced with assumed indifference over the details of the examination of Daniel Mann, while she devoured its meaning with an agonising closeness of scrutiny. The passage which concerned her most was the following:—

"—— Questioned, If he were known to the deceased Eily O'Connor; answereth, He hath met such a one in Garryowen, but knoweth nothing farther. Questioned, If he heard of her death; answereth, Nay. Questioned, If he knoweth a certain Lowry Looby, living; answereth, Yes. Questioned, Whether Eily O'Connor did not lodge for a time in the house of Philip Naughten, Killarney; answereth, How should he be aware of his brother-in-law's lodgers? Saith, He knoweth not. Questioned, If he were not present in said Naughten's house, when said Eily, deceased, said Looby being then in Naughten's kitchen, did give a letter to Poll Naughten, sister to prisoner, addressed to Dunat O'Leary, hair-cutter, Garryowen, and containing matter in the handwriting of said Eily; answereth, How should he (prisoner) see through a stone wall? Saith, He was in the kitchen. Saith, Looby was a fool, and that his eyes were not fellows. Saith, He knoweth not who was in the said inner room. Questioned, Why he was discharged out of the employment of his master, Mr. Hardress Cregan; answereth, He knoweth not. Questioned, Where he hath been residing since he left his master's service; answereth, It is a token that examinant doth not know, or he would not ask. And the like impertinent and futile answers, with sundry speeches little to the purpose, hath the prisoner responded to all subsequent inquiries."

With a feeling of relief, Mrs. Cregan returned the book to the clerk, and glancing towards the prisoner, observed that his eye was fixed on hers with a look of shrewd and anxious inquiry. To this glance she returned one equally comprehensive in its meaning. It told him she was fully in the counsels of her son, and prepared him to be guided by her eye.

At the same moment the sentinel was heard presenting arms at the door, and a corporal entered to say that Mr. Warner's messenger had returned, and that the witnesses might be expected in a few minutes.

"All's right, then," said Mr. Warner, who entered on a scrutiny of this kind with the same professional goût which might make Xenophon find excitement amid the difficulties and intricacies of his famous retreat. "Remove the prisoner. We shall examine them apart, and see if their stories will bear the jangling. If they are all as much given to the negative as this fellow, I am afraid we shall find it hard to make them jar."

This was a moment of intense anxiety to Mrs. Cregan. She saw no probability of being able to communicate with the prisoners (for such were all the witnesses at present); and she comprehended all the importance of preventing, at least, the chance of Hardress's name being mingled up with the account of the unknown visitor at the cottage of the Naughtens.

A little experience, however, in the proceedings of Irish law courts would have given her more courage and comfort on this subject. The peasantry of Ireland have, for centuries, been at war with the laws by which they are governed, and watch their operation in every instance with a jealous eye. Even guilt itself, however naturally atrocious, obtains a commiseration in their regard from the mere spirit of opposition to a system of government which they consider as unfriendly. There is scarcely a cottage in the south of Ireland where the very circumstance of legal denunciation would not afford, even to a murderer, a certain passport to concealment and protection. To the same cause may be traced, in all likelihood, the shrewdness of disguise, the closeness, the affected dulness, the assumed simplicity, and all the inimitable subtleties of evasion and of wile which an Irish peasant can display when he is made to undergo a scene of judicial scrutiny, in which he will frequently display a degree of gladiatorial dexterity which would throw the spirit of Machiavelli into ecstasies.

While Mrs. Cregan remained endeavouring to control the workings of her apprehension, a bustle was heard outside the door, in which the sound of a female voice, raised high in anger and remonstrance, overtopped the rest in loudness, like a soprano voice in a chorus.

"Let me in!" she exclaimed in a fierce tone. "Do you want to thrust your scarlet jacket between the tree and the rind? Let me in, you tall ramrod, or I'll pull the soap and powder out of your wig. If I had you on the mountains, I'd cut the pig's tail from your pole, and make a show o' you. Do, do—draw your bay'net on me, you cowardly object! It's like the white blood o' the whole of ye! I know fifty lads of your size, that would think as little of tripping you up on a fair-green, and making a high road of your powdered carcass, as I do of snapping my fingers in your face! That for your rusty bay'net, you woman's match!" Here she burst into the room and confronted the magistrate, while the sentinel muttered, as he recovered his guard, "Well, you're a rum one, you are, as ever I see!"

"Danny a'ra gal! Oh vo, ohone, achree, asthora! is that the way with you? What did you do to 'em? What's the matther?"

"Dat de hands may stick to me, Poll, if I know," returned the prisoner, while she moaned and wept over him with a sudden passion of grief. "Dey say 'tis to kill some one I done. Dey say one Eily O'Connor was a lodger of ours westwards, an' dat I tuk her out of a night an' murdered her. Isn't dat purty talk? Sure you know yourself we had no lodgers."

"Remove that prisoner," said Mr. Warner; "he must not be present at her examination."

"I'll engage I have no longin' for it," returned Danny. "She knows right well that it is all talk, an' 'tis well I have found a friend at last dat'll see me out o' trouble."

Danny was removed, and the examination of Poll Naughten was commenced by the magistrate. She had got but one hint from her brother to guide her in her answers, and on all other topics she came to the resolution of admitting as little as possible.

"Your name is Poll Naughten? Stay, she is not sworn. Hand her the book."

She took the volume with an air of surly assurance, and repeated the form of the oath.

"She did not kiss it," whispered Mr. Houlahan, with a sagacious anxiety; "she only kissed her thumb. I had my eye upon her."

"Had you? Well, gi' me the book till I plase that gentleman. Is that the way you'd like to lip the leather?" she said, after a smack that went off like a detonating cap. "Is that done to your liking, sir?"

Mr. Houlahan treated this query with silence, and the examination proceeded.

"Poll Naughten is your name—is it not?"

"Polly Mann they christened me for want of a betther, an' for want of a worse I took up with Naughten."

"You live in the Gap of Dunloe?"

"Iss, when at home."

"Did you know the deceased Eily O'Connor?"

"Eily who?"

"O'Connor."

"I never knew a girl o' that name."

"Take care of your answers. We have strong evidence."

"If you have it as sthrong as a cable you may make the most of it. You have my answer."

"Do you know a person of the name of Looby?"

"I do, to be sure, for my sins, I believe."

"Do you remember his being in your house in last autumn?"

"I do, well; an' I'd give him his tay the same night if it wasn't for raisins."

"Did you give him a letter on that evening?"

"He made more free than welcome, a dale. I can tell him that."

"Answer my question. Did you give him a letter?"

"Oyeh, many's the thing I gev him, and I'm sorry I didn't give him a thing more along with 'em, an' that's a good flakin'."

"Well, I don't deny you credit for your good wishes in that respect, but still I wait to have my question answered. Did you give Looby a letter on that evening?"

"Listen to me now, plase your honour. That the head may go to the grave with me——"

"Those asseverations, my good woman, are quite superfluous. You should remember you are on your oath."

"Well, I am; sure I know I am upon my oath, an' as I am upon it, an' by the vartue o' that oath, I swear I never swopped a word with Lowry Looby from that day to this."

"Whew!" said the magistrate, "there's an answer! Hear me, my good woman. If you won't speak out, we shall find a way to make you speak."

"No use in wasting blows upon a willing horse. I can do no more than speak to the best of my ability."

"Very well. I ask you again, therefore, whether Looby received a letter from you on that evening?"

"Does Lowry say I gev him a letther?"

"You will not answer, then?"

"To be sure I will. What am I here for?"

"To drive me mad, I believe."

"Faiks, I can't help you," said Poll, "when you won't listen to me."

"Well, well, speak on."

"I will, then, without a word of a lie. I'll tell you that whole business, and let Lowry himself conthradict me if he daar to do it. 'Tis as good as six years ago, now, since I met that boy at one o' the Hewsan's wakes."

"Well, what has that to do with an answer to a plain question?"

"Easy a minute, can't you, an' I'll tell you. He behaved very polished that night, an' I see no more of him until the day you spake of, when he came into the cottage from Killarney."

"Woman," said the magistrate, "remember that you have sworn to tell the whole truth; not only the truth, but the whole truth."

"Ah, then, gentleman an' lady, d'ye hear this? Did anybody ever hear the peer o' that? Sure it's just the whole truth I'm tellin' him, an' he won't listen to the half of it."

"Go on," said Mr. Warner in a tone of resignation.

"Sure that's what I want to do, if I'd be let. I say this, an' I'll stand to it: Lowry gave me impidence that I wouldn't stand from his masther; an' I did (let him make the most of it), I admit it, I did give him a sthroke or two. I did. I admit it."

"And after the sthrokes, as you call them, you gave him a letter?"

"What letther?"

"I see, you are very copious of your admissions. Are you Philip Naughten's wife?"

"I am."

"Ay, now we're upon smooth ground. You can give an answer when it suits you. I'm afraid you are too many for me. What shall we do with this communicative person?" he said, turning to the other gentlemen.

"Remand her," said Captain Gibson, whose face was purple from suppressed laughter, "and let us have the husband."

"With all my heart," returned Mr. Warner. "Take that woman into another room, and bring up Philip Naughten. Take care, moreover, that they do not speak upon the way."

Poll was removed, a measure which she resented by shrill and passionate remonstrances, affecting to believe herself very ill-treated. Her husband was next admitted, and from his humble, timid, and deprecating manner, at once afforded the magistrate some cause of gratulation, and Mrs. Cregan of deep and increasing anxiety.

He approached the table with a fawning smile upon his coarse features, and a helpless, conciliating glance at every individual around him.

"Now we shall have something," said Mr. Warner; "this

fellow has a more tractable eye. Your name is Philip Naughten, is it not?"

The man returned an answer in Irish; which the magistrate cut short in the middle.

"Answer me in English, friend. We speak no Irish here. Is your name Philip Naughten?"

"The wisha, vourneen——"

"Come, come—English. Swear him to know whether he does not understand English. Can you speak English; fellow?"

"Not a word, plase your honour."

A roar of laughter succeeded this escapade, to which the prisoner listened with a wondering and stupid look. Addressing himself in Irish to Mr. Cregan, he appeared to make an explanatory speech, which was accompanied by a slight expression of indignation.

"What does the fellow say?" asked Mr. Warner.

"Why," said Cregan, with a smile, "he says he will admit that he couldn't be *hung in English before his face*,* but he does not know enough of the language to enable him to *tell his story* in English."

"Well, then, I suppose we must have it in Irish. Mr. Houlahan, will you act as interpreter?"

The clerk, who thought it *genteel* not to know Irish, bowed, and declared himself unqualified.

"Wisha, then," said a gruff voice at a little distance, in a dark corner of the room, "it isn't but what you had opportunities enough of learning it. If you went to foreign parts, what would they say to you, do you think, when you'd tell 'em you didn't know the language of the country where you were born? You ought to be ashamed o' yourself, so you ought."

This speech, which proceeded from the unceremonious Dan Dawley, produced some smiling at the expense of the euphuistic secretary, after which the steward himself was sworn to discharge the duties of the office in question.

The preliminary queries having been put and answered, the interpreter proceeded to ask, at the magistrate's suggestion, whether the witness was acquainted with the deceased Eily O'Connor.

But if it had been the policy of Mrs. Naughten to admit as little as possible, it seemed to be the policy of her husband to admit nothing at all. The subterfuge of the former in denying a knowledge of Eily, under her maiden name (which, she imagined, saved her from the guilt of perjury), was an idea too brilliant for her husband. He gaped upon the interpreter in silence for some moments, and then looked on the magistrate as if to gather the meaning of the question.

"Repeat it for him," said the latter.

Dawley did so.

"'Tis the answer he makes me, plase your honour," he said, "that he's a poor man that lives by industhering."

"That's no answer. Repeat the question once more, and tell him I shall commit him for trial if he will not answer it."

Again the question was put, and listened to with the same plodding, meditative look, and answered with a countenance of honest grief, and an apparent anxiety to be understood, which would have baffled the penetration of any but a practised observer. So earnest was his manner, that Mr. Warner really believed he was returning a satisfactory answer. But he was disappointed.

"He says," continued the interpreter, "that when he was a young man he rented a small farm from Mr. O'Connor, of Crag-beg, near Tralee. He has as much thricks in him, plase your honour, as a rabbit. I'd as lieve be brakin' stones to a pavior as putting questions to a rogue of his kind."

Threats, promises of favour, lulling queries, and moral expedients of every kind were used to draw him out into the communicative frankness which was desired. But he remained as adamant. He could or would admit nothing more than that he was a poor man, who lived by his industry, and that he had rented a small farm from Mr. O'Connor, of Crag-beg.

The prisoners, therefore, after a short consultation, were all remanded, in order that time might be afforded for confronting them with the friends of the unhappy Eily. Mrs. Cregan, with

* A common phrase, meaning that the individual understood enough of the language to refute any calumny spoken in his presence, which, if uncontradicted, might leave him in danger of the halter. The acute reader may detect in this pithy idiom a meaning characteristic of the country in which it is used.

the feeling of one who has stood all day before a burning furnace, hurried to the room of Hardress to indulge the tumult which was gathering in her bosom; and the gentlemen, by a special invitation (which could no more be declined without offence; in the Ireland of those days, than in a Persian cottage), adjourned to the consolations of Mrs. Chute's dining-parlour. Separate places of confinement were allotted to the prisoners; a sentinel was placed over each; and the remainder of the party, notwithstanding the remonstrances of Captain Gibson, were all entertained like princes in the servants' hall.

CHAPTER XL.

HOW HARDRESS TOOK A DECISIVE STEP FOR HIS OWN SECURITY.

THE hospitalities of Castle Chute were on this evening called into active exercise. If the gravest occasion of human life, the vigil of the dead, was not in those days always capable of restraining the impetuous spirit of enjoyment so much indulged in Irish society, how could it be expected that a mere anxiety for the interests of justice could interrupt the flow of their social gaiety? Before midnight the house rang with laughter, melody, and uproar, and in an hour after every queue in the servants' hall was brought into a horizontal position. Even the three that stalked on guard were said to oscillate on their posts with an ominous motion, as the bells in churches forebode their fall when shaken by an earthquake. Hardress continued too unwell to make his appearance, and this circumstance deprived the company of the society of Anne Chute, and, indeed, of all the ladies, who took a quiet and rather mournful cup of tea by the drawing-room fire. The wretched subject of their solicitude lay burning on his bed, and listening to the boisterous sounds of mirth that proceeded from the distant parlour with the ears of a dreaming maniac.

The place in which his boatman was confined had been a stable, but was now become too ruinous for use. It was small and roughly paved. The rack and manger were yet attached to the wall, and a few slates, displaced upon the roof, admitted certain glimpses of moonshine, which fell cold and lonely on the rough unplastered wall and eaves, making the house illustrious, like that of Sixtus V. Below, on a heap of loose straw, sat the squalid prisoner, warming his fingers over a small fire heaped against the wall, and listening in silence to the unsteady tread of the sentinel before he strode back and forward before the stable door, and hummed, with an air of suppressed and timid joviality, the words,—

"We won't go home till morning,
We won't go home till morning,
We won't go home till morning,
Until the dawn appears!"

A small square window, closed with a wooden bar and shutters, was to be found above the rack, and opened on a hay-yard, which, being raised considerably above the level of the stable floor, lay only a few feet beneath this aperture. Danny Mann was in the act of devouring a potato, reeking hot, which he had cooked in the embers, when a noise at the window made him start, and set his ears like a watch-dog. It was repeated. He stood on his feet, and crept softly into a darker corner of the stable, partly in superstitious apprehension, and partly in obedience to an impulse of natural caution. In a few minutes one of the shutters was gently put back, and a flood of mild light was poured into the prison. The shadow of a hand and head was thrown with great distinctness of outline on the opposite wall; the other shutter was put back with the same caution, and in a few moments nearly the whole aperture was again obscured, as if by the body of some person entering. Such, in fact, was the case; and the evident substantiality of the figure did not remove the superstitious terrors of the prisoner, when he beheld a form wrapped in white descending by the bars of the rack, after having made the window close again, and the apartment, in appearance, as gloomy as ever.

The intruder stood at length upon the floor, and the face, which was revealed in the brown fire-light, was that of Hardress Cregan. The ghastliness of his mouth and teeth, the wildness of his eyes, and the strangeness of his attire (for he had only wrapped the counterpane around his person), might, in the eyes of a stranger, have confirmed the idea of a supernatural appearance. But these circumstances only tended to arouse the sympathy and old attachment of his servant. Danny Mann advanced towards him slowly, his hands wreathed together, and extended as far as the sling which held the wounded arm would allow; his jaw dropped, half in pity and half in fear; and his eyes filled with tears.

"Masther Hardress," he said at length, "is it you I see dat way?"

Hardress remained for some time motionless as a statue, as if endeavouring to summon up all his corporeal energies to support him in the investigation which he was about to make.

"Won't you speak to me, masther?" continued the boatman. "Won't you speak a word itself? 'Twas all my endeavour since I came hether to thry an' get 'em to let me speak to you. Say a word, masther, if it is only to tell me 'tis yourself dat's dere!"

"Where is Eily?" murmured Hardress, still without moving, and in a tone that seemed to come from the recesses of his breast, like a sound from a sepulchre. The boatman shrank aside, as if from the eye of Justice itself. So suddenly had the question struck upon his conscience, that the inquirer was obliged to repeat it before he could collect his breath for an answer.

"Masther Hardress, I tought, after I parted you dat time——"

"Where is Eily?" muttered Hardress, interrupting him.

"Only listen to me, sir, one moment——"

"Where is Eily?"

"Oh, vo! vo!"

Hardress drew the counterpane around his head, and remained for several minutes silent in the same attitude. During that time the drapery was scarcely seen to move, and yet he raged beneath it. A few moans of deep but smothered agony were all that might be heard from time to time. So exquisite was the sense of suffering which these sounds conveyed, that Danny sank trembling on his knees, and responded to them with floods of tears and sobbing.

"Masther Hardress," he said, "if dere's anything dat I can do to make your mind aisy, say de word. I know dis is my own business, an' no one else's. An' if dey find me out itself, dey'll never be one straw de wiser of who advised me to it. If you tink I'd tell, you don't know me. Dey may hang me as high as dey like; dey may flake de life out o' me, if dey plase; but dey never'll get a word outside my lips of what it was dat made me do it. Didn't dey try me to-day, an' didn't I give 'em a sign o' what I'd do?"

"Peace, hypocrite!" said Hardress, disgusted at a show of feeling to which he gave no credit. "Be still, and hear me. For many years it has been my study to heap kindnesses upon you. For which of those was it that you came to the determination of involving me in ruin, danger, and remorse for all my future life—a little all it may be, certainly?"

It would seem, from the manner in which Danny gaped and gazed on his master while he said these words, that a reproach was one of the last things he had expected to receive from Hardress. Astonishment, blended with something like indignation, took place of the compassion which before was visible upon his countenance.

"I don't know how it is, Masther Hardress," he said. "Dere are some people dat it is hard to plase. Do you remember saying anything to me at all of a time in de room at de masther's, at Killarney, Masther Hardress? Do you remember divin' me a glove at all? I had my token surely for what I done."

So saying, he drew the glove from his waistcoat, and handed it to his master; but the latter rejected it with a revulsion of strong dislike.

"It ought I had ears to hear at dat time, and brains to understand," said Danny, as he replaced the fatal token in his bosom, "an' I'm sure it was no benefit to me dat dere should be a hue and cry over de mountains after a lost lady, an' a chance of a hempen cravat for my trouble. But I had my warrant—dat was your very word, Masther Hardress—warrant, wasn't it? 'Well, when you go,' says you, 'here is your warrant;' an' you ga' me de glove. 'Worn't dem your words?"

"But not for death," said Hardress. "I did not say for death."

"I own you didn't," returned Danny, who was aroused by what he considered a shuffling attempt to escape out of the transaction. "I own you didn't; I felt for you, an' I wouldn't wait for you to say it. But did you mane it?"

"No!" Hardress exclaimed with a burst of sudden energy. "As I shall answer it in that bright heaven, I did not. If you crowd in among my accusers at the judgment-seat, and charge me with that crime, to you, and to all, I shall utter the same disclaimer that I do at present. I did not mean to practise on her life. As I shall meet with her before that Judge, I did not. I even bade you to avoid it. Did I not warn you not to touch her?"

"You did," said Danny Mann, with a scorn which made him eloquent beyond himself, "an' your eye looked murder while you said it. After dis, I never more will look in any man's face to know what he manes. After dis, I won't believe my senses. If you'll persuade me to it, I'll own dat dere is noting as I see it. You may tell me I don't stand here, nor you dere, nor dat de moon is shining trough dat roof above us, nor de fire burning at my back, an' I'll not gainsay you after dis. But listen to me, Masther Hardress. As sure as dat moon is shining, an' dat fire burning, an' as sure as I'm here an' you dere, so sure de sign of death was on your face dat time, whatever way your words went."

"From what could you gather it?" said Hardress with a deprecating accent.

"From what! From everything. Listen hether. Didn't you remind me den of my own offer on de Purple Mountain a while before, an' tell me dat, if I was to make dat offer again, you'd tink different? An' didn't you give me de token dat you refused me den? Ah! dis is what makes me sick, after I putting my neck into de halter for a man. Well, it's all one. An' now to call me out o' my name, an' to tell me I done it for harm! Dear knows, it wasn't for any good I hoped for it, here or hereafter, or for any pleasure I took in it, dat it was done. And talkin' of hereafter, Masther Hardress, listen to me. Eily O'Connor is in heaven, an' she has told her story. Dere are two books kept dere, dey tell us, of all our doings, good an' bad. Her story is wrote in one o' dem books, an' my name (I'm sore afeerd) is wrote after it; an' take my word for dis, in whichever o' dem books my name is wrote, your own is not far from it."

As he spoke these words with an energy beyond what he had ever shown, the fire fell in, and caused a sudden light to fill the place. It shone ruddy brown upon the excited face and uplifted arm of the deformed, and gave him the appearance of a fiend denouncing on the head of the affrighted Hardress the sentence of eternal woe. It glared likewise upon the white drapery of the latter, and gave to his distorted and terrified features a look of ghastliness and fear that might have suited such an occasion well. The dreadful picture continued but for a second, yet it remained engraved upon the mind of Hardress, and, like the yelling of the hounds, haunted him, awake and dreaming, to his death. The fire again sank low, the light grew dim. It came like a dismal vision, and like a vision faded.

They were aroused from the pause to which this slight incident gave occasion by hearing the sentinel arrest his steps as he passed the door, and remain silent in his song, as if in the act of listening.

"All right within there?" said the sentinel, with his head to the door.

"All's right your way, but not my way," returned Danny sulkily.

In a few minutes they heard him shoulder his musket once again, and resume his walk, humming with an air of indifference the same old burden,—

> "We won't go home till morning,
> Until the dawn appears."

Hardress remained gazing on his servant for some moments, and then said in a whisper,—

"He has not heard us, as I feared. It is little worth, at this time, to consider on whom the guilt of this unhappy act must fall. We must at least avoid the shame, if possible. Could I depend upon you once again, if I assisted in your liberation, on the understanding that you would at once leave the country?"

The eyes of the prisoner sparkled with a sudden light. "Do you tink me a fool?" he said. "Do you tink a fox would refuse to run to earth wid de dogs at his brush?"

"Here, then," said Hardress, placing a purse in his hand; "I have no choice but to trust you. This window is unguarded. There is a pathway through the hay-yard, and thence across the field, in the direction of the road. Depart at once, and without farther question."

THE SENTRY AND THE GHOST.

"But what 'll I do about dat fellow?" said Danny. "Dat sentry comes constant dat way; you hear him now asking me if all 's right."

"I will remain here and answer for you," said Hardress, "until you have had time to escape. In the mean time use your utmost speed, and take the road to Cork, where you will be sure to find vessels ready to sail. If ever we should meet again on Irish soil, it must be for the death of either, most probably of both."

"An' is dis de way we part after all?" said Danny. "Well, den, be it so. Perhaps, after you tink longer of it, master, you may tink better of me." So saying, he sprang on the manger, and ascended, notwithstanding his hurt, with the agility of a monkey to the window. A touch undid the fastening, and in a few moments Hardress became the sole occupant of the temporary dungeon.

He remained for a considerable time leaning with his shoulder against the wall, and gazing with a vacant eye upon the decaying fire. In this situation the sentinel challenged several times in succession, and seemed well content with the answers which he received. But the train of thought which passed through the mind of Hardress became at length so absorbing that the challenge of the soldier fell unheard upon his ear. After repeating it without avail three or four times the man became alarmed and applying the butt of his musket to the door, he forced it in without much effort. His astonishment may be conceived when, instead of his little prisoner, he beheld a tall figure wrapped in white, and a ghastly face, on which the embers shed a dreary light. The fellow was a brave soldier, but, like all people of that class in his time, extremely superstitious. His brain, moreover, was heated with whiskey punch, and his imagination excited by numberless tales of horror which had been freely circulated in the servants' hall. Enough only remained of his presence of mind to enable him to give the alarm, by firing his musket, after which he fell senseless on the pavement. Hardress, no less alarmed, started into sudden energy, and climbing to the window with an agility even surpassing that of the fugitive, hurried off in the direction of his sleeping chamber.

There were few in the house who were capable of adopting any vigorous measures on hearing the alarm. Hastening to the spot, they found the sentinel lying senseless across the stock of his musket, the stable door open, and the prisoner fled. The man himself was enabled, after some time, to furnish a confused and broken narrative of what he had seen; and his story was in some degree confirmed by one of his comrades, who stated that, at the time when the shot was fired, he beheld a tall white figure gliding rapidly amongst the haystacks in the little inclosure, where it vanished in the shape of a red heifer.

The sentinel was placed under arrest in an apartment of the castle until the pleasure of his officer could be known respecting him. Captain Gibson, however, in common with the other gentlemen and the greater number of his soldiers, was at this moment wholly incapable either of conceiving or expressing any opinion whatsoever.

This story, as usual, was circulated throughout the country in the course of the following day, with many imaginative embellishments. Amongst other inventions, it was said that the ghost of Eily O'Connor had appeared to the sentinel to declare the prisoner's innocence and demand his liberation. Many persons adduced the well-known character of Eily as a ground for lending credence to this fiction. "It was like her," they said; "she was always a tender-hearted creature."

The evidence remaining against the other prisoners was now so immaterial, that their dismissal became a necessary consequence. Several efforts were made to draw them into some confession of their participation in the offence alleged; but if they were cautious in their admissions while the murderer was in custody, they would make no admission whatever after hearing of his escape. Equally unavailing were all the exertions made for the recapture of the suspected fugitive, and in a few weeks the affair had begun to grow unfamiliar to the tongues and recollections of the people.

Notwithstanding the assurances of Danny, and the danger which he must incur by remaining in the country, a doubt would frequently cross the mind of Hardress whether he really had availed himself of his recovered freedom to leave it altogether. He had money; he had many acquaintances; and he was an Irishman—an indifferent one, it is true, but yet possessing the love of expense, of dissipation, and the recklessness of danger, which mingle so largely in the temperament of his countrymen. It was almost an even question whether he would not risk the chances of detection, for the sake of playing the host among a circle of jolly companions in the purlieus of his native city. These considerations, often discussed between Hardress and his now miserable mother, made them agree to hasten the day of marriage, with the understanding that, by an anticipation of the modern fashion, the "happy pair" were to leave home immediately after the ceremony. The south of France was the scene fixed upon for the commencement of their married life—the month of honey.

CHAPTER XLI.

HOW THE ILL-TEMPER OF HARDRESS AGAIN BROUGHT BACK HIS PERILS.

A CIRCUMSTANCE which occurred during the intervening period once more put Hardress to a severe probation. It was not less severe, moreover, that it came like the accesses of a nervous disorder, suddenly and from a cause extremely disproportioned to its violence.

He had been conversing with his intended bride, on that day which was fixed upon as the penultimate of their courtship, with a more than usual appearance of enjoyment. Anne, who looked out for those breaks of sunshine in his temper as anxiously as an agriculturist might for fair weather in a broken autumn, encouraged the symptom of returning peace, and succeeded so happily as to draw him out into quick and lively repartees, and frequent bursts of laughter. Unfortunately, however, in her ecstasy at this display of spirits, she suffered her joy to hurry her unwisely into the forbidden circle which enclosed his secret, and their music turned to discord. She thought this holiday hour afforded a fair opportunity to penetrate into the blue chamber of his heart, from which he had so often warned her, and which a better impulse than curiosity urged her to explore. She did not know that the interior was defiled with blood.

"Well, Hardress," she said, with a smile that had as much of feeling as of mirth, "is not this a happier score for counting time than sitting down to shut our eyes and ears to the pleasant world about us, and opening them on a lonesome past or a foreboding future?"

If the clouds of the past and the future both had met and mingled in the mid-heaven of consciousness, they could not have cast a darker or more sudden shade than that which now overspread the brow of Hardress. The laughter darkened on his cheek, his eye grew stern and dull, and his whole being, from the inmost feeling of his nature to the exterior on which those feelings were indicated, seemed to have undergone an instantaneous change.

Anne perceived her error, but did not cease to follow up her claim upon his confidence.

"Do not let me feel," she said, "that I have brought back your gloom. Dear Hardress, hear me still without uneasiness. My sole intention is that of procuring your health and peace of mind; and surely it should not be considered an intrusion that I desire your confidence. Do you fear to find in me anything more foreign than a near and interested friend? Believe me you shall not, Hardress. I am driven upon this inquiry in spite of me. There is something hidden from me which it would be kinder to reveal. I see it prey upon your own health and spirits day after day. I see it even fixing its cruel hold at length upon my aunt. You meet with a consciousness in your eyes, and you both glance from time to time at me, as if I were a stranger, or—I should not say it, perhaps—a spy. If I come upon you when you speak together, there is a hush at my appearance, and sometimes an embarrassed look; and I have often seen trouble in your eyes, and tears in hers. Tell me, my dear Hardress, what is the cause of this? You either apprehend or you have endured some terrible misfortune. It is not now the time to treat me as a stranger."

She ceased to speak, and seemed to expect an answer; but Hardress said not a word. He remained with his hands crossed on the back of the chair, his cheek resting upon these, and his eyes fixed in gloomy silence on the floor.

"Or, if you do not think me worthy of a confidence," Anne resumed with some warmth, "at least—— Nay, but I am ill-tempered now," she added, suddenly checking herself. "I should not say that; I would say, Hardress, if you really find yourself prevented from admitting me into your confidence, at least assure yourself of this. If it is anything in your present situation—in—in—I fear to say too much—in your engagement with myself, that interferes with your peace of mind, I—I—had rather suffer anything—than—than—be the cause of suffering to you."

She turned away as she said these words, to hide from him the burst of tears with which they were accompanied. She pressed her handkerchief against her lips, and used a violent, though silent, effort avoid the convulsive utterance of the grief that struggled at her heart.

It often happens that the most sensitive persons are those who are most blind to, and make least allowance for, the susceptibility of others. The long habit of brooding over his own wants and sufferings made Hardress incapable, for the moment, of appreciating the generous affection which this speech evinced. He answered gloomily that "there were many things in the minds of all men which they would hide, if possible, even from themselves, and which therefore they could not reasonably be expected to communicate over-readily to another, however undeniable the claim to confidence might be."

With this cold answer the conversation ceased. A little, yet but a little, warmed to find her generous proposal (a proposal which cost her so much agony) thus unhandsomely received, Anne dried her tears, and remained for some minutes in that sorrowing and somewhat indignant composure to which, in virtuous breasts, the sense of unmerited injury gives birth. Subduing, however, as she had long since learned to do, her personal feelings to a sense of duty, she forced herself to assume an air of cheerfulness, and once more resumed the tone of conversation which had preceded this unfortunate failure. Again her wonted spirits arose at her desire, and again she was successful in withdrawing Hardress from his mood of dismal meditation.

One remarkable feature in the mental disease of Hardress (for such it might now be justly termed) was, as we have before remarked, the extreme uncertainty and arbitrariness of its accesses. His existence seemed to be without a basis, his mind without a centre or a rest. He had no consciousness of duty to support him, no help from Heaven, and no trust in man. Even the very passion that ate up his soul was incapable of affording to his mind that firmness of purpose and false strength which passion often gives; for his was merely retrospective, and had no object in the future. He became a passive slave to his imagination. Frequently, while enjoying a degree of comparative tranquillity, the thought would suggest itself to his fancy that "perhaps this very day, secure as he believed himself, might see him manacled and in a dungeon." Instead of quietly turning his attention away to an indifferent subject, or baffling the suggestions (as a guiltless person might) by resigning himself to a directing Providence, he combated it with argument; it increased and fastened on his imagination, until at length his nerves began to thrill, his limbs grew faint, his brow moist, and his whole being disturbed as at the presence of an actual danger. At other times, when sitting alone, it would occur to him that his servant might, notwithstanding his caution, have abused his confidence and remained in the country. The idea of the danger, the ruin, which would most probably attend such disobedience, frequently produced so violent an effect upon his mind, that he would spring from his seat in a transport of frenzy, sink on one knee, and press both hands with his utmost force against the ground, as if in the act of strangling the delinquent. Then, hearing the footstep of Anne or his mother approaching the door he would arise suddenly, covered with shame, and reach his chair exactly in time to avoid detection.

Soon after the conversation we have above detailed Mr. Cregan entered, and some questions arose on the escape of Mr. Warner's prisoner, and the possibility of his recapture. This led naturally to a disquisition on the nature of the crime alleged against him, and of capital punishments in general.

"People have hinted," said Mr. Cregan, "that this might have been a case of suicide, and for my part I don't see the impossibility."

"I should think it *very* unlikely," said Anne. "Suicide is a very un-Irish crime. The people are too religious for it, and people say too miserable."

"*Too* miserable!" exclaimed Mr. Cregan. "Now, I should think that the only cause in the world *for* suicide—the only possible palliative."

"I am not metaphysical enough to account for it," returned Anne with a smile, "and I only repeat a sentiment which I heard once from Hardress. But their misery, at all events, is a cause for their piety, and in that way may be a cause of their resignation also."

"Of all crimes," said Mr. Cregan, "that is the most absurd and unaccountable, and I wonder how jurymen can reconcile it to themselves to bring in their shameful verdicts of insanity so constantly as they do. When you hear of a fellow's cutting his throat, look at the inquest, and if you can't laugh at the evidence, you have nothing in you. 'The deceased was observed to be rather silent and melancholy the day before; he wore his hat on one side, a fashion which his nearest acquaintances had never observed him to use till then; he called his wife out of her name, and went into the rain without an umbrella.' I should like to see how far such evidence would go to prove a case of lunacy in Chancery."

"Then you would, I suppose, uncle, have the law put in force in all its rigour—confiscation of property, and impaling the body on a cross-road?"

"Impaling the bodies!" exclaimed Cregan in a transport of zeal. "I would almost have 'em impaled alive! Why do you laugh? A bull, is it? Adad, and so it is. Then it is time for me to cut and run." So saying, he made his exit with the utmost speed, while his niece leaned aside and laughed.

Hardress heard all this with what might be supposed the sensation of one who finds himself struck by death while witnessing a farce; but he succeeded in concealing his emotions from the observation of his young friend.

The time was now arrived for their customary morning walk, and Anne arranged her bonnet and cloak before the large pier-glass, while she continued from time to time to address herself to Hardress. He had already taken his hat and gloves, and not liking the subjects on which she was speaking, paced up and down the room in gloomy and fretful impatience.

"What a dreadful death hanging must be!" said Anne, as she curled up a wandering tress upon her fingers. "I wonder how any temptation can induce people to run the risk of it."

"Come," said Hardress, "the morning will change if you delay."

"An instant only. If you would but deliver yourself up for a moment to such a day-dream, you may imagine something of the horror of it. Suppose yourself now, Hardress, marching along between two priests, with a hangman after you, and the rope about your neck, and a great crowd of people shouldering each other to obtain one glance at you—and——"

"There's a rain-cloud in the west," said Hardress: "we shall lose the best part of the day."

"I am just ready," returned Anne; "but let me finish my picture. Imagine yourself now at the place of execution; that you feel your elbows tied behind, and that shocking cap put down upon your eyes."

"Yes, yes, it is very pretty," said Hardress peevishly; "but I wish you would think of what you are about."

"You ascend, and there is a dreadful buzz amongst the people; your heart beats, your brain grows dizzy, you feel the hangman's iron fingers on your neck—the drop seems unfirm beneath your feet."

"You will drive me mad!" roared Hardress, stamping on the floor in a paroxysm of fury. "This is intolerable! I bid you make yourself ready to walk, and instead of doing so, you talk of death and hangmen, halters and ignominy, as if there were not real woe enough on earth, without filling the air around us with imaginary horrors. Forgive me, Anne," he added, observing the air of astonishment and sudden reserve with which she regarded him, as alarming as it was ominous—"forgive me for this ill-tempered language. You know my very being hangs upon you; but I am sick and sad, and full of splenetic thoughts."

"Hardress," said Anne after a long pause, "I have borne a great deal from you, but——"

"Nay, Anne," said Hardress, taking her hand with much anxiety and submissiveness of look, "do not say more at present. If I could tell you what is passing in my mind, you would pity, and not blame me. You are almost the only thing in this world, in my present state of ill-health, in which my heart is interested, and if you look cold upon me my life will indeed grow wintry. This will not, I hope, continue under a sunnier sky and more serene air. You must not be angry with me for having a set of irritable nerves."

After an interval of silent reflection Anne took his arm without reply, and they proceeded on their walk. She did not, however, cease to meditate seriously and deeply on the scene which had just taken place.

The morning was fair, and freshened by a gentle wind. The boats sped rapidly along the shores, the sea-gull sailed with wings outspread and motionless upon the breeze; the sea-lark twittered at the water's edge; the murmur of the waves, as they broke upon the strand, sounded sweet and distant; the green leaves quivered and sparkled against the sunshine; the peasants laughed and jested at their labour in the fields; and all was cheering, tender, and pastoral around them.

On a sudden, as they approached an angle in the road, the attention of our loiterers was caught by sounds of boisterous mirth and rustic harmony. In a few seconds, on reaching the turn, they beheld the persons from whom the noise (for we dare not call it music) proceeded—a number of young peasants, dressed out in mumming masquerade, with their coats off, their waistcoats turned the wrong side outward, their hats, shoulders, and knees decorated with gay ribbons (borrowed for the occasion from their fair friends), their faces streaked with paint of various colours, and their waists encircled with shawls and sashes, procured, most probably, from the same tender quarter. Many of them held in their hands long poles, with handkerchiefs fluttering at the top, and forming a double file on either side of half a dozen persons, who composed the band, and whose attire was no less gaudy than that of their companions. One held a piccolo, another a fiddle, another a bagpipe. A fourth made a dildorn * serve for

* A vessel used in winnowing wheat, made of sheepskin stretched over a hoop.

a tambourine, and a fifth was beating with a pair of spindles on the bottom of an inverted tin can, while he imitated, with much drollery, the important strut and swagger of the military kettle-drum. Behind, and on each side, were a number of boys and girls, who, by their shrill clamour, made the discord that prevailed among the musicians somewhat less intolerable. Every face was bright with health and gaiety, and not a few were handsome.

They came to a halt, and formed a semicircle across the road, as Anne and Hardress came in sight. The musicians struck up a jig, and one of the young men, dragging out of the crowd, with both hands, a bashful and unwilling country girl, began to time the music with a rapid movement of heel and toe, which had a rough grace of its own, and harmonised well with the rough-hewn exterior of the peasant.

It is the custom at dances of this kind for the gentleman to find a partner for his fair antagonist after he has finished his own jig, and that partner, if he be a person of superior rank, is expected to show his sense of the honour done him by dropping something handsome, as he is going, into the piper's hat. Neither is it in the power of a stranger to decline the happiness that is offered to him, for the people have a superstition that such a churlishness (to say nothing of its utter want of politeness) is ominous of evil to the lady, betokening the loss of her lover at some future day. Hardress was compelled, though much against his will, to comply with the established usage, the bashful fair one insisting with a great deal of good humour on her claim, and appealing to Miss Chute for her influence with a supplicating tone and eye.

While he was dancing Anne passed the May-day mummers (for so were the merry-makers termed), and strolled on alone. On a sudden the music ceased, and she heard a clamour commence, which had the sound of strife. Turning hastily round, she beheld a strange hurry amongst the crowd, and Hardress in the midst, griping one of the mummers by the throat, and then flinging him back with extreme violence against the dry stone wall on the roadside. The man rose again, and looking after Hardress, tossed his hand above his head, and shook it in a menacing way.

Hardress hurried away from the group, many of whom remained gazing after him in astonishment, while others gathered around the injured man, and seemed to inquire the cause of this singular and unprovoked assault. The same inquiry was made by Anne, who was astonished at the appearance of terror, rage, and agitation that were mingled in the demeanour of Hardress. He made some confused and unsatisfactory answer, talked of the fellow's insolence and his own warm temper, and hurried toward the castle by a shorter way than that which they had taken in leaving it.

The wedding-feast was appointed for the evening of the following day, and it was determined that the ceremony should take place early on the morning after the entertainment. The articles had been already signed by Anne with a pale cheek and a trembling, though not reluctant, hand. These circumstances made it impossible for her to think of altering her intentions; nor did she, with consciousness, even admit the idea to fasten on her mind. Still, however, her anxiety became every hour more trying and oppressive; and when she retired to rest upon this evening she could not avoid murmuring, in the words of the plebeian elector of Coriolanus, "If 'twere to give again—but 'tis no matter."

CHAPTER XLII.

HOW MR. WARNER WAS FORTUNATE ENOUGH TO FIND A MAN THAT COULD AND WOULD SPEAK ENGLISH.

ABOUT sunset on the evening of the following day, while Castle Chute and its vicinity were merry as wedding times could make them, Mr. Warner, the magistrate, was quietly enjoying a bowl of punch with a friend at his own table. That table was spread at the distance of about eight miles from the castle, and that friend was Captain Gibson. Another individual, Mr. Houlahan, the clerk, was seated at a distant corner of the table, imbibing his fluid in silence; but as he was seldom spoken to, and never ventured to mingle in the conversation himself, he could scarcely be considered as one of the company.

"Come, captain," said Mr. Warner, filling his glass and passing the bowl to the gallant officer, "I will give you the bride."

"I shall drink it with all my heart," returned the captain. "The bride," he added, raising the glass to his lips, and honouring the toast with a draught of proportionable profundity.

"And talking of the bride," continued Mr. Warner, "though I rejoice at it on my own account, as it gives me the pleasure of your society, yet it puzzles me to know, captain, why you are not at the wedding to-night."

"For the best of all reasons," returned Mr. Gibson, "because I wasn't asked."

"You may be certain, then, that there was some mistake in that, for the Chutes have always kept an open house."

"I am sure of it. Well, what do you say if I give you the bridegroom in return for your bride?"

"I don't know. I had rather drink the lady."

"Oh! so should I, for that matter; but we have drunk her."

"There's something mystical in that haughty young man that I cannot like. His conduct, on many occasions lately, has given me anything but a favourable indication of his character. I have sometimes been tempted to think—but no, no," he added, suddenly interrupting himself; "I should not indulge in those surmises, which, after all, may be the suggestion of prejudice and rash judgment. Come, sir, I will drink the bridegroom; and allow me to add a sentiment. The bridegroom; and may he show himself worthy of his fortune."

As he said these words the parlour door was opened, and a servant appeared, to say that a stranger wished to speak with Mr. Warner on judicial business.

"Pooh!" said the magistrate; "some broken head or sixpenny summons. Let him come to me to-morrow morning."

"He says his business is very pressing, sir; an' 'twill be more your own loss than his if you let him go."

"What! is that the ground he goes on? Then I suppose we must hear him. Captain, I know all these examinations are amusing to you. Shall I have him in here?"

"You could not do me a greater pleasure," said the officer. "These people are the only actors on earth."

The stranger was accordingly shown up. His story seemed to be almost told by his appearance, for one of his eyes was blackened and puffed out, so as nearly to disguise the entire countenance. There was in his tread and action an appearance of gloomy determination which had something in it impressive, and even chilling. The magistrate perceived at a glance that the affair was of a more serious nature than he had at first suspected.

"Well, my good man," he said in a gentle tone, "what is your business with me?"

"I'm not a good man," said the stranger, "as my business wid you will show. Arn't you de crowner dat sot upon Eily O'Connor?"

"I am."

"Did you find the murtherers yet?"

"They are not in custody, but we have strong information."

"Well, if you have, maybe you don't want any more?" said the man contemptuously, and seeming about to depart.

"No, no; the more we obtain, the stronger our case will be, of course."

"Den listen to me," said the stranger, "and I'll make it strong enough for you."

"This instant," returned Mr. Warner. "Mr. Houlahan, will you prepare your writing materials, and take down this examination in the regular form?"

"Do," said the stranger. "Give me de book, an' swear me: put every sentence in your book, for every word I have to say is goold to you an' to de counsellors. An' write down first dat Eily was surely murdered, an' dat I, Danny Mann, was the one that done de deed."

"Mann!" exclaimed the magistrate. "What! our fugitive prisoner?"

"I was your prisoner till I was set at liberty by one dat had a raison for doing it. I'm now come to deliver myself up, an' to tell de whole truth, for I'm tired o' my life."

The magistrate paused for a moment in strong amazement.

"I think it my duty," said he, "to warn you on one point. If you have been a principal in the murder, your confession will not entitle you to mercy as an approver, while it will be used as evidence against yourself, voluntarily tendered as it is."

"I don't want mercy," returned the stranger; "if I did, it isn't in coorts I'd look for it. If I valued my life, it was in my own hands already, an' 'tisn't here you'd find me now. It was not the fear of death, nor the hope of pardon, that brought me hether, but because I was desaved and disappointed in one dat I tought more of dan of my own life a hundred times. Do you see dat mark?" he added, stepping out into the light, and raising one shoulder so as to bring the defect in his spine more strikingly into view. "All my days dat was my curse. Didn't dey give me a nickname for it, an' usen't some laugh, and more start and shiver, when I'd come in sight of 'em? In place of being, as I ought to be, fighting at de fair, drinking at the wake, an' dancing at de jig-house, dere 's de figure I cut all my days! If anybody vexed me, an' I'd even sthrike him, he wouldn't return the blow; for who'd take notice o' the little lord? If I sat down by a girl, you'd think by her looks dat she wasn't shure of her life until she got away. An' who have I to tank for dat? Mr. Hardress Cregan. 'Twas he that done it to me, an' I a little boy. But if he did, he showed such feeling after—he cried so bitter, an' he cared so much for me, that my heart warmed to him for my very loss itself. I never gev him as much as a cross word or look for what he done, nor never spoke of it until dis minute. I loved him from dat very time, twice more dan ever; but what's the use o' talking? He's not de same man now. He met me yesterday upon de road, an' what did he do? He sthruck me first, but dat I'd bear aisy; he called me out o' my name, an' dat I didn't mind; but I'll tell you what druv me wild—he caught me by de troat, an' he flung me back again' de wall, just de same way as when he ga'e me my hurt, an' made me a cripple for life. From dat moment a change come in me towards him. He doesn't feel for me, an' I won't feel for him; he had his revenge, an' I'll have mine. Write down," he added, wiping the damp from his brow, and trembling with passion, "write down Danny Mann for de murderer of Eily, an' write down Hardress Cregan for his adviser."

Both the gentlemen started, and gazed on one another.

"Ye start!" cried the deformed with a sneer; "an' ye look at one another as if ye tought it a wonder a gettleman should do de like—but dere 's de difference. A gettleman will have a bloody longing, an' he'll hide it for fear of shame. Shame is de portion of de poor man, an' he'll ease his longing when he can, for he has notten to lose. A gettleman will buy de blood of his inimy for goold, but he'll keep his own clane gloves and slender fingers out of it. A poor man does his own work wid his own hands, an' is satisfied to damn his own soul only. All the difference I see is this—that a gettleman, besides his being a murderer, is a desaver an' a coward."

"If you really mean," said the magistrate, "to impeach Mr. Hardress Cregan with this crime, you do not strengthen your testimony by evincing so much vindictive feeling. His character stands high, and we know that the highest have often had their steps beset by serpents, who have no other motive for the sting they give than private malice or revenge, such as you avow."

The wily taunt succeeded. The stranger turned on the magistrate a scowl of indescribable contempt.

"If I could not afford to avow it," he said, "I had wit enough to hide it. I knew your laws of old. It isn't for noting that we see de fathers of families, de pride an' de strength of our villages, de young an' de old, de guilty an' de innocent, snatched away from dere own cabins, an' shared off for transportation an' de gallows. It isn't for noting our brothers, our cousins, an' our friends are hanged before our doores from year to year. Dey taich us something of de law—we tank 'em. If I was trusting to my own confessions, I knew enough to say little of what brought me here. A counsellor would tell you, Mister Magistrate, dat I'll be believed the sooner in a coort for daling as I done. But I have oder witnesses. Eily O'Connor was Hardress Cregan's wife. You start at dat, too. Dere 's the certificate of her marriage. I took it out of her bosom after I——"

He suddenly paused, placed both hands upon his eyes, and shuddered with so much violence that the floor trembled beneath him. The listeners maintained their attitude of deep and motionless attention.

"Yes," he at length continued, letting his hands descend, and showing a horrid smile upon his lip, "de poor crature kep' her hand in her bosom, an' upon dat paper, to de last gasp, as if she tought it was to rob her of dat I wanted. Little she mattered her life in the comparison. De priest dat married

'em died de moment after—a black sign for Eily, an' a blacker sign, perhaps, for de weddin' dey're goin' to have to-morrow mornin'. Dat's a good witness. Write down dat in your book; an' den write down Phil Naughten and his wife, for havin' Eily in their house, an'—but let 'em tell their own story. When you have dem wrote, put down Lowry Looby after, an' den Myles Murphy, an' after, Mihil O'Connor, de father; and, last of all, if you want a real witness, I'll tell you how you'll make it certain. Be de first yourself to lay a hand on Hardress; tell him you heerd of his doin's, an' look into his face while you are speakin', an' if dat doesn't tell de whole story, come back and call me liar."

"It is clear!" said Mr. Warner, starting from his seat. "Captain, I need make no excuse to you for stirring. Mr. Houlahan remain and see this man confined. What, Horan! bring the horses to de door this instant. Captain, you will, perhaps, accompany me, as the service may possibly be dangerous or difficult on such an occasion. We will first ride for a guard to your quarters (though that will cost some time), and then proceed to arrest this gentle bridegroom. Horan, quick with the horses! I thought there was something in him not so orthodox. I am sorry for it; 'tis a shocking business— a mournful transaction."

"And will require, I think," said the captain, "that we should proceed with great delicacy. So amiable a family, and such a shock——"

"With great delicacy, certainly," returned the magistrate, "but likewise with a firmness becoming our trust. Mr. Houlahan, look closely to the prisoner. He left our vigilance at fault on another occasion. Come, captain, here are the horses."

They rode rapidly away; and Mr. Houlahan, slipping out of the room, locked the door on the outside, and went to prepare some suitable dungeon upon the premises for the prisoner.

The unfortunate man remained for several minutes standing on the floor, his hands clasped and elevated before him, his ear inclined as if in the act of listening, and his eye set in stolid, dreamy wonder. The window opened on a craggy field, and was fortified by several bars of iron. He did not, however, even cast a glance at this formidable impediment. Every faculty of his spirit seemed for the moment to be either absorbed by one engrossing image, or to be suspended altogether by a kind of mental syncope.

While he remained thus motionless, and while the house was quiet and still around him, he suddenly heard a rough, but not unmelodious voice singing the following verses outside the window:—

> "But for that false and wicked knave,
> Who swore my life away,
> I leave him to the Judge of heaven,
> And to the judgment day.
>
> "For gold he made away my life;
> (What more could Herod do?)
> Nor to his country, nor his God,
> Nor to his friend, proved true."

The verses seemed to be sung by one in the act of passing the window, and, with the last line, the singer had proceeded beyond hearing. The verses, though containing a common ballad sentiment, characteristic of the peculiar notions of honour and faith held among the secret societies of the peasantry, seemed as if directed immediately against the informer himself; at least his conscience so received it.

He might become one day the subject of such a ballad. He, too, had his sense of shame and of honour, as all men have, regulated by the feelings of the class in which he moved. It would tell nothing against him there that he had died by the hangman's hands. Every petty village had its Tell and its Riego, and they had made that death no more disgraceful in the peasant's eye. Their names were cherished amongst the noblest recollections of his heart; they were sung to his ancient melodies, and made familiar sounds in the ears of his children. But to be branded as an informer—that character which, combining as it does the vices of bad faith, venality, and meanness, is despised and detested by the Irish peasantry beyond all social sins—that was a prospect which he could not bear so well. And then he turned to Hardress, and thought of his feelings—of his old kindness and affection. He made excuses for his sudden passion, and he thought how those kindnesses would be dwelt upon in the ballad which was to immortalise the guilt and penitence of Hardress and his own treachery.

He started from his reverie, and gazed around him like a forest lion in a trap. He rushed to the door, and gnashed his teeth to find it locked. He drew back to the other side of the room, and dashed himself against it with all his force. But it was a magistrate's door, and it resisted his efforts. He turned to the window, dashed out the frame, and shivered the glass with his foot, and seizing the iron railing with both hands, swung himself from it, and exerted his utmost strength in endeavouring to wrench it from its fastening in the solid masonry; but he might as well have set his shoulder to displace the centre of gravity itself. Baffled, exhausted, and weeping with vexation and remorse, he hung back out of the railing, his face covered with a thick damp, and his limbs torn and bleeding from the fragments of the broken glass.

We shall leave him to suffer under all the agonies of suspense, augmented by the double remorse under which he now began to labour, and turn our eyes in the direction of the castle.

CHAPTER XLIII.

HOW THE BRIDE WAS STARTLED BY AN UNEXPECTED GUEST.

INVITATIONS, numberless as the sibyl's leaves, had been dispersed throughout the country on the occasion of the wedding at Castle Chute. Among the rest the Dalys were not forgotten, although certain circumstances in the history of both families, with which the reader is already acquainted, made it appear probable that they would be merely received as things of form. It was, therefore, with feelings of strong surprise and of secret confusion (though arising from very different causes), the bridal pair understood that Kyrle Daly intended to be amongst the guests.

The popularity of the bride amongst the tenantry on the estate was manifested by the usual demonstrations of festive enjoyment. Bonfires were lighted on the road before the avenue gate, and before every public-house in the neighbourhood. The little village was illuminated, and bands of rural music, followed by crowds of merry idlers, strolled up and down playing various lively airs, and often halting to partake of the refreshments which were free to all who chose to draw upon the hospitality of the family.

Before sunset the house was crowded with blue coats and snow-white silks. Several of the guests strayed in groups upon the demesne, and young gentlemen, fashionably dressed, might be seen hovering around the ladies, and endeavouring to make havoc of all, by enchanting those who were near them by their conversation, and those at a distance by the elegance and grace of their gesticulations.

Mrs. Cregan was in the drawing-room, among the elder guests, pale, worn, and hollow-eyed, but still preserving the same lofty, courteous, and cordial demeanour to her friends, by which her manner had been always marked.

The bridegroom, habited in a splendid suit, that seemed to sit upon his frame as the shirt of Dejanira upon the shoulders of Hercules, glided like a spectre through the laughing crowd, the most envied and the most miserable of all the throng.

A few of the most intimate female connections of the bride were admitted into the garden where Anne herself, leaning on the arm of a bridesmaid, was watching the last sun that was to shine upon her freedom. Her dress was a simple robe of white, and her hair, for the last time dressed in the maiden fashion of the day, hung loose upon her neck. As she glided to and fro among the walks, her fair companion endeavoured by every species of raillery to draw her out of the low-spirited and anxious mood which had been hourly increasing upon her since the morning. But as, in a disease of the frame, an injurious determination to the part afflicted is said to be occasioned by merely directing the attention towards it, so, in our moments of nervous depression, the jest that makes us feel it is observed serves only to augment its heaviness.

At a turn in the walk, hedged round by a pear tree neatly trained, the lovely friends were suddenly met, and one of them startled, by the appearance of a young man attired in a wedding costume, and handsome, but with a pale serenity upon his features that might have qualified him to sit as a study for Camillus. The lady who started at his appearance was the bride; for in this interesting person she recognised her old admirer, Mr. Kyrle Daly.

It was the first time they had seen each other since the day on which their conversation had been attended with so much pain to both. It would have little served to confirm the newly-acquired tranquillity of Kyrle Daly if he had known how often, and with what feelings how unconsciously altered, his conduct had been compared by Anne with that of Hardress during the last few months. True this was a subject of meditation on which she never wilfully suffered her mind to repose for an instant. It was a forbidden land, on which her wandering thoughts alone would steal at intervals; but these unlicensed musings had tended to qualify her old opinions in a degree more striking than she herself believed. Of all this Kyrle Daly, of course, knew nor imagined nothing, and therefore was he here. He came secure in the consciousness of a right intention, and believing that his own appearance of quiet and cheerfulness of mind would afford a real satisfaction to his fair, and only poetically cruel, friend.

He advanced towards the ladies with an easy cordiality, and that total absence of consciousness in his own demeanour which was most certain to restore quietness to Anne, for self-possession is often as contagious as embarrassment. He addressed her in the tone of an interested friend, inquired for her health, spoke of her mother, even of Hardress, whom he said he had not yet been fortunate enough to meet, then of the weather, of the scene around them, of the company, of every subject that was at the same time amusing and indifferent. The same attentions, and with a tone so studiously similar that the ear of Petrarch only might have found a difference, he addressed to Miss Prendergast, the bridesmaid, who also was an old acquaintance. Finally, he gently contrived to separate the ladies, and, giving an arm to each, they continued to tread the garden walks, while he divided between them the same cheerful conversation on indifferent subjects. His spirits flowing freely, and supported by those of the lively bridesmaid, proved too much for Anne's depression, and she became cheerful almost without perceiving it.

After some time Miss Prendergast, beckoned by a fair friend in a neighbouring walk, deserted her companions for some moments. Both stopped to await her return, and Kyrle, perceiving the embarrassment of the bride beginning to return, took this opportunity of entering on something like an explanatory conversation.

"You see, Miss Chute," he said with a smile, "you were a better prophetess than I believed you. If you were one that could be vain of your influence, I should not do so wisely, perhaps, in making such an admission, but you are not. I have not, as you perceive, found it so difficult a task to master my old remembrances."

The eyes of Anne fell unconsciously upon the worn cheeks and figure of the speaker. He saw the secret suspicion which the glance implied, and he reddened slightly; but he saw likewise that it was involuntary, and he did not seem to have observed it.

"There are some feelings," he continued, "though looked upon as harmless, and even amiable in themselves, which ought to be avoided and repelled with as much vigilance as vice itself. I once thought it a harmless thing to turn my eyes on past times, and deliver myself up, on a calm evening, to the memory of my younger hours, of sunny days departed, of faces fled or changed, of hearts made cold by death or by the world, that once beat fervently beside my own; to lean against some aged tree in the twilight, and close my eyes and ears to the lonely murmur of the woods around me, and fancy I heard the whoop of my boyish friends, or the laugh of my first love along the meadows. But I have learned to think more vigorously. I was young then, and fond; but age has taught me wisdom, at least in this respect. I shun these feelings now as I would crime. They are the fancies that make our natures effeminate and weak—that unfit us for our duty to Heaven and to our fellow-creatures, and render us in soul what the sensualist is in frame. I have meditated long enough to know that even my feelings toward yourself at one time, exalted as they were by the excellence of the object, were still unworthy, and deserved to be disappointed. I think, and I fear not to let you know, that if I were again to become a suitor, my sentiments should be governed by a higher feeling of duty, and I could bear the trial of a sudden repression with greater firmness and a more submissive spirit."

"You will give me credit, then," said Anne, with much relief and real pleasure, "for some knowledge of your character?"

"No, no; it was not in me then," said Kyrle with a smile, "or the occasion would have brought it into action. Hardress could tell you what a mournful evening—— But wherefore should he trouble you?" he added, suddenly interrupting himself. And apropos of Hardress—his health appears to suffer, does it not?"

"Daily and hourly."

"And without a cause?"

"The physicians," said Anne, "can find none."

"Ay," returned Kyrle, "it is a distemper that is not to be found in their nosology. It is the burning of an honourable mind beneath an undeserved and self-inflicted imputation. He knew of my—my—regard for his fair cousin. I forced a confidence upon him, and he feels this transaction a great deal more acutely than he ought."

Anne started at this disclosure, as if it shed a sudden light upon her mind. Her eyes sparkled, her face glowed, and her whole frame seemed agitated by a solution of her doubts which appeared so natural, and which elevated the character of Hardress to that noble standard at which she always loved to contemplate and admire it.

"It must be so!" she said with great animation, "and I have done him wrong. It is like his fine and delicate nature. He is still, then, what I have always thought him, fine-minded, sensitive, and generous as——" She suddenly turned, and extending her hand to Kyrle, said, in an altered tone, "As yourself, my excellent friend!"

Kyrle took the hand which was tendered to him with as little appearance of emotion as he could command, and resigned it again almost upon the instant.

At this moment Hardress appeared upon the walk. His step was troubled and rapid, his eye suspicious and wandering, his hair neglected, and his whole appearance that of a person at fearful odds with his own thoughts. He stopped short as he approached them, and glanced from one to another with a look of wildness and irresolution.

"I have been looking for you, Anne," he said in a weak voice; "Mrs. Chute has been wishing to speak with you about your preparations."

"Do you leave Ireland so soon?" asked Kyrle with some interest.

"To-morrow morning, we leave home," replied Anne trembling, and slightly confused.

"Then," said Kyrle, resuming the hand which he had so hastily resigned, "permit me to offer my good wishes. Be assured, Anne," he added, accompanying her to a little distance along the walk, and using a tone which Hardress could not overhear, "be assured that I am perfectly, perfectly contented with your happiness. Let me entreat you to forget altogether, as I myself will learn to do henceforward, that I have ever proposed to myself any higher or happier destiny. That scheme has fallen asunder, and left no deeper an impression on my reason than a love dream might upon my heart. I desire only to be remembered as one who imagined himself the warmest of your admirers, but who found out, on a little examination, that he was only your friend."

Anne remained silent for a moment, deeply penetrated by the anxiety for her peace of mind which Kyrle evinced in all his conduct and his conversation.

"Mr. Daly," she replied at length, and with some agitation, "it is impossible for me now to say all that I feel with respect to your consideration of me on every occasion. I am proud of the friendship that you offer me, and if we meet again I hope you will find me worthy of it."

She hurried away, and Kyrle, returning on his steps, resumed his place before the bridegroom. The picture which was formed by the two figures might have challenged the united efforts of a Raphael and an Angelo to do it justice. Kyrle Daly, standing erect, with arms folded, his face pale and bright with the serenity of triumphant virtue, his mouth touched by a smile of forgiveness and of sympathy, and his eye clear, open, and seraphic in its character, presented a subject that might have pleased the eye of the pupil of Perugino. Hardress, on the other side, with one hand thrust into his bosom, his shoulders gathered and raised, his brow knitted, rather in shame and pain than in sternness or anger, his eyes not daring to look higher than the breast of Kyrle, and his face of the colour of burnt sienna, would have furnished a hint for the sterner genius of Buonarrotti.

"Hardress," said Kyrle, with an air of sudden frankness, "confess the truth, that you did not expect me here to-day."

Hardress looked up surprised, but made no answer.

"I am come," continued Kyrle, "to do justice to you and to myself. That I have something to complain of, you will not deny—that I have not so much as I imagined, I am compelled to admit. My resentment, Hardress, has been excessive and unjustifiable, and with that admission I toss it to the winds for ever."

The surprise of Hardress seemed now so great as to master even his remorse and his anxiety. He looked with increasing wonder into the eyes of Daly.

"Knowing as I did," continued the latter, "what passion was, I should have made more charitable allowances for its influence on another; but all charity forsook me at that moment, and I thought it reasonable that my friend should be a cold philosopher where I was a wild enthusiast. I have not even to reproach you with a want of confidence; for it now appears, from my unreasonable expectations, that I could not have deserved it. We are both, perhaps, to blame. Let that be a point agreed upon, and let all our explanations resolve themselves into these two words—forgive, forget."

Saying this, he gave his hand to Hardress, who received it with a stare of absent wonder and confusion. Some indistinct and unintelligible murmurs arose to his lips, and died in the act of utterance.

"I know not," continued Kyrle, "and I shudder to think how far I might have suffered this odious sentiment to grow upon me, if it were not for an occasion of melancholy importance to us all, which arrested the feeling in its very bud. I have even sometimes thought that my unaccomplished sin might possibly have been the cause of that——" Here he shuddered, and stopped speaking for some moments.

Before he could resume, the sound of the dinner-bell broke short the conference. Kyrle, glad of the relief, hastened to the house, while Hardress remained as if rooted to the spot, and gazing after him in silence. When he had disappeared the bridegroom raised his eyes to the heavens, where already a few stars twinkled in the dying twilight, and said within his own mind,—

"In that world which lies beyond those points of light, is it possible that this man and I should ever fill a place in the same region?"

CHAPTER XLIV.

HOW MORE GUESTS APPEARED AT THE WEDDING THAN HAD BEEN INVITED.

LIGHT and laughter, mirth and music, plenteous fare and pleasant hearts to share it, were mingled in the dining-room on this occasion. Mrs. Chute presided. The "old familiar faces" of Mr. Cregan, Mr. Creagh, Mr. Connolly, Dr. Leake, and many others were scattered among the guests, and every eye seemed lighted up to contribute its portion of gaiety to the domestic jubilee. A cloud of vapour, thin and transparent as a peri's sighs, arose from the dishes which adorned the table, and was dissipated in the air above. The heavy moreen window-curtains were let down, the servants flew from place to place like magic, the candles shed a warm and comfortable lustre upon the board, and the clatter of plates, the jingling of glasses and decanters, the discomfiture of provision, and the subdued vigour with which all this was accomplished, considering the respectability of the guests, were really astonishing. Without any appearance of the havoc and carnage which are displayed on such occasions in humbler life, it is a question whether there were not actually more execution done in a quiet, determined way. It furnished a new instance of the superior advantages of discipline.

Towards the close of the feast the manliness of Kyrle Daly was put to a cruel test, by one of those unfeeling jests which are the sport of fools in every country. The reader may smile at the circumstance as trifling, but it was not so in its effects upon the heart of the forlorn lover. A young lady, who was considered a wit among her country friends, and feared accordingly, put a willow-leaf upon a slice of cream cheese, and handed it to Kyrle Daly with an unconscious face. Some months before, a jest of this kind would have put his temper to its severest trial, and even now he felt as if he had been stung by a serpent. He did not, however, betray the least emotion, but took revenge by going near the lady as soon as circumstances permitted, and making mock love to her during the night.

The spirit of the scene produced its effect upon the mind of Hardress himself, who, yielding to its influence, adopted a degree of gaiety that surprised and delighted all who were interested in his fortunes. It is true that, from time to time, a fear struck at his heart like the shock of an alarm, and the glassy eyes of a corpse seemed at intervals to stare at him from among the crowd; but he turned his eyes and his thoughts away to happier objects, and, as if in defiance of the ghastly interruption, became more gay than before.

Mrs. Cregan did not smile to see her son so far forget his misery. A feeling of nervous apprehension had lain upon her spirits throughout the day, and became more oppressive and insupportable according as the time approached for Hardress's departure. The more certain his escape became, the more did her anxiety increase, lest it should, by some unlucky circumstance, be yet prevented.

While Hardress, in the full fling and zest of his false spirits, was in the act of taking wine with a fair friend, he felt a rustling as of some person passing by his chair, and a low voice whispered close to his ear, "Arise, and fly for your life."

The wine-glass fell, untasted, from his hand, and he remained a pale and motionless image of terror. There was some laughing among the company, who perceived the accident; and many ingenious omens were deduced, not very favourable to the prospects of the lady. But the agitation of the bridegroom was attributed to mere embarrassment.

The cloth soon after was removed, some songs were sung, and the ladies rose to depart. Hardress, with the mysterious warning still ringing in his ear, was about to follow in their train, when a rough grasp was laid upon his arm, the door was shut with violence, and he beheld Hepton Connolly standing with his finger raised in an attitude of menace and reproach. Hardress felt his heart sink at the thought that this interruption might cost him his life.

"Let me go, my dear Connolly," he said in an anxious voice. "It is of the last importance to me."

"The last importance!" repeated Connolly, with a suspicious smile. "I'd consider it a disgrace to me, my dear Hardress, if you were to go to bed sober after being in my company to-night, the last that you are to spend in the country. Come, come, Hardress, don't look fierce; you will have Miss Chute long enough, but here are a pleasant set of fellows, whom, perhaps, you may never see round the same table on earth again."

"But, Connolly!"

"But, Hardress!"

"What's the matter there?" cried a rough voice from the head of the table. "Anybody sneaking? Bring him up here by the collar. If any man leaves this room sober to-night I shall make it personal with him."

The speaker, who was no other than the culprit's father, added an oath, and the room rang with acclamations. Hardress, faint with fear and anxiety, was compelled to return to the table, and the bowl was shortly circulated with that enthusiasm which was considered appropriate to the occasion. The wine which he drank, and the conversation in which he was compelled to mingle, gradually stole him back into his revel mood, and in a little time he became more loud and seemingly mirthful than ever. The voice which he heard might be ideal as the visions he had seen. He thought no more of it.

He became engaged in a violent dispute with Creagh as to whether the cascades of Killarney were the better or worse for being without basins. Hardress contended that the want was a defect, inasmuch as it left the beholder without that delightful sensation which he might gather from the contrast of those two most perfect images of tumult and repose, a roaring cataract, with clouds of foam and mist, and a smooth expanse of water, with its glancing and streaky light, and its lulling motion, like the heaving of a sleeping infant's bosom. Creagh, on the other hand, held, and he defended the idea stoutly, as he happened to hit on it by accident, that the very mystery attending the disappearance of the stream, when the spectator saw it hurry downward by his feet, still foaming and roaring on, until it was hidden from his view by the closing thicket below, gave a greater idea to the mind than could be produced by the contrast which Hardress admired.

The latter had his hand raised, with a *cascade* of eloquence just bursting from his lips, when a warm breath came to his ear, and the same low voice murmured in a tone still lower than before, "Arise, I tell you! The army is abroad, and your life is in danger."

It could not now be an illusion, for the tresses of the speaker had touched his cheek, and the dress had brushed his feet. He dashed his chair aside, and standing suddenly erect, looked round him for the warner. A female dress just glanced on his eye as he stared on the open door which led to the hall. He followed it with so much rapidity that no one could find time to interfere; but the hall was empty of living figures. He only saw the cloaks and hats of the visitors hanging against the wall, while the dusky flame of a globe-lamp threw a gloomy and dispiriting light upon the walls and ceiling. On one side the floor was shaken by the dancers, and the ear stunned with the music of the bagpipe, violin, and dulcimer; on the other, he heard the bacchanalian uproar of the party he had left. At a distance in the kitchen he could distinguish the sound of one solitary bagpipe, playing some air of a more rapid and vulgar character; while the voice of a villager, penetrating in triumph through a two-foot wall of stone and mortar, was heard singing some wild and broken melody, which was meant for mirth, but in which a stranger ear might have detected a greater depth of pathos and of feeling than the composer probably intended. Snatching his hat and coat, and trembling in every joint, Hardress was about to hurry down a narrow staircase leading to the yard door, when his mother with a bridesmaid met him on the way.

"Come this way, Hardress," she said; "I have a partner engaged for you."

"Mother," said Hardress, with the horrid sense of oppression which one feels in a dream of danger and vain resistance, "take your hand from my arm and let me pass."

Mrs. Cregan imagined that as, in compliance with an established superstition, patronised by some of the old people, the bridegroom was not to sleep in the house on the night before the bridal, Hardress was thus early preparing to comply with the old custom.

"You must not go so soon," returned Mrs. Cregan. "Come, Miss Prendergast, make that arm prisoner, and lead him to the ball-room."

Hardress, with a beating pulse, resigned himself to his fate, and accompanied the ladies to the dancing-room. Here he remained for some time, endeavouring, but with a faint spirit, to meet and answer the gaiety of his companions. After dancing a minuet with a good deal of silent approbation, he led his fair partner to her seat, and, taking a chair at her side, began to entertain her as best he could, while other dancers occupied the floor. His chair was placed a few yards distant from an open door, at which a crowd of servants and tenants appeared thrusting in their heads, and staring on the dancers for the purposes of admiration or of satire, as the occasion might arise.

One of these, a handsome country lad, had encroached so far as to get within a foot or two of Hardress's chair, and to be recognised by him with some appearance of kindness.

"Master Hardress," he said, stooping to his ear, "did Syl Carney tell you anything?"

"No," said Hardress, turning suddenly round, and neglecting to finish some observation which he was in the act of making to his fair companion.

"Why, then, never welcome her!" said the lad. "I told her to slip in a word to you some way, to let you know that Danny Mann has given information, and the army are out this night."

Hardress trembled as if the hangman's grasp had been laid upon him.

"What a shocking dance that hornpipe is!" exclaimed the lady. "I am always reminded, when I see it, of the dampers of a piano."

"Precisely, indeed," said Hardress, with a smile like death;

KYRLE DALY'S REWARD.

"very ridiculous indeed. Tell me how you know of this?" he said apart to the boy. "Speak low and quickly."

"From a little hunchback in bridewell at magistrate Warner's," returned the lad. "He bid me—— But the lady is talking to you."

"I beg your pardon," said Hardress, turning quickly round.

"It was not I," said the fair dancer: "it was Mrs. Cregan called."

He looked at his mother, and saw her holding towards him a small basket of confectionery and oranges, while she glanced towards the ladies. Hardress rose to perform this piece of gallantry with a sensation of gloomy resignation, and with a feeling of bitterness towards his unhappy parent, as if she ought to have known that she was knotting the cord upon his life.

When it was done he hurried back to his seat; but the servants were all gone, and the door was closed. He stole from the apartment to the hall, once more resumed his hat, and ascending the small flight of steps leading to the chamber so often mentioned, he was once more upon the point of freedom.

But the grasp of an avenging Providence was laid upon his life. In the middle of this chamber he encountered the bride alone.

"Hardress," said she, "are you leaving us for the night?"

"I am," he murmured in a faint voice, and passed on.

"Stay, Hardress!" said Anne, laying her hand upon his arm. "I have something to say, which you should know immediately."

This last interruption completed the confusion of the bride-groom. A sudden faintness fell on his whole frame, his brain grew dizzy, his senses swam, and he reeled, like one intoxicated, into a vacant chair.

"Well, Anne," said he, "anything—everything—my life itself, if you think it worth your while to require it."

"I owe it to my own peace, and even to yours, Hardress," said Anne, "to tell you that I have discovered all."

"Discovered all!" echoed Hardress, springing to his feet.

"Yes—all. A generous friend—generous to you and me alike—has given the whole history of your cause of suffering, and has left me nothing to regret but that Hardress should not have thought it worth his while to make Anne a partner in his confidence. But that I have forgotten likewise, and have only now to say that I regret my own conduct as much as I once was grieved for yours. I must have added to the pain which—— Hark!"

"What do you hear?" cried Hardress, crouching fearfully.

"There is a tumult in the drawing-room. Good Heaven, defend our hearts! What is that noise?"

The door of the room was thrown open, and a female figure appeared, with hair disordered, and hands outspread with an action of warning and avoidance.

"Hardress, my child!"

"Well, mother?"

"Hardress, my child!"

"Mother, I am here! Look on me! Speak to me! Do not gasp, and stare on your son in that horrid way! Oh, mother, speak, or you will break my heart!"

"Fly, fly, my child! Not that way! No! The doors are defended. There is a soldier set on every entrance. You are trapped and caught. What shall we do? The window! Come this way—come—quick—quick!"

She drew him passively after her into her own sleeping-chamber, which lay immediately adjoining. Before Anne had made one movement from the attitude of sudden fear and wonder to which this strange occurrence had given rise, Mrs. Cregan again appeared in the chamber, showing in her look and action the same hurried and disordered energy of mind.

"Go to your room!" she said, addressing the bride. "Go quickly to your room; stop not to question me——"

"Dear aunt——"

"Away, I say! You will drive me frantic, girl! My reason is already stretched to its full tension, and a single touch may rend it. Go, my dear child, my love! my wretched—— Ha!"

"Anne Chute! Where's Anne?" exclaimed an anxious voice at the doorway. "Where is the bride?"

"Here, here!" said Mrs. Cregan.

Kyrle Daly rushed into the room, his face paler than ever, and his eye filled with anxious inquiry.

"Come this way, Anne!" he said, taking her hand, while his own were trembling with anxiety. "Unhappy bride! Oh, horrid, fearful night! Come—come!"

"I will not stir!" exclaimed the bride, with vehemence. "What mean those words and actions? There is some danger threatens Hardress. Tell me, if there is——"

"Take her away, good Kyrle."

"He shall not take me hence. Why should he? Why does he call me an unhappy bride? Why does he say this night is horrid and fearful? I will not stir——"

"They are coming! Force her hence, good Kyrle," muttered the expectant mother.

Struggling in his arms, and opposing prayers, threats, and entreaties to the violence which he employed, Kyrle Daly bore the affrighted bride away from the apartment. He remained by her side during the whole evening, often soothing her anxiety by his ready eloquence, and watching every movement of her mind and feelings with the tender vigilance of a near and devoted relative.

Mrs. Cregan, meanwhile, remained alone in the room, her ear bent to catch the first sounds of approaching danger, and her frame made rigid with the intensity of feeling. Her hands were employed, while in this attitude, in arranging her hair, and removing, as far as possible, every appearance of disorder from her dress. At length the clatter of muskets and the tramp of many feet were heard in the little hall. A momentary convulsion shook her frame. It passed away, and she rose to her usual height and her customary stateliness of eye and gesture.

At the same moment the door opened, and Mr. Warner, accompanied by Captain Gibson and the military party, appeared upon the little staircase. The first mentioned seemed surprised and somewhat embarrassed at the sight of Mrs. Cregan. He murmured something of his regret at being compelled to do what must be so painful to her, and was proceeding to recommend that she should retire, when she cut short the speech.

"Talk not to me, sir," she said, "of your regret or your reluctance. You have already done your worst to fix a stigma on our name, and a torture in our memories. For months, for weeks and days, my son spoke with you, laughed with you, and

walked freely and openly among you, and then you laid no hand upon his shoulder. You waited for his wedding-day to raise your lying cry of murder; you waited to see how many hearts you might crush together at a blow. You have done the worst of evil in your power; you have dismayed our guests, scattered terror amid our festival, and made the remembrance of this night, which should have been a happy one, a thought of gloom and shame."

"My duty," murmured the magistrate, "obliged me to sacrifice——"

"Complete your duty, then," said the mother haughtily, "and do not speak of your personal regrets. If justice and my son are foes, what place do you fill between them? You mistake your calling, Mr. Magistrate; you have no personal feelings in this transaction. You are a servant of the law, and, as a servant, act."

Mr. Warner bowed, and directed the soldiers to follow him into the inner room. At this order Mrs. Cregan turned her face over her shoulder with a ghastly smile.

"That," she said in a tone of calm reproach, "that is my sleeping-chamber."

"My duty, madam."

"Be it so," said Mrs. Cregan in a low voice, and turning away her face with the same painful smile, while her heart crept and trembled.

The party entered the room.

"I hope," said Captain Gibson, who really began to think that Mrs. Cregan had a great deal of reason, "I hope Mrs. Cregan will not blame me for my part in this transaction."

"I do not blame you," said the mother with a scornful smile; "it is your trade."

At this portentous moment Mr. Cregan, Mr. Connolly, and two or three other gentlemen came reeling into the apartment, excessively intoxicated, and retaining consciousness enough to feel a sense of injury not wholly understood, and a vague purpose of resistance.

"Dora," said Mr. Cregan, staggering towards her, and endeavouring to look sober, "what are you doing here? What's the matter?"

Mrs. Cregan, her whole soul absorbed by the proceedings in the inner room, did not even appear to be conscious of his presence.

"Very—very extraordinary conduct," he said, turning an unsteady eye upon the captain. "Soldiers, officers, eh, Connolly?"

"Very—very extraordinary conduct," echoed Connolly.

"Do they take the house for a barrack?" continued Cregan. "Captain, withdraw your soldiers."

Captain Gibson, already annoyed by the taunt of Mrs. Cregan, returned this demand by a stern look.

"Stand by me, Connolly. Your swords, gentlemen!" cried Cregan as he drew his own.

The others imitated his example. Captain Gibson, without condescending to unsheathe his own weapon, turned to his men, and, beckoning with his finger, said,—

"Disarm those drunken gentlemen."

His orders were obeyed upon the instant, a few slight scratches being all that was sustained by the soldiers in the drunken scuffle that ensued. The gentlemen were placed, with their hands tied, on chairs at the other side of the room, and the bundle of rapiers was laid upon the window-seat.

"Very well, sir, very well," said Mr. Cregan; "I shall remember this, and so shall my friends. I am a gentleman, sir, and shall look for the satisfaction of a gentleman."

"Expect the same from me," said Connolly, swinging his person round upon the chair.

"And me," said a third.

"And me," echoed a fourth.

"I little expected to meet with such a return as this for our hospitality," continued Mr. Cregan.

"For shame, for shame, Cregan!" said the unhappy mother. "Do not degrade yourself and your friends by such remonstrances. The hand of an enemy is raised against us, and let not the unworthy being think that he can sink us as low in mind as in our fortunes."

Captain Gibson, who took no notice of the gentlemen, again seemed hurt to the quick, perhaps not wisely, by this allusion from the lady.

"Mrs. Cregan," he said, "it is one of the most painful duties of a gentleman in my situation that he must sometimes be subjected to such insinuations as those; and it is only the peculiar circumstances in which you are placed that would prevent my forming a very harsh judgment of any lady who could use them."

"Sir," said Mrs. Cregan, lowering her head with a smile of the most bitter irony, "your consideration and your forbearance are extraordinary. All the events of this night bear witness to it. It must have surely been with much violence to that fine gentlemanly spirit that you chose a moment like this for your investigation. But I see you are impatient, sir, and I will desist; for you are a soldier, and I am but a female, and it is easy to see who would have the best of the argument."

"Madam——"

"Our friends dispersed, our mirth so quickly changed to terror, this scene of confusion at our domestic festivity—everything, sir, bears testimony to your forbearance. That sensitive and gentlemanly nature that is so tender of insinuations appears in all the actions of this night. My husband tied there like a malefactor, and my poor son—— Ah, shield and hide us, Earth! I hear his voice!"

A bustle was heard in the inner room, and the wretched lady, throwing her arms high above her head, uttered a shriek so loud, so shrill and piercing, that the stoutest soldier started like a maiden, and the flush of anger on the officer's cheek was changed to a deathlike paleness. Half sobered by the fearful sound, the intoxicated father rose from his chair, and turned a dull eye upon the room door, while every figure on the scene expressed, in various degrees, the same feeling of commiseration and anxiety.

"The prisoner is here!" cried Warner, hurrying into the room.

"Is he?" shrieked the distracted and almost delirious mother. "Dark blood-hound, have you found him? May the tongue that tells me so be withered from the roots, and the eye that first detected him be darkened in its socket!"

"Peace, shocking woman!" said the magistrate. "Your curses only add to the offence that Heaven has already suffered."

"What!" cried the unhappy parent, "shall it be for nothing, then, that you have stung the mother's heart, and set the mother's brain on fire? I tell you, no! My tongue may hold its peace, but there is not a vein in all my frame but curses you! My child—my child!" she screamed aloud, on seeing Hardress at the door. She rushed, as if with the intent of flinging herself upon his neck but; checking the impulse as she came near, she clasped her hands, and sinking at his feet, exclaimed, "My child, forgive me!"

"Forgive you, mother!" replied her son in a wretched voice. "I have destroyed you all!"

"The crime was mine," exclaimed the miserable parent; "I was the author of your first temptation, the stumbling-block between you and repentance. You will think bitterly of me, Hardress, when you are alone."

"Never!" said Hardress, raising her in his arms. "Still honoured, always well-meaning and affectionate, I will never think of you but as a mother. My eyes are open now. For the first time in many weary months, the first thought of peace is in my heart; and but for you, and those whom I have made wretched with you, I would call that thought a thought of joy. Grieve no more, mother, for my sake. Grieve not, because it is in vain. The bolt has sped, the victim has been struck, and earth has not a remedy. Grieve not, because I would not have it otherwise. A victim was due to Justice, and she shall no longer be defrauded. I had rather reckon with her here than in a future world."

"I cannot part with you," murmured his mother, while her head rested on his shoulder; "do not put away my hands awhile. It is tearing my very heart up!"

"Dear mother, let me go," said Hardress, gently disengaging himself. "We shall meet again, I hope. In the mean time hear my farewell request, as you have heard all that I have ever made: waste not your days in idle retrospection, but pray for me with fervour; be kind to those whom I have loved, and remember that my death, at least, was happier than my life."

"I threatened you with poverty," muttered Mrs. Cregan, while her memory glanced wildly through the past.

"Dear mother——"

"I bade you leave my house or do my pleasure——"

"Why will you vex my soul at such a moment?"

"I have tied the cord upon your throat! I slighted your scruples. Your own dread words come back upon me now. Those words which I heard with so little emotion at Dinis, and in this hall before, now ring like the peal of dead-bells in my ear. I have been your fellest foe. You drank in pride with my milk, and passion under my indulgence. I have destroyed you for this world, and——"

"My dear, dear mother!" cried Hardress, clasping her to his breast, and bursting into tears of shame and penitence, "forget, I implore you, those impious and reproachful words; they were the ravings of my madness, and should not be regarded. Hear me now, in the full and calm possession of my judgment, and let those words only be remembered. Do you hear me, my dear mother?"

"I do—I am listening. Speak, my child; I will remember well."

Hardress stooped to her ear, and murmured in a low voice, "In a secret drawer of my cabinet you will find a paper unsealed. Give it to"—he paused and bowed down a moment in deep agitation—"to Anne Chute. I am glad she bears that name—glad of her fortune in escaping me. Let her read that paper. I have penned it with the view of rendering justice to a confiding friend, whose confidence I have betrayed. Oh, memory! memory! But I must look forward now, not back. Ah, mother! if I had really known how to value your affectionate counsels in my childhood—if I had only humbled my heart to a belief in its own weakness, and a ready obedience to your will in my younger days, I should not die in my youth a shameful death, and leave you childless in your age."

"Ay," said Mrs. Cregan, "or if I had done the duty of a mother; if I had thought less of your worldly, and more of your eternal, happiness. My brain is scorched! I——"

"My dear fond parent, will you add to my agony?"

"You will hate me in your prison."

"Never!"

"I know what you will say when they are dragging you to the scaffold. 'It is my mother,' you will say, 'who has bound these cords upon my limbs.' The people will stare on you, and you will hang your head, and say that I was the author of your shame. And in the moment of your death——"

"I will pray for you," said Hardress, pressing her to him, and kissing her forehead, "as you will do for me." While he spoke he felt the arms that encircled his neck grow rigid, and the face that looked up to his was overspread with a damp and leaden paleness.

"Farewell, dear mother, for the present," he continued; "and remember—— Oh! she is growing cold and weak. Remove her—remove her quickly, gentlemen!"

She was borne out in a half-fainting condition, and Hardress, surrendering himself to the hands of the soldiers, prepared to depart. Turning round once more before he left the room, he said aloud,—

"Hear me, and testify against me, if it shall please you. Lest my returning feebleness, or the base love of life, should tempt me once again to shun my destiny, I am willing here to multiply my witnesses. I am guilty of the crime with which you charge me—guilty, not in act, nor guilty even in word, nor positive, implied assent—but guilty beyond even the wish of pardon. I am glad this hideous dream at length is ended—glad that I have been forced to render up her right to Justice, even against my will, for I was sick of my anxieties."

He ceased, and the party proceeded down the narrow staircase leading to the hall door, Hardress being placed in the centre. In a few minutes the lighted chambers of the castle, its affrighted revellers, its silenced musicians, the delirious mother, the drunken father and his band of brawlers, the bewildered bride, and all the scattered pomp of the espousal, were lost to the eye of the unhappy Hardress.

Some apprehension was entertained lest any injudicious person amongst the peasantry should occasion the useless loss of lives by attempting a rescue before the party left the neighbourhood; but no symptoms of such an intention were manifested by the people. The whole transaction had been conducted with so much rapidity, that the circumstance of the bridegroom's capture was not generally known, even in the castle, for some time after his departure.

CHAPTER XLV.

HOW THE STORY ENDED.

IT only remains for us to inform the reader, in general terms, of the subsequent fortunes of the various actors in this domestic drama. Such is the fate of the historian, regarded only as the chronicler of events or feelings in which he has no share: his claim to attention rests only upon these. While they continue to awaken interest he may toy and dally as he pleases; he may deck his style with flowers, indulge his fancy in description, and even please his vanity with metaphysical speculation; but when the real matter of the tale is out, farewell his hobbies! Stern and brief must thenceforth be the order of his speech, and listlessness or apathy become the guerdon of his wanderings. He is mortified to find that what he mistook for interest was only patience, and that the attention which he imagined to be bestowed upon himself was only lavished on the automata which his fingers exercised.

Stern and brief, then, be the order of our speech henceforward. Unhappily a portion of our incidents will fit that manner well.

The remorse of Hardress led him even to exaggerate his own share in the transaction on which the foregoing measures were founded. Nevertheless, when all the circumstances of the case had been fully considered, the mercy of the executive power was extended to his life, and a perpetual exile from his native land was the only forfeit which he paid to the outraged law. But before this alteration in his destiny had been announced to him, Hardress had learned to receive it with great indifference. With the austerity of an ancient penitent, he persisted in refusing to hold personal communication with any of his friends, his mother only excepted; and even she was cheated (by a necessary device, for her health could not have sustained it) of the last parting interview.

The mitigation of punishment, which was intended to save his life, had only the effect of sparing him the ignominy of such a fate. An occurrence which took place on the day of his departure completed the ruin which ill-health had long been making in his constitution.

The convict-ship which was to bear him from his home had cleared out of port, and lay at anchor in that part of the river which, from its basin-like appearance, has received the appropriate denomination of the Pool. In the grey of a summer morning the prisoners, Hardress amongst the number, left the jail in King's Island, where they had been confined, for the purpose of occupying their places on board. Arrived at the river side, the party halted with their guard, while a small boat was let down from the vessel's stern, and manned for the shore. It touched the strand, and received its lading of exiles. It could not hold the entire party, and Hardress, who felt a sudden, and to him unaccountable, reluctance to leave his native soil while it was possible for him yet to feel its turf beneath his feet, petitioned to be left until the return of the pinnace.

He looked to the misty hills of Cratloe, to the yet silent and inactive city, and over the face of the gently-agitated waters. The fresh, cool light of the morning only partially revealed the scene; but the veil that rested on the face of nature became more attenuated every instant, and the aërial perspective acquired, by rapid yet imperceptible degrees, a greater scope and clearness. Groups of bathers appeared at various distances on both sides of the river, some plunging in headlong from the lofty quays, some playing various antics in the water, and some floating quietly on the surface of the tide in the centre of the stream; while others, half dressed and shivering at the brink of the sloping strands, put in a hand or foot to ascertain the temperature of the refreshing element before venturing to fling off their remaining habiliments, and share in the salutary recreation.

In other respects the scene was nearly the same in appearance as it has been described in the third chapter of this volume. Nature, always the same calm and provident benefactress, had preserved her mighty heart unchanged throughout the interval, and the same joyous serenity was still visible upon her countenance. The passions of men may convulse the frame of society; the duration of human prosperity may be uncertain as that of human woe; and centuries of ignorance, of poverty, and of civil strife may suddenly succeed to years of science, and thrift, and peace; but still the mighty mother holds her course unchanged. Spring succeeds winter, and summer spring, and all the harmonies of her system move on through countless ages with the same unvarying serenity of purpose. The scene of his happy childhood evinced no sympathy with the condition of the altered Hardress.

He turned with an aching heart from the contemplation of the landscape, and his eye encountered a spectacle more accordant to his present feelings. The row of houses which lined the quay on which the party halted consisted, for the most part, of coffin-makers' shops, a gloomy trade, although, to judge by the reckless faces of the workmen, it would appear that "custom had made it with them a property of easiness."

Only one of those dismal houses of traffic was open at this early hour, and the light which burned in the interior showed that the proprietor was called to the exercise of his craft at this unseasonable time by some sudden and pressing call. The profession of the man was not indicated, as in more wealthy and populous cities, by a sculptured lid, or gilded and gaudy hatchment suspended at a window-pane. A pile of the unfinished shells, formed for all ages from childhood to maturity, were thrust out at the open window, to attract the eye of the relatives of the newly dead. The artificer himself appeared in the interior of his workshop, in his working dress, and, plane in hand, was employed in giving the last touch to an oaken coffin, placed lengthways on his bench. Its size denoted that the intended occupant had died in the full maturity of manhood.

While Hardress watched him plying his melancholy trade in silence, a horseman rode up to the door, and dismounted with some awkwardness and difficulty. He was a small, red-haired man, and Hardress thought that the face and manner were not altogether new to his observation. Another horseman followed, and alighted with more ease and alertness. He was tall and well formed, and Hardress shrank aside from his gaze, for in this person he recognised one of the persons who appeared against him at his trial. Leaning against one of the short posts used for the purpose of holding the cables of the shipping, and once more turning his face towards the river, Hardress listened to the conversation which ensued.

"Servant kindly, Mr. Moran," said the smaller man. "Well, is the coffin ready?"

"What time will it be wanted?" was the reply.

"The car will be here in half an hour. Father Edward bid me to step on before, in dread you wouldn't have it done. If it wasn't out of regard for him and his, indeed, I'd rather be spared the jaunt, for I was always a poor horseman, and I think it jolting enough I'll get between this and the churchyard."

"And where'll he be buried?"

"At Mungret church, westwards. His people are all buried at St. John's; but he took it as a delight to be buried at Mungret, because it was there his daughter was buried before him."

A deep groan escaped the second horseman as he said these words.

"No wonder for you to be heart-broken!" exclaimed the first. "Old and good friends were parted when they were taken from you. The poor old man! 'twas enough to convert a Turk to hear him on his deathbed giving his forgiveness to all the world, and praying for his enemies. A year since, as you know well, Miles Murphy, Mihil O'Connor and his daughter were a happy pair; but he never raised his head from the day she left his floor. Well, well, 'tis thrue for Father Edward what he says, that this world would be good for nothing if there was not another."

At this moment a soldier touched the arm of Hardress, and pointed to the pinnace, whose keel just grated on the gravelled strand. With a rigid and terrified countenance Hardress arose, and was about to hurry down the steps leading from the quay, when his strength suddenly failed him, and he would have fallen headlong to the bottom, but for the timely aid of his escort.

When he recovered from the confusion which this attack occasioned in his brain, he found himself seated on the deck of the vessel, her canvas wings outspread, and the shores of his native soil fleeting rapidly away on either side. He looked, as the ship went on, to the cottage of the Dalys. Two or three of the children, in deep mourning, were playing on the lawn; Lowry Looby was turning the cows into the new-mown meadow; and Mr. Daly himself, also in deep black, was standing, cane in hand, upon the steps of the hall door. The vessel still swept on, but Hardress dared not turn his eyes in the direction of Castle Chute. The dawn of the following morning beheld him tossed upon the waves of the Atlantic, and looking back to the clifted heads of the Shannon, that stood like a gigantic portal opening far behind. The land of his nativity faded rapidly on his sight; but before the vessel came within sight of that of his exile, Hardress had rendered up the life which the law forbore to take!

His mother lived long after in the practice of the austere and humiliating works of piety which her Church prescribes for the observance of the penitent. Her manner, in the course of time, became quiet, serene, and uncomplaining; and though not so generally admired, she became more loved among her friends and her dependents than in her days of pride and haughtier influence.

One circumstance may be mentioned as affording a striking proof of the deep root which her predominant failing had taken in her character. After reading the paper which Hardress had left in his cabinet, and finding that it was written under what she conceived a too humiliating sense of his unworthiness, she refrained from bestowing it as he desired. It was not until the salutary change above mentioned had been wrought in her character, and after the purpose which the document was intended to accomplish had been brought to pass by other means, that she complied with her son's parting wishes.

It was a circumstance which placed the character of Anne Chute in a noble point of view that, from the moment of the fearful discovery recorded in the last chapter, she never once upbraided her unhappy relative with the concealment which had so nearly linked her fate with that of one whose conduct she had so much cause to view with horror. Much as she had loved Hardress, and shocked as she was by the terrible occurrences of that night, she could not look back without the feeling of one who has escaped a great and hidden danger. It would have been denying her a virtue which she ought not to have wanted, if we said that the generosity and disinterested-ness of Kyrle Daly failed eventually to produce that effect upon her feelings which it had long since done upon her reason. It was long, indeed, before this favourable indication could be suffered to appear; but it did appear at length, after the remembrance of this unhappy story had grown faint in the course of time, and the tumult which it had left in many bosoms had been stilled by years, by penitence, or death. They were then united, and they were as happy as earth could render hearts that looked to higher destinies and a more lasting rest. They lived long after in the practice of the duties of their place in life, and of that religion to which the guilty and the neglectful owe their deepest terrors, and good men their dearest consolations.

The wretched partner in the crime of Hardress died amid all the agonies of a remorse, which made even those whose eyes had often looked upon such scenes shrink back with fear and wonder. He owed his fate to an erring sense of fidelity, and to the limited and mischievous course of education too common in his class; while Hardress might be looked on as the victim of his cherished vanity and pride of self-direction.

These events furnished Lowry Looby with matter for a great fund of philosophical eloquence, which he was fond of indulging at even, when his pipe lit freely and the fire shone bright upon the hearth. This faithful servant lived long enough to enjoy the honours of a freehold in his native county of Clare, and to share it with the careful housewife who was accustomed to provide for his wants with so much affectionate care at the dairy cottage. His name, I understand, was found upon the poll-books at the late memorable election in that county; but on which side of the question he bestowed his voice is more than my utmost industry has enabled me to ascertain.

Reader, if you have shuddered at the excesses into which he plunged, examine your own heart, and see if it hide nothing of the intellectual pride and volatile susceptibility of new impressions which were the ruin of Hardress Cregan. If, besides the amusement which these pages may have afforded, you should learn anything from such research for the avoidance of evil, or the pursuit of good, it will not be in vain that we have penned the story of our two COLLEGIANS.

NARRATIVE.

The real occurrence which suggested the plot of the "Colleen Bawn; or, the Collegian's Wife," though furnishing little more than the ground-work of that tale, was in itself little inferior in interest. THE FOLLOWING NARRATIVE OF IT IS TAKEN FROM THE *New Monthly Magazine;*—

The river Shannon, in its passage westward towards the Atlantic, expands, about forty miles below the city of Limerick, int a capacious sheet of water resembling an estuary, and making a distance of ten or twelve miles from bank to bank. At the northern or county of Clare side, is the town of Kilrush. Upon the opposite shore, adjoining the borders of the counties of Limerick and Kerry, is the town of Tarbert; and a few miles higher up the stream the now inconsiderable village of Glyn— the same from which a branch of the Fitzgeralds originally took their ancient, and still honoured, title of "Knights of Glyn." None of these places make any kind of show upon the banks, which, besides, are pretty thickly planted almost down to the water's edge. The river itself in this part presents few signs of human intercourse. In the finest summer weather the eye may often look round and search in vain for a single bark or boat to break the solitude of the scene. The general desolation is, in fact, at times so complete that, were an adept in crime to be in quest of a place where a deed of violence might be perpetrated under the eye of God alone, he could not select a fitter scene than the channel of the river Shannon, midway between the points I have just described.

One morning, a little after sunrise, about the latter end of July, in the year ——, two poor fishermen, named Patrick Connell and —— Driscol, who lived at Moneypoint, a small hamlet near Kilrush, went down to the river side, according to their custom, to attend to their occupation. As they walked along the strand in the direction of their boat, they came upon a human body, which had been washed ashore by the last tide. It was the remains of a young female, and had no clothing or covering of any kind, excepting a small bodice. Who or what she had been they could not conjecture, but how she came by her death was manifest. They found a rope tied at one end as tightly as possible round the neck, and at the other presenting a large loop, to which they supposed that a stone, or some other weight, had been attached, until the working of the stream had caused it to separate. From the general state of the body, and more particularly from the teeth having almost all dropped out, they concluded that it must have been under the water for several weeks. After a short consultation the two fishermen resolved upon proceeding without delay to Kilrush, to apprise the civil authorities of the circumstance; but, in the mean time, they could not bear to think of leaving the remains exposed, as they had found them, on the shore, and liable to be borne away again by the tide before they could return. They accordingly removed the body to a little distance beyond high-water mark, and gave it a temporary interment.

The magistrates of the neighbourhood having ascertained, from the report of the fishermen, that a dreadful crime had been committed, set immediate inquiries on foot for the discovery of the offender. The exertions of the magistrates in the present instance were so successful that a considerable mass of circumstantial evidence was in readiness for the coroner's jury that was summoned to inquire into the identity of the deceased, and the cause of her death. The details were voluminous; and I shall, therefore, select only the most striking and material.

The most important and ample information was communicated by a young woman named Ellen Walsh. A few weeks before the finding of the remains this person, being at Kilrush, went down to the river side in search of a passage across to Glyn, where she resided in service with a lady. It was then approaching sunset. Upon arriving at the shore she found a small pleasure boat on the point of putting off for Tarbert. Six persons were in the boat—a Mr. S——, a young woman who was addressed as Mrs. S——, Stephen Sullivan, Mr. S——'s servant, and three boatmen of the town of Kilrush. There was also on board a trunk belonging to Mrs. S——. The only one of the party of whom Ellen Walsh had any previous knowledge was Sullivan, whose native place was Glyn; and, upon addressing herself to him for a passage across, she was permitted to enter the boat. They immediately got under weigh, expecting to reach Tarbert before dark; but before they had proceeded any distance on their way across, they discovered that this was impracticable. In addition to an adverse tide, it came on to blow so hard against them that the boat made little or no way, so that they were kept out upon the water the whole of the night. Towards morning a heavy shower of rain fell, but the wind having moderated, the rowers succeeded in reaching a small place below Tarbert, called Carrickafoyle. Here the party landed as the day began to dawn, and, taking the trunk along with them, proceeded to a small public house in the village to dry themselves, and obtain refreshment. After breakfast the boatmen, who had been hired for the single occasion of rowing the boat across the river, were dismissed, and returned towards their homes. The boat, which (it afterwards appeared) had been purchased a few days before by Mr. S—— remained. Shortly after the departure of the boatmen, Mr. S—— and Sullivan went out (they said to search for change of a note), and were absent about an hour, leaving Mrs. S—— and Ellen Walsh together in the public-house.

And here it was that some particulars observed by the latter, when subsequently recalled to her recollection and disclosed, became of vital moment as matters of circumstantial evidence. It has been already stated that the body found by the fishermen was without any covering save a small bodice, so that no direct evidence of identity could be established by ascertaining what particular dress Mrs. S—— wore; but indirectly a knowledge of this fact, (as will appear in the sequel), became of the first importance. Upon this subject Ellen Walsh was able to give some minute and accurate information. She had forgotten the colour of the gown Mrs. S—— wore when they landed at Carrickafoyle; but she well remembered that she had on a gray cloth mantle, lined with light blue silk, and with welts of a particular fashion in the skirts. She also wore a pink-coloured silk handkerchief round her neck, and had on her finger two gold rings—one plain, the other carved. These Ellen Walsh had observed and noted before Mr. S—— and his servant left the public-house; but, during their absence, Mrs. S—— opened the trunk, and, with the natural vanity of a young female, exhibited for her admiration several new articles of dress which it contained. Among other things, there were two trimmed spencers—one of green, the other of yellow silk; two thin muslin frocks—one plain, the other worked; and a green velvet reticule, trimmed with gold lace.

Upon the return of Mr. S—— and Sullivan to the public-house, the weather having now cleared, they proposed to Mrs. S—— to go on board the boat. Ellen Walsh, understanding that Tarbert was their destination, desired to accompany them; but Sullivan, taking her aside, recommended her to remain where she was until the following morning, adding (and this last observation was in the hearing of his master), that in the meantime "they would get rid of that girl" (Mrs. S——), and then return and convey her to Glyn. This Ellen Walsh declined, and followed the party to the beach, entreating to be at least put across to the other side of a certain creek there, which would save her a round of several miles on her way homewards. At first they would not consent, and put off without her; but seeing her begin to cry, Mr. S—— and Sullivan, after a short

consultation, put back the boat, and taking her in, conveyed her across the creek, and landed her about three miles below the town of Glyn. They then sailed away in the direction of the opposite shore, and she proceeded homewards. Early next morning, Ellen Walsh having occasion to go out upon some errand, was surprised to see Sullivan standing at the door of his mother's house in Glyn. She entered the house, and the first thing she perceived was Mrs. S——'s trunk upon the floor; she asked if Mrs. S—— was in Glyn; Sullivan replied "that she was not, that they had shipped her off with the captain of an American vessel." Two or three days after, Ellen Walsh saw upon one of Sullivan's sisters a gray mantle, which she instantly recognized as the one Mrs. S—— had worn at Carrickafoyle. There was a woman at Glyn named Grace Scanlon, with whom Mr. S——, when he went there, was in the habit of lodging. In this person's house Ellen Walsh some time after saw the silk handkerchief, one of the spencers, and the two muslin frocks which Mrs. S—— had shown her at Carrickafoyle. (These it appeared from other evidence had been sold to Grace Scanlon by Sullivan, who accounted to her for their coming into her possession, by stating that Mrs. S—— had run away from Kilrush with an officer, and left her trunk of clothes behind her.) Finally, about a fortnight after the disappearance of Mrs. S——, Ellen Walsh, going one evening into Grace Scanlon's house, found Mr. S—— and Sullivan sitting there. The former had on one of his fingers a gold carved ring, precisely resembling that worn by Mrs. S——; they both were under the influence of liquor, and talked much and loud; among other things, Sullivan asked his master for some money, and on being refused observed emphatically, "Mr. John, you know I have as good a right to that money as you have."

Such were in substance the most material facts (excepting one particular hereafter mentioned) that had fallen under Ellen Walsh's observation; and upon the magistrates being apprised that she had such evidence to give, she was summoned as a witness upon the inquest. She accordingly attended, and accompanied the coroner's jury to the place where the remains had been deposited by the fishermen. The circumstances she detailed were pregnant with suspicion against Mr. S—— and his servant. A young and defenceless female had disappeared: upon the last occasion of her having been seen, she was in their company, in an open boat, on the river Shannon; a declaration had been made by the servant, "that she was to be got rid of." On the very next day her trunk of clothes is seen in their possession; and soon after a part of the dress she wore in the boat on the servant's sister, and one of her rings on the master's finger; add to this the mysterious allusion to the money, "Mr. John, you know I have as good a right to that money as you have;" a few weeks after, a body is washed ashore, near to the place where this young woman had last been seen, the body of a young female, who had manifestly been stript and murdered, and flung into the river, and exhibiting symptoms of decay, according to the report of the fishermen, that exactly tallied with the time of her suspected death. But, on the other hand, there were some circumstances in the case, as detailed by Ellen Walsh, which justified the magistrates in considering that a jury should pause before they pronounced her evidence to be conclusive. Of Sullivan they had no knowledge; but his master they knew to be a young gentleman of some territorial property, of respectable parentage, and nearly allied by blood with more than one of the noble families of Ireland. This naturally compelled them to entertain some doubts. Then, upon the supposition that he and his servant had concerted the murder of the young woman Ellen Walsh had seen with them, what could be more clumsy and incautious than their previous and subsequent conduct? The inference from her story of the transaction was, that the time and manner of executing their deadly purpose was finally determined upon during their absence from the public-house at Carrickafoyle. Yet the very first thing they do upon their return is to inform her, without any kind of necessity for the communication, "that they want to get rid of that girl;" a declaration consistent enough with their subsequent account of her disappearance, but almost incredible, if considered as a gratuitous disclosure by persons meditating the perpetration of an atrocious crime. They next permit the same person, as if determined that she should be a further witness against them, to see them bearing away their victim to the very scene of execution; and finally they appear the next day in the town of Glyn, and publicly exhibit themselves and the evidences of their crime to the very person from whose scrutiny and observation, upon the supposition of their guilt, they must have known they had so much to apprehend.

These conflicting views did not escape the attention of the magistrates who had undertaken the investigation of this affair. They saw that the case would continue involved in mystery, unless it could be unequivocally made to appear that the young woman seen by Ellen Walsh and the murdered person were the same. For this purpose, before they allowed the body to be disinterred for the inspection of the jury, they used the precaution of reinterrogating Ellen Walsh as to even the minutest particular she could recall respecting the personal appearance of Mrs. S——. The witness stated that she was extremely young, not more, she imagined, than fifteen or sixteen, and that her figure was short and slight. So far her description corresponded with that of the fishermen, who were also in attendance; but this would have been too feeble and general evidence of identity for a court of criminal inquiry to act upon with safety. The witness further stated, that Mrs. S—— was remarkably handsome, and gave the coroner's jury a minute description of her face; but no comparison of feature could now be availing. In the remains over which the investigation was holding every natural lineament of the countenance must long since have been utterly effaced by death, and by the equally disfiguring operation of the element to which she had been exposed. At length, however, the witness distinctly called to her recollection one peculiarity about Mrs. S——'s face, which, if she and the deceased were the same, might still be visible. The teeth were not perfectly regular. *Two of the upper row, one at each side, projected considerably.* This important clue having been obtained, the remains were disinterred, and found in the condition which the fishermen had described. The mouth was, of course, the first and chief object of minute inspection. The teeth of the upper jaw had all dropped out; but, upon a careful examination of the sockets, two of the side ones were found to be of such a particular formation as satisfied the jury that the teeth belonging to them must, of necessity, have projected as the witness had represented. Upon this fact, coupled with the other particulars of her testimony, they returned a verdict, finding that the deceased had· been wilfully murdered by John S—— and Stephen Sullivan.

Warrants were immediately issued for the apprehension of the parties accused, neither of whom, and this was not an immaterial circumstance, had been seen in public since the finding of the remains on the shore. The servant succeeded in concealing himself. The master was traced to a particular farm-house in the county of Limerick, and followed thither by the officers of justice, accompanied by a party of dragoons. They searched the place ineffectually, and were retiring, as from a fruitless pursuit, when one of the dragoons, as he was riding away, stuck his sabre, more in sport than otherwise, into a heap of straw that lay near the house. The sword met with no resistance, and the dragoon had already passed on, when a figure burst from beneath the straw, and called out for mercy. It was Mr. S——.

From some passages in the statement of Ellen Walsh, it was sufficiently obvious that the deceased could not have been the wife of Mr. S——, and who she had been remained to be discovered. Before the lapse of many days, this point was ascertained. There was an humble man, named John Conroy, who had followed the trade of a shoemaker, in one of the small towns in the county of Limerick. This person had humanely protected an orphan niece, named Ellen Hanlon, and brought her up from her infancy in his own house as one of his own children, till she attained her sixteenth year. He was in the habit of visiting Cork annually to purchase articles in the way of his trade, and a few weeks previous to the circumstances above detailed, was about to proceed there, when the young creature he had loved and protected as his own child disappeared from his home. He made inquiry for her in every direction, but never heard of her after; until on reading the description of the person of the young woman found on the shore of the Shannon, near Moneypoint, he knew her to be his lost niece.

The trial came on at the ensuing assizes for the county of Limerick. A clear case of circumstantial evidence, consisting mainly of the foregoing facts, was made out against the prisoner, who had nothing save the ingenuity of his counsel, to offer in his defence. When the issue was handed up to the jury, it was supposed that they would return a verdict of conviction without leaving the box; but, contrary to expectation, they retired, and continued long engaged in consultation.

At length, late in the evening, a verdict of guilty was found. Sentence of death was pronounced, and the prisoner ordered for execution on the next day but one succeeding his conviction. Some very unusual incidents followed. Before the judge left the bench, he received an application sanctioned by some names of consideration in the county, and praying that he would transmit to the Viceroy a memorial in the prisoner's favour. The judge, feeling the case to be one where the law should sternly take its course, refused to interfere. He was then solicited to permit the sentence to be at least respited to such a time as would enable those interested in the prisoner's behalf to ascertain the result of such an application from themselves. To this request the same answer was, for the same reason returned. There being however still time, if expedition were used, to make the experiment, a memorial, the precise terms of which did not publicly transpire, was that evening despatched by a special messenger to the seat of government.

The hour beyond which the law had said that this guilty young man should not be permitted to exist was now at hand, and the special messenger had not returned. Yet, so confident were the prisoner's friends that tidings of mercy were on their way, that the sheriff humanely consented to connive at every possible procrastination of the dreadful ceremony. He had already lived for more than two hours beyond his appointed time, when an answer from the Castle of Dublin arrived. Its purport was to bid him prepare for instant death. I have heard from a gentleman, who visited his cell a few minutes after this final intimation, that his composure was astonishing. His sole anxiety seemed to be to show that he could die with firmness. An empty phial was lying in the cell. "You have been taking laudanum I perceive, sir," said the gentleman. "I have," he replied; "but not with the object that you suspect. The dose was not strong enough for that—I merely took as much as would steady my nerves." He asserted his innocence of all participation in the murder of Ellen Henlon, and declared that if ever Sullivan should be brought to trial, the injustice of the present sentence would appear.

The friends of the prisoner were, for many and obvious reasons, desirous that he should be conveyed in a close carriage to the place of execution. Expecting a reprieve, they had neglected to provide one, and they now found it impossible to hire such a conveyance. Large sums were offered at the different places where chaises and horses were to be let; but the popular prejudice prevailed. At last an old carriage was found exposed for sale, and purchased. Horses were still to be provided, when two turf-carts, belonging to tenants of the prisoner, appeared moving in the town. The horses were taken from the carts, and harnessed to the carriage. To this the owners made no resistance; but no threats nor entreaties could induce either of them to undertake the office of driver. After a further delay, occasioned by this difficulty, a needy wretch among the bystanders was tempted, by the offer of a guinea, to take the reins and brave the ridicule of the mob. The prisoner, accompanied by the gaoler and clergyman, was put into the carriage, and the procession began to advance. At the distance of a few hundred yards from the gaol, a bridge was to be passed. The horses, which had shown no signs of restiveness before, no sooner reached the foot of the bridge than they came to a full stop. Beating, coaxing, cursing, all were unavailing; not an inch beyond that spot could they be made to advance. The contest between them and the driver terminated in one of the horses deliberately lying down, amidst the cheers of the mob. To their excited apprehensions, this act of the animal had a superstitious import. It evinced a preternatural abhorrence of the crime of murder, a miraculous instinct in detecting guilt, which a jury of Irish gentlemen had taken hours to pronounce upon. Every effort to get the carriage forward having failed, the prisoner was removed from it and conducted on foot to the place of execution. It was a solemn and melancholy sight as he slowly moved along the main street of a crowded city, environed by military, unpitied by the populace, and gazed at with shuddering curiosity from every window. For a while the operation of the laudanum he had drunk was manifest. There was a drowsy stupor in his eye as he cast it insensibly around him. Instead of moving continuously forward, every step he made in advance seemed a distinct and laborious effort. Without the assistance of the jailer and clergyman, who supported him between them, he must, to all appearance, have dropped on the pavement. These effects, however, gradually subsided; and before he arrived at the place of execution, his frame had resumed its wonted firmness.

At the place of execution the prisoner was solemnly adjured by the clegyman in attendance to admit the justice of his sentence; he as solemnly reasserted his innocence. The cap was drawn over his eyes, and he was about to be thrown off. An accidental interruption occurred. The clergyman raised the cap, and once more appealed to him as to a person upon whom the world had already closed. The answer was, "I am suffering for a crime in which I never participated. If Sullivan is ever found, my innocence will appear." Sullivan *was* found before the next assizes, when he was tried and convicted upon the same evidence adduced against his master. Sullivan was a Catholic, and after his conviction made a voluntary and full confession. It put the master's guilt beyond all question. The wretched girl, according to his statement, had insisted upon retaining in her own hands a portion of some money which it appeared she had taken from her uncle when she deserted him; To obtain this, and also to disembarrass himself of an incumbrance, her seducer planned her death. Sullivan undertook to be the executioner. After setting Ellen Walsh on shore, they returned to an unfrequented point near Carrickafoyle, where the instruments of murder—a musket and a rope—lay concealed. With these and the unsuspecting victim, Sullivan put out in the boat. The master remained upon the strand. After the interval of an hour the boat returned, bearing back Ellen Hanlon unharmed. "I thought I had made up my mind," said the ruffian, in his penitential declaration. "I was just lifting the musket to dash her brains out; *but when I looked in her innocent face, I had not the heart to do it.*" This excuse made no impression upon the merciless master. Sullivan was plied with liquor, and again despatched upon the murderous mission: the musket was once more raised, and—the rest has been told.

THE END.

16 AP 61

WINCHESTER: PRINTED BY HUGH BARCLAY, HIGH STREET.

1985